"In America, the prosecutor, often known as the District Attorney or State's Attorney, is the central figure in the operation of the criminal justice system. It is he or she who determines whether a suspect will be charged with a crime, decides what crime is levied, obtains and presents the evidence for conviction, and is often significant in advising on the ultimate sentence. Prosecutors are governed in their work by their responsibility to make sure that justice is done and the community is protected. Charles Stimson and Zack Smith show in *Rogue Prosecutors* that when these officials abdicate their responsibilities and substitute their own ideas for what the law actually provides, the result is not only a breakdown of the system, but also massive increases in crime and the destruction, fear, and civic incivility that is now being experienced in many of our largest cities. This is a highly readable book which reveals how renegade billionaires can manipulate elections to place in office insidious zealots who undermine public safety under the false narrative of 'social justice.' It is an invaluable contribution and a must-read for anyone interested in the safety of our citizens."

—**Edwin Meese III,** Former Attorney General of the United States

"Trading on the fictions of a mass-incarceration crisis driven by systemic racism, American progressives drew from their deep wellsprings of funding to execute a scheme as ingenious as it is destructive: overwhelm the electoral competition to capture district-attorney posts in the nation's cities, and place law-enforcement power in the hands of radicals committed to non-enforcement. The results, as Zack Smith and Charles Stimson painstakingly document in *Rogue Prosecutors*, are a windfall for hardened criminals, the savaging of urban communities, and the evisceration of America's existential commitment to the rule of law."

—**Andrew C. McCarthy**, Former federal prosecutor, bestselling author, and Contributing Editor, *National Review*

"You no longer have to win a majority in the state legislature or the governor's mansion to significantly impact public safety policy in America. Instead, radical groups only need to win local, county, or city-wide prosecutor elections that typically fly under the radar. *Rogue Prosecutors* highlights the benefactors and players across our country that are cherry-picking laws to enforce, ignoring crime, and making our communities less safe. Most importantly, the book provides a voice too often ignored in our debate on criminal justice reform in America: the victims."

—**Jason Miyares,** Attorney General for the Commonwealth of Virginia

"*Rogue Prosecutors* is hard to read—not because it is poorly written, it is in fact lucid—but because it lays out with such unflinching detail the horrific crimes that have resulted from left-wing prosecutors' refusal to apply the criminal law. These opponents of law and order have enacted elaborate charging and sentencing policies that make it almost impossible to bring justice for victims and to prevent future crimes. The rogue prosecutor movement rests on race-based lies about America's criminal justice system, lies that the media and academia relentlessly amplify. George Soros funded and provided organizational help to this destructive movement. *Rogue Prosecutors* is essential reading for anyone who wants to organize and to take back America's streets."

—**Heather Mac Donald,** The Thomas W. Smith fellow at the Manhattan Institute and author of *The War on Cops* and *When Race Trumps Merit*

"An unvarnished and unapologetic takedown of the so-called 'progressive prosecutor' movement, *Rogue Prosecutors* reveals this misguided trend for what it is: an ideological distortion of the prosecutorial role that ignores the separation of powers, decades of thoughtful criminal justice reform, and—most tragically—the very communities it purports to serve."

—**Andrew Lelling,** United States Attorney for the District of Massachusetts 2017-2021

"The push to capture local prosecutors' offices by criminal justice reform advocates pursuing decarceration is still an underexplored phenomenon, given the movement's electoral success. Smith and Stimson deliver an important and timely investigation of this movement, its component parts, and its potential effects on our most important societal commodity: public safety."

—**Rafael A. Mangual,** Senior Fellow and Head of Research, Policing & Public Safety Initiative, Contributing Editor, *City Journal*, The Manhattan Institute, author of *Criminal (In)Justice: What the Push for Decarceration and Depolicing Gets Wrong and Who It Hurts Most*

# ROGUE
# PROSECUTORS

## HOW RADICAL SOROS LAWYERS ARE DESTROYING AMERICA'S COMMUNITIES

# ZACK SMITH and
# CHARLES D. STIMSON

BOMBARDIER
BOOKS

Published by Bombardier Books
An Imprint of Post Hill Press
ISBN: 978-1-63758-653-2
ISBN (eBook): 978-1-63758-654-9

Rogue Prosecutors:
How Radical Soros Lawyers Are Destroying America's Communities
© 2023 by The Heritage Foundation
All Rights Reserved

Cover Design by Conroy Accord

Post Hill Press
New York • Nashville
posthillpress.com

Published in the United States of America
1  2  3  4  5  6  7  8  9  10

To the millions of nameless victims and their families who suffer under this failed social experiment.

# CONTENTS

# INTRODUCTION

I magine the horror: your wife wakes up for an early morning jog and a few short hours later, instead of her arriving home ready to tackle the rest of her day, you get a call that she's in the hospital after having been beaten, choked unconscious, raped, and robbed by a complete stranger.

Unfortunately, for one forty-three-year-old New Yorker and her family, they don't have to imagine this scenario because they lived it.[1]

But that should not have happened in the first place. This New Yorker's assailant should not have been free to victimize her. He should have been behind bars.[2]

New York City authorities were already looking for him in connection with two previous sexual assaults with eerily similar fact patterns. But more shockingly, officials had arrested him at least twenty-five prior times for a variety of offenses—many of them the so-called "quality of life" crimes, such as petit larceny, assault, and drug-related offenses—that so-called "progressive" prosecutors around the country are refusing to enforce because, according to them, these crimes don't harm the communities where they take place.

Let's be clear: These prosecutors are not progressive, and neither are their policies. They're rogue. They harm their communities, benefit criminals, and rip away justice from victims.

Wherever rogue prosecutors implement these policies, the same results follow.

Consider that only a few months before the New York jogger suffered her horrific assault, another woman on the other side of the country, in Los Angeles County, California, experienced a similar traumatic attack by a repeat violent offender who should not have been free to roam the streets.[3]

On the evening of July 31, 2022, Marissa Young finished her shift at a restaurant in Torrance, California, when she took her two dogs out for a brief walk. Suddenly her world changed. A man tackled her, wrestled her to the ground, and began mercilessly pummeling her. He raped her and assaulted her for over thirty minutes. As one report said, after "the attack, he left her on the ground, bloodied and naked from the waist down...."[4] The attack left her "with missing teeth, broken bones, deep bruises and physical and emotional scars."[5] On top of all that, for "about a month afterward, she was partially blind."[6]

The worst part? Like the New York attack, it never should have happened. In some ways the circumstances surrounding this attack are even more egregious than those surrounding the attack in New York. Why? Her alleged attacker, a forty-six-year-old homeless man, had been arrested for unlawfully possessing a dagger. Rogue prosecutors released him only hours earlier on his own recognizance, which is essentially his word that he will show up to court and not commit any offenses pending his trial.

Marissa Young rightly expressed anger "that the suspect had been released from jail so soon after this earlier arrest."[7] She said, "It's horrifying to think that they were holding this guy with a huge knife that was taken off him that's illegal and he was let go the next day even though he has a record...."[8]

She continued, "Once something like this happens to you, it sort of changes your mind as to what the laws should be...."[9]

## BLAME GEORGE SOROS FOR THIS NATIONWIDE PROBLEM

The rogue prosecutor movement was started and funded by George Soros in 2015. Two lawyers, one of whom worked for George Soros and another who worked for the American Civil Liberties Union (ACLU), concocted a devious scheme to replace law and order prosecutors with zealots opposed to the death penalty. The Soros employee convinced Soros to give over $1 million to set up "Safety and Justice" political action committees to help elect two small-town district attorneys in Louisiana and Mississippi and reelect a third in Mississippi, all of whom were against the death penalty.

When each candidate won, Soros and his team decided to go big and not only fund candidates opposed to the death penalty but also procriminal, antivictim zealots. They hired a national public relations firm and started funding district attorney candidates across the country, starting with Kim Foxx in Chicago in 2015.

Of our nation's thirty cities with the highest murder rates, at least fourteen of them have rogue prosecutors backed or inspired by Soros. The murders in those fourteen cities accounted for 68 percent of the homicides in the thirty top homicide cities through June 2022.[10]

Recent estimates show that *at least* seventy-two million Americans suffer under the rule of rogue prosecutors. That's one in five Americans. In fact, rogue prosecutors reign in almost half of America's fifty most populous cities.[11] And they have overseen almost 40 percent of all homicides.[12]

## VICTIMS ARE MOSTLY MINORITIES

But why are these prosecutors refusing to do their job and hold criminals accountable?

These prosecutors and their supporters have bought into two myths: 1) that we have a mass incarceration problem in our country, which we don't, and 2) that our criminal justice system is systemically racist. It's not. These are the animating features of the movement, as we explain in detail in the next chapter.

In the abstract, the idea of sending fewer people to prison is laudable. But it's not new.

For many years, traditional prosecutors have worked to ensure that only those who need to be incarcerated are kept behind bars. But instead of working to further improve existing programs (such as drug courts, veterans courts, and various diversionary programs that have contributed to community safety while making sure individuals are not needlessly incarcerated), the rogue prosecutor movement uses populist shibboleths to conceal a virulent scheme to destroy the criminal justice system as we know it.

The sad irony of it all is that many of the so-called reforms championed by these so-called progressives have actually harmed the very people they are supposed to help. Minorities, especially young black men, are disproportionately the victims of violent crime. So, when the number of violent crimes increases, the number of minority victims also increases. It's the dirty secret these radicals won't, and don't, talk about.

There is really no way of knowing the exact number of crimes that have been committed as a direct result of rogue prosecutors' policies. But when you compare the average number of crimes committed in the five years before a rogue prosecutor was elected to the five years (or more) after he/she has been in office, you see a distinct pattern: crime explodes.

We added up the total number of murders, rapes, robberies, thefts, motor vehicle thefts, and burglaries for each city in the five years before each prosecutor was elected and compared those totals to the same crimes committed in the years since they have been elected.[13]

We then evaluated whether there were additional or "extra" crimes in each city above the previous five-year rolling average and, if so, what that extra number was.

Based on our conservative estimations, across the eight cities featured in this book, there have been *at least* an additional 3,090 homicides, 3,580 rapes, 7,500 robberies, 14,800 motor vehicle thefts, countless thousands of nonfatal shooting victims, and hundreds of thousands of other crimes (and victims) in those cities between 2015–2021. And of those 3,090 extra murders, over 75 percent of the victims were minorities.

## The Blame Game—Lies and More Lies

Defenders of progressive prosecutors suggest that crime has been increasing all across the country, and, as such, one cannot reasonably tie the increase in crime to their procriminal, antivictim policies.

But that's a lie.

Crime has not increased in every large city across the country anywhere near the degree it has in rogue prosecutor cities, and crime rates have in fact remained flat or decreased in cities with prosecutors committed to law and order, like San Diego, as we show below.

Another favorite talking point of progressive prosecutors and their enablers is that crime only started to increase in 2020.

Another lie.

What the data actually shows is that once a rogue prosecutor was elected and unveiled his/her policies, crime started to increase in his/her city. Every rogue prosecutor in this book, with the exception of New York's Alvin Bragg, was elected before 2020, and crime in their cities spiked well before 2020.

When you stop to think about it, the indisputable uptick in crime in cities with rogue prosecutors is a natural and predictable outgrowth and byproduct of their policies. Despite their protestations and denials that the crime rate in their cities is due to their policies,[14] it doesn't take a criminologist or crime expert to realize that when you enact policies that give criminals repeated passes on breaking the law, they commit more crimes with impunity, crime rates go up, and more people become victims of those crimes.

This is common sense, yet the movement expects you to ignore or suspend your common sense when it applies to their approach to "reimagining" prosecution. But try a thought experiment here. Imagine that you're a parent. Like most families, you have rules that you expect your children to follow, such as flush the toilet, brush your teeth, make your bed, go to school, do your homework, don't stay up late on school nights, eat healthy food, and the like. If you told your kids that they didn't have to follow the rules for a week, do you honestly think they would choose to follow the rules of their own volition? Of course, they wouldn't. Yet this is exactly what the rogue prosecutor movement wants you to believe is happening in their cities: they give society, including career criminals, a pass on following the law and want you to believe that people will still follow the law. They actually want us to believe that if we do this, crime actually will go down!

It's ludicrous, yet they repeat this stuff over and over and claim to have "data and science" to back up their radical approach.

Another lie.

Here's the thing: as a general rule, state legislatures pass criminal laws to signal to anyone in that state that it is unlawful to commit a particular act. In some states, like California, the voters themselves vote on ballot initiatives related to criminal laws or penalties, as we discuss in the chapter on George Gascón. Regardless of how those criminal laws came into force, each is an expression of the values, morals, and sentiments of the populace.

Ignorance of the law, as the saying goes, is not a defense. Yet everyone knows by the time they reach a certain age that it is wrong to steal, lie, assault, injure, maim, rob, sexually assault, or murder another human being. We learn, early in life, that breaking rules has consequences, like it or not, because humans must self-govern.

The criminal law in each state is, in a way, the formal codification or logical extension of an entire genre of less important rules we learn as youngsters, rules such as the requirement to brush your teeth, make your bed, do your homework, go to school, don't lie, cheat, or steal, don't hit your siblings or classmates, and the like.

As we mature into adulthood, each of us decides whether and what rules to follow, and every person engages in a cost-benefit analysis of the risks and rewards of following or not following customs, practices, norms, and rules. How many times have you exceeded the speed limit while driving your car, or jaywalked, or paid a bill late, or turned in an assignment past its due date? In each of these instances, and other similar behaviors, you had a choice to make, and in making that choice, you weighed the rule and the possible punishment or ignominy you would suffer if caught.

Fortunately, most people choose not to commit serious crimes, as the fear of being caught, punished, and sentenced to jail or prison, or other draconian consequences, far outweighs the marginal benefit of committing the crime.

Until the perverse rogue prosecutor movement was born, that was the social construct in which most people operated. To use an overused expression, they didn't "commit the crime because they didn't want to do the time." It's a simplification of the same concept renowned American psychologist B. F. Skinner put forward in his book *Science and Human Behavior*.[15] According to Skinner, the law, "by creating unpleasant effects, for others as well as for the individual himself, reduces the probability that any individual will engage in a particular behavior. The individual receives 'aversive stimulation' that influences his behavior response."[16]

But what happens when those "unpleasant effects" or punishments or consequences disappear as applied to most criminal behavior? The incentive to follow the law disappears, and antisocial behavior, including engaging in criminal acts, increases.

And that is exactly what has happened in every city that has a rogue prosecutor.

The chapters that follow catalogue the breakdown of law and order in many of our nation's biggest cities. While each city has experienced this breakdown in its own unique way, common themes—like a disproportionate number of minority victims—do emerge.

But the picture is likely worse in many of these cities than the one painted by the official crime statistics. Why? Because part of the playbook employed by the eight rogue prosecutors featured in this book and across the movement is the wholesale refusal to prosecute entire categories of crime, especially misdemeanors. Since there is no prosecution for crimes such as simple assault, theft, resisting arrest, possession with intent to distribute illegal drugs, breaking and entering, malicious destruction of property, driving offenses, and the like, there are no convictions for those crimes.

Furthermore, police in those cities, knowing that the district attorney won't prosecute those crimes, have no incentive to arrest offenders who commit those crimes. Why waste the time and paperwork on those cases when the rogue district attorney won't let the prosecutors in his or her office prosecute anyone who commits those offenses? Invariably, the number of arrests goes down for those crimes, while the number of actual instances of those crimes likely skyrockets. This, in turn, gives rogue prosecutors the ability to tout the reduction in arrests for the very crimes that they are enabling and allows them to suggest—without any verifiable studies—that not prosecuting these crimes does not result in more of these crimes being committed.

But it's more difficult to hide or ignore dead bodies, armed robberies, carjackings, burglaries, and other violent crimes. Rising crime rates, especially violent crime rates, are the Achilles' heel of the rogue prosecutor movement, as the data, incomplete as it is, proves.

Throughout this book, we trace the ideological underpinnings of the rogue prosecutor movement, to the people and money funding it, to the real-world consequences this movement has inflicted on cities where the eight featured rogue prosecutors have been in power: 1) Baltimore (Marilyn Mosby), 2) Chicago (Kim Foxx), 3) Philadelphia (Larry Krasner),

4) San Francisco (Chesa Boudin), 5) St. Louis (Kim Gardner), 6) Los Angeles (George Gascón), 7) Boston (Rachael Rollins), and 8) New York City (Alvin Bragg).

While we take a deeper dive later in the book into the policies each of these prosecutors has implemented—and the harmful consequences that have resulted—a quick overview here shows the scope and severity of the problem.

## BALTIMORE

In Baltimore, in the eight years before Marilyn Mosby was elected, homicides averaged 229 per year. Every year since Mosby has been in office, that average has risen to 333.1 homicides per year, a whopping increase of 104 killings per year. Under Mosby's watch, 89.2 percent of homicide victims were black.

Put another way, during Mosby's tenure (2015 through 2021), there were 2,332 homicides in Baltimore. That represents an extra 832 people who were slaughtered.

As of November 30, 2022, Baltimore had 307 homicides, thanks in large part to Mosby.

Rapes, aggravated assaults, and robberies have predictably gone up under Mosby's watch too.

For the five-year period before Mosby was elected, Baltimore City residents suffered 292 rape cases annually. After Mosby was elected, the average increased to 330 per year. In other words, an extra 190 people were raped in the first five years of Mosby's tenure compared with the five years before she assumed office.

In the five years before Mosby was elected, 23,707 aggravated assaults were committed. In the five years since she was elected, there have been 26,519 aggravated assaults, representing an "extra" 2,812 such assaults in total or 562 additional aggravated assaults per year.

In the five years from 2010 through 2014, there were 17,809 robberies in the city, averaging 3,562 per year. After Mosby arrived, between 2015 and 2019, there have been a staggering 25,350 robberies in the city, averaging 5,070 robberies per year.

Put another way, 7,541 extra people were robbed, many at gunpoint, while Mosby acted as Baltimore's gatekeeper to the criminal justice system.

Robberies are so ubiquitous in the city that even the deputy police commissioner and his wife were robbed at gunpoint in 2019.[17] In fact, in 2019, Baltimore was the number-one city in America for robberies, topping out at 95 robberies for every one hundred thousand residents.[18]

# CHICAGO

In Chicago, in the six years before Kim Foxx took office as the state's attorney for Cook County, there was an average of 445 homicides per year (2010–2015).

And although 445 homicides per year sounds like a high number (it is), it was still much better than the carnage that took place in the early 1990s. Between 1991–1998, there was an average of 845 homicides per year, with a whopping 947 in the year 1992 alone, and 709 in the year 1998.

In 2015, there were 493 homicides. But in 2016, when Kim Foxx took office, homicides spiked to 778 in her first year, and through 2021, have averaged 680 per year. Over 75 percent of homicide victims during Foxx's tenure have been black, and the majority of those (approximately 87 percent) were men.

In other words, there have been an extra 1,412 homicides in Chicago during Foxx's tenure (and counting), an average of 235 more deaths per year.

To put this carnage into perspective, between 2003–2010, there were 3,481 Americans killed in action in Iraq, an average of 435 a year.

In the war in Afghanistan, between 2001 and 2014, there were 1,833 Americans killed in action, an average of 141 per year.

In other words, the City of Chicago's annual murder rate is worse than the number of US military personnel annually killed in action in Afghanistan and Iraq. In parts of Chicago, on any given weekend, it is—literally—a domestic war zone.

Unfortunately, just like Baltimore, Chicago has seen a spike in other crimes, too, since its rogue prosecutor was elected.

In the six years before Foxx was elected, there were 8,316 rapes reported to the police, an average of 1,386 per year.

During Foxx's tenure (2016–2021), there were 10,310 rapes reported to the police, an average of 1,718 per year. That means that there were an extra 1,994 rapes in Chicago (and counting) during Foxx's tenure.

# PHILADELPHIA

Larry Krasner has been a disaster as the Philadelphia district attorney since he was elected. By any measure, he has been a complete and utter failure, if one measures the "success rate" of a district attorney by low crime rates. When asked by a reporter about the massive spike in crime in Philadelphia under his policies in the fall of 2022, Krasner responded, "It's working."[19]

The only things working more in Philadelphia since Krasner took over are undertakers, homicide detectives, emergency room doctors, paramedics, and other collateral victims of his dystopian scheme.

In the five years before Larry Krasner became the district attorney in Philadelphia, there were 1,356 homicides, an average of 271 per year. Since Krasner took office in 2018, there have been 2,286 homicides,[20] an average of 457 per year. In other words, there have been 930 extra dead bodies in Philly (and counting) since Krasner took over, an average of 186 extra bodies per year.

Philadelphia is setting all-time-high murder records—even higher than the much-touted crime epidemic of the late '80s and early '90s.[21] In 2021, 561 people were murdered in Philadelphia.

Moreover, 83 percent of the victims in Krasner's killing fields are black, 90 percent of whom are male.

But even if you aren't killed in Krasner's Philadelphia, you are much more likely to be shot than before he took office.

In the three years before Krasner took office, there were 3,143 non-fatal shootings, an average of 1,047 per year. In the five years Krasner has been in office, there have been 7,711 nonfatal shootings, or 1,588 per year. That's 4.24 people shot each day for five years. Thanks to Krasner's policies, an extra 501 people (and counting) have been shot per year since he was elected.

Aggravated assaults while armed with a handgun (AAG) also have mushroomed during Krasner's reign. In the five years before he took office, there were 11,048 AAGs, averaging 2,209 per year. Since he took office, AAGs have totaled a whopping 15,582, an average of 3,116 per year. That means an extra 4,534 AAGs under Krasner, an average of 906 extra AAGs per year, or 2.4 per day.

As we detail in our chapter on Krasner, retail thefts have snowballed as well, resulting in downtown city stores, such as Wawa convenience stores, closing because theft (with no consequences) has made it impossible to stay in business.

In the five years before he took office, there were 37,061 instances of retail theft, an average of 7,412 events per year. Since he took office, there have been a stupefying 45,424 retail thefts, or 9,084 per year. That means an extra 8,363 retail thefts under Krasner, an average of 1,672 extra retail thefts per year, or 4.5 per day. No wonder many retailers have left downtown Philadelphia.

Auto thieves also have been enjoying a free-for-all under Krasner. In the five years before he took office, there were 28,455 auto thefts, an average of 5,691 per year. But since Krasner, who thinks thefts are mere "quality of life" crimes that aren't worthy of prosecution, took office, there have been 43,327 auto thefts, an average of 8,665 per year.

That means there have been an extra 14,872 auto thefts during his tenure, an average of 2,974 extra auto thefts per year (and counting), or 8.1 per day. Don't park your car in Philadelphia—if you want to keep it.

## SAN FRANCISCO

San Francisco is arguably the most beautiful city of the eight we feature in this book. Located on the eastern shore of the cold, icy cerulean waters of San Francisco Bay, San Francisco is the gateway to the East and the Pacific. Resplendent with world-class art museums, architecture, and cuisine, the "City by the Bay" is home to many of the world's top technology companies, banks such as Wells Fargo, venture capitalists, and entrepreneurs. Tourists from around the world flock to San Francisco, ride the famed cable cars, tour Alcatraz, eat chocolate at Ghirardelli Square, and enjoy the parks, sights, and sounds of a truly unique city.

Unfortunately, from 2011 until July 2022, San Franciscans, tourists, and visitors had to survive in a city that had not one but two rogue prosecutors. George Gascón was the district attorney from 2011 to 2019, and Chesa Boudin was the district attorney from 2020 until he was fortunately recalled from office in July 2022. During their combined tenure, crime, especially rape, retail theft, and rampant drug sales and usage, exploded.

Parts of the city, especially the Tenderloin District, have deteriorated into a dystopian scene akin to a Mad Max movie.

In the five years before Gascón took office in San Francisco, there were 757 reported rapes—an average of 151 per year. In his last five years in office, after his policies had taken root, there were a stunning 1,731 rapes, an average of 346 per year. In 2017 alone, there were 367 rapes, and every year from 2014 to 2019, the year he left office, there were more than three hundred rapes per year.

During Chesa Boudin's three years in office (2020–2022), there were 659 rapes, an average of 211 per year, well above the pre-Gascón era of 151 per year.

In summary, there were approximately 1,216 extra rapes during Gascón's tenure and 180 extra rapes during Boudin's tenure, for a total of at least 1,396 extra people who were raped during their eleven-year reign of terror.

Aggravated assaults also went up dramatically under Gascón's watch as San Francisco DA. In the five years before he took office, there were 11,921 aggravated assaults, an average of 2,384 per year. In his last five years in office, there were 13,070 aggravated assaults—an average of 2,614 per year.

Aggravated assaults did not increase under Boudin's short tenure, but burglaries exploded compared to the five-year pre-Gascón average of 5,339 burglaries per year. Under Boudin's hands-off approach, there were 7,587 burglaries in 2020 and 7,330 in 2021, for a two-year average of 7,458.

The most shocking crime statistic, and no doubt the one that ultimately led to the residents of San Francisco recalling Boudin from office, is the tsunami of thefts, including retail thefts. In the two years before Gascón took office, there was an average of 24,152 thefts, or sixty-six per day.

During the combined tenures of Gascón and Boudin, both of whom refused to prosecute theft cases, retail and garden variety theft became an everyday reality for storekeepers, shoppers, apartment and home owners, and virtually anyone who came to the city. During the Gascón-Boudin eleven-year reign of terror, there was an average of 35,443 thefts per year, an average of 97.1 per day. In 2017, there were 46,733 thefts alone, or 126.9 per day.

That means there were approximately 124,201 extra thefts under these two rogue prosecutors. It's not difficult to see why retailers such as Walgreens and others have shuttered stores in San Francisco, depriving many inner-city residents of a neighborhood store in which to buy groceries and other necessary items.

## SAN DIEGO

But it didn't have to be this way. Some prosecutors understand the importance of enforcing law and order in their cities—to the benefit of the citizens whom they were elected to serve.

Tied with Philadelphia as the seventh largest city in the United States, the city of San Diego sits on the southern tip of California and abuts Mexico. Interstate 5 runs from the Mexican border, through the spine of San Diego, northward through Los Angeles, San Francisco, Portland, and Seattle, and ends at the Canadian border. Like its counterpart on the East Coast, Interstate 95, I-5 is a major illegal drug corridor up and down the West Coast.

Like Philadelphia, San Diego has gangs, drugs, prostitution, and turf wars in the city and county. The County of Philadelphia encompasses the City of Philadelphia, just like San Diego County encompasses the City of San Diego.

But unlike Philadelphia, where Larry Krasner is the rogue district attorney, San Diego has had, and continues to have, a law-and-order, real prosecutor by the name of Summer Stephan. A career, independent-minded, fair-but-tough prosecutor who leads the second-largest DA's office in California (three-hundred-plus attorneys and total staff of one thousand), Stephan has worked tirelessly with the public defender's office, law enforcement, community members, and the judiciary to keep crime rates low. She holds criminals accountable by using San Diego's drug courts, domestic violence courts, teen courts, the nation's first Family Justice Center, and dozens of community programs to give offenders alternatives to incarceration and a path to a successful life. She is a model district attorney and the gold standard for the country.

Stephan was elected district attorney in June 2018. Her predecessor, Bonnie Dumanis, also ran a first-rate office and kept crime rates in check during her tenure from 2003 until 2017.

While crime exploded in cities that elected rogue prosecutors, crime rates remained constant or decreased in many categories in San Diego.

From 2012 to 2021, the number of homicides in San Diego County averaged 92.1 per year. In the City of San Diego, there were 57 homicides in 2021 compared to 562 in the City of Philadelphia!

Furthermore, whereas Philadelphia, Chicago, Baltimore, Los Angeles, and St. Louis saw huge increases in the number of homicides per year once their rogue prosecutors were elected, the number of homicides in San Diego County has remained relatively steady, ranging from 104 in 2012 to a high of 118 in 2021.

Similarly, the number of robberies in San Diego has gone down from a high of 3,200 in 2012 to a ten-year low of 2,418 in 2021. Residential burglaries have plummeted over the ten-year period from a high of 9,375 in 2012 to a low of 3,226 in 2021. Residential and non-residential burglaries have gone down from their peak in 2012 of 14,076 to a ten-year low of 7,149 in 2021.

There was no crime spike in San Diego County after the police-involved shooting of Michael Brown in 2015, nor any other high-profile case where a black man was shot by the police in any subsequent year.

There was no appreciable crime spike in San Diego County in 2020 after the COVID-19 pandemic caused the country to shut down.

In 2019 and again in 2020, there were 115 homicides in San Diego County and only a slight uptick to 118 homicides in 2021.

Unlike all the rogue prosecutors featured in this book, Stephan did not fire anyone upon taking office, nor did prosecutors quit out of disgust for her policies or during the pandemic. Based on our interviews with deputy district attorneys in the office, and from speaking with Summer

Stephan herself, morale in the office is high, and there is tremendous job satisfaction. This stands in sharp contrast to the culture of the offices featured in this book.

## RECIDIVISM AND BAIL-REFORM INSANITY

One of the ubiquitous myths peddled by rogue prosecutors, the Soros machine, and their enablers, like Fair and Just Prosecution, is that by "promoting a justice system grounded in fairness, equity, compassion, and fiscal responsibility," crime will go down over time.[22] They argue, and would have voters believe, that their approach to prosecution protects the public both from crime and saves them money by reducing the need for expensive prisons and jails.

The dangerous social experiment they have unleashed across the country includes a push to require that most persons charged with crimes be released immediately, regardless of their criminal record. Fair and Just Prosecution actually has argued that "local prosecutors can help make communities safer and the justice system safer by supporting the elimination of a money bail system, which penalizes defendants who cannot afford to post bond."[23]

That's just silly talk, dangerous, and frankly stupid.

Fair and Just Prosecution tries to sell the public on this idea by writing that "common sense dictates that people should not be held in jail or penalized simply because they cannot afford a monetary payment."[24] They even have a cute little phrase they use to sum up their position: the "poverty penalty."

On its face, that sounds reasonable, until you start thinking about it. But what if the person is dangerous? Violent? A career criminal? A sex offender? A repeat offender? Is it common sense to let them walk out of the back of the jail after arrest?

What they frame as a "poverty penalty" is, in reality, a common sense, proven way to keep people in jail pending trial to ensure public safety. Judges must have a way to assess the risk that offenders pose to their communities. That's often missing, or shockingly anemic, in most bail-reform proposals.

Noticeably absent from the *New York Times* and other articles decrying the criminal justice system's so-called mass incarceration and the "lack of fairness" is a serious discussion of recidivism rates based on facts and data and peer-reviewed studies.[25] The reason for that is quite clear: the recidivism rates for local, state, and federal prisoners are shockingly high. Re-offending, that is, choosing to commit more crimes while out on probation, parole, court supervision, or pending a trial, is gender, age, and race neutral.

But common sense and data have nothing to do with the rogue prosecutor movement, despite their ad nauseam assertions to the contrary.

The fact is that in places that have enacted bail reform, recidivism rates have skyrocketed, including for violent crime. Most people don't know this because the press and advocates for bail reform fudge numbers, studies, outright lie, or simply ignore reality to push through and justify their procriminal bail reform fantasies.

## THE CHICAGO AND NEW YORK BAIL REFORM DISASTERS

Until recently, there haven't been many empirical studies on the effects of bail reform. That changed in July 2017, when the chief judge of the Cook County Circuit Court, Timothy Evans—an attorney who served on the city council before taking the bench in 1992—announced that starting in September of that year, felony bond judges would be required to determine whether a suspect is dangerous in order to impose bail. If a judge determines that the suspect is not dangerous but has a reason to believe that he may not return to court, the judge would be required to ensure that the defendant can afford the amount of bail.[26]

Of course, even when judges professed to consider an accused's dangerousness when deciding whether to grant bail, this dangerousness consideration was often so circumscribed as to essentially be meaningless.[27]

Chief Judge Evans said that he made this change because Kim Foxx and other officials agreed that whether someone was held in pretrial custody should not depend on the person's ability to pay.[28] Sound familiar?

Eighteen months after the new program went into effect, Chief Judge Evans published a study entitled "Bail Reform in Cook County." It claimed that the new pretrial reforms led to an increase in the percentage of defendants who were released pretrial—from 72 percent to 81 percent of all defendants.

The more titillating finding was this: the study claimed that the new, more lenient release procedures did not increase crime.[29] That finding was significant because, in ensuing years, it has been cited repeatedly by other rogue prosecutors and their supporters.

The problem with that finding, however, is that it just wasn't true. In fact, the opposite was true.

In one academic study analyzing that data, researchers found that the "number of released defendants charged with committing new crimes increased by about 45%" after the new program was implemented.

More damning was this: the number of "pretrial releases charged with new violent crimes increased by about 33%."[30] The *Chicago Tribune* also analyzed Chief Judge Evans's report and found "flaws in both the data underlying Evans' report and the techniques he used to analyze it."[31]

Evans limited violent crime to only six offenses for the study and excluded assault with a deadly weapon, armed violence, and reckless homicide, among other crimes commonly understood to be violent offenses. The *Tribune* noted that the "report's underlying data also was flawed in multiple ways that led to an undercount of murders and other violent crimes allegedly committed by people out on bail."[32]

In other words, the "study" is garbage. But that hasn't stopped Fair and Just Prosecution from touting the program.[33] They don't mention the empirical study casting doubt on the Cook County program or any of the other negative reports on the abysmal failure of bail-reform efforts and recidivism rates.

Moreover, although the Cook County program has been a complete failure, that hasn't stopped them from continuing to use it.

Not to be outdone by Cook County, New York state lawmakers passed a controversial bail reform law in April 2019 that went into effect on January 1, 2020.

Prior to that time, when an individual was arrested and charged with a crime, he was brought before a judge who, in turn, had to decide whether the charged person would be released prior to his trial, and if so, what conditions (if any) he would require of the person in exchange for allowing him to be outside of jail prior to trial.

Under the law at that time, the judge's decision could only be based on whether he thought the accused was a flight risk—not based on his criminal record or whether he posed a high risk of reoffending during the pretrial period.

The tools available to judges at that time were: (1) allowing an accused to be released on his own recognizance or (2) requiring an accused to post bail. In general, bail is "a security such as cash or a bond…required by a court for the release of a prisoner who must appear in court at a future time."[34]

Contrary to what progressives want everyone to believe, most people in New York City did not rot away in jail pending trial simply because of a "poverty penalty." In fact, "only about 10% (26,350) of the more than 250,000 individuals arrested by the New York Police Department (NYPD) in 2018 went to jail after failing to make bail at their initial court appearance. Of those defendants who entered jail, 70% (approximately 18,445) made bail within a week, and another 17% (approximately 4479) made bail within a month."[35] As the Manhattan Institute's Rafael Mangual notes, "in other words, just over 3,100 defendants spent more than 30 days in pretrial detention in 2018."[36]

Most criminal defendants across the state were also released pretrial. But that fact didn't dissuade New York lawmakers and then-Governor Andrew Cuomo from amending the state's bail law, codified in Article 500 of New York's Code of Criminal Procedure.[37] This law virtually eviscerated judicial discretion, placed limits on the conditions judges could impose, and required judges to articulate, on the record, any rationale for imposing any pretrial conditions.

Under the new regime, cash bail is prohibited for all individuals charged with misdemeanor offenses, except misdemeanor sex offenses, criminal contempt of court, or some domestic violence misdemeanors, regardless of their criminal history. It is also prohibited for virtually all nonviolent felony defendants, again regardless of the accused's criminal history.[38]

In a narrow class of serious cases, cash bail and pretrial detention are options for trial judges, most notably for those accused of having committed most violent felonies and certain sex-related offenses. But judges are not required to put any conditions on such defendants if they don't want to.

One of the most restrictive new rules is that for most offenses, judges must release defendants on their own recognizance unless that defendant poses a risk of flight. This essentially neuters the judge, as he is in the best position to weigh whether it is in the best interests of the public at-large to let this defendant, with the criminal record he may have, roam the streets prior to trial. Defendants in New York are no different than those in Cook County, as you might have guessed.

The law did not restrict the ability of judges to put defendants on supervised release, impose travel restrictions, require electronic monitoring, and, naturally, restrict firearms possession.

After blowback from law enforcement officials and others, New York legislators slightly revised the bail law to allow judges to expand the list of qualifying offenses where bail could be set, but that "expansion" was marginal at best.

New York is the only state that forbids judges from basing "any decision regarding a defendant's pretrial release on the public safety risk he poses."[39] To sum up: this new law does not allow a judge to deny pretrial release to a defendant who poses a public safety risk, and it prohibits judges from considering the public safety risk when setting monetary or nonmonetary conditions on those granted pretrial release.

Even Illinois, California, New Jersey, Maryland, Washington, DC, Rhode Island, Washington State, and Wisconsin, all notable for their lax bail laws, allow judges to consider public safety risks when making a decision about whether to impose cash bail or nonmonetary conditions of release.

The results of New York's bail reform law have been as disastrous as they were predictable. One in every five (20 percent) defendants arrested for burglary or theft in New York in 2021 was rearrested on a felony charge within sixty days of being released back into the streets, according to New York City Police Department statistics.[40]

Even more troubling is the fact that these same statistics show recidivism rates "as high as three times what they were in 2017…before New York's controversial bail-reform law took effect in 2020."[41]

According to the *New York Post*, "suspects arrested last year [2021] for misdemeanor petit larceny amid the city's ongoing shoplifting spree went on to quickly commit more serious crimes, with 21.6% charged with felonies less than two months later."[42]

The NYPD's "five-year comparisons show 23.7% of last year's burglary suspects were rearrested within 60 days, up from 7.7% in 2017—an increase of 208%."[43] A similar pattern was seen with grand larceny—19.7 percent up from 6.5 percent; auto thieves, 21 percent up from 10.3 percent.[44]

Professor Eugene O'Donnell of the John Jay College of Criminal Justice said that state lawmakers "didn't level with people when they did bail reform."[45] No doubt aware of the large body of literature that shows that when negative behavior receives immediate negative consequences,[46] O'Donnell added, "There used to be a cooling off period where someone was arrested and held. The bad guys are literally beating the arresting officers back to the neighborhood."[47]

Recidivism rates are also through the roof for defendants on supervised release in New York. According to data compiled by the New York State Office of Court Administration and the state Division of Criminal Justice Services, 23 percent of those who were out of jail on supervised release were rearrested on felony charges between January 2020 and June 2021. When you factor in new misdemeanor arrests, the number skyrocketed to 41 percent. And that's just the criminals who were caught, which is a fairly low number compared to the actual number of misdemeanors and felonies committed each day in New York.

The numbers speak for themselves. New York's bail-reform law was a risky gamble, and it has failed, but those invested in this type of procriminal policy continue to stand behind the reforms or try to shift the blame of its failure on—you guessed it—the COVID-19 pandemic. Insha Rahman, a former public defender who joined the Vera Institute as vice president of advocacy and partnerships, surmised that the number of rearrests could be related to COVID-19, saying that the "supervised release program was forced to temporarily shut down when the pandemic first emerged…it is therefore no surprise that the program's ability to serve people effectively was compromised."[48]

So instead of placing the blame where the blame should be placed—on the repeat offenders, who probably shouldn't have been released in the first place—Rahman blames the pandemic and lack of resources. Rahman, no doubt speaking for other cheerleaders for the progressive prosecutor playbook, said that the risk of rearrest is worth the price of reducing the harm by pretrial incarceration.[49]

Tell that to the thousands of unnecessary victims of crimes by these recidivists who should have been in jail pending their new charges, based not only on their flight risk but also their dangerousness and prior criminal record.

These recidivism results are not unique to Illinois or New York.

In California, after the outbreak of the COVID-19 pandemic, Governor Gavin Newsom declared a state of emergency, part of which was an executive order to stay at home issued on March 19, 2020. A statewide emergency bail policy was instituted on April 19, 2020, which set bail at zero dollars for most misdemeanors and nonviolent felonies.

Even though California's judicial council voted to end the statewide emergency bail schedule on June 10, 2020, individual counties were allowed to make their own decisions.

Yolo County, near Sacramento, kept the policy in place until May 31, 2021. Yolo County, in conjunction with the district attorney's office and other law enforcement, released a report on the recidivism of the 595 unique individuals who were released from custody in Yolo County under the emergency bail guidelines.

Not surprisingly, 420—70.6 percent—were rearrested after being released, including for the following crimes:[50]

- Homicide (1)
- Attempted homicide (5)
- Kidnapping (5)
- Robbery (32)

- Carjacking (4)
- Assault to commit rape (1)
- Assault with a deadly weapon (46)
- Domestic violence (29)

Five people were arrested on the day they were released. Fourteen (2.4 percent) were arrested within a day. Forty-six (7.7 percent) were arrested within seven days of being released. One hundred and four people (17.5 percent) were arrested within thirty days of being released. A whopping 288 (48.4 percent) were arrested within 180 days of being released. Many individuals were arrested on more than one charge during the timeframe.

Recidivism rates are real. The three examples featured above are by no means unique. Career criminals commit crimes at an astounding rate. Most of the time, they get away with it.

Finally, time in prison or jail does have an impact on recidivism rates. Contrary to the nonsense spewed by rogue prosecutors and their supporters, there is ample evidence that the longer a criminal serves in prison, the lower the recidivism rate is for that person once he emerges from prison.

In their latest report on the length of incarceration and recidivism, the United States Sentencing Commission (USSC) examined 32,135 federal offenders who reentered the community during 2010 after discharging their sentence of incarceration.[51]

The USSC found that the odds of recidivism were approximately 29 percent lower for federal offenders sentenced to more than ten years of incarceration compared to a matched group of federal offenders receiving shorter sentences. And the odds of recidivism were approximately 18 percent lower for offenders sentenced to more than five years up to ten years of incarceration compared to a matched group of federal offenders receiving shorter sentences.

The USSC concluded: "This study found that offenders confined for longer periods of incarceration had lower odds of recidivism."

The USSC 2022 findings were virtually identical to prior USSC research examining federal offenders released in 2005.

As you read this book and consider the policies of each rogue prosecutor, ask yourself this: Does this policy, standing alone, make the community and/or victims safer? Does the policy hold offenders accountable for their crime(s)? Would a first-time offender be dissuaded from committing more crimes based on the way his case was handled? Do the residents of the county where this rogue prosecutor presides live in safety, knowing that their elected district attorney cares about them more than the criminals? Do these policies promote justice?

The answer to each of these questions, sadly, is a resounding no.

But that doesn't matter to these rogues, given their radical roots, radical belief system, and ultimate goal—to tear down and to fundamentally reimagine and reengineer our criminal justice system from the ground up.

# CHAPTER 1

# THEIR ORIGINS, BELIEFS, AND PLAYBOOK

*"...imagine a world without prisons."*[52]

**Angela Davis**

*"Getting rid of police, prisons and jails, sur-veillance, and courts."*[53]

**Patrisse Cullors**

T he progressive prosecutor movement, which we call the "rogue prose-cutor" movement, is the organic and predictable outgrowth of efforts by earlier radicals, including American Marxists and Communists, to for-ever alter—abolish—the American way of life as we know it.

Long before there was a rogue prosecutor movement—which began in earnest around 2015—there were radical activists who argued for the abolition of capitalism, prisons, corporations, and called for the redistri-bution of wealth, socialized healthcare, and reparations for slavery.

To understand how and why the rogue prosecutor movement came into being, and why rogue prosecutors implement the polices they do, you have to go back in time well before the first rogue prosecutor was hand selected and installed into office.

The intellectual lineage of the abolitionist movement, occupying the shadowy corners of the radical left, went essentially unnoticed by the pub-lic, the media, and most Americans. That's because for most Americans on the right or mainstream left, the ideas espoused by these activists were so far out of the norm as to be almost laughable. Their ideas were antithetical to a democratic republic, where capitalism, the rule of law, individual responsibility, and a constitution that grants the federal government only limited and enumerated powers and places limitations on state governments, too, were conjoined to make the United States.

The fact that most of the abolitionists' ideas have not attracted widespread attention or support among mainstream politicians and have failed to garner support from the public has not dissuaded them from writing, holding conferences, agitating, and nurturing and further developing their ideas and arguments. These intellectual ancestors of the rogue prosecutor movement have thrived in a self-contained, self-nurturing, and self-absorbed ecosystem, regardless of whether any of their nutty (and often dangerous) ideas eventually were commonly accepted.

But significant cultural events, real and perceived, such as the rise in crime and incarceration rates, the existence of the death penalty, and the obsession by the media, activists, and academics

on race and police misconduct, laid the groundwork for the idea to replace independent, law and order, elected prosecutors with hand-selected activists who were procriminal and antivictim.

## ABOLITIONIST ROOTS

If you listen to the proponents and activists in the rogue prosecutor movement, including the district attorneys themselves, you will think that their movement was inspired by and created to be an antidote to the so-called "tough on crime" prosecutors, the death penalty, and "mass incarceration." On one level, that is true. They came into existence, as detailed below, precisely to act as a counterweight to law-and-order prosecutors, to abolish the use of the death penalty no matter the crime, and to stop sending most criminals to jail.

But on a deeper level, the truth is that their efforts are merely the latest tactic, albeit highly sophisticated, well-funded, and effective, of those in the abolitionist movement and other radical agitators.

At the root of the abolitionist movement is the belief that our country, and its institutions, including capitalism, is racist. Mark Levin made the case in his book *American Marxism* that "the progressive intellectuals of the late 1800s and early 1900s laid the foundation for the present day acceptance and indoctrination of the Marxist ideology throughout academia, society, and the culture.[54] They made clear their hostility toward capitalism and the constitutional-republican system that established barriers against tyrannies of various kinds, including that which is born from the mob or centralized autocracy—and, of course, what would become known as progressivism."

Those progressive intellectuals of long ago inspired modern radicals and movements such as Herbert Marcuse, Students for a Democratic Society (SDS), Jean Anyon, Marcus Garvey, the Black Panthers, the Black Power movement, the Black Liberation Army, Stokely Carmichael, Huey Newton, Angela Davis, Malcolm X, and JoAnne Chesimard, among others.

But progressivism doesn't really capture the intellectual underpinnings of this rogue prosecutor movement. Many can regard progressivism as misguided, perhaps, but benign. Our Heritage colleague Mike Gonzalez makes clear the intellectual godfathers of the "progressive prosecutor" movement aren't really progressives. They're full-blown Marxists. In his book *BLM: The Making of a New Marxist Revolution*, Mike says they "embraced both Marx's ideas and Lenin's means, with an additional dose of Red Guard Maoism." It's bad stuff all around.

The modern-day heirs of these intellectuals argue that America was built on the backs of slaves and their slave labor. They believe that even though we fought a Civil War to end slavery, passed and ratified the Thirteenth Amendment, abolished Jim Crow laws, passed the Civil Rights Acts, brought Supreme Court cases like *Brown v. Board of Education* and more, that the entire United States, all corporations, American capitalism, and the criminal justice systems in all fifty states and the federal government are systemically racist. To them, the only solution is a radical transformation of our entire system of government, including the norms and practices of civil society. Only then can we erase and cleanse ourselves as a just country from the original sin of slavery.

Of course, this narrative is wrong. But as Levin chronicled in *American Marxism*, "The period of the late 1950s to the early 1970s gave rise to the New Left movement on America's college campuses, [and is] much heralded by today's Marxists. Students for a Democratic Society (SDS), among the most prominent of the New Left Groups, was founded in 1959 and issued its political manifesto, The Port Huron Statement, in 1962"[55] which condemned capitalism and endorsed revolution.

One of the leaders of the modern abolitionist movement is Angela Davis. She wrote the highly influential book, *Are Prisons Obsolete?* In it, Davis unabashedly calls on us to "imagine a world without prisons."[56] She equates prisons to modern-day slavery and opines that "the prison has become a black hole into which the detritus of contemporary capitalism is deposited," and that throwing people into prisons "relieves us of the responsibility of seriously engaging with the problems of our society, especially those produced by racism and, increasingly, global capitalism."[57]

It's hard to overstate how influential Davis's advocacy and writings have been on the rogue prosecutor movement, and how she, in a way, is one of the intellectual bridges between the radicals of old and today. She decries the "prison industrial complex" and wrote that "prisons are racist institutions"[58] filled with "enormous numbers of people [who] are in prison simply because they are, for example, black, Chicano, Vietnamese, Native American or poor, regardless of their ethnic background."[59]

Two other women who have had an enormous influence on the abolitionist movement, and whose work and ideas influenced the rogue prosecutor movement, are Patrisse Cullors and Alicia Garza (aka Alicia Schwartz).

Cullors is a radical militant. Her adopted father abandoned her, and her biological father spent time in prison. Cullors herself went to jail for illegal drug use. She grew up as a Jehovah's Witness in the San Fernando Valley. While there, she studied apartheid and communism. After she graduated from high school, "a history teacher told her about a radical seven-day camp, the Brotherhood-Sisterhood social justice camp, and Cullors enrolled in it. She studied more about 'systems of oppression' and was encouraged to celebrate her lesbianism."[60]

In his book on BLM, Mike Gonzalez outlines what happened next: Cullors joined the Labor/Community Strategy Center, which was the brainchild of Eric Mann of the Weather Underground. Mann, a convicted felon himself, calls the Labor/Community Strategy Center the "Harvard of Revolutionary graduate schools." In 2008, he told students at the University of California, San Diego, that the center's purpose is "to build an anti-racist, anti-imperialist, anti-fascist united front."[61]

Cullors put her revolutionary graduate training to work and founded Dignity and Power Now, which, according to its website, is a "Los Angeles based grassroots organization founded in 2012 that fights for the dignity and power of all incarcerated people, their families, and communities." It says, "Our mission is to build a Black and Brown led abolitionist movement rooted in community power."[62]

According to their website, Dignity and Power Now is "founded and chaired by Black Lives Matter (BLM) Cofounder Patrisse Khan-Cullors."[63]

In a 2019 *Harvard Law Review* article about abolition and reparations, Cullors praised the work of Angela Davis, writing that she is a "philosopher, Marxist, and former Black Panther whose work on prisons, abolition, and Black struggle has proven relevant over time—has informed our movements and communities for decades. Her political theories and reflections on anticapitalist movements around the world have sought not only to transform U.S. society by challenging white supremacy in U.S. laws, institutions, and relationships, but also to act as a catalyst toward building a broader antiracist and antiwar movement internationally."[64]

Alicia Garza, another co-founder of BLM (along with Patrisse Cullors and Opal Tometi), is a towering figure in the abolitionist movement, and is also a devotee of Angela Davis. Born in 1981 in Los Angeles, Garza is a vocal and vituperative critic of capitalism and the rule of law in the United States. At the Left Forum in 2015, a gathering of Marxists from around the world, sponsored by the John Jay College, City University of New York, Garza said, "It's not possible for a world to emerge where black lives matter if it's under capitalism. And it's not possible to abolish capitalism without a struggle against national oppression and gender oppression."[65]

In that same speech at the Left Forum, Garza said that the Black Lives Matter movement is "an organized network, in 26 cities, globally. It's also intended to be a tactic to help rebuild the Black Liberation Movement. BLM. BLM." In her telling, BLM was created as a response to "police terrorism."

Garza wasn't done yet, though. Later, in the same speech, Garza said, "Black folks have been murdered since we were brought here. This is not a new phenomenon…. It's part of a plan to subvert, to oppress, and in some cases, many cases especially now, to extinguish black lives. To get rid of us."

She noted that Black Lives Matter started in 2013 when George Zimmerman was acquitted of the "murder" of Trayvon Martin. But she suggests that the inspiration for the movement preceded the formal creation of Black Lives Matter, saying: "If we root this in historical conditions, Black Lives Matter was present when Oscar Grant was murdered [in 2009] three blocks from my house. Black Lives Matter was present when Rodney King was brutally beaten on television in 1992. When Sean Bell was murdered [in 2006] on his wedding day. When Amadou Diallo was shot forty-one times [in 1999]."

She continued, "Criminalization is the way that black bodies have been forced from the formalized economy. It's also a way to subvert and abolish the Black Liberation Movement. Our brother Mumia, our sister Asada, our brother Herman Bell, and so many more, are behind bars because of the vision they espoused."[66]

To give you a sense of those supposedly oppressed because of "the vision they espoused," consider the case of Mumia Abu-Jamal (aka Wesley Cook). He was a member of the Black Panther Party and a "journalist" in Philadelphia when, in 1981, he shot and killed Philadelphia police officer Daniel Faulkner after Faulkner pulled over his brother during a traffic stop. He was convicted and sentenced to death in 1982. In 2011, his conviction was upheld, but the death sentence was overturned. He was resentenced to life in prison.

Like most cop killers, Abu-Jamal/Cook is a hero and victim to members of the hard left like Angela Davis, Patrice Cullors, and Alicia Garza.

During a 2017 interview on PBS with Angela Davis, Garza heaped praise on Davis for her work exposing the "carceral state," and called on others to "enter into it to dismantle it."[67]

Make no mistake. They want killers like Cook freed.

# THE BIRTH OF THE ROGUE PROSECUTOR MOVEMENT

But what's the best way to accomplish these goals? Two years before the PBS interview with Garza and Davis, the rogue prosecutor movement was born.

Like a lot of movements, it wasn't a national movement at first but started locally, with a test run, if you will. Like many nascent movements, this movement started out with a narrow focus, and only after finding success achieving its narrow goals did the early leaders decide to expand their reach and goals nationally.

This brings us to Whitney Tymas and Chloe Cockburn.

In 2015, Whitney Tymas went to work for George Soros, the liberal billionaire who had been funding liberal causes for years. An African American female, Tymas had worked as a public defender in Harlem and the Bronx, and then, moved to Richmond, Virginia, where she was an assistant commonwealth's attorney (a line state prosecutor).

As Emily Bazelon notes in her book *Charged*, Tymas not only was the lead on a project for the National District Attorney's Association on community prosecutors, but she also worked at the Vera Institute of Justice where she focused on "the role of prosecutors in perpetuating racial disparity."[68]

It was during her first week working for Soros that Tymas met Chloe Cockburn, who at the time was working at the ACLU as advocacy and policy counsel, and working to end "mass incarceration." A graduate of Harvard University and Harvard Law School, Cockburn did a summer clerkship with the Public Defender Service for the District of Columbia, worked for a year at the Vera Institute of Justice, became a program officer in criminal justice at the left-wing Open Philanthropy Project, and just recently (2021) founded and became the CEO of Just Impact Advisors, "a grantmaking and donor advisory group devoted to ending mass incarceration and building autonomous political power of communities most impacted by mass incarceration."[69]

Cockburn had all the right credentials and contacts when she met Tymas, and they hit it off immediately. They talked about the role of prosecutors, how elections for local prosecutors were low visibility races, and how, according to an ACLU poll, "half of sixteen hundred voters said they didn't know the D.A. was elected."[70]

Both are opponents of the death penalty, so they decided to take advantage of this information and do something. They realized that if they could help unseat an elected DA who supported the death penalty and replace him with an antideath-penalty DA, they would be advancing their beliefs. Essentially, they wanted to short circuit the system. It didn't matter what death penalty laws were on the books if an antideath-penalty prosecutor refused to enforce them. So, Cockburn and Tymas got in touch "with a group of death penalty opponents around the country who aimed to unseat prosecutors who sought execution frequently."[71]

According to Scott Bland, George Soros "put over $1 million into 'Safety and Justice' groups that helped elect two anti-death penalty district attorneys in Louisiana and Mississippi and re-elect a third—Hinds County, Miss., DA Robert Shuler Smith."[72]

Death penalty opponents targeted those races because these areas "had the highest death sentence rate[s] per capita of any county in the nation. The jurisdictions were relatively small, but the races showed it was possible to defeat incumbents known for overzealousness"[73]—or at least what Cockburn, Tymas, and their ilk perceived to be overzealousness.

"With three wins in Mississippi and Louisiana, the time seemed right to go bigger…Tymas launched an operation for local DA races like the one the Democratic Congressional Campaign Committee ran for house races, working with the political consulting firm Berlin Rosen."[74]

What began as a modest goal—to unseat prosecutors who sought the death penalty—grew into a national movement with more ambitious goals. And their timing was good: the country had elected, and reelected, the first black president, Black Lives Matter was coming to national attention, and a handful of high-profile shootings by the police of black Americans occurred.

Emily Bazelon sums up the realization of Tymas, Cockburn, and others at the birth of the rogue prosecutor movement: "Change who occupies the prosecutor's office, and you can make the system operate differently."[75] Like Angela Davis, the unabashed prison abolitionist, these authors of the rogue prosecutor movement sought to abolish the traditional concept of a prosecutor who enforced the law as written and to instead "choose prosecutors who will open the locks"[76] of prisons.

Backed by the deep pockets of George Soros, Dustin Moskovitz (a tech billionaire), and others, Tymas set her sights on a national campaign.

Enter Kim Foxx and the then-Cook County State's Attorney Anita Alvarez, the elected DA (state's attorney) of Chicago. But why Chicago? On its face, it just didn't make sense.

A Hispanic Democrat, Alvarez was a career prosecutor, starting in the Cook County state's attorney's office in 1986. She rose through the ranks, trying more than fifty felony jury trials and serving in leadership positions in the narcotics and gang units. Twenty-two years into her career in the office, she ran for state's attorney as a Democrat and won. She was the first Hispanic female elected to an office that, until then, had elected only white males dating back to 1896.

But to Tymas and her growing coterie, Alvarez was vulnerable because of her support for mandatory minimum penalties for gun crimes, her initial refusal to file charges against Chicago police officer Jason Van Dyke for shooting and killing seventeen-year-old African American Laquan McDonald, and her lack of support for releasing the police dash cam video of the shooting.

Black Lives Matter and the Open Philanthropy Project pushed for police accountability. They demanded that the mayor, Rahm Emanuel, and Alvarez release the video. Emanuel and Alvarez resisted.

Initial reports from the police indicated that McDonald had been walking down the middle of the street armed with a knife, was acting odd, and when ordered to drop the knife, lunged at the police. Over a year later, after a court ordered the video to be released, the public saw what really happened: McDonald was walking away from the police when he was shot sixteen times by officer Van Dyke. Van Dyke was charged with first-degree murder, and after a trial, was found guilty of second-degree murder.

"With the polls showing that Alvarez was beatable, Soros contributed $400,000 to create the Illinois Safety and Justice PAC, which also received $300,000 from the Civic Participation Action Fund, a nonpartisan funder that seeks to engage people of color in the democratic process," according to Emily Bazelon.[77]

They recruited Kim Foxx, a former prosecutor who grew up in the Chicago projects, to run against Alvarez in the primary. Foxx, flush with cash from the Illinois Safety and Justice PAC and others, amassed $3.8 million and beat Alvarez in the March 2016 primary 58.3 percent to 28.7 percent. Not surprisingly, in the heavily Democratic city of Chicago, Foxx won the general election 72 percent to 28 percent in November 2016.

And so, the national movement was born.

## COUNTING ON VOTER AMNESIA

Advocates for electing rogue prosecutors have been successful in large part because they have relied on voters' general ignorance of the fact that crime (especially violent crime) and incarceration rates have been going down dramatically over the past twenty-five years.

There's a lot of historical amnesia about the cause of prison expansion, a mistaken sense that it was all about drugs or race and has very little to do with serious crime.[78] This ignores the facts.[79] As Barry Latzer points out in the *Wall Street Journal*, "Between 1960 and 1990, the rate of violent crime in the U.S. surged by over 350 percent, according to FBI data, the biggest buildup in the country's history."[80]

Prison populations swelled during that time, but that was because of violent crime. By the middle of the 1990s, as the charts below show, crime began to drop, as did incarceration rates.

## U.S. VIOLENT AND PROPERTY CRIME RATE HAVE PLUNGED SINCE 1990s, REGARDLESS OF DATA SOURCE

U.S. Violent and Property Crime, 1993-2019

Note: FBI figures include reported crimes only. Bureau of Justice Statistics (BJS) figures include unreported and reported crimes. 2006 BJS estimates are not comparable to those in other years due to methodological changes.

SOURCES: U.S. BUREAU OF JUSTICE STATISTICS (BJS); FEDERAL BUREAU OF INVESTIGATION (FBI); PEW RESEARCH CENTER, WWW.PEWRESEARCH.ORG/FACT-TANK/2020/11/20/FACTS-ABOUT-CRIME-IN-THE-U-S/.

☎ heritage.org

Progressives decry the "war on drugs" and argue that it was primarily responsible for mass incarceration. But that just isn't true either. As Michael Shellenberger writes in his book *San Fransicko*, "During the 1990s and 2000s, an estimated 50 percent of the increase in state prisons came from those convicted of violent offenses,"[81] citing the Justice Department's Bureau of Justice statistics. Violence, not stricter drug sentences, drove so-called mass incarceration.[82]

But facts and real data don't stop rogue prosecutors from peddling the idea that mass incarceration still exists and that the increased incarceration rates of the past are (were) the prosecutors' fault.

As Jeffrey Bellin noted in his review of Emily Bazelon's book *Charged: The New Movement to Transform American Prosecution and End Mass Incarceration*, "Contrary to prominent voices quoted throughout *Charged* and in the academic literature, mass incarceration did not arise because increasingly aggressive prosecutors seized too much power from hapless legislators and judges. Rather, the phenomenon came about through a slow-developing consensus among those, including prosecutors, who were supposed to check the State's power to punish."[83] Bellin noted that the rise in incarceration rates happened because of rising crime rates and the response to them by legislators, judges, police, governors, and voters.[84]

Today, incarceration rates in the United States are at a thirty-year low.[85] Even in 1997, just 1 percent of all prisoners were in for a first or second nonviolent drug offense, and only 4 percent of state prisoners were drug "kingpins."[86]

According to Shellenberger, "Of the people convicted of drug offenses, 62 percent never went to prison and one-third never went to prison or jail. And while 43 million drug arrests between 1980 and 2012 sound like a lot, over the same period there were 445 million total arrests, making drugs less than 10 percent of all arrests."[87]

According to the Bureau of Justice Statistics, as noted by Shellenberger, "The data reveals that just 3.7 percent of state prisoners are there for nonviolent drug possession, and that 14.1 percent of state prisoners are locked up for any nonviolent drug offense.... Over half of all prisoners in state prisons are there for violent offenses like murder, rape and robbery."[88]

Shockingly, the US homicide rate is seven times higher than the combined rates of twenty-one Western nations plus Japan, according to a 2011 study by researchers of the Harvard School of Public Health and the UCLA School of Public Health.[89] Of course high rates of homicide destroy the fabric of cities and communities.[90]

Proponents and advocates for the progressive prosecutor movement realize that rising crime rates are the Achilles heel of their movement. As Rachel Barkow acknowledges in the introduction to her book, *Prisoners of Politics: Breaking the Cycle of Mass Incarceration*, the movement could falter if crime rates rise.[91] Others, like Emily Bazelon, disagree but also seem not to grasp the amount of violent crime that happens in our country, writing, "Some people commit truly violent crimes—not that many, relatively speaking, but some—and a subset cause unconscionable harm."[92]

As later chapters will demonstrate, Bazelon and all of the eight rogue prosecutors featured in this book have their heads in the sand on rising crime rates and the connection between the policies they espouse and the meteoric rise in those numbers.

One of the most common tactics of rogue prosecutors is the refusal to prosecute possession of marijuana cases, even in states where marijuana possession is a misdemeanor. They give all sorts of excuses for the failure to hold people accountable for this behavior. Again, playing on the public's ignorance of what is really happening in the criminal justice system, they say they are not prosecuting simple possession of marijuana cases because no one should go to jail or prison for that offense—suggesting by their excuse that people actually ARE in jail for simple possession.

Dr. Kevin Sabet, who worked in the Office of National Drug Control Policy in the Clinton administration, chronicled some of the more outlandish false statements about the pot-to-prison narrative in his book *Reefer Sanity: Seven Great Myths about Marijuana.*[93]

For example, NPR reporter and host of a show on Boston Public Radio, Margery Eagan, opined, "Though there aren't enough cells for violent criminals, marijuana smokers and small-time dealers are going to prison by the thousands—sometimes for life."[94] In another, Eric Schlosser, author of *Reefer Madness*, wrote, "We are a nation overrun with robbers, rapists, murderers, wife beaters, child molesters. We say we're petrified of them. Yet we're releasing them first from overcrowded jails so dope smokers can take their cells."[95]

Eagan's and Schlosser's comments are "fear-based, hyperbolic statements"[96] and not based on the facts. As Sabet notes, "The reality, according to studies by the Bureau of Justice is that only one-tenth of one percent of people in state prisons are serving sentences for first-time marijuana possession. Just three-tenths of one percent of people in state prisons are serving time for marijuana possession if they have prior offenses, and only 1.4 percent of people are in jail for offenses involving only marijuana-related crimes."[97]

Furthermore, twenty-two states and territories have legalized marijuana, twenty-seven states have decriminalized marijuana, and forty-two states and territories have so-called "medical" marijuana laws. Hardly anyone in law enforcement, including prosecutors, wants to throw anyone in jail or prison for possessing small amounts of marijuana.[98] And, on the federal side, data has shown that the median amount of marijuana for those convicted of marijuana possession is 115 pounds—or 156,000 marijuana cigarettes.[99] Someone convicted with that kind of weight obviously isn't simply Cheech and Chong[100] or Spicoli from *Fast Times at Ridgemont High*.[101]

To sell the candidates to voters, especially liberal inner-city voters, the backers of rogue prosecutors have created an entire vocabulary of poll-tested words and phrases, designed to buttress and exploit white guilt and self-loathing liberals. These words and phrases include: mass incarceration, correction free lunch, carceral state, overpolicing, structural racism, school-to-prison pipeline, youth interrogation, overincarceration, poverty penalty, decarcerate, shrink the justice system, the old law-and-order script, and many other words and phrases. Many of these ideas come directly from the abolitionist movement.

In practice, however, the policies of rogue prosecutors, discussed in detail throughout this book, have been devastating to African Americans and other minorities in the inner city. Tens of thousands of minorities have been murdered, shot, raped, burgled, and assaulted. Minority businesses in the inner city have been decimated, their livelihoods destroyed, because of thefts of goods and property damage. Residents of the inner city, who, like anyone else, want to feel safe, want their kids to get a good education, and strive for a better life, live in fear and have suffered the brunt of the lawlessness emblematic of rogue prosecutors' policies.

The irony of the movement, which is supposed to help minorities by not holding people fully accountable for their crimes, is that more minorities are harmed.

## THEIR BELIEFS

Drawing inspiration from the Marxist-inspired abolitionists discussed above, supporters of the rogue prosecutor movement believe that the entire criminal justice system is systemically racist. Conveniently, they also push the idea that they have the solution to fix it. Rachel Barkow, a law professor, author, and a former member of the US Sentencing Commission, has summed up the goal of the progressive prosecutor movement (which she enthusiastically supports) as follows: "To reverse-engineer and dismantle the criminal justice infrastructure" that currently exists.[102]

Barkow is widely revered on the left and an enthusiastic cheerleader for the movement. Her encapsulation of the movement's goals is not hyperbole, nor is this the mere musings of a random outlier professor. She is the author of one of the more influential books on so-called "mass incarceration," a vice dean at NYU's law school, and a former member of the US Sentencing Commission, which sets sentencing policy and guidelines for federal courts throughout the United States. In other words, Barkow is one of the most influential defenders of and advocates for the movement.

Miriam Aroni Krinsky, is the executive director of Fair and Just Prosecution, the umbrella organization that provides resources, education, and funding for rogue prosecutors, and is the chief mouthpiece for the movement nationwide. Krinsky is also the author of the book *Change from Within: Reimagining the 21st Century Prosecutor*, published in 2022. In the introduction to the book, she recounts a trip she led to Berlin Germany with rogue prosecutors. During the trip, they visited Nazi concentration camps where Hitler and his genocidal regime exterminated over six million Jews during WWII. Of that experience, Krinsky wrote: "Scholars of the Nazi regime describe the complicity of inaction by judges, lawyers, and other esteemed community members who sat by silently and enabled horrific things to happen. The antidote is Zivilcourage, 'everyday moral courage,' or the willingness to speak out and work to defy injustice, even at personal risk. In the face of unjust laws and our own country's history of atrocities, we are all called to have the Zivilcourage to reckon with the past and work toward a more righteous future."[103]

Krinsky, the putative leader of the rogue prosecutor movement, is conflating the current United States carceral system with the Nazi regime and the final solution. In her mind, traditional prosecutors are Nazis, and her acolytes are the ones with the moral courage to end the nightmare.

And the only way for advocates of the movement to achieve that ambitious goal—in their minds—is to eliminate independent and traditional prosecutors who enforce the law and seek justice by convicting the guilty and protecting the innocent—the very thing the American Bar Association says is a prosecutor's duty.

The movement consists of donors, candidates for district attorney, elected rogue prosecutors, academics,[104] and activists.[105] Those recruited by the movement to run for office tout their "progressive" bona fides and suggest that we need to "reimagine"[106] a better criminal justice system. Sound familiar?

As we detail in the next chapter, it is a serious movement in large part because leftist billionaires like George Soros and others have dumped and continue to dump tens of millions of dollars into specific DA races, often through dark-money PACs that identify, recruit, and fund criminal defense attorneys to run against independent law-and-order prosecutors.[107] Academics, mostly in the form of law review articles, support and defend the movement.

When we first started looking into this movement, we were struck by the moniker "progressive prosecutor." To us, the word "progressive" denoted forward progress, a new approach, or achieving an old goal in a new way.

We weren't far off. In Merriam-Webster's dictionary, the word *progressive* means "making use of or interested in new ideas, findings, or opportunities."[108] But as we discovered, and as you will discover throughout this book, there is nothing "progressive" about the rogue prosecutor movement.

The only thing that is "new" about this dangerous movement is its members' approach, which has caused crime to explode in the cities where rogue prosecutors reign, harming the very people about whom they profess to care the most.[109]

The *real* progressives are the independent traditional prosecutors who have created thousands of new diversionary programs across the country; have started conviction integrity units in their offices; and have created drug courts, domestic violence courts, and teen/peer courts,[110] prostitution diversion courts,[111] veterans courts, mental health courts,[112] family justice centers,[113] community prosecutors,[114] and more, all of which we discuss in detail in our last chapter. They started these new initiatives because they are charged with keeping their communities safe and are constantly trying new ways to tackle old problems in a better, more cost-effective way within the bounds of the law. Given these welcome developments, it is no surprise that for many of these prosecutors, crime rates in their jurisdictions have gone down, as have incarceration rates.

Rogue prosecutors, on the other hand, call themselves progressive, but they have not started any new collaborative programs like drug, domestic violence, teen, or prostitution courts. Nor did they invent anything like conviction integrity units within district attorney offices. The only thing new about the rogue prosecutor movement is the radical idea of replacing independent, true progressive and traditional prosecutors with criminal defense attorneys, or defendant-oriented attorneys, who pretend to be prosecutors but do the bidding of the elitist billionaire class, with George Soros-funded organizations taking point.

In recent years, a cottage industry of law review articles backing the idea that the whole criminal justice system is racist has sprung up. For example, many of these articles claim that independent and traditional prosecutors are "reluctant to criticize the police,"[115] are "unable or unwilling to bring charges or seek convictions against police officers,"[116] and are "complicit in officer perjury."[117]

A student note in the *Harvard Law Review* opined that the entire criminal legal system "is a racial caste system."[118] The author contends that the criminal justice system is a "fundamentally rotten system" and that "progressive prosecutors seek to rebalance the use of prosecutorial discretion."[119] The system, the author writes, "was never intended to keep marginalized people safe."[120] The irony is that marginalized people, especially people of color, suffer the worst in cities that have elected rogue prosecutors.

Another ill-informed law student wrote that "progressive prosecutors do more than simply churn through cases; they also often consider whether an alternative to incarceration is best for a particular defendant."[121] Whether this student knows it or not, thousands of diversionary programs across the country have been around for decades and were begun by independent, real progressive and traditional prosecutors.

In practice, however, the policies of rogue prosecutors, discussed in detail throughout this book, have been devastating to African Americans and other minorities in the inner city.

# THEIR PLAYBOOK

## *Replacing Independent Law-and-Order Prosecutors with Procriminal DAs*

This well-funded and organized movement is not about liberal versus conservative, Democrat versus Republican, black versus white, or one law-and-order prosecutor against another. This movement is about power. It is about a handful of progressive billionaires manipulating the criminal justice system with large amounts of cash.

The unspoken quid pro quo is that those elected to office must implement elements of the rogue prosecutor playbook. And they have done so with remarkable discipline, to the detriment of law and order and victims, especially minorities.

Rather than run antilaw enforcement candidates for sheriff, the movement realized that a quicker way to implement their radical goals is to run well-financed criminal defense attorneys, or defense-oriented attorneys, for district attorney in liberal cities. The movement is keenly aware that prosecutors, not police, have the final say as to whether charges are filed against people who are arrested, and because prosecutors occupy that unique position, by eliminating independent progressive and traditional prosecutors and replacing them with attorneys who are beholden to a movement that sees defendants as victims, you "reverse-engineer" and "dismantle" the criminal justice system as it currently exists.

It is no coincidence that Soros, his various PACs, and allies have given huge financial support to rogue candidates in liberal cities, as they have the best chance of being elected by a disinterested electorate.[122] One study recently found that even though there are over 2,300 separate state felony prosecutor's offices in the country, and even though incumbents win reelection 95 percent of the time,[123] "incumbents are unlikely to run in contested elections…and…all prosecutor elections are unlikely to be contested."[124] The same study showed that "the larger the jurisdiction, the more likely the election was contested."[125]

Even in district attorney races that are contested, there is usually a relatively small amount of money spent by both sides. Knowing this, the Soros-backed rogue prosecutor movement spends heavily to buy elections, investing vast sums of money to back candidates of their choice, knowing that traditional candidates typically cannot begin to match the infusion of cash that the movement provides.

Ironically, one of the written goals of Soros's Open Society Foundations is to reduce "the undue influence of money in politics" even as they are buying district attorneys who are beholden to their dismantling of the independent truly progressive and traditional prosecutorial system.[126] So much for standing by your principles and working to rid elections of dark money.

For example, when the Philadelphia district attorney's seat became open, seven people ran for office in an open primary. Larry Krasner, featured in Chapter 5, received almost $1.45 million in campaign spending from George Soros.[127]

Immediately after he was elected and sworn into office, Krasner fired thirty-one career prosecutors in the office, many of whom were in the homicide division and highly experienced.[128] Because deputy district attorneys in the Philadelphia DA's office serve at will and do not enjoy civil service protection, Krasner's move was legal, but it was still extraordinary. Firing independent progressive and traditional career-line prosecutors is a recommendation commonly made by leftist members of the academy.[129]

Finally, although big-city district attorneys are the most visible targets for the rogue prosecutor movement, the movement has trained its sights on smaller jurisdictions as well because (1) they account for a large percentage of defendants being sentenced to prison[130] and (2) the financial investment needed to buy a district attorney seat by backing a rogue candidate is small.

"[P]ut simply," in the words of one law review article, "in order for prosecutor elections to serve as an antidote to mass incarceration, more candidates will have to run in rural districts."[131]

Emily Bazelon made clear that "about 40 million Americans, more than 12 percent of the population, lived in a city or county with a D.A." who falls into the progressive prosecutor category.[132] That estimate is now much higher with recent figures showing that one in five Americans, or approximately seventy-two million people, "including half of America's 50 most populous cities and counties" are under the rule of rogue prosecutors.[133]

## *Abusing Their Office by Prosecutorial Nullification*

One of the hallmarks of the rogue prosecutor movement has been its blatant usurpation of the constitutional role of state legislatures. Elected rogue prosecutors have refused to prosecute entire categories of crimes that are on the books in their states, claiming that they are empowered to refuse under the fig leaf of "prosecutorial discretion."

Usurpation of legislative power by refusing to prosecute entire classes of crimes is dangerous. It violates the separation of powers between the executive branch and the legislative branch. In doing so, it distorts the entire legal system by disrupting the equipoise between separate but equal branches of government.

In this regard, separation of powers is not merely a legal technicality. The Framers understood that the quickest path to a democratic republic's destruction would be the accumulation, in a single set of hands, of the power to legislate and to enforce the laws.[134]

A prosecutor's discretion to refrain from bringing cases is not limitless. The principle requires enforcing laws as the legislature has written them, except when the prosecutor believes in good faith that an applicable law is unconstitutional.[135] And their authority does not give them the power to redefine crime and punishment.[136] By refusing to prosecute entire categories of crime and not weighing each case and each offender on a case-by-case basis, they are in effect repealing criminal statutes.[137] Only legislatures can do that, not executive branch employees who swear an oath to uphold the law.

One commentator has called the practice of refusing to prosecute valid laws on the books "taking items off the menu," as if prosecutors are merely cooks at a restaurant.[138] But that's just an attempt at a clever spin for what in reality is prosecutorial nullification.

Defenders of this practice utterly fail to muster strong arguments in support of this abuse of power. In his review of Bazelon's book *Charged*, Jeffrey Bellin wrote that prosecutors who refuse to enforce certain laws on the books act "as a check on the State's power to punish."[139] It's a form of prosecutorial lenience, according to the author.

The author of another law review article applauds the "prosecutorial veto" exercised by rogue prosecutors, writing that there is a "disparity between the state legislature that passes criminal law and the local community where criminal law is enforced."[140] A "non-prosecution policy" therefore "acts…against the democratic inadequacies of the legislative system."[141]

The author suggests in a not-so-subtle manner that rural white legislators pass criminal laws that are used against black inner-city defendants, claiming that "rural residents, who are predominately white, carry disproportionately greater representation in the legislature than urban residents" and that "white and rural populations [therefore] have relatively greater influence in the writing of criminal laws than the residents of the areas most affected by crime."[142]

So, it's the supposedly racist white state legislators who are to blame? Come on.

The lawful use of prosecutorial discretion gives prosecutors license to exercise judgment, taking into consideration a variety of factors, in deciding how to proceed in a particular case with a particular defendant and given his track record, what actions to take under the circumstances.

Valid and proper prosecutorial discretion takes myriad forms: from telling police officers that they do not have probable cause to refusing to file charges in cases where the evidence is weak; telling a victim that the case cannot be proven beyond a reasonable doubt; refusing to file charges where the accused's Fourth, Fifth, and/or Sixth Amendment rights were violated; dropping prior convictions at sentencing to lower the overall exposure of a convicted criminal; agreeing to a plea to a lesser included offense; deferring on a sentence recommendation; limiting the number of charges despite the fact that the accused committed other crimes; providing discovery to the defense beyond what is legally required; and more.

Misdemeanor prosecutors, given the volume of cases they have, exercise discretion every single day by dropping cases, holding them in abeyance, or offering a multitude of diversionary programs to those who are accused of minor crimes.

Real prosecutors engage in this type of prosecutorial discretion thousands of times a day.

When we allow for the chronic violation of laws and social norms, though, we erode the foundation of our cities and civilization.[143] If we are not safe, if our cities are not livable, then we don't have a civilization.[144]

Imagine, for example, a different rogue prosecutor movement called the XYZ movement whose goal was to elect prosecutors who would refuse to enforce laws they found distasteful or racist or discriminatory. The XYZ movement might refuse to prosecute all federal or state environmental laws, all insider trading laws or all white-collar crimes, and child sex crimes; refuse to add hate crimes enhancements to charges no matter the circumstances; or refuse to prosecute every criminal violation of fish and wildlife statutes.

From the standpoint of legislative usurpation, there is no difference between the current rogue prosecutor movement and this hypothetical XYZ movement. Both movements are lawless and rogue, trample on the separation of powers, and lead to disastrous consequences. But the rogue prosecutor movement is real, and the XYZ movement is not.

Prosecutorial discretion was never meant to be the talisman that progressives have made of it.[145] But invoking prosecutorial discretion as a cover for what is a scheme to gut and distort applicable laws is an executive usurpation of legislative power[146] and a practice that has led to disastrous results as you will soon learn in later chapters.

## Eliminating Cash Bail

The rogue prosecutor movement cannot claim credit for starting the movement to end cash bail,[147] but ending cash bail is one of the movement's central goals.

Cash bail is a guarantee by a defendant, or a person acting on behalf of a defendant, that the defendant will show up for trial or hearings. The amount of cash money required to "post bail" varies by jurisdiction and by crime, and judges usually have the authority to waive cash bail. Those who cannot afford to post bail remain in custody pending trial. Those who post bail and fail to show up for hearings or trial forfeit the cash.

One of the main arguments against cash bail is that many people, especially people of color, cannot afford cash bail, and the requirement therefore has a disproportionate effect on minorities.[148] The American Civil Liberties Union (ACLU) claims that cash bail does not work because the inability of a person to leave jail pending trial hinders his ability to fight the charges.[149]

The National Association of Criminal Defense Lawyers (NACDL), the nation's premier organization of criminal defense attorneys dedicated to "identifying and reforming flaws and inequities in the criminal justice system," opposes pretrial detention in most cases and notes that "over 75% of those detained in local jails have not been convicted of a crime."[150]

Rogue prosecutors, once elected, have a major say in whether to ask for cash bail, depending on the state and its law.

A major proponent for eliminating cash bail is Chesa Boudin, the former district attorney in San Francisco. He ran on the promise that he would end all cash bail, and once elected, he did just that.[151] Boudin "believes that no one should be in jail simply because they are too poor to post bail to get out."[152] Under his new policy, "if someone poses a serious public safety risk, the District Attorney's office will ask that the person remain in jail while waiting for the case to resolve or go to trial."[153] Boudin touted his no-cash-bail policy as the most progressive in the country and an "important step towards ending the criminalization of poverty and stopping mass incarceration."[154]

Of course, it is not easy to identify everyone who poses a "serious public safety risk," and opinions naturally will vary as to which particular defendant poses or does not pose such a risk. Rogue prosecutors tend to side with defendants, whom they view as victims of a structurally racist criminal justice system and racist police departments. As a result, they are eager not to request cash bail.

Rachael Rollins, the former DA in Boston, who was inspired by the rogue prosecutor movement and who was recently appointed US Attorney by President Biden, established a new policy on cash bail and pretrial release in her policy memo: "Presumptive recommendation of release on personal recognizance without conditions. This presumption will only be rebutted if there is clear evidence of a flight risk."[155] Not to be outdone by other progressive prosecutors, Rollins ordered that her office apply her cash bail and pretrial release policy retroactively to anyone held on "an amount of cash bail $25,000 or less and re-assess bail through this release presumption framework."[156]

Many police organizations, traditional independent law-and-order prosecutors, and legislators think cash bail is appropriate for select defendants and oppose the wholesale abolition of cash bail as a pretrial precautionary device.[157] In response to Rollins's bail policy, a commission in Massachusetts charged with looking at the issue of cash bail recommended keeping cash bail because it "continues to play an important role."[158]

If these core beliefs were the extent of their procriminal policies, we would not have written this book. Radical as those ideas are, they would not, in practice, even when combined, have fundamentally "reverse-engineered" the entire criminal justice system. In reality, the movement has gone well beyond these core beliefs and transformed the office of the district attorney into what Larry Krasner bragged is a "public defender with power."

Rather than feature the eight rogue prosecutors in the order they were elected, we decided to start with George Gascón of Los Angeles for one simple reason: his policies not only effect current and future cases but past convictions and are the most radical, procriminal, antivictim policies of the bunch.

But first, we explain how George Soros and other liberal billionaires have supported many of these prosecutors and bankrolled the movement.

# CHAPTER 2

# THE MONEY AND INDIVIDUALS BEHIND THE PLOT

*"...Democratic mega-donor George Soros has directed his wealth into an under-the radar...campaign to advance one of the progressive movement's core goals—reshaping the American justice system."*[159]

**Scott Bland—*Politico* Reporter**

*"The prosecutor exercises the greatest discretion and power in the system. It is so important."*[160]

**Andrea Dew Steele—President of Emerge America**

While it is important to understand the goals of the rogue prosecutor movement, it is also important to understand who is funding the movement, the goals of these funders, who some of the recipients of these funds are, and the consequences for the unfortunate citizens who have to endure these rogue prosecutors' lawless decisions to abdicate their duties.

## NO MOVEMENT WITHOUT GEORGE SOROS

Let's be clear: the rogue prosecutor movement would not exist without the massive financial backing provided by George Soros. In June 2022, the Law Enforcement Legal Defense Fund (LELDF) reported that as of that date, "Soros ha[d] spent more than $40 million on direct campaign spending over the past decade to elect prosecutors."[161] But given his largesse to help put in place "policy infrastructure" such as "media relations, sponsored academic or think tank papers, lobbying campaigns, and grassroots organizing," to bolster rogue prosecutors' efforts, the group estimates that "all told, Soros has contributed hundreds of millions of dollars—possibly well over a billion dollars—to organizations directly and indirectly that constitute the progressive prosecution infrastructure on top of the more than $40 million in campaign financing."[162] That's an eye-popping and outcome-altering amount of cash—especially for local district attorney races, which traditionally have been low-profile, low-dollar affairs. Rather than simply cutting a check to many of his preferred candidates, Soros instead "uses a series of shell organizations, affiliates, and pass-through committees to steer contributions to both candidates and his robust support network for" these prosecutors.[163] LELDF found that the "web of Soros-linked and financed criminal justice reform groups is both deep and wide to include 527 political action committees (PACs), and 501(c)(4) 'social welfare' advocacy organizations or what some on the left call 'dark money' groups, charitable foundations as well as dozens of traditional 501(c)(3) nonprofit organizations who conduct research, provide technical training, and conduct advocacy campaigns."[164] It's a tangled web that can be—and likely was purposefully set up to be—very difficult to untangle. Sometimes Soros contributes directly to candidates. Other times, he contributes to third-party groups who then make independent expenditures on behalf of his preferred candidate. Still other times, the candidates and officials receive benefits from third-party organizations that are funded directly or indirectly by Soros. Regardless, the result is largely the same.

## OTHER LEFTIST BILLIONAIRE CO-CONSPIRATORS

But Soros isn't alone in using his vast wealth to push his radical agenda for so-called criminal justice reform. Some other billionaires who have been involved in his space are familiar names such as Facebook (now Meta) CEO Mark Zuckerberg.[165] Others may not be as familiar, like Facebook co-founder Dustin Moskovitz and his wife, Cari Tuna, and Patty Quillin, the wife of Netflix CEO Reed Hastings.

While George Soros might be the most well-known liberal backer of rogue DAs, Moskovitz and Tuna have provided significant funding as well, most notably through their Open Philanthropy Project. The Open Philanthropy Project says on its website that:

> We have funded a lot of work in the prosecutor space. An example of a specialty organization for prosecutors is Fair and Just Prosecution. We tend to think that funding work for particular policy reforms… may have limitations…when system actors are able to quickly adapt and push different policies that may have the same effect, and [this approach avoids] the danger of signaling too clearly to anti-change forces what the intended target is.[166]

The reach of Moskovitz and Tuna's Open Philanthropy Project is vast—and may even rival Soros's influence. For instance, a May 2018 *Los Angeles Times* article noted that the Open Philanthropy Project "directed $6.6 million toward 'prosecutorial reform' or similar terms" from 2014 to 2017.[167] A review of the project's grants database shows that from 2019 through October 15, 2020, it has recommended making criminal justice-related grants totaling $60,796,100, with approximately $21,987,300 of this amount related to prosecutorial "reform" efforts.[168] From November 2020 through December 2021, it recommended making a whopping $65,344,300 in criminal justice-related grants, with $50 million going to Just Impact, an organization that is "working to end mass incarceration and increase racial equity" to combat the "scale of harm caused by America's unique obsession with incarceration."[169] Its director and lead strategist is Chloe Cockburn, who also pulls double duty as the head of criminal justice reform for the Open Philanthropy Project itself.[170] Overall since December 2013, the Open Philanthropy Project has recommended making at least $199,574,123 in grants to impact the criminal justice space.[171]

# ORGANIZATIONS BEING SUPPORTED

These grants have helped to put into place a vast infrastructure that provides support to the prosecutors who support these billionaires' radical agenda. For example, as noted above, the Open Philanthropy Project named Fair and Just Prosecution as a specialty organization it supports. What does this benignly named organization do? Well, according to its website, Fair and Just Prosecution is an organization establishing a network of prosecutors committed to building a better criminal justice system.[172] In reality, it's a national clearinghouse that helps disseminate radical ideas and policies to its members. It garners support for these ideas by asking its members to sign onto letters and statements supporting its agenda. Andrew Warren, a local prosecutor around the Tampa, Florida, area signed onto two such Fair and Just Prosecution letters, where he and other prosecutors pledged not to enforce certain laws.[173] Florida Governor Ron DeSantis cited Warren's signature on these letters, among other issues, when suspending him from office.[174]

Fair and Just Prosecution (FJP) also acts as a pseudo-reward system for rogue prosecutors who support the radical national agenda it pushes. When FJP says they are highlighting "inspiring new leaders redefining prosecution in the 21st Century," they actually mean they're using their donors' money to reward these prosecutors for sticking to the company line. For instance, in "2019, over two dozen Soros-linked DAs traveled (all expenses paid) on FJP junkets to Scotland, Germany, Portugal, and Kenya."[175] Some of them, such as St. Louis's Kimberly Gardner and Baltimore's Marilyn Mosby, did not properly disclose their trips.[176] Because Fair and Just Prosecution bills itself as a "fiscally-sponsored project of The Tides Center," which itself receives money from George Soros and other left-leaning activists,[177] it is hard to decipher the exact state of its finances.[178] Again, this is by design. Soros has relied on organizations like Tides, "a San Francisco-based group that acts almost like a clearing house for other donors, directing their contributions to liberal non-profit groups"[179] to spread his donations around in a way that can be difficult to decipher. Still, we know that in 2018, for example, Tides "hosted campaign donors for Soros and the ACLU and racial-justice activists from Color of Change to talk about steering nonprofit money toward the cause [of criminal justice reform]."[180] Moreover, in July 2020, the Black Lives Matter Global Network (BLM) gave notice that it intended "to transfer the fiscal sponsorship of BLM and the funds and associated assets it has held for the BLM Project to The Tides Center, a leading provider of nonprofit fiscal sponsorship services."[181]

Photo taken December 7, 2018 at the Harris County District Attorney's Office with Hostess Kim Ogg, Harris County District Attorney. Fair & Just Prosecution Event. Front row, L to R: Unknown male; unknown female; Rachael Rollins, District Attorney, Suffolk County, MA; Andrea Harrington, District Attorney, Berkshire County, MA; Beth McCann, District Attorney, Denver, CO; Unknown female; Satana DeBerry, District Attorney, Durham County, NC; Carol Sieman, District Attorney, Ingham County, MI; Mark Gonzalez, District Attorney, District Attorney, Nueces County, TX; Kim Gardner, Circuit Attorney, City of St. Louis, MO; John Creuzot, District Attorney, Dallas County, TX; Marilyn Mosby, State's Attorney, City of Baltimore, MD; Tori Verber Salazar, District Attorney, San Joaquin County, CA. Back row, L to R: Channing D. Phillips, former U.S. Attorney for the District of Columbia; Unknown male; Joe Gonzalez, District Attorney, Bexar County, TX; Michael Dougherty, District Attorney, Boulder County, CO; Eric Gonzalez, District Attorney, Kings County, NY; Kim Foxx, State's Attorney, Cook County, IL; Kim Ogg, District Attorney, Harris County, TX; Stephanie N. Morales, Commonwealth's Attorney, Portsmouth County, VA; Mark A. Dupree, Sr., District Attorney, Wyandotte County, KS; Unknown male; Spencer B. Merriweather III, District Attorney, Mecklenburg County, NC; Unknown male.

Soros has also partnered with the ACLU before to pursue his radical policy objectives, including making a $50 million donation "to mount an eight-year political campaign across the country to make change of criminal justice policies a key issue in local, state and national elections."[182] In fall of 2017, other large-dollar left-wing donors were encouraged to support a similar agenda after "a panel on prosecutor races at the closed-door retreat of Democracy Alliance, a coalition of groups and leaders who pool their resources behind liberal causes."[183] A number of groups have benefitted. For instance, Color of Change is "an online organizing organization" that employs web-based "campaigns…to advocate for liberal policies,"[184] and its Color of Change PAC has been actively supported by George Soros and others to advocate in favor of electing certain rogue prosecutors such as Manhattan's Alvin Bragg.[185] Other beneficiaries include organizations such as the Accountable Justice Action Fund and the Real Justice PAC, that directly or indirectly support rogue prosecutors and candidates. The Accountable Justice Action Fund "supports criminal justice reform, with a focus on reforming prosecution and equipping local and national groups to increase accountability in prosecutorial elections," with an eye to ending mass incarceration.[186] Its treasurer, once again, is Chloe Cockburn, the head of criminal justice reform for the Open Philanthropy Project.[187] The Real Justice PAC states that it wants to utilize tactics "pioneered" by the Bernie Sanders Campaign to "[e]lect prosecutors who will fix our broken criminal justice system."[188] Their endorsements read like a who's who of rogue prosecutors and rogue prosecutor wannabes.[189] Moreover, the organization was co-founded by Shaun King, an activist with a history of making false accusations and threatening statements against police officers.[190]

The increased funding and prominence of these organizations show that by deploying massive amounts of cash to "level the playing field" in favor of candidates willing to shill their radical policies, these billionaires are seeking to dismantle and to fundamentally transform the criminal justice system.

## ROGUES SUPPORTED

So, how many individual candidates have Soros and others supported and who are they? The Law Enforcement Legal Defense Fund estimates that there are "at least 75 Soros-Backed social justice [rogue] prosecutors, supported through campaign dollars and/or Soros-funded progressive infrastructure groups."[191] And they are located across the nation in both large and small jurisdictions. Between 2014, when the movement was in its infancy, through May 2018, Soros "spent more than $16 million in 17 county races in [states other than California]...."[192] During that same time period, he spent more than $2.7 million in California alone.[193] The *Wall Street Journal* reported that in the 2016 election cycle alone, Soros "contributed at least $3.8 million to political-action committees supporting candidates for district attorney in Arizona, Colorado, Florida, Georgia, Illinois, Missouri, New Mexico, Texas, and Wisconsin...."[194] But more recently, from "2018 to 2021, Soros spent $13 million on just 10 prosecutors' races, where his organizations were by far the biggest spender in the race and comprised the majority of the [rogue] candidate's spending—as much as 90% in some cases."[195] And again, it's estimated that overall he has spent "more than $40 million on direct campaign spending over the past decade to elect prosecutors."[196]

In 2019, Soros backed Buta Biberaj to be the commonwealth's attorney in Loudoun County, Virginia—the chief prosecutor in this DC suburb. She received a total of $922,000 through Soros-related entities,[197] $861,000 from the "solely Soros funded Justice and Public Safety PAC" and $61,496 from the New VA Majority, "which Soros substantially funds…." Soros has funneled many of his contributions to support rogue DAs through the Justice & Public Safety PAC, as well as related state-level Justice & Public Safety PACs.[198] Importantly, excluding Biberaj's own contributions to her campaign, "Soros funds constituted 84% of [her] total contributions."[199] Close by in the DC Suburb of Fairfax County, Virginia, Steve Descano received $659,000—or nearly 70 percent of his campaign contribution—from Soros-backed entities.[200]

While not included in the $13 million number above, Soros also spent heavily in 2019 to help Parisa Dehghani-Tafti win her bid to become Arlington County's commonwealth's attorney. A week before her primary election, the *Washington Post* reported that "[t]he Justice and Public Safety PAC has donated about $583,000 to Parisa Dehghani-Tafti…."[201] The article went on to say that the "donations represent the lion's share of the roughly $744,000" she had raised to date.[202] To put that in perspective, Soros's donations accounted for approximately 78 percent of Deghani-Tafti's war chest at that time. For even more perspective, by that same point, Deghani-Tafti's opponent, the incumbent Arlington County commonwealth attorney, had raised only $191,000. Not surprisingly, Dehghani-Tafti won her race with that kind of backing.

The next year, in 2020, Soros-backed entities poured money into the campaign coffers of former San Francisco DA George Gascón to support his race to become the next Los Angeles County district attorney. Soros donated almost $2.5 million to the California Justice & Public Safety PAC, which supported Gascón.[203] That was after Soros had donated approximately $2.5 million to that same PAC in 2018.[204] This is in addition to the almost $2 million in contributions the PAC received from the independent expenditure group Run, George, Run: George Gascon for LA DA 2020,[205] which is notable since the wife of Netflix's CEO had previously made a $1 million donation to that organization.[206] The *Los Angeles Times* estimated that the amount she contributed directly or indirectly to help Gascón get elected was second only to Soros's contributions.[207] That same year, Soros pumped $2 million into the Illinois Justice & Public Safety PAC to help Cook County State's Attorney Kim Foxx win her bid for reelection.[208] She had received "$708,000 of Soros help in her first run in 2016."[209] In 2020, the Soros-supported Missouri Safety and Justice Committee spent $116,000 to help St. Louis Circuit Attorney Kim Gardner win reelection. She had received $208,000 from this same group four years earlier.[210]

Fast forward to 2021 where Philadelphia's Larry Krasner "received a combined $1,259,000 from Soros-funded groups" in his bid for reelection. This was after he had received $1.7 million from Soros-funded groups when he first ran for DA in 2017. In 2017, Soros support accounted for 90 percent of Krasner's funding.[211] How else could this defense-attorney-turned-prosecutor who had no experience prosecuting cases and who was pushing a radical agenda waltz into office? In 2021, Soros-backed groups also put at least "$1,072,000…via the New York Justice and Public Safety PAC and Color of Change PAC" to help Alvin Bragg get elected as Manhattan's new district attorney.[212]

Of course there are more rogue prosecutors backed by Soros—some successful, some not successful.[213] In November 2019, Soros funneled $1 million to the Pennsylvania Justice & Public Safety PAC, which helped Jack Stollsteimer win election as the Delaware County district attorney in a Philadelphia suburb.[214] Similarly, in 2020, Soros-linked groups helped push Monique Worrell to victory in the Democratic primary to become the state attorney responsible for prosecuting crimes in and around Orlando, Florida. According to the *Orlando Sentinel*, "Records show that a new political committee raised more than $2.2 million and spent more than $1.5 million" in just two weeks in support of Worrell.[215] At least "$1 million [came] from Democracy PAC, a political committee set up by Soros" after "Soros [had] spent more than $1.3 million in the closing weeks for the 2016 campaign to elect the current state attorney, Aramis Ayala, who is not running for reelection."[216] Ayala infamously refused to seek the death penalty in cases that her office prosecuted, and this led two Florida governors to take the drastic step of reassigning capital cases to a different state attorney's office.[217] Also in Florida in 2020, Soros supported Joe Kimok in his bid to become the state attorney overseeing Broward County. Although Kimok lost the primary, among all of the Democratic candidates, he was the "biggest beneficiary of PAC money, by far...."[218] In three weeks, "the Florida Justice & Public Safety PAC...raised more than $750,000 for his effort."[219] Before that, Soros-backed entities had contributed $1,584,000 to Geneviéve Jones-Wright in her bid to unseat Summer Stephan as San Diego's district attorney.[220] Jones-Wright ultimately lost because, though outmatched financially, Stephan was able to receive enough support to get her own message out to voters.[221]

## SOROS SHOWS NO SIGNS OF SLOWING DOWN HIS CONTRIBUTIONS

The flood of money has continued unabated since Soros made his first contributions to elect rogue prosecutors, and it shows no signs of slowing down. While the movement itself has encountered resistance from voters in places like San Francisco, who recalled Chesa Boudin, and Baltimore, who declined to reelect Marilyn Mosby, Soros has struck a defiant tone. In a summer 2022 *Wall Street Journal* op-ed, Soros defended the radical policies of the rogue prosecutor movement and his funding of it.[222] He says that he has supported these prosecutors "transparently," despite the web of organizations that make the cash difficult to follow and that he has "no intention of stopping." And he went on to say that the "funds I provide enable sensible reform-minded candidates to receive a hearing from the public," when in reality his tsunami of cash in these races often overwhelms local politics and drowns out opposing voices. Currently, one in five Americans live in a jurisdiction where a rogue prosecutor holds power.[223] That's approximately seventy-two million Americans. As we'll see throughout this book, the consequences for these Americans—for all Americans—have been devastating.

# CHAPTER 3

# GEORGE GASCÓN: LOS ANGELES

## THE WORST OF THE WORST

*"So my community becomes a petri dish for some-
one's social experiment. I'm not OK with that."*
**Andrew Lara (D)—Pico Rivera City Council Member**[224]

*"What they're trying to do is dismantle the criminal jus-
tice system as we know it and using the false canard
about systemic racism and mass incarceration and all
these buzzwords that are in the political sphere."*
**Alex Villanueva (D)—Former Sheriff of Los Angeles County**[225]

In 2014, ten-year-old Sara[226] walked into the ladies room at a Denny's restaurant. As she was drying her hands at the sink, a male stranger came toward her. Afraid, Sara started backing up toward the handicap stall. The man told her, "Take your pants off," but Sara said, "No, I want my mommy." By now, Sara had backed up into the handicap stall, where the man followed her into it, and closed and locked the door. He grabbed her and placed his hands around her neck, threatening, "If you don't do what I say, I will choke you." Terrified, Sara followed his commands and pulled down her shorts but she left her underwear on. The man jammed his hand down under Sara's underwear and rammed his index finger into her. As he digitally penetrated Sara, he leaned down to kiss Sara, but she turned her head away. The man was breathing hard and looking at Sara with a blank stare.

Fortunately, an adult women walked into the ladies room. The man, realizing that someone had come into the bathroom stopped, told Sara to stay quiet, and went into another stall. He eventually fled the restaurant.

Someone called the police, and Sara accompanied them to the hospital. Medical professionals took vaginal swabs to collect potential DNA evidence. They entered the DNA evidence into the national DNA database (CODIS), in the off chance the monster who did this to Sara would be found later on.

Fast forward to 2019 in Idaho where police arrested a man for battery. Police took his DNA and ran it through CODIS, where they got a "hit" from the 2014 California sexual assault of Sara. The perpetrator was James Tubbs. Tubbs, who was born on January 19, 1996, had been just shy of his eighteenth birthday when he digitally raped Sara in 2014, and he was now going by the name Hannah Tubbs. Because of the many complications from the global COVID pandemic, Tubbs was not transferred to California to face charges until November 2021.

By then, George Gascón had been elected district attorney for Los Angeles County and had issued his new policies (called "special directives"), including one that prohibited all minors from being prosecuted in adult court, and, he required prosecutors under his command to only file one charge per incident, no matter how many crimes the person committed or no matter how serious the conduct. Had former Los Angeles district attorney Jackie Lacey, the first black female elected district attorney in the county, remained in office, Tubbs would have been tried as an adult and, if convicted, been sentenced to decades in prison.

But Tubbs lucked out, as you will see.

On January 4, 2021, the day before charges were to be filed against Tubbs, Los Angeles County Deputy District Attorney (DDA) Shawn Randolph emailed DDA Maria Ramirez to alert Ramirez to facts about the case and to seek guidance.

Randolph wrote: "This is a media case. This email is FYI so you can see my analysis and decision. Please advise if I get it wrong and you have different expectations."[227] Randolph included Tubbs's adult criminal record:

- 3/18/20 arrest and conviction in California for Assault with a Deadly Weapon. He received a four-year state prison sentence.

- 6/25/19 arrest and conviction in California for Possession of Controlled Dangerous Substances. He got nine days in jail and thirty-six months of probation.

- 10/13/18 arrest and conviction in Washington State for Domestic Violence. He got 364 days in jail.

- 9/21/17 arrest and conviction in Washington State for Felony Assault. He got eighty-six days in jail and twelve months of "community custody."

- 9/21/17 arrest and conviction in Washington State for Resisting Arrest. He got fifty days in jail and twenty-four months of probation.

- 11/12/16 arrest and conviction in Washington State for Unlawful Recreational Fishing. He got ten days in jail.

- 7/27/14 arrest and conviction in Washington State for Criminal Trespass, Malicious Mischief, and Theft. He got 364 days in jail.

- 7/16/14 arrest and conviction in Washington State for two counts of Theft. He got 364 days in jail.

Randolph expressed her dissatisfaction with Gascón's juvenile charging policies, writing that "Gascón's policy, strictly read, will require us to file one non-strike offense. I believe this case warrants a filing of forcible penetration by a foreign object. I believe the policy listing forcible rape as an exception under [Policy Directive] 20-09, and not listing other forcible sex crimes such as forcible sodomy, forcible penetration with a foreign object, and forcible oral copulation was an oversight, as it makes no sense to include one but not the other, and in all policy directives by this office preceding 20-09 and in virtually all Penal and Welfare and Institutions Code lists, these crimes are always listed together."

In imploring her superior to make an exception to Gascón's blanket directive on youths, Randolph continued, writing: "Therefore, I have directed our office to file one count of Forcible Sexual Penetration of Victim Under 14 by a Foreign Object, which is a strike. It will make this former minor eligible for DJJ [Department of Juvenile Justice], and if he is committed to DJJ, he will have to register as a sex offender. There is no alternative, non-strike offense available that, [according to the new directive] 'corresponds to the alleged conduct....' As such, I see our options are to file a strike or to not file at all. This former minor appears to me to be an extreme public safety risk. Accurate charges are imperative, as is DJJ and a record of this offense."

Randolph's professional judgment—that Tubbs was "an extreme public safety risk"—was spot on. Gascón spurned the advice and judgment of his career deputy district attorneys, and Angelenos have paid the price with their lives, their livelihoods, and their sense of peace.

Randolph noted that "there are zero options available to treat this extremely dangerous former minor," that it is "extremely important that a record of this offense be created, as this minor has the hallmarks of a sexual predator," and her "serious concern" that the office is "setting ourselves up to limit our ability to prove the charges against this minor." Randolph begged her supervisor to allow her to "plead alternate charges so that when we are in the middle of the adjudication, we can ensure our best ability to prove this case" with the victim, whom she noted, "is desirous of prosecution."

But Randolph's request—like those of her fellow career prosecutors—fell on deaf ears. Ramirez emailed a curt two-sentence reply, stating that "only one charge may be filed per incident."

After the charges were filed against Tubbs in Juvenile Court, but before he was sentenced by the judge, Tubbs placed several calls from jail to his father, which were, unbeknownst to him, recorded. Tubbs gloated about his plea deal. While talking about Sara to his dad, he called her a "piece of meat." He was elated that he would not have to register as a sex offender and suggested that his "transition" to being a woman was a scam so that he could be housed with biological women in jail.

Jail officials gave those audiotaped recordings to Gascón's office before Tubbs's sentencing. They wanted the DA's office, and the DA himself, to know what Tubbs had been saying, no doubt in an effort to get Gascón to reconsider sending Tubbs to adult court, where he belonged, or at least to inform the judge about the real James Tubbs.

Shockingly, Gascón and his top lieutenants, including DDA Alisa Blair and DDA Sharon Woo, knew about the calls before the sentencing hearing. How do we know this? Because Blair was on a video conference call (called a "Webex") during a hearing regarding possible punishment of Tubbs after the guilty pleas. During that Webex call, DDA Shea Sanna brought up, in general terms, the jailhouse calls in open court to alert Judge Mario Barrera.

Both Blair and Woo—like Gascón—were not real prosecutors. Blair had been a career deputy public defender, who Gascón brought over to the DA's Office, and Woo had served as Gascón's chief of staff for eight years when Gascón was the district attorney in San Francisco.

On that same day as the status hearing, DDA Blair emailed DDA Sanna and the entire chain of command (excluding Gascón) and directed DDA Sanna to provide the recorded jailhouse calls to senior management. DDA Sanna sent them to senior management that day, providing headings for each of the calls and describing each sickening call in detail.

But Blair, Woo, and Gascón didn't do anything after reviewing those calls. Tubbs, now twenty-six years old, was sentenced to six months to two years in juvenile detention. He was eligible to be released in June 2022.

About a month after the sentencing, all hell broke loose. Someone leaked the audio version of the calls to the press. When the public heard Tubbs talking to his father, laughing about the juvenile sentence, and calling Sara "meat," there was an immediate backlash.

The press asked Gascón's office if Gascón or anyone in leadership knew about Tubbs's calls. They lied and said no. Not only that, but they also said the victim in the case did not want to testify. But then someone leaked the emails from DDA Sana to Blair and Woo to the press, showing not only that senior management knew about the calls but that Gascón had heard them. To make matters worse, the email from DDA Randolph to DDA Ramirez contained the following sentence about the victim: "She is desirous of prosecution."

Here we start to see a pattern. When Gascón is caught in a lie or when a rigid blanket policy backfires (as most of them have), at first, he ignores the fact that he lied. When the spotlight gets too hot, he carves out minor exceptions to his iron-fisted policy.

Gascón first came out and said that Tubbs's recorded telephone calls didn't change his mind—a tacit acknowledgment that, in fact, he had heard them. About a week later, after extensive media blowback, Gascón acknowledged that the "current iteration" of the juvenile system was not appropriate for Tubbs. Gascón issued a change in policy. Prosecutors could now submit a transfer motion filing evaluation memorandum that would be reviewed by a newly formed Juvenile Alternative Charging Evaluation (JACE) Committee. Importantly, Alisa Blair, the special advisor for Juvenile, Diversion, and Collaborative Courts, is on that committee, and Sharon Woo has the final word.

In May 2022, while serving his sentence in juvenile detention, Tubbs was charged with first-degree murder in California's Kern County. According to police reports, Tubbs and a co-conspirator robbed another person, shot him, and then threw him into the Kern River. The murder took place in 2019 when Tubbs was nineteen years old. Since Tubbs has at least one strike under California law, if convicted of first-degree premeditated murder, he would get fifty years to life in prison.

And for those of you who think that Gascón's treatment of Tubbs was fair, consider this: Gascón, Blair, and Woo knew that Tubbs had been accused of sexually assaulting Sophia,[228] a four-year-old girl, a year before he sexually assaulted Sara. According to the police report,[229] in August 2013, at a public library in Bakersfield, California, Tubbs exposed his penis to a four-year-old girl and put it onto her lips against her will. The girl ran away to her mother, who called the police. Tubbs was immediately identified, questioned, and detained by the police for the sexual assault. Tubbs denied placing his penis on the girl's mouth. Police took Tubbs's DNA. The case was referred to juvenile authorities but ultimately not pursued.

For Gascón, the Tubbs case is just the tip of the iceberg.

Gascón's policies, including his "youth justice" policies, have had far-reaching, deadly, and disastrous consequences. Gascón's campaign, his published policies, and the visceral and public pushback from across the community provide a richer body of material to write about than that available for most other rogue prosecutors. Unlike Gascón's policies, those of the other rogue prosecutors discussed in this book are either not publicly available in writing or are less comprehensive.

We feature only a handful of the most radical special directives, describe who created them, what they require, and then let the facts from actual cases tell the story of why we call George Gascón the "King of Rogue Prosecutors."[230] If you want to read more about all of Gascón's directives, what they do, and why they are each procriminal and antivictim, we recommend reading our Heritage Foundation Legal Memorandum.[231]

## WHO IS GEORGE GASCÓN?

At first blush, Gascón was an unlikely candidate for the Soros machine to back.

As Ari Ruiz, political vice president for Stonewall Young Democrats told the *Los Angeles Blade* after the Los Angeles County Democratic Party endorsed Gascón for DA in 2019 over Jackie Lacey, the first African American female-elected district attorney in LA, "I'm shocked that they endorsed Mr. Gascón whose history as a Democrat is quite new. He had been a registered Republican well up into the first two years of the Obama presidency. He became a Democrat in or around 2010."[232]

As the *Blade* article noted, Lacey had "top tier endorsements, including Rep. Adam B. Schiff, LA Mayor Eric Garcetti, four members of the Board of Supervisors, law enforcement unions—and San Francisco Mayor London Breed." Breed's endorsement was a bitter swipe at Gascón, because Gascón was the former DA in San Francisco until he was recruited to run for DA in Los Angeles.

So, what special qualifications did Gascón have that brought him to the attention of the Soros network?

Was he chosen because he was the former chief of police in both San Francisco and Mesa, Arizona? Not likely.

Was he chosen because, like Barack Obama, he was a gifted orator? Not really.

Gascón doesn't come across in his public speeches or interactions with the press or public as a uniquely gifted orator. He was born in Cuba, so his first language is Spanish. But even when you listen to what he says in Spanish, he is not prone to lofty turns of phrase or soaring rhetoric. He is also somewhat awkward in dealing with the press and public.

So, was he chosen because he was an experienced trial attorney? Not really.

Although he has a law degree from Western State University College of Law, he has never prosecuted or defended a criminal case in court, even when he was the district attorney in San Francisco.

Was he chosen because he had an outstanding track record as the district attorney of San Francisco? Not really.

If prosecutorial accomplishments mattered (i.e., prosecuting the guilty and protecting the innocent), Gascón would never have been anointed to run for Los Angeles DA in the first place.

Even a cursory examination of his record as San Francisco DA from 2011–2019 shows that he was an abysmal failure. Under his tenure as the San Francisco DA,[233] crime exploded. Ask virtually any resident of San Francisco, and they will tell you how dangerous the city became under Gascón's tenure.[234]

Next to the rapists themselves, Gascón was a rape victim's worst enemy in San Francisco. In the five years before he took office in San Francisco, there were 757 reported rapes—an average of 151 per year.[235] In his last five years in office, after his policies had time to take root, there were a stunning 1,731 rapes, an average of 346 per year. Three times as many women and men were raped in the City by the Bay under Gascón.

In 2017 alone, there were 367 rapes, and every year from 2014 to 2019 there were more than three hundred rapes per year. Gascón cannot explain why rapes went up under his tenure,[236] but there is little doubt that anything other than his lax policies was to blame.

Keep in mind that nationwide, all crime, including violent crime, had been going down for decades.[237] But not in George Gascón's San Francisco.

Aggravated assaults also went up dramatically under Gascón's reign as San Francisco DA. In the five years before he took office, there were 11,921 aggravated assaults, an average of 2,384 per year. In his last five years in office, there were 13,070 aggravated assaults—an average of 2,614 per year.[238] That means that more than 1,150 more people—many of whom were LGBTQ, minorities, Asians, and tourists—were violently assaulted as a result of Gascón's soft on crime approach. Gascón has no explanation for why aggravated assaults went up during his tenure.

But what is clearly a track record of prosecutorial failure as the head lawman in San Francisco to most people was just the opposite to the

Soros-backed or inspired movement. Gascón's criminal-friendly approach to being the DA was a resume enhancer. Soros saw Gascón, a Democrat (albeit a recent convert) from a large liberal city, who also had the patina of being prolaw enforcement because of his career as a police officer, as someone who might—might—be willing to go "all-in" and unleash the most comprehensive set of "reform" policies written by defund the police activists, special interests, and other radicals.

The Soros machine was politically astute. They evaluated and measured not just the person as a potential candidate, but also, as we detailed in the first chapter, the political landscape and the vulnerability of incumbents. Even with the political waters roiling over race, police shootings, and the election of Foxx, Krasner, and others, something, anything, had to happen in LA to give Gascón a fighting chance.

That something was the death of Kenneth Ross.

## BENDING A KNEE TO BLACK LIVES MATTER

By 2019, there had been several high-profile deaths of black men at the hands of police around the country, including Eric Garner (2014), Michael Brown (2014), Tamir Rice (2014), and Freddie Gray (2015). Those killings, regardless of the circumstances, gained national attention, both in the public square, academia, the news, and, understandably, the political realm.

But one of those high-profile, police-involved shootings happened in Los Angeles and was the beginning of the end for incumbent Jackie Lacey. The incident paved the political yellow-brick-road for Gascón.

On April 18, 2018, career criminal Kenneth Ross Jr. was running through the streets in the City of Gardena firing a handgun in broad daylight at people and buildings. Numerous witnesses saw Ross. Someone called 911. Police arrived and chased Ross, who continued to fire his weapon. Ross refused to drop his weapon and died when Officer Michael Robbins shot him.

Black Lives Matter (BLM), which was started in 2013 as a Marxist-inspired organization, became a more vocal and potent national movement after these incidents, stirring the flames of racial division, joining with other radical groups like Antifa. After each incident, BLM took to social media and to the streets, claiming that the police were executing unarmed black men across America. And when Ross was killed by Officer Robbins, BLM demanded that he be prosecuted by Jackie Lacey.

After a thorough investigation, the LA DA's office—headed by Lacey at the time—declined to prosecute Robbins, finding that Ross was to blame and that Robbins shot Ross in self-defense.[239] Lacey's refusal to prosecute Officer Robbins infuriated BLM, so they decided to attempt to intimidate and bully Lacey into changing her mind.

By now, BLM had used all sorts of tactics, lawful and unlawful, to achieve their political ends. By refusing to accede to BLM's demands, Lacey became target number one in Los Angeles for BLM. Hyperagitators, and politically savvy, BLM of LA had to find the right time to turn the tables on Lacey and pave the way for a DA candidate who was more to their liking.

They selected the night before the Democratic primary to make their move.

On March 2, 2020, BLM showed up at Jackie Lacey's house in a quiet LA neighborhood with bullhorns, drums, and signs. Starting in the middle of the afternoon, they started yelling and screaming at Lacey to come out of the house to meet with them, screaming, "Bye bye Jackie Lacey" and other trite sayings. Nightfall came, and Lacey hadn't appeared. They continued to disturb the peace and scream outside Lacey's house.

Around 3 AM the next morning, the group's leader, Melina Abdullah,[240] an admirer of the anti-Semite[241] Louis Farrakhan, and the co-founder of BLM Los Angeles, trespassed onto Lacey's property, marched up to her front door, pounded on it, and demanded that Lacey come out. Lacey's husband, who at the time was using a cane, opened the door armed with a handgun, telling Abdullah, "Get off of my porch."

Switching to a soft, reasonable-sounding voice, Abdullah sweetly asked David Lacey, "Are you going to shoot me?"

David Lacey said, matter-of-factly, "Yes, I will shoot you." Abdullah got exactly what she wanted. The daughter of a trained Marxist, Abdullah had her smartphone out and recorded the confrontation. She promptly tweeted it out on the @BLMLA Twitter page.[242]

Textbook tactics. Threaten violence, violently protest, potentially commit a crime, and then engage in time-tested projection by reversing roles and playing the victim. The political table was now set. Mission accomplished.

Political knees started bending to BLM immediately.

Within days, Lacey lost the political support of the entire Democratic establishment, in large part, because, as Andrew Lara, a city council member from Pico Rivera, put it, "She didn't bend a knee to BLM…and she wasn't prosecuting police officers."[243] Gascón, armed with talking points from the Soros-backed or inspired groups like Fair and Just Prosecution, and a good public relations team, had a populist message that rode the tide of the moment. Gascón talked about the so-called "cradle-to-prison pipeline," police killings of black men, mass incarceration, and the utterly vacuous phrase, "reimagining prosecution."

Nonetheless, Lacey rightly stood her ground.[244] She was not willing to jettison her prosecutorial independence, even in the face of massive amounts of Soros money funneled into Gascón's campaign coffers.[245]

On November 6, 2020, Gascón won his race against Lacey by 53 percent to 46 percent.

Ironically, he was sworn into office a month later, on the same day the Japanese Imperial Navy launched a surprise attack against the United States Pacific Fleet at Pearl Harbor, resulting in the deaths of over three thousand sailors in 1941. What Angelenos didn't realize in voting for Gascón was that they had just unleashed another "sleeping tiger" on the City of Angels, resulting in murder, mayhem, gang infestation, looting, robbery, and misery.[246]

## RADICAL TRANSITION AND POLICY TEAMS

Immediately after he was elected, Gascón announced what he described as an "all-star" transition team—stellar, that is, from the perspective of a public defender's office.[247] A real all-star transition team for a district attorney's office would have included former prosecutors, former judges, law enforcement personnel, and other community leaders who would help the incoming district attorney assess the efficacy of current policies, and evaluate current and future programs designed to protect crime victims and keep the community safe. But not George Gascón.

The members of his transition team, many with direct ties to Soros, were antilaw-and-order activists and zealots. Of the thirty-eight people on his transition team, only one was a career prosecutor, and only one was a former judge.

None had any connection to nationally recognized prosecution organizations, such as the California District Attorneys Association,[248] the National District Attorneys Association,[249] the Association of Prosecuting Attorneys,[250] or any of the dozens of other law-and-order organizations in California and across the country.[251]

That is because Gascón and his team did not have a prosecutorial background and did not associate with career professional prosecutors. Gascón clearly bought into the idea articulated by Larry Krasner, the rogue Philadelphia DA, that prosecutors are and should be "public defender[s] with power."[252]

Gascón's transition team was littered with leading proponents of ending cash bail and eliminating the death penalty, and were anti-incarceration zealots, pro-illegal alien agitators, prison abolition activists, and more. The transition team was organized into thirteen units, each of which took the lead in drafting a special directive in their area of advocacy.[253] None of the transition teams reached out to or worked with any of the division heads in the Los Angeles DA's office, nor did they seek or accept any input from them, despite the fact that several senior career prosecutors offered to assist. In reality, the transition team had been recruited from the Soros network during the campaign and had already been secretly drafting policy proposals for Gascón, enabling Gascón to announce his "all-star" team the day he was elected and to publish his controversial, and lengthy, special directives the minute after he was sworn into office.

At the top of transition-policy team hydra was "The Steering Committee." It was composed of four people, none of whom had extensive managerial experience as a prosecutor or extensive ties to law enforcement or other proprosecution organizations. Cristine Soto DeBerry was the executive director of Prosecutors Alliance, a California-based nonprofit that "supports and amplifies the voices of" California's rogue prosecutors.[254] Jamarah Hayner is a public affairs consultant who previously worked for then-San Francisco DA Kamala Harris.[255] Joseph Iniguez is a deputy district attorney in the Los Angeles DA's office who initially ran against Jackie Lacey but dropped out and backed Gascón.[256] Iniguez had no significant trial or managerial experience. And Max Szabo is a lawyer who worked as a communications professional who was "previously a senior adviser to [Gascón in San Francisco] where he served as an assistant district attorney and director of communications and legislative affairs."[257]

## THE BLOODY CONSEQUENCES OF NO-CASH BAIL

The bail committee was composed of two individuals vehemently opposed to cash bail. Both have dedicated part of their professional careers to ending cash bail and championing more permissive standards for pretrial release—meaning more individuals, *even dangerous ones*, would be released based on nothing more than their word that they will show up to court and not commit any additional crimes. Dolores Canales was the community outreach director for the Bail Project, an organization dedicated to eliminating bail for all criminals, and a former Soros Justice Fellow.[258] Robin Steinberg is the founder and CEO of the Bail Project. She was a public defender for thirty-five years who has expressed the desire to transform "the pretrial system in the US."[259]

Their handiwork was Special Directive 20-06 entitled "Pretrial Release Policy."[260] A more accurate title would be "Let Everyone Out of Jail and End Cash Bail."

The California Constitution (Art. I. Se. 28(f)(3)) and state law (Penal Code section 1275(a)(1)) provide guidance with respect to the setting of bail: "In setting, reducing, or denying bail, a judge or magistrate shall take into consideration the protection of the public, the safety of the victim, the seriousness of the offense charged, the previous criminal record of the defendant, and the probability of his or her appearing at trial or at a hearing of the case. The public safety shall be the primary consideration."

Gascón's special directive on bail violates both the California Constitution and long-established state law.

In a subsection entitled "The Unfairness of Cash Bail," Gascón's directive notes that even though an initiative to eliminate cash bail in the state failed, "[W]e will not wait for statewide reform before imposing meaningful changes in the use of cash bail."[261] Cash bail, according to his directive, creates a "two-tiered system of justice" and leads to "unnecessary incarceration" that harms "individuals, families and communities."[262] In other words, Gascón is saying that even though Californians had just voted to keep cash bail, he will not obey the will of the voters and will not follow the law.

Gascón's directive goes on to declare, "Unaffordable cash bail eviscerates the bedrock of our democracy and undermines our principles of justice, fairness and equality under the law."[263] According to Gascón, "Freedom should be free."[264]

What the directive does not mention is that certain criminals—especially career criminals—pose a significant risk of danger to the community; that cash bail is a tool that works to ensure their appearance at future court dates; and that, in appropriate cases, pretrial detention protects the public by keeping the accused off the streets while awaiting trial.

The bail directive theorizes that it is "exceptionally rare that individuals willfully flee prosecution or commit violent felony offenses while released pretrial."[265] This statement cites no data—and runs counter to what prosecutors, judges, courtroom clerks, and police observe across the country every day. Crooks often reoffend even when they do make their court appearances.

A similar idea, Proposition 25, was rejected by California voters in 2020. Proposition 25 would have replaced current bail laws, replacing monetary bail by establishing a risk-assessment tool designed to ensure the public is protected. Gascón's policy does not provide any risk-assessment tool and prohibits prosecutors from asking for bail in most cases.

For example, Gascón's prosecutors are prohibited, regardless of the extent of an accused's criminal history, from requesting cash bail for any misdemeanor, nonserious felony (at least as defined by Gascón), or nonviolent offense. And in the event that a deputy district attorney gets supervisor approval to request cash bail, the prosecutor must presume a defendant is indigent and ask only for minimal bail, regardless of the defendant's actual financial means.[266] Further, Gascón forbids his prosecutors from relying solely on scores from risk-assessment tools for detention,[267] even though such tools have been used for decades, are quite sophisticated, and are part of the First Step Act passed by Congress last year.[268]

To make matters worse, Gascón's prosecutors are not allowed to oppose a defense counsel's motion to remove or modify a defendant's conditions of release,[269] nor can prosecutors oppose a defense counsel's request to waive a client's appearance at "nonessential" court appearances (at least as defined by Gascón),[270] nor can prosecutors oppose a defense counsel's request that a judge not issue a bench warrant against the defendant for not showing up in court.[271] In essence, Gascón has decreed that there should be two defense attorneys for each defendant. This last directive is bad policy because each court appearance gives the defendant's lawyer, the judge, and pretrial supervision officers another chance to make contact with the defendant and to ensure any issues are being addressed. And while a defendant may not need to be present for every court hearing, that issue typically is, and should be, resolved on a case-by-case basis if a defendant does not appear without prior notice. In our experience as former prosecutors, prosecutors typically do not immediately ask a judge to issue a bench warrant for an absent defendant. Defense attorneys are given a few days' notice to produce their clients.

To top it off, these policies applied *retroactively*. Anyone who was currently incarcerated in Los Angeles County on cash bail benefited.[272] And again, Gascón prohibited his prosecutors from objecting to their release.[273]

The court has a bail schedule that sets the presumptive bail for every crime. Bail schedules were devised, in part, to eliminate the possibility of judges either favoring or disfavoring any particular defendant based on race or any other improper factor. Bail schedules are race-neutral. The amount of bail goes up as the severity of the charged crime increases. The 2022 Felony Bail Schedule for the Superior Court for the County of Los Angeles is available online.[274] As former Los Angeles County deputy district attorney Kathy Cady wrote in a blog post, "The bail schedule takes into account the enhancement allegations for additional facts of the crime such as the infliction of great bodily injury (PC 12022.7), use of a deadly weapon (PC 12022(b)(1)), use of a gun (PC 12022.53), or when the crime was committed at the direction of a gang (PC 186.22). The bail schedule also takes into account enhancement allegations based on prior criminal convictions of recidivist offenders. The law requires a judge to consider the following when setting bail: the defendant's prior record including convictions for serious or violent felonies (PC 667(a)(1) and 1170.12(a)-(d)); prior prison commitments; and the commission of new felony crimes committed while out on bail (PC 12022.1)."[275]

But since Gascón thinks "freedom should be free," and he cannot tolerate "unaffordable bail," the directive requires there to be a presumption in favor of pretrial release. Everyone arrested "shall receive a presumption of their own recognizance release without conditions."[276] Pretrial detention "shall only be considered" when "clear and convincing evidence" shows a substantial likelihood that the defendant's release would result in great bodily harm to others or his flight to avoid prosecution.[277]

The consequences of this policy are epitomized by the preventable murder of Alejandro Garcia.[278]

Jonathan Madden was a career criminal long before he executed Alejandro Garcia. In 2001, he was convicted of felony robbery, was given a second chance, and got probation. The next year, he was convicted of burglary and grand theft. In 2006, he was convicted of robbery again. In 2009, he was convicted of possessing drugs—while in prison. In 2018, he was caught with a weapon and was convicted of being a felon in possession of a firearm and possession with intent to distribute cocaine. He amassed this impressive resume prior to Gascón becoming DA.

On February 4, 2021, Madden was again caught with a gun in his possession. He was charged with being a felon in possession of a firearm. Under California law, prosecutors are required to file any prior violent/serious felony convictions under Penal Code section 667(a). But because of another one of Gascón's special directives, to be discussed later, prosecutors were not allowed to allege Madden's prior convictions on the current charging document. Nor were they allowed to tell the judge about Madden's violent criminal past. In essence, the judge would assume, incorrectly, that Madden was a criminal virgin when setting bail. To make matters worse, Gascón's policies prohibited prosecutors from asking for the correct amount of bail (at least $160,000 under the bail schedule) because they could not consider any prior violent convictions. Since the judge didn't know about the priors, he set the bail at $30,000, and Madden paid the bail bondsman $3,000 (10 percent of the bail) and walked out of jail.

Three months later, while still released on the minimum bail, Madden was arrested and charged with selling narcotics, a felony. Under California law, if a person is out on bail when he commits a new crime, a sentencing enhancement can be added to his new charges, but since Gascón's new policies didn't allow for any such enhancements to be used by prosecutors, they couldn't file the enhancement. And again, instead of facing a bail of at least $190,000, the judge set bail at only $100,000. Madden quickly bailed out again, after posting $10,000, which is not much for a drug dealer.

Seven months later, on January 8, 2022, while out of custody on two grants of minimal bail, Madden showed up at a Taco Bell in South Los Angeles. He tried to pay for his food with a counterfeit twenty-dollar bill, but the cashier at the drive-through window spotted the fake currency and told Madden he could not accept the bill. So Madden then shot and killed the cashier, a forty-one-year-old husband and father of three children, even though, as a convicted felon, he had no right to possess a firearm, much less to kill someone with it. Perhaps there are a few holes in Gascón's operating theory that charged defendants do not reoffend.

Madden, and thousands like him, should have been in jail pending trial. But because of Gascón's blatant disregard for the laws of California, an utter lack of common sense, and the radical combination of no cash bail and no enhancements, criminals roam the streets of Los Angeles instead of awaiting trial behind bars, resulting in the death of innocent human beings.

## ENHANCEMENTS AND ALLEGATIONS NULLIFICATION

Gascón's so-called "Enhancements, Three Strikes, and Charging Committee" proposals were drafted by one person, whose entire career has been dedicated to upending the law in California by eliminating enhancements, weapon allegations, and the three-strikes and one-strike laws that were passed by the California legislature and upheld numerous times by the California Supreme Court. His name is Michael Romano, who, according to his bio, is the founder and director of the Three Strikes and Justice Advocacy Project at Stanford Law School.[279] Gascón could not have selected a more inappropriate person to outsource the review, revision, and promulgation of policies in a district attorney's office on these topics than Romano. The result of Romano's handiwork was Special Directive 20-08.[280]

This directive had an immediate and deadly impact, as we detail below. But first, some background.

Over the years, the California legislature has passed various sentencing enhancements, providing for increased penalties or mandatory incarceration for individuals who commit certain crimes against specific classes of individuals, such as children, the elderly, and others, when certain aggravating circumstances, such as using a firearm or other deadly weapon, are present or when someone is a repeat offender.

In 1994, in response to rampant crime and gang activity in California by career violent felons, the legislature passed the Three Strikes Law,[281] which gave prosecutors the ability to seek a life sentence for anyone who commits a qualifying offense and has two qualifying prior convictions. Over the years, the legislature has passed laws detailing the special circumstances that would make a criminal eligible for life without parole (LWOP) or the death penalty in homicide cases.[282] California prosecutors, including deputy district attorneys in the Los Angeles DA's office, exercised their discretion accordingly, adding enhancements when appropriate, and when necessary, seeking guidance from supervisors in the most violent cases in deciding whether to seek LWOP or the death penalty in murder cases. In exercising this discretion, prosecutors sought the death penalty in only a small percentage of death-eligible cases.

Gascón's enhancement directive starts with the bold yet highly dubious assertion that the statutory sentencing ranges for criminal offenses "alone, without enhancements, are sufficient to both hold people accountable and also protect public safety."[283] In essence, Gascón is substituting his personal view for the will of California's voters and its legislature. California criminal statutes have sentencing ranges, which are often called a sentencing triad. Murder, however, does not have "statutory ranges." Experienced prosecutors know this. Gascón, having never actually prosecuted a case, apparently did not. The directive references "studies" that purport to conclude that each "additional sentence year causes a 4 to 7 percent increase in recidivism."[284] But one of the research papers cited to support this bald assertion was written by an economist (about criminals in only one county in Texas) who applied economic theory to modest sentences to see if the benefits of incarcerating people for shorter periods of time outweighed the costs of longer-term incarceration, taking into consideration higher recidivism rates and increased dependence on other governmental programs.[285] In short, the paper does not support what Gascón asserts it says.

The directive makes no mention of the groundbreaking study by the National Bureau of Economic Research entitled "Using Sentencing Enhancements to Distinguish between Deterrence and Incapacitation," which demonstrated that California sentence enhancements had a substantial deterrent effect and were cost effective.[286]

Professors Daniel Kessler and Steven Levitt of Stanford University and University of Chicago, respectively, tested their model using California's Proposition 8, which imposed sentence enhancements for a select group of crimes. They found that in "the year following its passage, crimes covered by Proposition 8 fell by more than 10 percent relative to similar crimes not affected by the law, suggesting a large deterrent effect."[287] More strikingly, they found that "three years after the law comes into effect, eligible crimes have fallen roughly 20–40 percent compared to non-eligible crimes."[288] They concluded that California sentence enhancements had a large deterrent effect and "may be more cost-effective than is generally thought."[289]

Those inconvenient facts aside, Gascón's directive prohibits prosecutors from adding any applicable and provable sentence enhancement to the charging documents that would trigger any additional punishment upon conviction. He further forced his prosecutors to *withdraw* such allegations that had been filed in all pending cases.

Despite the fact that enhancements, special allegations, and the Three Strikes Law keep violent, career felons off the streets for decades, thus protecting society from the worst of the worst, Special Directive 20-08 countermands California law and outright bans their use. His prosecutors cannot allege any "5-Year Priors" under California Penal Code § 667(a)(1) or "3-Year Priors" under California Penal Code § 667.5(a) and are required to dismiss such allegations in pending cases—moreover they cannot add "gang enhancements" against known violent gang members pursuant to California Penal Code § 186.22 and must dismiss such charges in pending cases.[290] Gascón's prosecutors are told, in essence, to ignore, if not violate, California law.

In contrast to these new proposals, the *Legal Policy Manual* that was in effect under former District Attorney Jackie Lacey included reasonable charging policy guidance for prosecutors in their use of enhancements and special circumstances. For example, Chapter 2.10 (Charging Special Allegations), now rescinded by Gascón, stated:

> When a complaint is filed, a deputy shall charge all applicable special allegations that enhance the penalty or result in the mandatory denial of probation (e.g., all prior serious or violent felony convictions, possession or use of weapons and the infliction of great bodily injury) whenever the policies on evidentiary sufficiency have been satisfied.[291]

Prosecutors were required, under Jackie Lacey, to file all applicable special allegations. Gascón has taken the opposite approach, banning the filing of special allegations.

Similarly, Chapter 3.02 (Three Strikes), now rescinded by Gascón, took a measured approach to filing three strikes, stating:

> The Three Strikes law, Penal Code §§ 1170.12(a)–(d), provides a powerful tool for obtaining life sentences in cases involving habitual criminal offenders. However, unless used judiciously, it also has the potential for injustice and abuse in the form of disproportionately harsh sentences for relatively minor crimes. The Three Strikes statutory scheme appropriately authorizes the use of prosecutorial discretion in its implementation. Deputies have a legal and ethical obligation to exercise this discretion in a manner that assures proportionality, evenhanded application, predictability and consistency. Moreover, the potential for coercive plea bargaining must be avoided.[292]

Section 12.05 (Three Strikes) in the Lacey Legal Policy Memo, now rescinded, stated:

> All qualifying prior felony convictions shall be alleged in the pleadings pursuant to Penal Code § 1170.12(d)(1). Prior to seeking dismissal of any strike, the prior strike case files shall be reviewed, if available, in order to fairly evaluate mitigating and aggravating factors. If it is determined that proof of a prior strike cannot be obtained or that the alleged strike is inapplicable, dismissal of the strike shall be sought after obtaining Head Deputy approval.[293]

Gascón's termination of the Three Strikes policy was not judicious, proportional, or evenhanded. It was and is reckless, especially because Los Angeles has a major gang and violent crime problem. The district attorney's office is charged with holding criminals, especially violent criminals, accountable. Keeping particularly dangerous criminals off the streets, for long periods of time, keeps the community safe from such offenders.

Deputy district attorneys, victims, and victims' groups reacted, understandably, with horror at this directive and spoke out repeatedly against it to the media and anyone who would listen. At first, Gascón stood his ground, but within eleven days, he issued an amendment, Special Directive 20-08.2.[294] The amended directive allows for allegations, enhancements, and alternative sentencing schemes in a small handful of cases with special victims, such as those involving hate crimes, elder and dependent abuse, child physical and sexual abuse, adult sexual abuse, human sex trafficking, and financial crimes, or in cases in which there is extensive physical injury or when a dangerous weapon was used and "exhibited an extreme and immediate threat to human life"—but only after getting a supervisor's permission.[295]

But given that there are over one hundred sentencing enhancements, allegations, and special circumstance laws in California, the vast majority of eligible criminals will now not be held to account under the full force of laws that were passed by the California legislature, and Los Angelenos will suffer as a result.

Prosecutors were ordered to never file special circumstance allegations that would result in an LWOP sentence and must dismiss or withdraw such allegations in pending cases. And, unlike other rogue prosecutors, Gascón has mandated that these rules apply *retroactively*. For defendants sentenced within 120 days of December 8, 2020, prosecutors were not allowed to oppose a request from defense counsel for resentencing in "accordance with these guidelines."[296] On February 18, 2022, in response to mounting criticism, Gascón had an epiphany. He issued a new special directive that stated, "I understand there may be the rare occasion where the filing of special circumstance allegations may be necessary. Accordingly, I will enact a committee to review the appropriateness of filing such enhancements in an extremely limited number of cases where the underlying facts are extraordinary and/or the victims are uniquely vulnerable." Of course, the people on that committee include individuals whom Gascón brought over from the Public Defender's Office: Shelan Joseph, Tiffiny Blacknell, and Joseph Iniguez, the latter of whom had a total of four felony trials under his belt when Gascón elevated him to be acting chief deputy.

The deputy district attorneys who work in the Los Angeles County District Attorney's Office are civil servants who have collective bargaining rights and as such, have a union called the "Association of Deputy District Attorneys for Los Angeles County," hereinafter "the Association." This stands in stark contrast to every other DA's office featured in this book, where line prosecutors are at-will employees and cannot speak out against their boss without risking termination for having done so.

The Association (composed of over eight hundred DDAs) sued Gascón over his new policy directives, which they described in their suit filed on December 30, 2020, as "not merely radical, but plainly unlawful."[297] In their lawsuit, filed in the Superior Court for the County of Los Angeles, these career prosecutors argued that some of the sentencing enhancements are required by law and that their boss did not have the legal authority to order prosecutors—each of whom is an officer of the court and member of the California bar—not to file those enhancements. The association argued that the law enacting the enhancements "made the prosecutor's duty to seek the Three Strikes enhancement absolute. In cases where the Three Strikes Law applies, the prosecutor has no discretion to refuse to seek the enhancement—he or she is bound by law to do so."[298]

In seeking relief from the court, the DDAs made four points of how Gascón's special directives require them to "violate California law, to violate their oaths of office, and to violate [our] ethical and professional obligations."

First, the Three Strikes Law requires the prosecutor to plead and prove each prior felony conviction.

Second, the special directives violate the DDA's specific duty to prosecute general laws under the California code, and that duty is mandatory, not discretionary. The DDAs argued that they have a "ministerial duty to enforce the law and to exercise their prosecutorial discretion in particular cases." Gascón, much less any prosecutor, cannot ignore entire categories of crime, which is, in effect, prosecutorial nullification, and then paper that over and call it a proper exercise of prosecutorial discretion.

Third, the special directives require DDAs to violate the law by requiring them to bring a motion (and refuse to oppose a motion at resentencing) to strike (get rid of) all prior convictions and special circumstances that might result in a sentence of life without parole in all pending cases where they were already alleged.

And finally, the special directives violate the Three Strikes Law by "wrest[ing] from the judiciary its legislatively mandated role in determining whether a prior conviction should be stricken in the 'interests of justice.'" In the situation where a prosecutor decides to file a motion asking a judge to get rid of (strike) a prior, the law gives the judge the duty to decide whether to do so or not. Gascón's directives run afoul of the law, because, they claim, in cases where a judge decides not to strike a prior (thereby frustrating Gascón's policy goal of not exposing criminals to long prison sentences), Gascón requires DDAs to file a new set of charges (called "an amended complaint") that omits the allegations in the first place.

On February 8, 2021, Judge James C. Chalfant ruled for the Association of Deputy District Attorneys for the most part, granting their request for a preliminary injunction.[299] In his ruling, Chalfant stopped (enjoined) Gascón's directives from, among other things, requiring DDAs not to plead and prove strike priors under the Three Strikes Law, compelling DDAs to move to dismiss prior strikes or any existing enhancement in a pending case, compelling DDAs to move to dismiss or withdraw special circumstance allegations that would result in a LWOP sentence upon conviction, or compelling DDAs not to use proven special circumstances in other types of cases.

Perhaps in retaliation, a month later Gascón disbanded the hardcore gang unit in his office. Composed of seasoned, tough, career prosecutors who had accumulated hundreds of years of experience learning about, investigating, targeting, and taking down many of the dozens of vilest gang members in the megalopolis, Gascón realized that by disbanding the gang unit, he would pay back BLM, who had been begging for him to do so. One prosecutor interviewed shortly after the announcement said, "We can already hear jail calls and interviews with officers on the street...that gang members are laughing."[300]

Andrew Lara, the city council member from Pico Rivera, said, "Right when I heard that we weren't going to charge enhancements, like gang affiliation enhancements, I said, 'What are you doing?' I don't understand why we haven't classified gangs as terrorist organizations. Period. They prey upon our kids. They prey upon property. They terrorize neighborhoods.... They are terrorist organizations. I don't know why we don't. Because they're Mexican?"[301]

Lara is half-Mexican and half-Native American. A Democrat who graduated from the University of Southern California, he grew up in the segregated neighborhood of Boyle Heights in East Los Angeles, the birthplace, according to Lara, of Mexican gangs in LA. "All of my friends, some good friends jumped into gangs."

He saw firsthand the allure of gang life, telling us, "The cool guys were the guys with nice cars, with the Chevy Impalas, with money, with a gun on them, with girls, and they sold drugs...those were the shot callers right? Everyone aspired to be that unfortunately."

He explained that in the 1990s, the Mexican mafia took over by bringing all the Mexican gangs together in Los Angeles and brokered a sort of pact by saying to them, "OK, we're going to tax you. You're gonna sell our drugs. You're gonna sell our drugs, and we are going to tax every single gang member a monthly charge…. If you don't pay your taxes, or you don't do what we say then all of your members in prison…we're going to shank them, we're going to beat them up or make life horrible for them." The Mexican mafia "control the prisons," so, "right away the vast majority of the Mexican gangs toed the line."

Gangs started recruiting younger and younger members to commit crimes for them, including murder. That's because, as Lara said, they told would-be youngsters who wanted to be cool and join the gang, "Look, you'll get caught, you'll put in work for the gang, you'll get a rep, and you'll be out [of juvenile detention] by twenty-five. You'll be a superstar. You'll come back as a superstar in the neighborhood. And that's how all these young kids were being set up."

But Lara knew something that Gascón and his inner circle refused to acknowledge or chose to ignore: "…it wasn't until Three Strikes, and it wasn't until they started prosecuting minors as adults…that we saw a lot of decreased gang activity here in Pico Rivera and East LA."

Not surprisingly, gang activity, especially gang-related violence and murders, has exploded since Gascón took office.

And although Judge Chalfant's injunction was welcome news, it came too late for many cases. That's because between December 7, 2020, and February 8, 2021, because of Gascón's lawless directives, thousands of criminals slithered through the cracks the directives mandated.

Two of those criminals included Emiel Lamar Hunt and Darryl Collins.[302]

Emiel Lamar Hunt had brutally abused his three-year-old son, putting him into a coma. Hunt was convicted in 2005 and sentenced to twelve years in prison. On March 1, 2019, Hunt and his girlfriend, Taquesta Graham, killed Trinity, Taquesta's daughter, and dumped her body on the side of the road in Los Angeles County. The two were arrested and charged. Because he had a prior 2005 felony conviction, Hunt would have faced fifty-to-life for the first-degree premeditated murder if he was convicted, versus the twenty-five-to-life for Taquesta. Prosecutors, however, were required to cite the prior conviction in the charging document against him for this enhancement to apply.

One week after Gascón took office, and his policies relating to prior conviction allegations were being enforced by his reluctant DDAs, Hunt's prior conviction was stricken from the indictment by a DDA. Now, both defendants face the same punishment for murdering Trinity, even though Hunt had a serious and violent record.

Or take the case of Darryl Collins, a murderer whom Gascón let off the hook by preventing his prosecutors from filing a special circumstances allegation, making him eligible for life without parole.

Collins murdered his girlfriend Fatima Johnson on July 2, 2021. He bound her, gagged her, and beat her to death. Collins, no stranger to the law, was arrested shortly thereafter. In 1992, he was convicted of attempted robbery, went to prison, but was let out early. Six years later, in 1998, he killed two people on two separate dates while engaged in a string of armed robberies. That should have been the end of the line for a guy like Collins. He pled guilty to both murders and was sentenced to fifty-years-to-life, but after serving over two decades in prison, the California Parole Board granted him parole and released him. Less than a year later, he murdered Fatima Johnson—Gascón was the DA.

Under Penal Code section 190.2, prosecutors can file a "special circumstance" allegation when someone like Collins has murdered more than one person in his life. If convicted of the new murder charge with a special circumstance, Collins would face either an LWOP sentence or a death sentence. But since Gascón prohibited all special circumstance allegations, Collins, if convicted, will not face either an LWOP or death penalty, which he richly deserves. Instead, the fifty-one-year-old will likely receive a sentence of twenty-five-to-life. And because of the Elder Parole law[303] in California, he likely will get out of prison around seventy years of age.

Two days after Judge Chalfant issued his injunction, Gascón released Special Directive 21-01 entitled "Revised Policies Pursuant to Preliminary Injunction," wherein he mischaracterized the judge's ruling and noted that the "office will be filing a notice of appeal."[304] Gascón knew he had to appeal because this directive was one of the cornerstones of his plan to dismantle the criminal justice system.

Gascón hired one of the most experienced appellate lawyers in the country.

A former acting solicitor general of the United States in the Obama administration, Neal Kumar Katyal filed the appeal on August 16, 2021. Katyal argued with vigor that Gascón had the power to order his DDAs to dismiss existing charges or enhancements and not file strikes—even though by doing so, Gascón was making an end-run around the judge. Yet this is the same Neal Katyal who, two years earlier, wrote an op-ed in the *New York Times* decrying the Justice Department's abandonment of the case against Michael Flynn, pontificating that "a prosecutor's say-so is not enough to drop a prosecution; it requires the approval of the court."[305] Katyal ended his *New York Times* op-ed, echoing an opinion by his friend and fellow liberal judge (current Supreme Court justice but on the District Court in Washington, DC, at the time ) Ketanji Brown Jackson the year before, writing, "Presidents are not kings, and federal courts have a vital role to play in protecting our democracy."[306] The same is true of state courts. A California appeals court panel agreed with that assessment, writing that the "district attorney overstates his authority.... He is an elected official who must comply with the law, not a sovereign with absolute, unreviewable discretion."[307]

At the time this book went print, the issue had not been resolved because Gascón asked the California Supreme Court to further review the case.

## IGNORING THE DEATH PENALTY

It won't surprise you that one of the requirements to be a Soros-funded rogue prosecutor candidate is refusal to enforce the death penalty, even if that sentence is authorized in the state where you are elected. Citizens may differ in their views about the death penalty, but the elected district attorney is not the moralist or ethicist-in-chief and has a more limited (albeit important) role: to faithfully enforce the law as written using appropriate, professional, informed prosecutorial discretion.

The death penalty is an authorized punishment in California. Even though California is a progressive state, the legislature and California voters have consistently authorized the death penalty for persons convicted of qualifying offenses. Much of death penalty law in California is by voter initiative, and every time Californians have voted on whether to abolish or retain the death penalty, they chose to keep it. In 2016, Californians voted 53 percent to 46 percent to keep the death penalty.

But the will of the people is irrelevant to Gascón. Gascón selected three of the most radical antideath penalty activists he could find to lead his death penalty committee. Stephanie Faucher was the deputy director of the 8th Amendment Project, an organization founded in 2014 to end the death penalty.[308] She worked in communications and previously worked at MoveOn.org, which has also been funded by George Soros.[309] Sean Kennedy was the executive director of the Center for Juvenile Law and Policy at Loyola Law School and a former federal public defender.[310] And Natasha Minsker was a consultant, a former American Civil Liberties Union (ACLU) attorney, and former director of the ACLU of California Center for Advocacy & Policy.[311] They wrote Special Directive 20-11 entitled the Death Penalty Policy.[312]

If truth in advertising was required, it should have been called the "No-Death-Penalty-Ever Policy." Like any policy document you would expect from a public defender's office, the directive states that "a sentence of death is never an appropriate resolution in any case."[313]

Of the 692 people currently on death row in California as of May 21, 2022, 215 were sentenced to death as a result of capital prosecutions in Los Angeles County.[314] According to Gascón's directive, 85 percent of those 215 criminals are people of color. This is proof, he claims in his directive, that the imposition of the death penalty in Los Angeles County resulted from racism. No further analysis is included.

His directive prohibits prosecutors from seeking the death penalty in all cases, including pending cases, and disbands the Special Circumstances Committee that determined when to seek capital punishment.[315] Further, Gascón's prosecutors were prohibited from seeking an execution date for any person currently on death row, and prosecutors were also prohibited from defending existing death sentences on appeal.[316]

Furthermore, Gascón has ordered his prosecutors to review all prior death sentences handed down in Los Angeles County with "the goal of removing the death sentence."[317] To be clear, that included serial killers like

Chester Turner, who was convicted of raping and murdering ten women in Los Angeles. He also killed a victim's unborn baby and was subsequently convicted in 2014 of four additional killings.[318]

And for those death sentence cases in which the DA's office is a not a party, and the death judgment arose within Los Angeles County, the office will "consult with the [California] Attorney General and seek his assistance with implementing the goals of this office."[319] Over time, Gascón's directive could result in most, if not all, 215 LA County death sentences being set aside, despite the fact that many of their direct appeals were rejected by the California Supreme Court years or decades ago.

One of the many victims of Gascón's policy was a little four-year-old named Anthony Avalos.

Born to Heather Barron and her ex-husband in Los Angeles, Anthony Avalos was neglected by his mom (Heather) and her live-in gang banger boyfriend, Kareem Leiva. Eventually, neglect turned to rage, and during the last few weeks of his life, Anthony was whipped repeatedly with a belt and a looped cord, had hot sauce poured on his face and into his mouth, was held upside down by his feet and dropped on his head over and over. Kareem and Heather made him kneel on uncooked rice for eight to ten hours a day and beat him to a pulp. They withheld food and water from him for weeks.

Kareem is an MS-13 gang member who had several MS-13 tattoos on his body. Kareem would make Anthony and his three siblings (Angel, Raphael, and Destiny) fight each other until they cried. Each was horribly abused by Heather and Kareem.

Shortly after noon on June 20, 2018, Heather called 911 to request an ambulance, saying that Anthony had suffered an injury after falling. When paramedics arrived on the scene, the door was closed, and nobody was out there, which was odd. When they finally gained access to the apartment, Anthony was lying on the ground in the living room. He wasn't breathing and had no pulse. His Glasgow Coma Scale was a three.[320] Paramedics saw multiple injuries all over Anthony's body, including actively bleeding knees, and abrasions and cuts from head to toe. It was obvious to the paramedics that Anthony did not suffer a mere fall.

When Anthony was taken to the hospital, a deputy sheriff called DDA Jon Hatami and said, "We have another Gabriel," referring to the infamous Gabriel Fernandez child torture and murder case that Hatami had tried and was part of a 2020 Netflix multipart series. By the time Hatami got to the hospital, Anthony was dead.

An autopsy was performed, and the forensic pathologist found that Anthony had died from blunt force trauma and child neglect and starvation. All of his internal organs had shut down, which meant he had been subjected to prolonged neglect and starvation.

Kareem Leiva was charged first with murder, torture, and intentional murder by torture (a special circumstance). Heather was charged with the same offenses.

DDA Hatami presented the case to the Los Angeles County Grand Jury. Over the course of three and a half weeks, Hatami presented sixty-five witnesses and over two thousand exhibits. The evidence of guilt was overwhelming, and the grand jury indicted both Heather and Kareem for murder.

Recognizing the brutality of the crimes committed against Anthony, including numerous acts of torture, Hatami sought permission to present the case to the Special Circumstances Committee in the DA's office. Composed of the most senior experienced career prosecutors in the office, handpicked by then-District Attorney Jackie Lacey, the Special Circumstances Committee reviewed all the facts and circumstances of the case, considered any possible mitigating evidence, and recommended to Jackie Lacey that her office seek the death penalty against Heather and Kareem.

In August 2019, the LA DA's office announced that they would be seeking the death penalty and filed capital charges. Heather and Kareem remained in jail pending trial without bail.

Enter Gascón and Special Directive 20-11.

Once Gascón was elected district attorney and Special Directive 20-11 was implemented, Hatami was required to call the victim's family members to tell them that he had to drop the special circumstances and would not seek either LWOP or the death penalty. He called Maria Barron, Anthony's aunt, and said, "I've got really bad news. The new DA has said not only do I have to remove the death penalty in the case, but I have to remove the special circumstances in this case." She started crying. He explained that by removing the death penalty and special circumstances, the most the defendants could get would be a twenty-five-to-life sentence. Further, they would now be eligible for bail and be able to get out of jail pending trial. If convicted, Heather and Kareem would be eligible for the Elder Parole law, meaning that they would be eligible for parole once they turned fifty years old.

Hatami had to make that same call to twelve family members in this case alone.

Of the ten or so death penalty cases in the office when Gascón came into office, Hatami had three. Each of those cases had been heavily investigated, had gone to the grand jury, and was headed to trial.

Gascón refused to meet with Hatami or any of the other prosecutors handling death penalty cases, refused to read the special circumstances memos that they had filed, and refused meet with the families of the victims. The death penalty was withdrawn from every pending case, and unless Gascón changes his mind, no death penalty charges ever will be filed under his watch

On March 7, 2023, after a weeks-long bench trial, both defendants were found guilty of first degree murder, the special circumstances allegation of torture, and other crimes. Their sentencing hearing is scheduled for April 25, 2023, where they both face a sentence of life without the possibility of parole. During his closing argument at the trial, Hatami called both defendants "evil" and "monsters."

Hard to argue with Hatami's characterization. Both defendants, in our opinion, deserved the death penalty.

## LETTING THIRTY THOUSAND FELONS OUT OF PRISON

The district attorneys featured in this book have policies that impact current and future cases. As you have seen in this chapter, and will see in the ones that follow, those edicts have had a devastating impact on the communities where they serve, emboldened criminals, exacerbated tensions with law enforcement officials, and ignored victims' rights. The one line they had not crossed is applying their policies retroactively to hard-earned convictions from their office.

That is, until Gascón was elected.

Gascón created a resentencing committee to figure out how to release thirty thousand-plus felons who had been previously convicted by the Los Angeles District Attorney's Office and who were still serving prison terms after their appeals were denied. This is not reform; it is not "progressive." It is not the job of a newly elected district attorney to undercut the hard work of the prosecutor's office, police, detectives, deputy sheriffs, and other stakeholders who worked together to earn these convictions. But Gascón doesn't care about that, as you can see from whom he appointed to head the committee, and his special directive.

The driving belief behind the work of this committee is that the only reason these felons are imprisoned is because of a systemically racist criminal justice system, including racist cops and prosecutors. Therefore, it is important to abolish their prison terms under the guise of resentencing each and every one of them.

This committee was composed of six diehard prison abolitionists. Hillary Blout is the founder and executive director of For the People and the Sentence Review Project. She worked briefly as deputy district attorney in San Francisco for both Gascón and Kamala Harris when each was the district attorney.[321] She also worked for the antiprosecution organization called Fair and Just Prosecution.[322]

Kate Chatfield is the director of audience engagement and senior legal analyst at The Appeal, which describes itself as a "nonprofit news organization dedicated to exposing how the U.S. criminal legal system fails to keep people safe and, instead perpetuates harm."[323] The Appeal decries the "economic costs of our expansive carceral system." She was formerly the director of policy at The Justice Collaborative, former policy director at Restore Justice, and a former public defender.[324]

Christopher Hawthorne is a law professor and director of the Juvenile Innocence and Fair Sentencing Clinic at Loyola Law School and a former criminal defense attorney.[325] Jennifer Hansen is a staff attorney at the California Appellate Project.[326] Paula Mitchell is the executive director of Project for the Innocent at Loyola Law School. Michael Romano, the one-man wrecking ball who wrote the policy to end the use of all enhancements, Three Strikes, and allegations, rounded out the committee.

The result of their work was Special Directive 20-14 and is entitled "Resentencing."[327] One of the most dangerous, wide-ranging and irresponsible of Gascón's directives, it should be called "We Love Murderers," "Fifteen Years Is the Most Time You'll Ever Serve," or "We Stand with Criminals."

First, Gascón's prosecutors are required to "reevaluate and consider for resentencing people who have already served 15 years in prison."[328]

Second, for pending cases that have sentence enhancements, prosecutors are required to "join in the Defendant's motion to strike all alleged sentence enhancements."[329] It is bad enough to force career prosecutors not to object to a defense motion to strike all alleged sentence enhancements when the defendant is eligible for each one based on his criminal conduct. It is offensive and insulting to order prosecutors to *join* in such a motion. In all cases in which a defendant is eligible for resentencing or recall of a sentence, prosecutors are prohibited under the directive from opposing the resentencing or sentence recall.[330] Again, Gascón's directives effectively put two defense attorneys in court.

If a criminal convicted of felony murder[331] seeks relief under Penal Code § 1170.95,[332] prosecutors who oppose sentencing relief "shall submit the reasons in writing to the Head Deputy" who will then consult with Gascón, who will make the final decision in accordance with his directive.

What does that mean in practice? For criminals who killed someone during a robbery, rape, or other serious felony and pled guilty pursuant to a plea agreement to a lesser charge of manslaughter, but who could have been convicted of the more serious crime of murder or attempted murder charges under certain theories (including felony murder), the directive makes them eligible for relief.[333] Essentially, they receive a double break. A felony murder is when someone commits a qualifying felony, and someone dies during the commission of that qualifying felony. A person convicted of participating in a felony murder will have the murder charges, as well as all sentencing enhancements, dismissed. What remains, if anything, will be any sentence for a lower-level crime such as robbery or burglary. The shorter length of these sentences will often result in the offender being eligible for *immediate release* based upon time already served.

Third, Gascón's directive states that the "default policy" of the office is that prosecutors "will not attend parole hearings and will support in writing the grant of parole" for every person who has "already served their mandatory minimum period of incarceration." Can you imagine telling the family of a murder victim that you are prohibited from attending the parole hearing to offer them the support they need and deserve or that you were required to file a document supporting the offender's release?

Moreover, if the defendant represents a "high" risk for recidivism, as determined by the California Department of Corrections and Rehabilitation, prosecutors "may, in their letter, take a neutral position on the grant of parole."

Gascón's directive goes on to state that prosecutors not only are prohibited from attending parole hearings, thus depriving the parole board of the prosecutor's point of view on the grant of parole, but the directive prevents prosecutors from using anything said by the convict at his own parole hearing—even if it is false—in future court proceedings. Gascón has decided that parole hearings are "coercive"[334] environments, and, as such, statements made by the offender during them are "unreliable and involuntary."[335] Therefore, Gascón says prosecutors cannot introduce statements made by criminals during parole hearings in court for any purpose.

The directive further provides that any criminal who comes up for parole who was under twenty-five years old when he committed his crime will now be allowed to present mitigating evidence at his parole hearing, something criminals were already allowed to do.[336]

Each month, there are approximately two hundred parole hearings for inmates convicted of crimes committed in Los Angeles County that his prosecutors are now not allowed to attend.[337] Gascón knows this. And he should also know a bedrock principle of the California Constitution defines victim's rights as found in Article I, Section 28, better known as Marcy's Law.

Those victim's rights include: to be treated with fairness and respect; to be reasonably protected from the defendant; to reasonable notice of and to reasonably confer with the prosecuting agency; to reasonable notice of all public proceedings including postconviction release; to be informed of all parole procedures, to participate in the parole process, to provide information to the parole authority.[338]

In response to this directive, former DDAs and pro bono victim's rights attorneys have stepped up and attended as many parole hearings as they can on behalf of victims. Furthermore, then-Sheriff Alex Villanueva sent a letter to Gascón in February 2021 notifying him that the Los Angeles County Sheriff's Office "will attend parole hearings in the absence of our prosecutors."[339] Villanueva wrote, "I cannot understand why your office is barring prosecutors from attending parole hearings," as it is "important to give a voice for the voiceless and keep our commitment in good standing in support of those who have been victimized by violent crime."[340]

Despite Villanueva, Kathy Cady (a former prosecutor-turned-victims'-rights attorney), and others who have stepped up to help with parole hearings, the majority of victims who appear at parole hearings each month don't have anyone standing by their side and enforcing their rights.

Fourth, perhaps the most radical aspect of this directive, and the one that has prosecutors, police, and victims' rights groups up in arms, is the establishment of a resentencing unit. The unit is charged with a "comprehensive review" of cases in which a defendant received a sentence that is "inconsistent" with the office's new policies.[341] Specifically, the unit is charged with conducting an expedited review of a "universe of 20,000 to 30,000 cases with out-of-policy sentences,"[342] which are defined as:

- Criminals who have already served five years or more;

- Criminals who are currently sixty years of age or older;

- Criminals who are at enhanced risk of COVID-19 infection;

- Criminals who have been recommended for resentencing by the California Department of Corrections and Rehabilitation, as allowed by a recent amendment to the California Penal Code, which extended the time for certain individuals and entities to request a recall of a sentence and for resentencing of an inmate;

- Criminals who were also victims of a crime; and

- Criminals who were under eighteen at the time they committed their crimes but were tried as adults.[343]

The directive also benefits—of all people—criminals sentenced to life without parole. In language that only a criminal defense attorney could write, the directive states that "parole is an effective process to reduce recidivism."[344] To ensure that the worst of the worst get out of prison, the directive states that "prosecutor's input at parole hearings" is limited, and as previously mentioned, prosecutors not only are prohibited from attending parole hearings, but they are now *required to support*—in writing—parole for any thug who has served his mandatory minimum period of incarceration.[345] The Manson family members and Sirhan Sirhan thank him.

Gascón is forcing career prosecutors, who have dedicated their professional lives to protecting the residents of Los Angeles County, to actively work to release violent criminals sentenced to life without parole.

And the criminals celebrate it.

In 2005, a gang member named Phillip Dorsett, armed with a .380 pistol, walked up to Jesse Fujino, a member of a rival gang named the Evil Klan. Fujino, also known as Mousey, asked Dorset, "Where you guys from?" Dorsett responded, "This is Muertos" (the Spanish word for murder), lifted the .380, and shot Mousey in the head from a foot away.

In 2007, Dorsett was convicted of second-degree murder and sentenced to forty-years-to-life. The case was overturned on appeal for technical reasons (not because Dorsett was innocent), and he was retried and convicted again of second-degree murder.

While serving his prison sentence in New Folsom State Prison, Dorsett and his cellmate heard about Gascón's resentencing directive and celebrated. Using a cell phone, Dorsett videotaped himself and his cellmate holding glasses of moonshine known as "white lightning," clinking the glasses together for a toast saying, "Some white lightning, a little cup, boom! Celebrating us going home on this Gascón directive. Whoop!"

The video made its way to the media. Gascón's office refused to comment, but the DA's Association issued a statement saying, in part, "CDAA calls on Gascón to abandon his reckless policies that put violent criminals like Dorsett back on the streets."

But Gascón ignored the pleas from his own DDAs.

In May 2022, Dorsett was resentenced on a giveaway charge of manslaughter, which resulted in his getting out of prison. And to add insult to injury, Gascón's office sent a convicted murderer and gang member to the hearing to speak for Dorsett (not the victim). Skipp Townsend, who still appears in the state's gang database, was hired by Gascón to be on the "Victim's Advisory Panel," and he gave an impassioned plea for mercy on behalf of Dorsett to the resentencing judge.

And that's just one case we know about.

Violent felons who were convicted by the LA DA's office and who are serving long sentences are getting resentenced all the time. There are over eighty cities in Los Angeles County. There are fifty-two offices of the LA County DA's Office across the county. There is no public information on how many and how often offenders are getting resentenced, and the DA's Office has refused to produce any information in response to Public Records Act requests. But they are happening every day.

And who is in charge of all of these resentencings? Diana Teran, who was "on loan" from the Public Defender's Office for several months before being hired full-time by Gascón. Teran is one of several former career deputy public defenders who were hired by Gascón to fill senior positions in the LA DA's office. The others include Alisa Blair, Shelan Joseph, and Tiffiny Blacknell. The DA's Association, along with former district attorneys Steve Cooley and Jackie Lacey, have sued Gascón claiming that these hires violated the civil service rules.

## JUVENILE FREE-FOR-ALL

Part of the quid quo pro in being a Soros bought-and-paid rogue prosecutor is that you have to pretend that murderers, rapists, child abusers, gang members, armed robbers, and other violent thugs who committed their crimes when they were younger than eighteen are "children." Ignore the fact that in California you can get a state-issued California learner's permit to drive a car (with an adult present) at fifteen-and-a-half, drive a car at sixteen, get married with your parents' consent if you're under eighteen, become legally emancipated from your parents at fourteen, work for pay before you're eighteen, and can get an abortion without parental notification or consent before you are eighteen. So, the California legislature has decided that minors have brains developed enough to drive a car, get married, terminate a pregnancy, and join the military (with their parents' permission), but, according to Gascón, don't have brains developed sufficiently to hold them fully accountable for committing violent crimes.

Gascón populated his juvenile committee to further the radical goals of never charging juveniles in adult criminal court—no matter how heinous or depraved the crimes—as well as other policies that will neither help juveniles nor keep the community safe. He could not have picked a more dangerous group of people to serve on this committee. Frankie Guzman is the director of the Youth Justice Initiative at the National Center for Youth Law and was a recipient of a Soros Justice Fellowship.[346] Michael Mendoza is the director of National Advocacy for the Anti-Recidivism Coalition.[347] Maureen Pacheco is a trainer for the Juvenile Division of the Alternate Public Defender's Office of Los Angeles and a former public defender.[348] Patricia Soung is an attorney at the Pacific Juvenile Defender Center, where she is the director of Youth Justice Policy. She was also a Soros Justice Fellow at Northwestern University Law School.[349]

What emerged from this crime-enabling group was Special Directive 20-09, entitled "Youth Justice."[350] A more accurate title would be "Violent Teens Never Go to Jail" or, alternatively, "The Gang Improvement and Recruiting Act" as the policies create incentives for gangs to enlist even more youth under eighteen years old to commit violent crimes.

Dressed up in more bumper sticker feel-good language like "care over cages" and "need over deed," the directive makes diversion the default for those under eighteen who commit crimes, with a goal of "keeping youth out of the juvenile justice system." Of course, the way Gascón keeps youth out of the juvenile justice system is simple: ignore their criminality and order his prosecutors to do the same.

The most radical aspect of this directive is this: Gascón's prosecutors are prohibited from asking judges to transfer youthful offenders to adult criminal court, no matter what crime they commit. That is why we featured the James (Hannah) Tubbs story at the beginning of this chapter.

The directive as it plays out means that a six-foot-three, 210-pound almost eighteen-year-old gang member who murders someone and later gets caught when he is eighteen and considered an adult is given an "adjudication" in juvenile court—and is essentially set free. Gascón ordered his prosecutors to withdraw all pending motions to transfer youthful offenders to adult court.

Furthermore, all youth accused of committing misdemeanor offenses are not to be prosecuted, unless it is "deemed necessary," and even those individuals must be offered the opportunity to participate in diversion programs. Youth who damage property and get in a "minor altercation with group home staff, foster parents and other youth" will not be charged. Undoubtedly, this will have a negative impact on whether people want to work in group homes or take in foster kids in LA.[351] Gascón also disbanded the school truancy unit and programs associated with chronic truancy. So much for encouraging kids to attend and stay in school in Los Angeles County.

Like prosecutors in adult court, Gascón's Juvenile Court prosecutors are prohibited from filing any "potential strike offense" for sixteen- and seventeen-year-old criminals, with the exception of forcible rape and murder. And even here, George Gascón's nomenclature is deceptively misleading, hiding the true impact of his directive. His exception specifies "rape" as an exception, but "rape" under California law means forcible penile penetration of a victim's vagina. "Rape" does not include forcible sodomy, forcible oral copulation, or forcible digital penetration. Those equally heinous crimes would not come within Gascón's exception. Details matter.

Therefore, a dangerous sixteen- or seventeen-year-old who is a gang member or has a long criminal record, who shoots someone but does not kill him, or who engages in physical or sexual abuse of a child, or who forcibly sodomizes a victim, or who commits another violent crime, will not be tried in adult court for his "adult" crimes and will not face adult punishment. Instead, he will have his case adjudicated in juvenile court, where the maximum punishment is being held in juvenile detention until the age of twenty-one. This creates a perverse incentive for gangs to step up their ongoing recruiting efforts to youth to carry out murders and other heinous crimes on their behalf.

As Andrew Lara noted in our interview, not charging gang enhancements and refusing to charge juvenile gang members as adults when appropriate results in those criminal minors coming back to "communities like mine. So my community becomes a petri dish for someone's social experiment. I'm not OK with that."

Then-Sheriff Alex Villanueva, when talking about not charging violent youthful gang members as adults and refusing to charge minors with felony theft, said, "It's profitable to do crime here in Los Angeles County. We're having people out of county, out of state, coming here to LA to do home invasion robberies, burglaries; we have foreign nationals coming here to do burglaries. We have posses of juveniles brazenly doing robberies, taking expensive watches from people in Beverly Hills and places like that, to the point where the City of LA is telling people, 'Don't wear expensive jewelry.' What kind of message are we sending? We are creating a dystopian society as we speak."[352]

Gascón and his cabal clearly don't care.

Gascón's prosecutors are also prohibited from objecting to a defense attorney's request to remove a client from the national sex offender public website if the offender was a youth at the time he committed the qualifying sex offense(s).[353] So a seventeen-year-old convicted of rape, child molestation, or any other qualifying violent sex offense, who has a history of deviant sexual assault and is on the sex offender registry, will not need to worry about a prosecutor objecting to him coming off the registry. Once he is off the registry, the public, including potential employers or landlords, will not have any way of knowing his criminal past unless he voluntarily discloses it, which is highly unlikely to happen.

Gascón's juvenile directive decrees that in juvenile court, much like adult court, the "presumption shall be against detention."[354] Detention in juvenile hall can only be sought where the accused ("child" in their lingo) "poses an immediate danger to others," and then only "for as long as the child represents a danger to others."[355] Prosecutors are prohibited from seeking detention for probation violations unless the youth commits a new, serious qualifying crime.[356] For youthful offenders who are illegal aliens, prosecutors "shall seek to avoid immigration consequences"[357] and cannot object when defense attorneys seek to seal the record, thereby virtually ensuring that no illegal alien criminal gets deported from LA, and no one will have knowledge about his or her crimes because the records are sealed.

# AT LEAST THIRTEEN CRIMES YOU CAN COMMIT IN LOS ANGELES

Special Directive 20-07 is entitled "Misdemeanor Case Management."[358] A more accurate title would be "Thirteen Crimes You Can Commit in Los Angeles with Impunity, Thanks to George Gascón."

Dressed up in the same psychobabble fuzzy language endemic to the rogue prosecutor movement, this directive implores the reader to "reimagine public safety,"[359] which, as we have discussed at length in our research,[360] is tantamount to ending public safety as we know it, favoring criminals, targeting police, and shunning victims. To that end, this directive states that "prosecution of low-level offenses will now be governed by this data-driven misdemeanor reform policy directive."[361]

The phrase "data-driven" is one that other rogue prosecutors use too. They want voters to believe that if you refuse to prosecute scores of crimes that crime will actually go *down*, and they have the "data" to prove it. But they usually do not.[362] And on those rare occasions when they actually do produce some data, a closer look behind how that "data" was generated, calculated, and interpreted often leads to vastly different conclusions.[363]

Rachael Rollins, the Soros-inspired former district attorney (and now the Biden-appointed United States Attorney for Massachusetts) in Boston, used the same "data driven" language in her "Rollins Policy Memo," which lists fifteen crimes you can now commit with impunity in Boston.[364] While she claims that ignoring these offenses will actually lead to less crime, the opposite has proven to be the case, according to recent crime statistics. The same is true in other cities with rogue prosecutors. This should hardly come as a surprise. Tell criminals they can commit certain crimes without being arrested or charged and, surprise, surprise, they will commit those crimes.[365]

Like Rollins, Gascón has decreed that thirteen misdemeanor offenses that are still on the books in California "shall be declined or dismissed before arraignment and without conditions,"[366] unless certain "exceptions" or other "factors" exist.[367] To make matters worse, the directive states that "these charges do not constitute an exhaustive list," and each prosecutor in Gascón's office is ordered to "exercise his discretion" to identify other offenses—out of the hundreds of misdemeanors in the California

Penal Code—that fall within "the spirit" of this directive and to proceed accordingly.[368]

The thirteen crimes the directive mentions by name that you can commit with impunity in Los Angeles as of December 8, 2020, are:[369]

- Trespassing
- Disturbing the peace
- Driving without a license/driving on a suspended license
- Criminal threats
- All drug possession
- All drug paraphernalia possession
- Minor in possession of alcohol
- Drinking in public
- Under the influence of a controlled substance
- Public intoxication
- Loitering
- Loitering to commit prostitution
- Resisting arrest

If the charge is not declined because it falls into a narrow exception, then prosecutors must follow a three-step process until the case is ultimately dismissed.[370] This process includes:

- Pre-arraignment diversion via an administrative hearing, then upon compliance with specified conditions, the charge will be formally dismissed.

- Post-arraignment, pretrial plea diversion. Once the criminal complies with conditions, the charge is dismissed without entry of a plea.

- Post-arraignment, post-plea diversion. Once the criminal complies with the conditions imposed pretrial, the charge is dismissed after the criminal withdraws his plea of guilty.

ZACK SMITH AND CHARLES D. STIMSON

For those misdemeanors not on the list of thirteen, pretrial diversion "shall be presumptively granted" for a period of six months and in no circumstance longer than eighteen months.

For those few misdemeanor cases that are not declined or subject to pretrial diversion, prosecutors are required to follow these rules when making plea offers:

- No offer can require a defendant to do jail time and community labor.

- No offer can require a defendant to do more than fifteen days of community labor.

- No offer can require a defendant to register on a public registry unless required by statute.

- Once a prosecutor makes an offer to a defendant, who then refuses the offer, the prosecutor cannot up the ante if the defendant decides to roll the dice by filing a pretrial motion (and loses) or decides he wants a jury trial, and then changes his mind once he gets closer to trial.

With respect to fines and fees, prosecutors are required to presume that *all* criminals are indigent and unable to pay a fine or fee.[371] Prosecutors must "actively support" a request by a criminal or his attorney to waive a fine or fee.[372]

When a defendant receives probation and, as a condition of probation, is required to pay a fine or fee or to participate in a program and then fails to make the payment or participate in the program, prosecutors are prohibited from arguing that the defendant violated the terms of his probation.[373]

## THE RESULT

The residents and voters in Los Angeles will decide whether this social experiment has been worth it. The once-invincible Gascón is now on his heels, as his antiprosecutorial, procriminal polices have taken a massive toll on Angelenos.

The tipping point for many residents of Los Angeles County, especially Democrats like Andrew Lara, was when Gascón lashed out at a press conference at a family whose loved one was murdered. Joshua Rodriguez was murdered in 2015 by a juvenile gang member who was tried, convicted, and sentenced in criminal court. Gascón's lenient policies towards juvenile murderers angered the family, and they wanted to meet with Gascón. But he refused. So, they showed up at one of his press conferences in December 2020 and started yelling at him. Instead of treating the family with respect, Gascón said to the family, including Rodriquez's mother, "It's unfortunate that some people do not have enough education to keep their mouths shut so we can talk." Those comments, which were caught on video, showed Gascón's real character and attitude toward crime victims—he didn't care about them, and considered them stupid and annoying.

When Andrew Lara saw the video on the news, he said to himself, "I was done. I was done." He and many others concluded that Gascón had to go. To see their progressive DA attacking a victim's family, on camera, was a bridge too far. Jackie Lacey or Steve Cooley, or anyone with a brain or sense of decency, would never have done that.

The DA's Association sued Gascón twice. Once for forcing prosecutors in his office, via his special directives, to violate the law and California bar ethics rules. And second for hiring career public defenders and violating the county civil service qualification and hiring rules in doing so. Those public defenders had no business working in the DA's office. Those lawsuits are ongoing.

The press, across the ideological spectrum, from ABC to NBC to CNN on the left, to Fox News on the right, have run hundreds of stories, day after day, week after week, about the consequences of Gascón's approach.

California has a process for recalling elected officials. According to guidance put out by the Office of the California Secretary of State, "Recall is the power of the voters to remove elected officials before their term expires. It has been a fundamental part of our government system since 1911 and has been used by voters to express dissatisfaction with their elected officials."

The first attempt to recall Gascón started after his first year in office, but organizers of that effort failed to collect enough signatures from registered voters to place the initiative on the ballot in the fall of 2021. They needed to get signatures from 10 percent of the registered voters in the county but came up short. Organizers were not fazed, got organized, and launched a second recall effort. They raised over $6 million, and as of June 2022, had gotten over 450,000 signatures from registered voters, well on their way to getting the 566,857 needed by July 6, 2022. While recall organizers submitted 715,833 signatures, which should have been more than enough to place Gascón's recall on the November 2022 ballot,[374] the "L.A. County registrar-recorder/county clerk's office said [only] about 520,000 of the signatures submitted were valid."[375] It's a good thing for Gascón because "if it had gone before voters, the recall had a good chance of winning," polls showed.[376]

Regardless, the cumulative impact of Gascón's policies will never be known. The criminal justice system in Los Angeles County is arguably the largest not only in the United States but also in the world. The county spans 502 square miles, has eighty-eight cities, and a population of over ten million residents. Although the headquarters of the Los Angeles District Attorney's office is in downtown LA, the office has fifty-two branch offices, serving thousands of courtrooms. The Los Angeles County Superior Court has 494 superior court judges, who handle hundreds of thousands of cases per year collectively.

According to then-Sheriff Alex Villanueva, in Gascón's first year in office (2021), the Los Angeles County District Attorney's office rejected 13,238 solid cases where his deputies arrested a person for committing a crime. That number does not include the number of cases that Gascón's office rejected from Los Angeles Police Department officers or the dozens of other police departments across the county.

There are no publicly available statistics that document how many misdemeanors have been dropped; how many felons serving long sentences have been set free or resentenced; how many death-eligible homicides have not been pursued as capital cases; how many minors committed violent crimes and should have been prosecuted in adult criminal court; how many billions of dollars have been stolen from stores, homes, or businesses, by individuals who acted with impunity; how many children have been sexually exploited on the internet; how many victims have had their rights abused; how many criminals have been paroled because the victim's voice—and the facts—were not allowed in the parole hearing; how many solid convictions earned by the office were kneecapped by the office because Gascón and his prodefendant cronies believed that the conviction resulted from "racial injustice"; or how many lives have been utterly ruined by Gascón's rogue approach.

But from the publicly available data, Gascón has been a nightmare as the DA. In just the City of Los Angeles alone, since Gascón took office in December 2020, homicides are up 41 percent, violent crime up 16 percent, property crime up 8 percent, and shooting victims are up 67 percent as of June 2022. The numbers are likely just as bad across the entire county.

As for the ideas behind Gascón and the entire rogue prosecutor movement, then-Sheriff Alex Villanueva summed it up best when he told us at our rogue prosecutor symposium in Los Angeles in the spring of 2022: "I think the public is starting to realize they're full of sh*t."

Today, Gascón is certainly one of the most well-known faces of the movement. But it all started six years earlier and two thousand miles away in the Windy City with the coronation of Kim Foxx.

# CHAPTER 4

# KIM FOXX: CHICAGO

## SOROS'S FIRST ROGUE PROSECUTOR: HANDPICKED BY THE BOSS TWEED OF CHICAGO POLITICS

*"Victims don't have anyone advocating for them."*[377]

**Lori Lightfoot (D)—Former Mayor of Chicago**

*"Kim Foxx is stupid, crooked and a joke—just as dishonest and bad as Smollett—embarrassment to Chicago and decent lawyers everywhere."*[378]

**Howard Tullman (D)—Chicago Entrepreneur, Venture Capitalist, Writer, Lawyer, andFounder of Twelve Companies**

As the popular television series *Empire* was heading into its fifth season in the fall of 2018, Jussie Smollett, who played Jamal Lyon on the show, was coming to the end of his latest contract with Fox Studios. Whether *Empire* would extend to a sixth season, and whether his character, a black gay rap artist, would remain a feature of the show, was an open question. An actor and model since childhood, Smollett hadn't broken into the upper tier of A-list actors and was getting anxious to make it big.

On January 22, 2019, Jussie Smollett says he received a letter at the Chicago studios where the television show is filmed. The letter allegedly contained white powder, a drawing of a stick figure hanging from a tree, and cutout letters stating, "Smollett Jussie you will die black f*ck."[379]

During an interview with ABC News, Smollett said that the return address was in large red letters and said MAGA, a reference to the Donald

Trump slogan "Make America Great Again." The case was turned over to the FBI.

A week later on January 29, 2019, at 2 AM, Smollett alleged that as he was walking to his residence in Chicago, he was "approached by two offenders who engaged in racial and homophobic slurs" directed at Smollett. The two men struck Smollett "about the face and body causing minor injuries," according to police reports that were released shortly after the alleged incident. The two assailants, one of whom, according to Smollett, was a white male, placed a rope fashioned like a noose around his neck and poured bleach on him. One of the men yelled, "This is MAGA country" at the actor, once again referencing the slogan made popular by former president Donald Trump.

Smollett called his production manager to report the attack, who then called the police. The Chicago Police Department sprang into action to find the hatemongers who had perpetrated the crime against the actor. Smollett gave Chicago Police Detective Kim Murray and Chicago Police Officer Muhammad Baig extensive information about the crimes mere hours after the alleged incident took place.

The crime drew not only national but also international attention. A hate crime against a prominent black actor—with overtones of white nationalism mixed in—with the strong feelings about President Donald Trump was just the thing for cable news. On January 31, Trump condemned the attack against Smollett, saying in an oval office interview that it was "horrible" and that "it doesn't get worse, as far as I'm concerned."[380] And who wouldn't agree based on Smollett's story?

Oddly, on February 9, 2019, Cook County State's Attorney Kim Foxx publicly announced, without stating why, that she would recuse herself from the case and delegated the handling of the case to First Assistant State's Attorney Joseph Magats, who would serve as the "Acting State's Attorney" and make all decisions with respect to the Smollett case.

That announcement would come back to bite her years later and shine a spotlight onto her character and fitness for public office.

Four days later, on February 13, 2019, the CPD arrested two brothers, Abimbola and Olabinjo Osundairo, as suspects in the crime. The brothers admitted that they were involved in the incident and revealed that it was actually a staged hate crime attack planned and directed by none other than Smollett himself. The brothers, both of whom are black, said that Smollett gave them a check for $3,500 on January 27, two days before the alleged attack, and that he also gave them a one-hundred-dollar bill on January 25, which they used to purchase the rope, gloves, face masks, a red hat, and other items.

Police recovered video surveillance that confirmed the two purchased those items at a store and checked their bank records and confirmed a deposit of a check for $3,500 from Smollett on January 28—one day before the assault.

The duo also told the police about the bleach. Police had recovered a bottle of El Yucateco Hot Sauce on February 7 at 406 North New Street, which the Osundairos later confirmed was the bottle they filled with bleach and poured on Smollett.

Police showed the Osundairos photos of Smollett's car. They admitted that the car in the photo was the same car Smollett used to drive them on two separate occasions right before the assault. The police reports also reference extensive video surveillance footage that refutes Smollett's claims and bolsters the case that he planned and staged the attack.

The case was a slam dunk, and a week later, on February 20, 2019, the Cook County State's Attorney's Office charged Smollett via a criminal complaint. He was arrested the next day.

A Cook County grand jury indicted Smollett on March 7, 2019, charging him with sixteen counts of false reports. The charges all centered around the activity on January 29 and related to knowingly transmitting false information to Chicago Police Detective Kim Murray and Chicago Police Officer Muhammad Baig.

But only nineteen days after the accused fraudster was indicted, Foxx's office and Smollett came to a highly unusual resolution to the case. Instead of a standard plea to one or more of the charges, where the defendant would admit guilt in exchange for a lesser sentence, the Cook County State's Attorney's Office essentially gave the case away. The deal had six parts, including:

- Dismissing the sixteen-count felony indictment
- No requirement that Smollett plead guilty

- No requirement that Smollett admit any guilt or wrongdoing—after his court proceeding on March 26, 2019, Smollett stated publicly that he was "completely innocent."

- The only punishment for Smollett was to perform fifteen hours of community service unrelated to the charged misconduct.

- Smollett was required to forfeit his $10,000 bond as restitution to the City of Chicago.

- No requirement that Smollett participate in the prosecutor's deferred prosecution program, which, if it had been a condition of the bargain, would have required a one-year period of judicial oversight over Smollett.

The judge took the "plea" and sealed the record, meaning that the public would not have access to the proceedings. The investigation by the CPD cost approximately $130,000.[381]

Many people were troubled by this turn of events. Then-Chicago Mayor Rahm Emanuel asked, "Where's the accountability in the system? You cannot have, because of a person's position, one set of rules apply to them and another set of rules apply to everyone else."[382]

The Chicago Fraternal Order of Police (FOP), disgusted by the deal, took a vote of "no confidence" against Foxx and called on her to resign. Chicago FOP President Kevin Graham said, "This is not just about the Jussie Smollett case, which undermined the public confidence and law enforcement's faith in [the] Cook County criminal justice system…this is about many cases that have gone un-prosecuted or had charges reduced, especially assaults against police officers."[383]

The National District Attorneys Association (NDAA), the membership organization that provides training and guidance to state and local prosecutors across the country, issued a stern statement about Foxx's handling of the notorious case.[384] First, they noted that "when Foxx, the elected state's attorney, recused herself from the case, the entire office should have been recused." Second, "Prosecutors should not take advice from politically connected friends of the accused. Each case should be approached with the goal of justice for victims while protecting the rights of the defendant." Rumors had been swirling at the time that Foxx had taken calls from politically connected friends of Smollett. A later investigation, discussed below, proved that those rumors were true.

Third, "When a prosecutor seeks to resolve a case through diversion or some other alternative to prosecution, it should be done so with an acknowledgement of culpability on the part of the defendant." And fourth, "Expunging Mr. Smollett's record at this immediate stage is counter to transparency. Law enforcement will now not be able to acknowledge that Mr. Smollett was indicted and charged with these horrible crimes and the full record of what occurred will be forever hidden from public view." The NDAA's use of the word *expunging* was referring to the judge's sealing of the record.

One local person who was particularly troubled by the events was retired Illinois Appellate Judge Sheila O'Brien. On April 1, 2019, she wrote the presiding judge of the Circuit Court of Cook County, Judge Michael P. Toomin, seeking the appointment of a special prosecutor to take over the matter. Judge O'Brien argued that once Foxx had recused herself from the case, the entire office was recused from the case, and thus, there was no state's attorney to preside over the case, making the proceedings a sham.

After briefing and a hearing, Judge Toomin issued an order on June 21, 2019, granting the request for appointment of a special prosecutor. He found that since Foxx recused herself from the case, her entire office was thus recused from the case. As such, there was "no duly elected State's Attorney" from the time of Smollett's arrest and indictment through the dismissal of the charges and the "plea" deal.[385] The judge said that the appointment of a special prosecutor was important to "restore the public's confidence in the integrity of our criminal justice system."[386]

Judge Toomin appointed Dan K. Webb, the former US Attorney for the Northern District of Illinois, as special prosecutor for Cook County. The Office of the Special Prosecutor (OSP) began its work on August 23, 2019, at the same time a special grand jury was empaneled. Judge Toomin directed Webb to determine two things: (1) whether Smollett should be further prosecuted for the false police reports, and (2) whether any person or office involved in the original case engaged in wrongdoing.[387]

In February 2020, the OSP requested that a Special Grand Jury indict Smollett, which it did, handing down a six-count indictment charging him with disorderly conduct stemming from making false police reports. Since the original charges had been dismissed by Foxx's office, there was a legal bar to prosecuting Smollett for the same conduct. A month later, the COVID-19 pandemic resulted in most of the United States shutting down, and jury trials across the country were put on hold. Smollett would have to wait eighteen months for his trial to start.

Despite the pandemic, Special Prosecutor Webb concluded his investigation into the State's Attorney's Office and Foxx's actions surrounding the Smollett case, and he delivered the report to Judge Toomin on August 17, 2020. As one would expect from a former United States Attorney, the report was exceedingly thorough and sober. Before delivering the report, the OSP conducted fifty-three interviews, issued over fifty subpoenas or document requests, and collected more than 120,000 pages of documents, including text messages and audio recordings.

The OSP report included five final conclusions and supporting findings, each of which shined a spotlight on Foxx's poor judgment, ethical lapses, and questionable leadership.[388]

The conclusions were as follows:

> (1) The State's Attorney's Office engaged in substantial abuses of discretion and operational failures in prosecuting and resolving the initial Smollett case. Abuses of discretion included poor decision making processes, a breach of its obligation to be honest and transparent about why the case was dismissed and the making of false statements about the same, substantial abuse of discretion and breach of obligation to be honest by Foxx and making false and/or misleading statements regarding her recusal to the public, and substantial abuse of discretion and breach of obligation to be honest and transparent when Foxx made false and misleading statements to the public that she had stopped communicating with Smollett's sister. Jurnee Smollett, Jussie's sister, and Foxx had communications between February 1 and February 13. The initial thrust of the conversations was Jurnee's concern about information being released to the public about the investigation. On February 8, Foxx learned that Jussie was a suspect, yet she continued to communi-

85

cate with Jurnee via five text messages, even though she made false statements to the media that she had ceased all communications with Jurnee.

(2) Foxx and lawyers in her office may have violated legal ethics rules relating to false and/or misleading public statements made about the prosecution or resolution of the initial case against Smollett. The OSP found that Foxx and/or her then-first assistant Joseph Magats made at least six false or misleading public statements relating to the nature and reason for the dismissal of the Smollett case.

(3) The OSP did not develop evidence that Foxx was involved in decision-making on the initial Smollett case after she recused herself but did find that she was provided with frequent updates about the case after her recusal.

(4) The OSP did not develop evidence that would support a criminal charge against Foxx or anyone working in the State's Attorney's Office.

(5) The OSP did not develop evidence of improper influence by any outside third parties in the decision-making by the State's Attorney's Office. The OSP did uncover communications between Foxx and Sherrilyn Ifill, the director and counsel for the NAACP Legal Defense Fund; Foxx and Tina Tchen, a victim advocate and former chief of staff to former First Lady Michelle Obama; and Jurnee Smollett, Jussie's sister. The OSP found that these communications did not influence or impact how the case was prosecuted or resolved.

After delivering the scathing report to Judge Toomin, Webb asked the judge to release it to the public. On two occasions, Toomin denied Webb's request, citing the inclusion of grand jury material as a reason to keep the fifty-nine-page report from the public eye. But on December 20, 2021, Judge Toomin granted Webb's request, and the report, which had not been turned over to Smollett's attorneys, was released to the public. The order to release the report was limited to the summary report and the grand jury material contained within the report but not other grand jury material gathered or possessed by the OSP.[389]

While this was happening, Smollett's trial began. On December 10, 2021, ten days before the report was released to the public, Smollett was convicted by a Chicago jury of five counts of lying to the CPD. In early March 2022, Cook County Judge James Linn sentenced Smollett to 150 days in jail, ordered him to pay $120,000 in restitution to the City of Chicago plus a $25,000 fine, and placed him on thirty months of probation. When handing down the sentence, Judge Linn scolded the unrepentant actor, accusing him of "throwing a national pity party for yourself."[390] After serving only six days in jail, an appeals court granted his defense attorney's motion to release him from jail while he pursues an appeal.[391] As this book was going to print, that appeal was still pending.

Shortly after Smollett's sentencing, but before the release of the OSP report, Foxx wrote an op-ed in the *Chicago Sun Times* lambasting the prosecution of Smollett.

Oblivious to the irony of her own words, Foxx wrote, "At its best, our justice system should make people safer, hold accountable those who seek to harm others and earn the trust of its citizenry. At its worst, the system can be easily manipulated in furtherance of thinly veiled political agendas…. Smollett was indicted, tried and convicted by a kangaroo prosecution in a matter of months."[392]

Mayor Lori Lightfoot (D), on the other hand, praised the conviction and sentence and said that the city feels "vindicated." Issuing a statement via her Deputy Press Secretary Ryan Johnson,[393] Lightfoot said, "The criminal conviction of Jussie Smollett by a jury of his peers and today's sentencing should send a clear message to everyone in the City of Chicago that false claims and allegations will not be tolerated."[394]

## THIS IS CHICAGO

So how did Kim Foxx come to occupy her position as Chicago's top prosecutor? It all started years earlier in the Mississippi Delta region.

Fresh off their three choreographed victories in Louisiana and Mississippi in 2015, as discussed in Chapter One, Whitney Tymas and Chloe Cockburn had proved to George Soros, who poured over $1 million into "Safety and Justice" groups to fund the races, that they had the mojo to do more. And that more, as we described in Chapter One, was to "change who occupies the prosecutor's office" so that you can "make the system operate differently."[395]

As the putative midwives of the rogue prosecutor movement, Soros's Tymas and the ACLU's Cockburn were desperate to realize Angela Davis's dream of abolishing prisons. But even Tymas and Cockburn, dyed-in-the-wool activists, realized that pushing openly to abolish prisons would fail. The better approach, in their minds, was to, in Emily Bazelon's words, "choose prosecutors who will open the locks."[396]

Armed with the realization that they needed to identify, recruit, and fund lawyers who would be willing to run for district attorney and then enact policies that would "open the locks" of jails and prisons, their next two logical questions were: What current district attorney was vulnerable, and in what city should they launch their first test case?

At that time, and now to a lesser extent, a "vulnerable" district attorney, at least in the eyes of the Whitney Tymases of the world, was an elected district attorney who (1) prosecuted "too many" minorities and (2) who didn't prosecute "enough" police officers.

Armed with the information the ACLU had collected over the years, and no doubt some additional sleuthing, Tymas and Cockburn set out to answer the first question: Which DA was vulnerable? They narrowed their list and eventually homed in on Anita Alvarez, the Cook County state's attorney. At first blush, she might not have seemed a ripe candidate to pick off. She was the first female elected state's attorney in Chicago, and she was a Democrat, elected in a solidly blue city.

But upon further inspection, Alvarez fit the bill, as her office prosecuted "too many" black men. Furthermore, as we outlined in Chapter One, Alvarez was for mandatory minimum sentences for gun crimes, and she initially refused to file charges against Chicago Police Officer Jason Van Dyke for shooting and killing seventeen-year-old Laquan McDonald. It was only after the release of the police car dashboard video, which she resisted at first, that Alvarez charged Van Dyke with first-degree murder thirteen months after the crime.

But just like in Los Angeles and Baltimore, where BLM and others agitated for charges and revenge after a police officer killed a black man, in Chicago, Alvarez's handling of the McDonald case made her politically vulnerable. The polls at the time confirmed that Alvarez's support among the electorate was waning. The primary was on March 15, 2016, so they needed to act fast.

The next question—and perhaps the most important of the two—was who to run against Alvarez? Tymas and Cockburn had to know that simply asking any current or former prosecutor to run against Alvarez was a fool's errand. Even if the person was well known, it was a gamble that he or she would win the race. The stakes were too high to lose. They needed more of a political sure thing. They not only needed to find a candidate who would appeal to inner city voters, they needed a political machine in that city that would deftly shepherd their chosen candidate to victory by paving the political field.

Enter Toni Preckwinkle, the Cook County board president. For at least six years, Preckwinkle had been a vocal critic of Alvarez and the way she operated as the state's attorney. She was a passionate advocate for criminal justice reform in Chicago and believed that Alvarez had a long history of "criminalizing people of color."[397] There was bad blood between the two women, and Preckwinkle wasn't a person who liked to lose battles.

Preckwinkle, a black female, made her way up the political ladder in Chicago over her twenty-five years in the arena. Described as the "Queen of Chicago politics," Preckwinkle has a long history of identifying and grooming "fresh talent within her administration" and then propelling them into office.[398] Her protégés included Christian Mitchell, an Illinois state representative who had served as her director of outreach and external affairs, and Kurt Summers, Chicago city treasurer who had served as her chief of staff. Preckwinkle's influence and power over Chicago politics has been described as "the iron fist in the velvet glove."[399] As the Queen of Chicago politics, Preckwinkle was exactly the type of person that was needed to grease the political skids for a candidate to run (and win) against Alvarez.

According to sources interviewed for this book, the linchpin between Toni Preckwinkle and Soros was Patrick Gaspard. Gaspard was the national political director for Obama for America in 2008. Once then-Senator Barack Obama became President Obama, Gaspard served as assistant to the president and director of the White House Office of Political Affairs from 2009 to 2011, and then was the executive director of the Democratic National Committee from 2011 to 2013. After serving as the US Ambassador to South Africa from 2013 to 2016, Gaspard became a vice president at Open Society, and on January 1, 2018, became president of the Open Society Foundation.[400] Gaspard was introduced to Soros while serving in the Obama White House. Gaspard got to know Preckwinkle through Chicago politics and working for Obama.

Today, Gaspard is the president and chief executive officer of the Center for American Progress, a far-left issue advocacy organization located in Washington, DC.[401]

Kurt Summers's replacement as Preckwinkle's chief of staff was, coincidently, a black female lawyer named Kim Foxx. But the kicker about Foxx was the fact that she had worked as an assistant state's attorney in the Cook County State's Attorney's Office under Anita Alvarez.

It's easy to see why Tymas and Cockburn were immediately drawn to Foxx. Not only was she Preckwinkle's acolyte and a former prosecutor, but also she had the perfect personal and professional pedigree. She had a personal story that would sell. Foxx was a native Chicagoan. She grew up in the notorious Cabrini-Green public housing complex. She was raised by a single mom, was homeless for a spell, and had been a victim of sexual assault not once but twice.[402]

Despite these odds, Foxx put herself through college and law school at Southern Illinois University. After leaving the Cook County State's Attorney's Office, where she worked for twelve years, and before she worked for Preckwinkle, Foxx served as the board chair for Planned Parenthood of Illinois, where, according to an article in *Mother Jones*, Foxx expanded access for "low-income women by adding evening and weekend hours to its Chicago clinics."[403] A Hollywood writer could not have come up with a more perfect character to run for state's attorney in Chicago.

Tymas got to work, helping to create the Illinois Safety and Justice PAC. George Soros, her boss, dumped $400,000 into the PAC, which also received an additional $300,000 from the Civic Participation Action Fund.[404]

The Civic Participation Action Fund was created by the Atlantic Advocacy Fund in 2014 and is one of several nonprofits created by Atlantic Philanthropies, the grant-making foundation started by the late liberal billionaire philanthropist Charles "Chuck" Feeney.[405] Gara LaMarche was appointed president of Atlantic Philanthropies in 2006. LaMarche is currently a senior advisor at The Raben Group, was a former president of Democracy Alliance, was the director of US programs for George Soros's Open Society Foundation, and, not surprisingly, worked for the ACLU.[406]

Meanwhile, the Cook County Democrats held their slating meeting on August 18, 2015, at the Erie Café to decide which of the three potential candidates to endorse in the upcoming primaries.[407] Each of the three potential candidates for Cook County state's attorney had five minutes to convince the party leaders that she should get their endorsement. Alvarez said that her concern was public safety, that she had cracked down on gangbangers, and that she had to make decisions that "might not be popular."[408] Kim Foxx took a different tack, saying that the office's mission is not "just about crime and violence" but rather "community and justice."[409] Donna More, a former state and federal prosecutor, vowed to leave politics out of prosecution. After the presentations, the party leaders decided not to endorse any of the candidates.[410] That was significant, as Alvarez was a Democratic incumbent who, under normal times, would have received her party's endorsement. What role, if any, the "Velvet Glove" had in that decision is anyone's guess.

By the time Kim Foxx formally announced her candidacy for Cook County state's attorney on December 12, 2015, at the Hilton Garden Inn in Evanston, Illinois, she had amassed significant political support. Foxx's announcement was more of a soft coronation than a neophyte entering the political fray. US Congresswoman Jan Schakowsky, a Democrat from Evanston who has represented Illinois' 9th Congressional District since 1998, introduced Foxx, saying, "We need someone who is going to be there and make sure justice is done in our county...we need change in that office."[411] Schakowsky was joined by two elected aldermen, several

Democratic committeemen, and four representatives to the Illinois General Assembly.[412]

During her remarks to the crowd, Foxx stated that she was "prepared for the task. I was being molded for this job, and I didn't even know it."[413] And the best was yet to come, because whether she knew it or not, Toni Preckwinkle was about to work her magic and turn the Cook County Democratic Party into Foxx's ally two months before the primary.

Not surprisingly, Preckwinkle served on the Cook County Democrat Committee, which had decided to remain neutral in the state's attorney's race in August. But Tymas and Cockburn selected Chicago and Foxx, no doubt, precisely because of Preckwinkle's influence, and it paid off big time. On January 14, 2016, behind closed doors, Preckwinkle presumably used her iron fist and convinced the Cook County Democrat Committee to endorse Foxx, which they did publicly that day.[414]

No one was surprised that Preckwinkle got the party to endorse Foxx, especially Donna More, the former federal prosecutor who had announced her campaign for Cook County state's attorney a week before the committee backed Foxx. Disgusted with party politics and this type of endorsement, Moore said of the Preckwinkle endorsement, "Toni Preckwinkle wants the power of indictment.... That's why she's endorsing her emissary in this office. It's a power play."[415]

The sentiment that Foxx was merely a pawn in Preckwinkle's political chess game was echoed by Alvarez after the Democrat Committee suddenly anointed Foxx, saying to the press, "I owe them nothing. Ask Ms. Foxx what she owes Toni Preckwinkle."[416]

In time, Foxx picked up the endorsements of former Illinois Governor Pat Quinn, the *Chicago Tribune*, the *Chicago Sun Times*, and the Chicago Teacher's Union, each of which catapulted Foxx from a relatively unknown attorney to the person to beat on March 15th—the date of Chicago's Democratic primary.

Politically shrewd and media savvy, Preckwinkle brushed to the side the rumors that Foxx was beholden to her and, if elected, would simply expand her power and ram through ideas that she had been pushing for years, saying, "I think there was a sense among a lot of us in the Democratic Party that Anita wasn't the right person for the job."[417]

But while Preckwinkle was a seasoned pro at brushing off awkward or uncomfortable questions, Foxx was a novice who made the mistake of acknowledging the truth when it came to Preckwinkle's bulldozing, saying, "I know, I tell people all the time, if I did not have the [Cook County Board] president's support, would people have paid attention to me? Would people have given me an opportunity, a platform to the degree that I've had? This is Chicago."[418]

And that support was more than meets the eye. Preckwinkle did what any political kingmaker might do: she spent $25,000 from her own campaign funds to take a poll, early in 2015, to see if Foxx had a chance.[419] Only after Foxx became a candidate and was required to file campaign finance reports did this donation come to light, because Foxx, a political freshman, neglected to mention the in-kind donation in her prior financial disclosure documents.

Two weeks before the primary, the Illinois State Board of Elections ruled unanimously that Foxx violated campaign finance law, found that she filed a quarterly report seventy-three days late and reported ten individual donations more than one day late, and assessed fines of $40,250 against Foxx for thirteen separate violations of campaign finance laws and regulations.[420] The fine was reduced to $19,450 by the board, which offered a discount, believe it or not, for a candidate's first and second offense.[421] Foxx, showing some signs of political savvy, said that she planned to appeal the ruling but added that "we're moving on."[422]

And move on she did, winning the primary on March 15, 2016, with 58.3 percent of the vote to Alvarez's 28.7 percent, and cruising to victory in the November general election against Republican Christopher E. K. Pfannkuche, 72 percent to 28 percent.

## PRECKWINKLE'S MASTERCLASS IN POLITICAL CHESS

On September 7, 2013, almost five years after Anita Alvarez was first elected as the state's attorney for Cook County, the University of Illinois at Chicago and the Crossroads Fund sponsored prison abolitionist Angela Davis for a symposium at St. James Cathedral in downtown Chicago. Davis's talk was entitled "If you want peace, fight for justice."[423] The topic of the symposium, held a year after Trayvon Martin was killed in Florida, and after recent school closings in Chicago because of racial unrest, could not have been more timely.

After recounting her version of the history of gun use by blacks in the United States and extolling historical figures such as Che Guevara, Fidel Castro, and Nelson Mandela, Davis pivoted to her main point: the long-term effects of the "prison industrial complex" or "PIC," a term she made famous in her 2003 bestseller, *Are Prisons Obsolete?*

At the crescendo of her speech, Davis said this: "The PIC is violence rendered legitimate by the law…we need to point out that solutions proposed to violence are responsible for cases of violence in the first place, make people more violent than when they are committed."[424] She urged those in the audience to "think beyond this moment, beyond the decade, and the century. Racism is still with us because too many of us think it can be wished away."[425]

A panel discussion followed Davis's diatribe. It was moderated by an NPR correspondent and none other than Toni Preckwinkle. During the discussion, Preckwinkle repeated one of Davis's familiar tropes, namely, that the United States has 5 percent of the world's population but 25 percent of the world's prison population. She bemoaned the fact that blacks and Latinos represent a large percentage of the prison population in the Cook County jail and talked about her efforts to reduce the number of people in jail who were "low risk."[426]

Problems with the Cook County jail were not new. In fact, the controversial facility had been operating under federal oversight since 1974. In 2007, the United States Justice Department launched an investigation into allegations of abuse and unlawful confinement, resulting in a 2010 consent decree that laid out what the Sheriff's Office, which ran the jail, had to do to come into compliance. It wasn't until June 2017 that US District Court Judge Virginia Kendall ruled that the Sheriff's Office was in compliance with the consent decree and order.[427]

Preckwinkle, who got her undergraduate and master's degree from the University of Chicago, had been interested in criminal justice and police accountability since she was first elected to the Chicago City Council in 1991. By then, the crime wave across the country was reaching its peak, and Chicago was not spared the carnage experienced in other large cities like New York and Los Angeles.

In November of 2010, Preckwinkle was elected Cook County board president. By then, Anita Alvarez had been the state's attorney for two years. The Great Recession of 2008 (also known as the Great Housing Recession) had affected the private and public sectors across the country, and Cook County was not immune to the fiscal calamity.[428] Shortly after taking office, Preckwinkle ordered a 16 percent budget cut across all departments, including Alvarez's office.[429]

Alvarez pushed back against the draconian cuts, saying the most she could do was an 8 percent cut. Even with that, she would have to lay off two hundred staff members, including prosecutors, which would impact public safety.[430] Preckwinkle was having none of it, saying that Alvarez could avoid laying off prosecutors by cutting administrative staff, and that she was going to hold Alvarez to a 10 percent cut.

By 2013, the Cook County jail population had climbed to over its capacity of ten thousand inmates, the highest level it had been in six years.[431] Jail overcrowding was, by then, one of Preckwinkle's pet peeves and political causes. She pressured county officials to come up with solutions to fix the problem and spared no one when they dragged their feet. One of her targets was Alvarez. But Alvarez, who had sparred and lost to Preckwinkle in the budget war of 2011, pushed back. Fabio Valentini, her top lieutenant in the criminal prosecution unit said, "Our mandate is public safety," adding, "we're not going to stop charging felonies tomorrow because the jail population has become too big."[432] Those were fighting words.

By the spring of 2015, even though the jail population had dropped to about eight thousand inmates, the topic of overcrowding and reform was front and center. And the acrimony between Preckwinkle and Alvarez had reached a boiling point, so the "Iron Fist" decided to do something about it. At a May 7 event featuring Preckwinkle, Cook County Circuit Court Chief Judge Timothy Evans, Sheriff Tom Dart, and Alvarez, among other stakeholders, Preckwinkle went out of her way to thank the courts, probation department, and even the public defender for helping to reduce the jail population.[433] She didn't mention Alvarez by name, even though the two women were sitting near each other. Moments later, when asked if she would support Alvarez's reelection, Preckwinkle blandly said, "I'm not prepared to talk about the state's attorney's race today."[434]

And right on cue, Kim Foxx, who was by her boss's side, told the reporter that she was "considering" running against Alvarez.

A month later, on June 15, Preckwinkle sat down with Mick Dumke from the *Chicago Tribune* to talk about reforms to the jail and criminal justice system.

Gifted politicians like Preckwinkle play three-dimensional political chess while less talented politicians do their best to play checkers. She excoriated Alvarez's reform efforts, saying, "She was one of the people who had to be dragged kicking and screaming through this reform process," adding that voters would be better off if they dumped Alvarez in next year's election and elected someone who is not stuck on the tough-on-crime policies of the past.

And then, like Gary Kasparov, Preckwinkle moved her first pawn in what became a nine-month virtuoso chess match as she suggested coyly, "If Kim Foxx decides to run, I will support her wholeheartedly."[435]

When asked about Preckwinkle's comment, Alvarez nonchalantly said, "Unless she's running Hillary Clinton against me, I think I'm going to be okay."[436] Little did she know what was coming.

After the Democratic party met in August and decided not to endorse anyone for the primary, Foxx did a series of interviews with friendly media. On October 28, 2015, the *Chicago Magazine*, a publication of the Tribune Publishing Company, which also owns the *Chicago Tribune*, ran a long story about Foxx. The first sentence was right out of central casting: "Kim Foxx, 43, has one of those life stories that is made for politics: She started out in Cabrini-Green with a father who wasn't around much and a mother who suffered from depression."[437]

The reporter pressed Foxx on the influence of Preckwinkle in her campaign, asking, "Why is Preckwinkle so adamant about getting Anita Alvarez out of that job and getting you into it? She seems to be a very major force in this story."[438]

Foxx demurred, saying, "I think she's a force, but I don't know about major."

But to anyone paying attention, not only was Preckwinkle a force, she was a force multiplier. After all, this was Chicago.

It was no coincidence that Foxx's top three goals were the same reforms that her boss had been pushing for years: (1) to bring back integrity in our criminal justice system, (2) to be "thoughtful on how we look at juvenile justice," and (3) to reallocate dollars spent on keeping people in jail "in a more responsible manner that will get us better outcomes than what we are doing right now." In other words, many prosecutors are bad, juvenile offenders should not be sent to adult court, and we need to open the prison doors.

A month later, Foxx did two back-to-back interviews. During the first, on Chicago's PBS station on November 17, 2015, Foxx touted her experience working for Preckwinkle "as her chief of staff and leading her criminal justice efforts; she had a chance to see me work firsthand on reforming our bond court system [and] on working on juvenile justice reform."[439] Sticking the knife in, Foxx added that Alvarez "has had seven years to make justice reform. ...The citizens of Cook County deserve better."[440]

The next day, Foxx sat down for an interview with Evan F. Moore of *Citizen Weekly*. When asked why now is the time to run against Alvarez, Foxx upped the temperature, saying, "It's long overdue. ...she hasn't put the needs of the community first."[441] She doubled down on her goal of not sending juveniles to adult court saying, "One of the things that was most heartbreaking to me was that we were sending kids into the criminal justice system at earlier and earlier ages."[442] She bemoaned the current system, saying that "our criminal justice system isn't mindful of how we treat" kids who were "doing things they shouldn't do" and "kids who were shooting people."[443]

Having moved her bishops, knights, and rooks into place, Preckwinkle then put Alvarez into check on December 2, 2015, when the *Chicago Tribune* published her op-ed entitled "Why Anita Alvarez Should Resign." Preckwinkle and co-author Chuy Garcia, a fellow Cook County commissioner, listed three main complaints, namely, "Laquan McDonald's execution" and how Alvarez "sat on this case and the evidence for 13 months," her failure to reduce the jail population "for people who are awaiting trial," and her failure to "build trust and confidence" with communities of color.[444]

They ended their screed on a hopeful note: "Imagine what progress we could make with a cooperative and collaborative approach from the state's attorney."[445] Imagine indeed.

Two days after Foxx unexpectedly trounced Alvarez by a two-to-one margin in the primary, Preckwinkle predicted that once elected in November, Foxx would have a "similar commitment to criminal justice reform" as she did, including, echoing Angela Davis, "ending the school to prison pipeline."[446]

Once elected, Foxx's policies weren't "similar" to Preckwinkle's policies. They were a carbon copy and worse. Preckwinkle, Soros, and Foxx were all on the same page.

As the first Soros-funded rogue prosecutor in a major city, Foxx was a test case, a prototype of sorts. Unlike others who came after her, such as Gascón, Rollins, and Bragg, Foxx did not unveil a blatantly radical set of policy proposals on her first day or weeks in office. Foxx wasn't a movement reformer. Instead, she was a black female former prosecutor who was elected as the state's attorney because of the guidance, mentorship, political savvy, and brute skill of Toni Preckwinkle—and the money of George Soros and others. Foxx didn't come to office as a change agent based on her own comprehensive criminal justice reform ideas. She absorbed Preckwinkle's ideas and the ideas of those who funded and backed her for office and implemented those ideas over the course of years.

As Rogue Prosecutor Model 1.0, Foxx blazed a trail for others to follow. The Soros machine, and those funded or inspired by him, like Fair and Just Prosecution and other social justice groups, no doubt learned from Foxx and shared that information in funded seminars, trips, or other gatherings of the nascent-but-growing movement.

## OPENING THE JAILHOUSE DOOR FROM DAY ONE

You would think that Kim Foxx, having been a prosecutor for twelve years in the second largest prosecutor's office in the country, would have the common sense to know that violent crime is perpetrated by a small percentage of career criminals, that most of them have or use guns to commit their crimes, and that by prosecuting them to the fullest extent of the law, you can work to reduce the crime rate in the city.

On the campaign trail, Foxx touted her extensive trial experience, telling potential voters that she had handled hundreds of trials and thus had the chops to be the top dog in the office. At one point in the campaign, she told the *Chicago Tribune* that she had handled about one hundred trials.[447] When the *Tribune* asked for a list of the one hundred cases, Foxx's campaign provided a list of fewer than twenty cases.[448] The *Tribune* then sent a state freedom of information act request to her old office asking for the number of trials Foxx tried as an assistant state's attorney.[449] The records indicated that she had tried two cases. Foxx retorted that she argued four felonies before a jury or judge but that she handled hundreds of other cases, most of which were guilty pleas.[450]

In her defense, Foxx had spent the majority of her time as a prosecutor in juvenile court. That not only explains her lack of jury trial experience, as all juvenile matters in Illinois are held before a judge, but also gives light to her goal to reduce the number of juveniles going to adult court.

After she won the general election in November 2016, but before she was sworn in on December 1st, Foxx appointed a transition team to develop recommendations on policies, challenges, and opportunities. The transition team was cochaired by Kamala Harris, who at the time was attorney general and senator-elect for the State of California, and Professor Ron Sullivan, director of the Criminal Justice Institute at Harvard University. In what became a model for Soros-funded prosecutors, members of the transition team included an all-star cast of professionals who, for the most part, had dedicated their professional careers to social justice causes.

Not a single one of the twenty-four-member transition team had been or was a career prosecutor.

On December 5, 2016, Foxx published the report from her transition team.[451] Only twelve pages in length, the report made twenty-one recommendations, including acknowledging the existence of racial inequalities in the justice system, the need to build an "expansive and effective diversion system for juveniles and emerging adults," and an exhortation to use tools to address the "school to prison pipeline."[452] Sound familiar?

Nowhere in the report does it mention targeting career felons for prosecution or any other commonsense approach to tackling violent crime.

## OPEN SEASON ON RETAIL STORES

Two weeks into the job, Foxx announced that she had raised the bar for prosecuting felony shoplifting from $300 per incident to $1,000 per incident, even though the law in Illinois was clear: felony shoplifting starts at $300. At the time she made the announcement, there were 101 people in Cook County Jail on felony retail theft charges, many of whom had been in custody for months.[453] Ali Abid, a staff attorney at the Chicago Appleseed Fund for Justice, said in response to Foxx's announcement, "I think this is a really positive step."[454] Abid's boss, Malcolm Rich, was the executive director of the Appleseed Fund for Justice[455] and on Foxx's transition team with Senator Kamala Harris.

But Rob Karr, the president of the Illinois Retail Merchants Association, said he was "extraordinarily shocked and disappointed" and Foxx's rewriting of the laws "sends a message that retail theft is victimless and not serious...this is tantamount to declaring open season on retail stores."[456]

By 2019, three years into Foxx's social experiment, Rob Karr was proved right. Since November 2016, retail theft reports had skyrocketed, up 20 percent across the city. In the ritzy Rush Street shopping district, reported incidents had more than doubled. And on State Street, retail theft cases were up 32 percent.[457]

In late August 2019, during a breakfast with about a dozen suburban mayors and other local officials, Toni Preckwinkle, still running point for Foxx, got an earful of complaints about retail theft and the lack of consequences for serial thieves. Mayor of the Village of Justice, located in Cook County, Kris Wasowicz told the "Iron Fist" that "people are not being prosecuted for stealing...my police officers are frustrated, my merchants are up in arms."[458] Thieves were taking up to $1,000 worth of goods at a time from small businesses, which, he added, "could be the profit margin for the month."[459]

Flossmoor Mayor Paul Braun tried to appeal to Preckwinkle's need for more property tax revenues saying, "Businesses don't want to locate out here because of crime."[460] But Preckwinkle wasn't going to undercut her understudy or her desire to drastically reduce the jail population in Cook County. So what if a few supposedly "rich" business people lost some merchandise to thieves?

## OPENING THE JAIL DOORS

Cook County Circuit Court Chief Judge Timothy Evans, an attorney who served on the city council before taking the bench in 1992, announced on July 17, 2017, that starting in September of that year, felony bond judges would be required to determine whether a suspect is dangerous in order to impose bail. If a judge determines that the suspect is not dangerous but has a reason to believe that he may not return to court, the judge would be required to ensure that the defendant can afford the amount of bail.[461]

Chief Judge Evans said that he made this change because Kim Foxx and other officials agreed that whether someone was held in pretrial custody should not depend on the person's ability to pay.[462]

Eighteen months after the new program went into effect, Chief Judge Evans published a study entitled "Bail Reform in Cook County." It claimed that the new pretrial reforms led to an increase in the percentage of defendants who were released pretrial—from 72 percent to 81 percent of all defendants.

The more titillating finding was this: the study claimed that the new, more lenient release procedures did not increase crime.[463] That finding was significant, because, in ensuing years, it has been repeated by other rogue prosecutors and their supporters.

The problem with that finding, however, is that it just wasn't true.

In fact, the opposite was true. In the only academic study to date analyzing that data, researchers found that the "number of released defendants charged with committing new crimes increased by about 45%" after the new program was implemented. More damning was this: the number of "pretrial releases charged with new violent crimes increased by about 33%."[464]

The *Chicago Tribune* also analyzed Chief Judge Evans's report and found "flaws in both the data underlying Evans' report and the techniques he used to analyze it."[465] Evans limited violent crime to only six offenses for the study and excluded assault with a deadly weapon, armed violence, and reckless homicide among other crimes commonly understood to be violent offenses. The *Tribune* noted that the "report's underlying data also was flawed in multiple ways that led to an undercount of murders and other violent crimes allegedly committed by people out on bail."[466]

By the end of Foxx's first year in office, liberal groups were growing frustrated with her for not doing enough to end "mass incarceration" and the "war on drugs." In a report entitled "In Pursuit of Justice for All: An Evaluation of Kim Foxx's First Year in Office," social justice activists urged Foxx to advance bail reform, increase transparency and accountability, lessen immigration collateral consequences for illegal aliens charged with crimes, end the "drug war," and reduce "overcharging."[467] Many of these things she had already done—but apparently she didn't go far enough or fast enough to appease her radical backers.

## THE CARNAGE ADDS UP YEAR AFTER YEAR

Even before the COVID-19 pandemic started in 2020, it was becoming obvious to residents, business owners, and community leaders that crime was out of control in the city, including homicides.

To put things into perspective, let's compare the number of Americans shot and killed in three war zones.

In one war zone, there were 3,481 Americans killed in action between 2003 and 2010, an average of 435 a year. In the second war zone, there were 1,833 Americans killed in action between late 2001 and 2014, an average of 141 per year. And in the third war zone, there were 4,724 Americans killed in action between 2011 and 2019, an average of 525 per year.

The first war zone was Iraq; the second was Afghanistan; the third is Chicago. If you think the number of homicide victims in Chicago is grotesque, consider the fact that in the two years before Foxx was elected state's attorney (2014–2015), there were 425 and 493 homicides, respectively. Right after Foxx was elected, homicides in Chicago exploded. In her first two years in office (2016–2017) there were 778 and 660.

The chart below shows the rate of homicides in Chicago in the years before Foxx was elected and every year since:

## CHICAGO HOMICIDES, BY YEAR

The number of people slain in 2022: 695

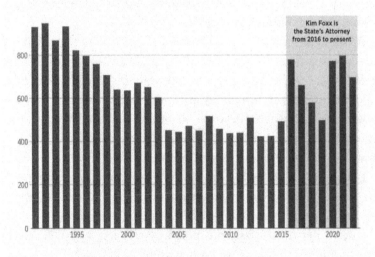

Kim Foxx is the State's Attorney from 2016 to present

SOURCES: CITY OF CHICAGO; *CHICAGO TRIBUNE*, WWW.CHICAGOTRIBUNE.COM/
NEWS/BREAKING/CT-CHICAGO-HOMICIDES-DATA-TRACKER-20220426-
IEDEHZUQ5JDOFBHWT3V2W6CJOY-STORY.HTML.

☎ heritage.org

In 2021 alone, there were 797 homicides, making Chicago one of the deadliest cities in the United States. Chicago hasn't seen that level of murder since the peak of the crime wave in the mid-1990s. Blacks constituted 80 percent of homicide victims in 2021, and black males accounted for 88 percent of homicide deaths.[468] There were at least 4,300 gunshot victims in the city, including those who suffered both fatal and nonfatal injuries in 2021, up from 2,800 in 2018.[469]

As Rafael A. Mangual notes in his must-read book, *Criminal [In] Justice: What the Push for Decarceration and Depolicing Gets Wrong and Who It Hurts the Most*, violent crimes are geographically and demographically concentrated.[470] Nationally, "while blacks constitute 13.4 percent of the population, they made up more than 53 percent of the nations' homicide victims in 2020."[471] The vast majority of those victims are male.

By 2019, three years into office, Foxx, her lieutenants, the chief of police, Preckwinkle, and other stakeholders surely knew this because they had real-time crime data establishing that homicides were concentrated in just a few areas in the city. Yet what did they do about it? Did Foxx crack down on and target repeat offenders, charge them with the most serious charges they could, prosecute them to the fullest extent of the law, and recommend maximum sentences? No.

As Mangual points out in *Criminal [In]Justice*, the national murder rate across the country in 2019 was 5.0 per 100,000 residents. In Chicago, the rate in 2019 was 18.2 per 100,000 residents. But shockingly, if you pinpointed the ten communities in Chicago with the highest number of murders in 2019, where "between 90 percent and 98 percent of the residents are either black or Latino, the homicide rates in 2019 ranged from a low of 40.8 per 100,000 to a high of 131.9 per 100,000."[472]

But instead of following the raw data and doing something about it, Foxx moved forward with her agenda of making sure fewer and fewer criminals, especially black and brown suspects, went to jail.

One of her most disastrous policies has been so-called "electronic home monitoring," otherwise known as ankle bracelets. In the wake of Foxx's efforts to pursue bail reform policies, more individuals have been placed on electronic home monitoring—apparently with no consequences for violating their bail terms.

By 2020, Chicago police identified the "skyrocketing use of electronic monitoring as a key factor in the city's shocking 50% rise in killings this year."[473] Foxx disputed the idea that those on electronic monitoring were responsible for the spike in the crime rate. She was joined by Chief Judge Evans, who also suggested that the data didn't support that claim.

But graphics depicted in the *Chicago Sun Times*, taken from data provided by the Cook County Sheriff's Office, tell a different story. As of August 9, 2020, forty-three people who were on electronic monitoring were charged with murder.[474] Additionally, 160 people charged with robbery and approximately one thousand charged with illegal gun possession were on electronic monitoring.

Chicago's gun violence also rose dramatically on Foxx's watch. In one weekend in September 2020, forty-five people were shot, ten of them fatally.[475] The next weekend fifty people were shot, nine of them fatally.[476]

Residents of Chicago have become accustomed to violent felons on electronic monitoring committing crimes of violence. For example, Joshua

Noah was the mastermind behind an armed home invasion that took place in the Riverside section of Chicago in 2020. According to prosecutors, he and two other armed men broke into a Riverside family's home, beat a man who owed them drug money, and dumped him into an alley. While in the house, one of the men pistol-whipped the man's mother and threatened the family.[477] But because of Foxx's predisposition to believing in the deterrent effect of electronic monitoring, even though he was charged with twenty-seven felonies, Noah was placed on electronic monitoring by the judge after posting $15,000 bail.

Two years later, while still awaiting trial, Noah went into a Mexican restaurant near Midway Airport armed with a gun, fired into the ceiling, and threatened five customers.[478] After Noah was arrested, the former police chief of Riverside, Tom Weitzel, said, "Noah is an extremely violent individual and should never have been out on bond or electronic monitoring."[479]

No doubt speaking for many across the city, Weitzel added, "The notion that this is somehow criminal justice reform and public safety is not affected by violent criminals on electronic monitoring is simply ridiculous."[480] The real-world anecdotes support the data that said the same thing.

One of the most high-profile examples of Kim Foxx refusing to do her job happened in late September 2021 on the city's west side when, in broad daylight, two gang members emerged from a car and started shooting at residents in a home. The residents returned fire. In all, seventy shell casings were found on the scene, one person died, two were injured, and three people were arrested. The entire event was caught on a street-mounted surveillance camera.

Amazingly, Foxx declined to press any charges, saying it was a case of "mutual combat."[481]

By now, Mayor Lori Lightfoot, a former federal prosecutor, though no law-and-order advocate herself, was fed up with Kim Foxx and her approach to solving the crime problem. After Foxx refused to file any charges against the shooters, Lightfoot held a press conference and said, "If they [criminals] do not feel like the criminal justice system is going to hold them accountable, we're going to see a level of brazenness that will send the city into chaos and we cannot let that happen."[482] But it had already been happening, and everyone knew it.

In 2020, the *Chicago Tribune*, one of the prominent papers that endorsed Foxx for state's attorney, broke a major story where they exposed the fact that Foxx had dropped more felony cases than her predecessor, Anita Alvarez.[483] The newspaper analyzed Foxx's first three years in office and looked at the percentage of cases her office dropped involving charges of murder and other serious offenses compared to the last three years of Alvarez's tenure in office. They found that Foxx's office dropped all charges against 29.9 percent of felony defendants versus 19.4 percent for Alvarez. In raw numbers, the paper found that 25,183 suspects had their felony cases dismissed under Foxx compared to 18,694 for Alvarez under the same time frame.[484]

Tellingly, Foxx did not disagree with the *Tribune*'s findings in general but suggested that her office was only dismissing cases against low-level, nonviolent offenders so that her office could concentrate on violent crimes.[485] This was, as you will see in later chapters, a standard talking point of rogue prosecutors.

The only problem is that it wasn't true.

The *Tribune* found that Foxx's higher rates of dropped cases included people accused of murder, shootings, sex crimes, attacks on police officers, and serious drug offenses.[486] The data showed that Foxx's office dropped 8.1 percent of homicide cases compared to 5.3 percent for Alvarez, and 9.5 percent of felony sex crimes compared to 6.5 percent for Alvarez.

As if those stats weren't bad enough, consider this: Foxx's office also dropped cases for aggravated battery and for aggravated battery with a gun against police officers at a rate of 8.1 percent compared to 3.9 percent for Alvarez.[487]

It's not hard to see why police departments, like the Chicago Police Department, started losing large numbers of officers to early retirement or transfers after Foxx became the state's attorney. It's also not hard to imagine why morale in police departments has tanked in cities with rogue prosecutors like Foxx, as they know, based on experience, that the criminal has the upper hand with policies like these.

To make matters worse, the Illinois legislature passed the Illinois Safety, Accountability, Fairness and Equity-Today Act (hereinafter SAFE-T) in early January 2021, which went into effect on July 1 of that year. Not only did the law eliminate cash bail, but it also, among other things, allowed certain prisoners who had served long prison sentences to receive a reduction in time and an early release. In that regard, the new law allowed prosecutors to request a reevaluation of sentences of select individuals whom the prosecutor thought were deserving of release from prison.

Less than a year after the law went into effect, Foxx jumped in to help release three long-serving violent felons who, to her mind, had done their time. When she announced her office's resentencing initiative, she framed it, as you might have guessed, in terms of race, saying, "Prosecutors can begin addressing the fact that many Black and Brown people are still incarcerated today under failed policies of the past, even though they have been rehabilitated and pose little threat to public safety."[488]

Foxx's office had partnered with, not surprisingly, a California-based nonprofit called For the People to "identify potential cases" for early release.[489] For the People's executive director and founder was Hillary Blout, who, as mentioned previously, worked for Kamala Harris and George Gascón when each was the district attorney for San Francisco. She also worked on the controversial California ballot initiative Proposition 47, which raised the threshold for felony theft and drug possession.[490]

But feel-good words and happy talk about rehabilitation didn't cut it with the first judge to hear a case under Foxx's scheme. Charles Miles was the defendant, and he had been sentenced to twenty-five years for committing two burglaries. When Assistant State's Attorney Nancy Adduci petitioned the court on behalf of Miles, citing the new law, Judge Stanley Sacks scowled, saying, "I've been doing this for 30-plus years. I make up my own mind, not Governor Pritzker, not Kimberly Foxx either."[491]

Judge Sacks asked why the defendant had a pro bono attorney when prosecutors were advocating for his release.[492] When the judge asked the prosecutor whether the governor, using his power of clemency, should be the one to release Miles, the prosecutor said, "That's one avenue, but that's mercy. There's also justice."[493]

Sacks, exasperated, said, "I'm not a social worker. All I know is, he commits burglaries…oh, he's changed in custody? We'll see."[494]

The next hearing with a different defendant before Judge Brian Flaherty didn't go well either. In another case with a third defendant, prosecutors withdrew their petition for early release before Judge Timothy Joyce could issue his ruling. As this book goes to print, no petitions have been granted, and no more petitions have been filed.

On May 6, 2022, Judge Sacks denied the prosecutor's request to release Miles from prison early, saying that he did not believe that the convicted burglar had been rehabilitated in prison.[495]

## THE IMPACT

The explosion of crime in the city of Chicago is a predictable and natural outgrowth of the policies and leadership coming from Kim Foxx, the governor, and the early policies of Lori Lightfoot. As Northwestern University Law Professor John O. McGinnis called them in an op-ed in the *City Journal*, they are "Chicago's Toxic Trio."[496] But with all due respect to the esteemed professor, we would suggest that it's a toxic quartet and would add Toni Preckwinkle, who paved the path for Foxx's ascension into office. Foxx is carrying out Preckwinkle's dream and that of Angela Davis and other Soros sympathizers to empty out the jails and prisons, one day at a time.

Lightfoot, sensitive to the fact that rising crime rates have potentially endangered her political career, has recently called for dramatic new steps to reverse Chicago's crime wave.[497] In a major speech on December 20, 2021, Lightfoot called for an end to electronic monitoring for criminals accused of murder, attempted murder, aggravated gun possession, felons in possession, sex crimes, illegal gun possession, vehicular carjacking, kidnapping, or other crimes of violence.[498] She noted that 2,300 suspects with those types of charges have been let out on electronic monitoring, which she said "defies common sense."[499] Of course, these views are a recent conversion for her.

In a line that must have stung Kim Foxx, Lightfoot said, "In 2021 alone, for example, well over 50 people have been arrested for a shooting or murder while on [electronic monitoring]."[500]

She called on US Attorney General Merrick Garland to do more, by sending more resources to the US Attorney's Office in Chicago, so they can prosecute felons in possession of guns in federal district court, a tacit acknowledgment that Foxx wasn't doing enough to disarm felons who were caught with guns.

The carnage on the streets of Chicago caught up to Lori Lightfoot on February 28, 2023, when she lost her bid for re-election. She was the first incumbent mayor of Chicago to lose reelction in over 30 years. And the reason she lost, according to exit polls, was crime.

But mayors, police chiefs, governors, legislators, and even the president of the United States have very little control over the discretion afforded the 2,300 elected district attorneys across the country. Kim Foxx, and those featured in this book, know that. They are the gatekeepers to the criminal justice system.

Kim Foxx remains in office to this day, though many, even within her own office, are starting to speak out. A twenty-five-year veteran of the office recently resigned, saying that he had "zero confidence" in Foxx's leadership and that she was "more concerned with political narratives and agendas than with victims and prosecuting violent crime."[501] And now that Lori Lightfoot was rejected by the voters because of Chicago's uncontrollable crime rates, Foxx might be next.

Meanwhile, two other rogue prosecutors who were elected after her have already been voted out of office by the voters in their cities. The people of Chicago watched as voters in San Francisco and Baltimore soundly rejected their rogue prosecutors. Foxx is up for reelection in 2024. Whether the issue of rising crime, a major issue in the minds of voters in 2022, will be front and center when they go to the polls in 2024, and how that will affect her political future, remains to be seen.

But the voters in the City of Brotherly Love reelected Larry Krasner, who considers himself a public defender with power. And the results are as predictable as they are deadly.

## CHAPTER 5

# LARRY KRASNER: PHILADELPHIA

## A DANGEROUS DISTRICT ATTORNEY WHO VIEWS HIMSELF AS A PUBLIC DEFENDER WITH POWER

*"We don't have a crisis of lawlessness, we don't have a crisis of crime, we don't have a crisis of violence."*[502]

**Larry Krasner—Philadelphia District Attorney**

*"[Those are] some of the worst, most ignorant, and most insulting comments I have ever heard spoken by an elected official."*[503]

**Michael Nutter—Former Philadelphia Mayor**

In a small overheated, second-floor ballroom in Philadelphia's William Way LGBT Community Center, fifty-six-year-old Larry Krasner strode to the stage declaring victory in the race to become Philadelphia's next district attorney.[504] In many ways, this was already a foregone, if not initially improbable, conclusion. George Soros-backed entities had spent nearly $1.7 million to elect Krasner, a career civil rights attorney and former public defender who had never prosecuted a case, in this typically low-dollar, low-profile race. But Krasner came to office intending to implement many radical new policies such as not prosecuting certain crimes, not seeking bail for many offenders, and not seeking lengthy sentences of incarceration in most circumstances. The negative consequences of Krasner's policies quickly became apparent.

But the consequences of Krasner's policies are more than just numbers on a page. While the crime statistics speak for themselves, each statistic

110

represents real lives impacted by his policy choices. Philadelphia Police Corporal James O'Connor's family knows that fact all too well. On the early morning of March 13, 2020, O'Connor and other officers entered a white two-story rowhouse on Bridge Street in Philadelphia's Frankford neighborhood to execute an arrest warrant for twenty-one-year-old Hassan Elliott, who was "wanted in a March 2019 robbery and murder around the corner from the house."[505] They found Hassan at the house, but before "they could reach him, more than a dozen bullets flew through the door."[506] One hit O'Connor, and doctors declared him dead thirty minutes later at a local hospital. But what outraged local officials was the fact that Elliott was even on the street at the time O'Connor and other officers were trying to arrest him. William McSwain, the US Attorney in Philadelphia at the time, said that "Corporal O'Connor's widow, his children, his brothers and sisters in law enforcement, and the entire city deserve to know why he died...."[507] And in a lengthy, detailed statement, he laid out the facts. Essentially, Hassan Elliott is a longtime member of the violent "1700" street gang, named for the blighted area of Philadelphia they terrorize. According to McSwain, this "gang is alleged to be responsible for many shootings in the area and is brazen about their access to firearms." Elliott himself was no stranger to committing crimes with guns.

On June 8, 2017—before Krasner entered office—Elliott was arrested and charged with threatening a neighborhood resident with a gun. Shortly after Krasner took office, he offered Elliott a lenient plea deal of a below-guidelines sentence of nine to twenty-three months' imprisonment followed by three years of probation. Elliott, of course, accepted this deal on January 24, 2018. He was released from prison the next day having actually spent only seven months and sixteen days behind bars.

After his release, the Philadelphia Probation and Parole Department labeled him a "high-risk" offender and required weekly visits and regular urine tests. Elliott failed numerous drug tests and failed to report to his parole officer multiple times. Because of these failures, the court scheduled a violation hearing for February 6, 2019. But before that hearing could take place, Elliott was arrested and charged with possession of fifteen packets of cocaine. As McSwain said, "This arrest was in direct violation of Elliott's parole, but the District Attorney's Office did not pursue a detainer against him or make any attempt to have Elliott taken into custody for this serious violation. The office allowed Elliott to be released on his own recognizance—no bail was set. This is stunning, considering that Elliott was on parole for his 2018 firearms conviction. Here, there was an arrest and multiple parole violations and the Krasner regime did nothing." On top of that, the Philadelphia Police Department had labeled Elliott as one of worst offenders in the city.

A little over a month later, on March 1, 2019, Elliott attended a hearing for his cocaine case, which was set for trial on March 27, 2019. As McSwain says, "It turns out that March 1 was a busy day for Elliott: after leaving his pretrial status listing, he allegedly murdered Tyree Tyrone on the 5300 block of Duffield Street. Elliott and another man, both armed with handguns, approached Tyrone, who was sitting in his car, and allegedly opened fire at close range. Video showed Elliott fleeing the scene and his fingerprints were found on one of the alleged murder weapons."

The day before Elliott's cocaine case was set to go to trial, the District Attorney's Office secured a warrant for Elliott's arrest for the Tyrone murder. The next day, March 27th, Elliott failed to appear for his cocaine trial. Inexplicably, when Elliott failed to appear, Krasner's office withdrew the cocaine case against Elliott, saying it was within their discretion to do so. The next time anyone from law enforcement saw Elliott was the day he murdered Corporal O'Connor. As McSwain said, "These facts paint a damning picture of a prosecutor's office that prioritizes 'decarceration' of violent offenders over public safety."[508]

To put it bluntly, O'Connor likely would be alive today if Krasner had done his job.

## TENSION WITH POLICE OVER FAILURE TO DO HIS JOB

But Krasner's failure to keep Corporal O'Connor's killer off the streets wasn't the beginning of his tension with local police and the community. The alarm bells first went off for many in law enforcement when Krasner won the Democratic primary race, which all but guaranteed his eventual election since Philadelphia overwhelmingly votes Democratic. It was at his primary-night election party in May 2017 where, as Krasner celebrated his primary-night victory, members of the crowd began to chant "F--- the FOP," the Fraternal Order of Police, which is the city's police union, and, "No good cops in a racist system."[509] While Krasner's campaign staffers tried to quiet the crowd, Krasner's response afterward did little to ease tensions. He said he was "a great believer in free speech," even if he might not "agree with everything that is said."[510] But Krasner himself has been unrelentingly critical of Philadelphia's police. The *Philadelphia Inquirer* reports that as an attorney, "Krasner has sued law enforcement or the government more than 75 times on behalf of clients."[511] The former US Attorney in Philadelphia said that there "is a culture of disrespect for law enforcement in [Philadelphia] that is promoted and championed by District Attorney Larry Krasner...."[512] After all, Krasner has said, "I just hate bullies...I hate bullies when they're on the street corner beating up on Grandma. I hate bullies when they're little kids. And I hate bullies when they happen to have a uniform on."[513]

## KRASNER'S BACKGROUND

One writer who profiled Krasner said that "in the legal world, there is an image, however cartoonish, of prosecutors as conservative and unsparing, and of defense attorneys as righteous and perpetually outraged. Krasner, who had a long ponytail until he was forty, seemed to fit the mold."[514] His father was a freelance writer and author of mystery novels, while his mother was an evangelical minister at one point in her life. Krasner has an elite academic pedigree, having majored in Spanish at the University of Chicago, and then having attended, and graduated from, Stanford University's law school.[515] While he applied for a job in the Philadelphia District Attorney's Office, he said he quickly decided that he couldn't work there, describing the interview as a series of questions about "Why aren't you in love with the death penalty?"[516] He instead became a criminal defense attorney, as both a public defender and in private practice. His years of experience as a trial lawyer show. He's confident, speaks without notes, and can articulate or obfuscate his true positions as it serves his purposes.[517] This can make it easy for him to pass the buck when the consequences of his policies become clear. Still, he clearly believes in the

policies he is promoting and clearly has antipathy for traditional prosecutors and for police officers, hence his comparison of them to "bullies."

# UNCLE LARRY COMES TO TOWN

But some have charged that Krasner has a soft spot for criminals—bullies who commit crimes. Like his counterparts in Los Angeles (George
Gascón), Boston (Rachael Rollins), and Manhattan (Alvin Bragg), Krasner
issued a memo to his staff shortly after taking office outlining some of his
goals.[518] He ordered the prosecutors in his office, as a rule, to:

- Decline to prosecute certain cases involving marijuana or
  prostitution

- Charge lower gradations of crimes (to make sure no bail
  is required)

- Divert more cases, including cases involving drug distribution

- Make plea offers at the bottom of the state's guidelines

- Inform the judge at sentencing about the financial cost to the state
  for each year of incarceration

- Request shorter probation and parole periods

- Request no more than six months for a technical parole violation
  (no matter how much "back-up time" the offender has)

- Request no more than two years for a regular parole violation
  (regardless of back-up time available)

- Charge no parole violation for a positive marijuana test or if the
  parolee is caught with marijuana

Krasner has justified this approach by saying that he has sought to prioritize more serious crimes over what he views as quality-of-life crimes.[519]
He called prosecuting people for "low-level crimes," such as marijuana
possession, a waste of resources.[520]

# GUN CRIMES AND HOMICIDES SURGE: COMMUNITIES OF COLOR SUFFER

Krasner also has adopted this hands-off approach with several more serious crimes, too, particularly those involving illegal gun possession. One news outlet reported that in a recently released report, "Krasner's office said the focus on illegal gun possession, at least in cases involving nonviolent offenders with no felony convictions, was about singling out people of color."[521] Krasner's report editorialized that "it does not appear that our state legislature's primary interest is in incarcerating people who carry firearms without a license. Our legislature's primary interest is in incarcerating Philadelphians, most of them Black and brown, in their far less diverse counties for the money and the power it brings them."[522] Of course Krasner isn't the only rogue prosecutor, or supporter of the movement, to make this argument. As we have previously written, others have made the same argument too.[523] And as we mentioned in chapter one, supporters of the rogue prosecutor movement argue, in essence, that rural white legislatures pass criminal laws that are used against black inner-city defendants. In their view, then, rogue prosecutors may appropriately "veto" laws through their nonprosecution policies to act "against the democratic inadequacies of the legislative system." Never mind that this principle has never before been recognized in American law—that prosecutors may generally veto duly enacted laws by simply refusing to enforce them—it also violates separation-of-powers principles and undermines the rule of law. As a practical matter, the consequences of these policies have produced disastrous results.

For instance, Krasner's statement comes as Philadelphia experiences a surge in violent crimes, particularly shootings, that can be attributed to his lax polices and his refusal to enforce the law. In 2022, Philadelphia experienced 4,041 shooting incidents. Police categorize a shooting incident as "any incident with a firearm discharge, with or without a victim struck, as determined by detective investigation."[524] In 2021, there were 4223 shooting incidents. In 2020, there were 3,884 shooting incidents, more than a 60 percent increase from the previous year. In 2019, there were 2,339 shooting incidents, and in 2018 there were 1,449. In 2017, the year before he took office, there were 1,263, down from 1,340 in 2016.

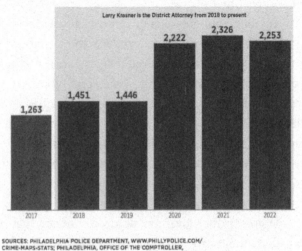

## SHOOTINGS VICTIMS, BY YEAR
Philadelphia

Larry Krasner is the District Attorney from 2018 to present

SOURCES: PHILADELPHIA POLICE DEPARTMENT, WWW.PHILLYPOLICE.COM/
CRIME-MAPS-STATS; PHILADELPHIA, OFFICE OF THE COMPTROLLER,
CONTROLLER.PHILA.GOV/PHILADELPHIA-AUDITS/MAPPING-GUN-VIOLENCE/
#/?YEAR=2020&LAYERS=POINT%20LOCATIONS

☎ heritage.org

Not every shooting incident results in a victim, but a lot do. In 2022, 2,253 people were shot in Philadelphia, down from 2,326 people shot in Philadelphia in 2021. In 2020, 2,222 people were shot. In 2019, 1,446 people were shot. In 2018, 1,451 people were shot.[525] And in 2017, the year before Krasner took office, *only* 1,263 people were shot. The trend line is clear: more shooting incidents and shooting victims under Krasner's watch.

## SHOOTINGS INCIDENTS, BY YEAR

Philadelphia

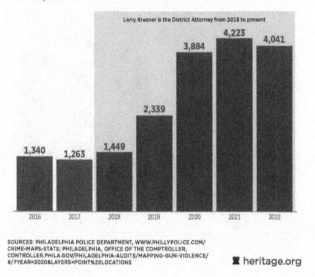

SOURCES: PHILADELPHIA POLICE DEPARTMENT, WWW.PHILLYPOLICE.COM/
CRIME-MAPS-STATS; PHILADELPHIA, OFFICE OF THE COMPTROLLER,
CONTROLLER.PHILA.GOV/PHILADELPHIA-AUDITS/MAPPING-GUN-VIOLENCE/
#/?YEAR=2020&LAYERS=POINT%20LOCATIONS

heritage.org

What's also clear is that the city is currently experiencing a murder crisis. In 2022, there were 516 murders in Philadelphia. In 2021, an all-time record of 562 people were murdered in Philadelphia, a 13 percent increase from the previous year. In 2020, 499 people were murdered in Philadelphia, a 40 percent increase from the previous year. In 2019, 356 people were murdered in Philadelphia, a 1 percent increase from the previous year. In 2018, 353 people were murdered in Philadelphia, a 12 percent increase from the previous year. And in 2017, the year before Krasner took office, *only* 315 people were murdered in Philadelphia. Again, the trend line is clear: more murders under Krasner's watch.

## MURDERS, BY YEAR
Philadelphia

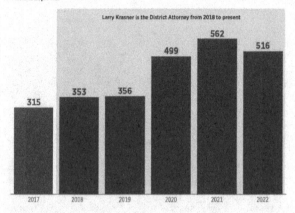

Larry Krasner is the District Attorney from 2018 to present

SOURCES: PHILADELPHIA POLICE DEPARTMENT, WWW.PHILLYPOLICE.COM/
CRIME-MAPS-STATS; PHILADELPHIA, OFFICE OF THE COMPTROLLER;
CONTROLLER.PHILA.GOV/PHILADELPHIA-AUDITS/MAPPING-GUN-VIOLENCE/
#/?YEAR=2020&LAYERS=POINT%20LOCATIONS            ♜ heritage.org

That's why community members and elected leaders were incensed when Krasner had the audacity to say toward the end of 2021 that "we don't have a crisis of lawlessness, we don't have a crisis of crime, we don't have a crisis of violence." He doubled down, saying, "It's important that we don't let this become mushy and bleed into the notion that there is some kind of big spike in crime."[526] The only thing bleeding in Philly under Krasner's reign as DA are wounded and dead bodies across the city. His hope that people wouldn't get the "notion" that there is a "spike in crime" is belied by the facts and incensed residents and politicians in Philly. Facts are stubborn things, and Krasner's block-and-bridge, political sleight of hand is losing its shine.

Former Philadelphia mayor Michael Nutter, a black Philadelphian, had heard enough. He called Krasner's comments "some of the worst, most ignorant, and most insulting comments I have ever heard spoken by an elected official."[527] He said:

> It takes a certain audacity of ignorance and white privilege to say that right now. As of Monday night [December 6, 2021], 521 people, souls, spirits have

been vanquished, eliminated, murdered in our City of Brotherly Love and Sisterly Affection, the most since 1960. I have to wonder what kind of messed up world of white wokeness Krasner is living in to have so little regard for human lives lost, many of them Black and brown, while he advances his own national profile as a progressive district attorney.

I'd like to ask Krasner: How many more Black and brown people, and others would have to be gunned down in our streets daily to meet your definition of a "crisis"? How many more children and teens have to die in record numbers to capture your attention, and be considered a "crisis"? How many more moms, dads, spouses, and friends need to shed tears over the loss of a loved one for you to call it a "crisis"?

Words matter. Words impact, and trigger, and hurt. Words mean something from elected officials. Krasner should publicly apologize to the 521 families of dead victims and the thousands of those maimed by gun wounds this year. He has ignored the pain of the living and insulted the memory of the dead.

Krasner should also use his words to send a message to the shooters, murders, and criminals of this city by committing to actually prosecute them, rather than coddle them, make excuses, reduce or drop charges. He should commit to locking them up for carrying illegal weapons or shooting people.[528]

The statistics support Nutter's claims that the increase in violence has disproportionately impacted minority members of the community. In 2021, 84 percent of Philadelphia's shooting victims were black,[529] and 9 percent were Hispanic, meaning 93 percent of the shooting victims were members of minority communities. In 2020, 83 percent of Philadelphia's shooting victims were black, and 10 percent were Hispanic, meaning 94 percent of 2020's shooting victims were members of minority communities. The trends for 2019 and 2018 are similar.

## UNCLE LARRY'S SOFT-ON-CRIME MESSAGE AND ATTEMPTS TO PASS BLAME

Rather than taking Nutter's advice and sending a message to the shooters, murders, and criminals of Philadelphia that their crimes will not be tolerated, Krasner instead has been sending the message that there will be little to no consequences for their actions. That's why the former US Attorney, Bill McSwain—the chief federal law enforcement officer in Philadelphia—said that "violent criminals in Philadelphia now refer to Krasner...as 'Uncle Larry' and view him as an ally."[530]

McSwain said, "When we arrest them federally, they are shocked and dismayed that 'Uncle Larry' is not there to 'hook them up,' as they put it."[531] "Hook them up" is street slang for bail them out or help them out.

Criminals who are charged by the federal government with being a previously convicted felon in possession of a firearm typically get sentenced to long prison terms if convicted. Those cases, referred to as "922g" cases, serve as a deterrent, sending the message that criminal activity will not be tolerated.[532] These 922g case prosecutions send exactly the message that Krasner should be sending to the criminals on the streets of Philly. Sadly, Krasner is sending the exact opposite message to those inclined to break the law.

Keep in mind, the primary responsibility for prosecuting these violent felons lies with the local district attorney, Krasner. There's only so much the feds can do. That's what makes the situation so frustrating for citizens and especially for law enforcement. At a recent symposium, the current head of the US Attorney's Office in Philadelphia made this same point. Local US Attorneys' Offices simply don't have the bandwidth to take on every 922g violation that occurs in their cities—especially in major metropolitan areas like Philadelphia.[533]

As shootings and murders have surged, Philadelphia's police officers have expressed particular frustration with Krasner and his policies. In March 2021, the *Philadelphia Inquirer* reported that "as Philadelphia's gun violence has surged to unprecedented heights, two troubling trends have quietly kept building: Thousands more people are being arrested for carrying guns illegally. But their chances of being convicted in court have fallen by nearly a quarter."[534] The paper said, "Put plainly, people accused of carrying illegal guns in recent years have had better than a coin flip's chance of beating their case in court."[535] You won't find odds that good in Vegas. Philadelphia's police commissioner, Danielle Outlaw, said that the criminal justice system has become a "revolving door" that leaves more criminals "on the street with their weapons, with little reason to fear the consequences of being caught."[536] She said, "If there's nothing to deter folks, if there's no consequences where people believe, 'If I do this, this is going to happen,' [then] there's no incentive to not carry a gun illegally, quite frankly...."[537] According to the paper, it's indisputable that "conviction rates for being caught with an illegal gun dropped after Krasner was sworn into office in January 2018."[538]

Naturally, Krasner sought to blame the police because, he said, they are submitting weaker cases or that witnesses would not show up for court.

But that comment, like many of Krasner's comments, makes no sense. If a police officer brings a weak case to the DA's office, the DA has a number of choices. The DA can tell the officer to go back and gather more evidence. The DA can tell the officer the case is too weak to prosecute. The DA can tell the officer that if he doesn't bring back more evidence, he won't file charges. What the Krasner comment above shows is this: he is trying to blame police officers for weak cases, when in fact, it's his job to bring trial-worthy cases to trial. If they weren't trial-worthy in the first place, then he shouldn't have filed charges.

Also, it's not the police officer's job to secure witnesses for trial: it's the job of the DA to secure witness testimony at a preliminary hearing or grand jury. It's the DA's job to track down witnesses; lock in their testimony; and provide them the security, assurances, or services they need prior to coming to court to testify, while they are testifying, and after they testify.

But since Krasner has never been a prosecutor prior to being elected, since he has never prosecuted a case, and since he will never, ever accept the blame for his lackluster leadership or rogue policies, he shifts the blame.

He also said, "If we're all going to focus on the questionable notion that everybody who possesses a gun is spending their time looking at data on what conviction rates are, then we're going to miss any solution that's actually going to be real and effective."[539] In other words, Krasner claims that conviction rates don't really matter, and higher conviction rates don't necessarily serve as deterrents to commit fewer crimes.

But officers on the street disagree. Nor does that comment pass the commonsense test, and it flies in the face of the latest study from the United States Sentencing Commission, which found that the odds of recidivism were lower for offenders sentenced to more than sixty months of incarceration compared to a matched group of offenders serving shorter sentences. The June 2022 study, the seventh in the recidivism series, showed that the odds of recidivism were approximately 29 percent lower for offenders sentenced to more than 120 months incarceration compared to a matched group of offenders serving shorter sentences.[540]

In other words: the longer the prison sentence, the less likely it is that a criminal, once released, will re-offend. The shorter the prison sentence, the more likely it is that a criminal, once released, will reoffend. This flies in the face of the entire ethos of rogue prosecutors and the movement behind them who argue that prison sentences, especially long ones, increase the crime rate, as we discussed in the last chapter. But the US Sentencing Commission reports on sentence length and recidivism undercut that argument.

And while Krasner may be correct that criminals don't spend a lot of time looking up actual conviction rates, word on the street matters, and criminals can readily determine whether criminals, including themselves, are being caught, prosecuted, and convicted or whether they are getting away with the crimes they have committed. Inspector Derrick Wood, a black police officer who commanded Philadelphia's Southwest Division, knows this. He attributed the rising gun crimes, in part, to "a growing lack of fear among people carrying guns due to dropping conviction rates and lower bails...."[541]

He said that he and his officers are encountering the same suspects time after time. He said, "They know there's no consequences for carrying a gun in Philly. It's zero to none...I don't care what kind of programs you come up with, what kind of money you put into prevention—if people are not held accountable, then people are going to keep carrying guns."[542]

Ironically, Krasner's response to Inspector Wood, Mayor Nutter, and his other critics is essentially that they are race and fear mongers. Krasner, who is white, is accusing the black leaders in Philly, and everyone else who is critical of his policies, of being racists! One news outlet described Krasner's response this way:

> "[These criticisms are] nothing more than a new version of the Southern strategy," Krasner said during an interview earlier this year [2022] at his office over a lunch of soup, potato chips, and a Diet Coke, referring to President Richard Nixon's appeal to a white majority frightened by scenes of civil unrest in the nation's cities. "It worked before. They've read their Republican history. They're saying 'big cities, lawless,' except all the big cities they're talking about are very Democratic and have huge Black and brown populations."
>
> In his view, the coded language of today is more subtle than that of the late 1960s. Instead of directly singling out minorities, his critics go after progressive prosecution, Krasner said.
>
> "I think politically, in many ways, it represents a good strategy," Krasner said. But, he added, it's "really about Black people. It's not about me."[543]

Some prominent black Philadelphians disagree. Former mayor Michael Nutter said that "Krasner portrays himself as the Great White Hope for Philadelphia's Black and brown communities, but if he actually cared about us, he'd understand that the homicide crisis is what is plaguing us the most."[544] And Uncle Larry is the primary cause of the plague.

# LET 'EM LOOSE LARRY

The plagues of the homicide crisis, the shooting crisis, and the overall increase in lawlessness in Philadelphia cannot be separated from Krasner's lenient bail policies. They are necessarily part of the problem too. When he originally ran for office, Krasner promised to eliminate cash bail in Philadelphia.[545] That's not surprising. Every criminal defense attorney wants his clients back out on the street. But once that criminal defense attorney becomes a prosecutor, his job responsibilities change: to protect the public from violent criminals. Appropriate bail plays a crucial role in protecting the public.

Shortly after taking office, Krasner took concrete steps to make good on the promise. He forbade his prosecutors from seeking cash bail for certain "low-level" offenses, including crimes like prostitution, drunk driving, and even some burglaries.[546] Still, bail magistrates and judges were imposing cash bail in some cases where prosecutors, following Krasner's orders, didn't ask for bail. In other cases, Krasner received political blowback, such as in the Hassan Elliott case, who was released without the prosecutor seeking bail, and went on to commit murder.

So Krasner, ever the clever and slick political operative, implemented "simulated no cash bail," what he called his "Bail Policy 2.0."[547] Krasner is eloquent, smooth, and media savvy, especially compared to counterparts like Baltimore's Mosby, St. Louis's Gardner, or LA's Gascón. His new policy essentially allowed him to game the system and have a ready-made scapegoat when something inevitably went wrong. As one columnist explained, here's how it works:

> After promising to dismantle bail, when the pandemic arrived in Philadelphia, Krasner pirouetted and started setting *million-dollar* bail for garden variety suspects.
>
> Well, not *million-dollar* [bail]. He was actually asking for $999,999 bail bonds, $1 less than $1 million, for many, many offenses.

What the heck happened? Did Krasner have some kind of a weird, pro-prosecution epiphany?

Of course not. He remained a SJW—Social Justice Warrior. His tactic was a trick to force magistrates to lower bail to normal levels—and then blame them for rising crime.

Why $999,999?

If bail was $1 million or more, "the prison would hold them in protective custody," which would *keep* them in jail, says [former Philadelphia magistrate Jim] O'Brien, 60. That would conflict with Krasner's desire to continue depopulating Philly's prisons.... As his $999,999 bail demand became the new normal, Krasner knew it would not mean more people would remain locked up.[548]

A slick serpentine, Krasner knew he could deflect blame. He has asked for bail commissioners, who are also known as arraignment court magistrates, to be removed from making bail determinations in shooting cases.[549] To justify this, he's cited two particularly problematic cases.

In April 2020, Tarik Bey shot two men and was himself shot in the head. Authorities investigated and issued an arrest warrant for him almost a year later. But they didn't apprehend him until October 2021. A bail commissioner set his bail at $175,000, and after an appeal, a municipal court judge lowered it further. Of course, he made bail and fled until he was apprehended again.

Feigning outrage, Krasner said that "this story is atrocious…I mean, there's no other way to put it."[550] He said, "This defendant's case is a stark example of why a money bail system simply fails to ensure public safety, particularly during a gun violence crisis that is being felt here in Philly and across the nation."[551] Of course, what he fails to mention is that his office sought bail just shy of the $1 million threshold mentioned above. As his statement shows, Krasner gets to have the best of both worlds. He asks for bail so high that he knows a local magistrate is unlikely to impose it. When the magistrate or judge lowers the bail, he gets to say essentially,

"See? I'm not the problem. They are," if that person, like Bey, later commits atrocious crimes. In most cases, though, he accomplishes his goal of getting relatively low, or no, bail set—just without his office's fingerprints on it. It's diabolical, and he knows it.

The same thing happened in another prominent case too. James White shot his ex-girlfriend. Although she was badly injured, fortunately, she didn't die. A bail commissioner held White without bail for this crime. "But officials say at the time of the shooting, White should have been in jail."[552] He had dozens of prior arrests and already had been arrested for pistol-whipping his ex-girlfriend and threatening her life. For those alleged crimes, Krasner's office requested $990,000 bail—again just shy of the $1 million threshold that would have resulted in White being held pending trial—which was ultimately lowered.[553] Again, Krasner gets to have the best of both worlds—feigned outrage when someone with reduced bail commits a heinous crime, while at the same time seeking relatively modest, or no, bail in most cases. A local news station reports that, somewhat ironically, "Krasner adds the most serious cases should have a scheduled hearing in front of an elected municipal court judge so that if people don't like how cases are being handled they can be voted out."[554]

## REAL-LIFE CONSEQUENCES OF KRASNER'S RADICAL POLICIES

Of course, Krasner's policies have troubling, real-life consequences, as the murder of Corporal O'Connor showed. Still there are many other stories of victims and their families suffering because of Krasner's radical policies.

For instance, there's the tragic murder of twenty-one-year-old Temple student Samuel Collington.[555] A few days after spending a quiet Thanksgiving with his family, Collington returned to Philadelphia and parked his mom's SUV around 1:30 PM on a Sunday afternoon, when "a gunman approached him in an apparent robbery and carjacking."[556] The gunman shot him twice in the chest, and he died thirty minutes later. So, who is the suspected gunman? It's seventeen-year-old Latif Williams,[557] who was no stranger to Philadelphia's criminal justice system. One commentator said that for "a teenager, Williams has quite a rap sheet, as well as [an] amazing record of success when being prosecuted by the D.A.'s office under...Larry Krasner."[558] Williams' record included:

On July 20, 2019, Williams was locked up for selling drugs. On Aug. 21, 2020, the D.A.'s office under Larry Krasner withdrew the charges against him.

On May 31, 2020, during the George Floyd riots, Williams was arrested for burglary, rioting[,] and looting. According to the police, Williams kicked a police car window out and spit on the cops.

On Sept. 18, 2020, the D.A.'s office under Larry Krasner withdrew all those charges against Williams.

On Nov. 6, 2020, Williams was arrested for selling drugs. On Sept. 10, 2021, the D.A.'s office under Larry Krasner withdrew those charges.[559]

And sadly, we know the rest of the story. Two months later, in cold blood, he allegedly murdered Sam Collington.

There are many other similar stories, such as the case of "Razique Bumpas, whom [sic], after Krasner's office failed to approve two arrest warrants for, shot and killed Ishan Charmidah Rahman, a 39 year-old pregnant woman; her unborn baby also died."[560]

Or the case of "Taray Herring, a convicted sex offender with a dozen arrests on his rap sheet whom Krasner let out of jail because the D.A. was afraid he'd catch Covid [sic], [who] allegedly killed, hacked up[,] and dismembered the body of Peter Gerold, 70, a licensed masseuse."[561]

And, there's the case involving Gladys Coriano. Her ex-husband, Adriano Coriano, violated a protection order Gladys had against him. He repeatedly stalked, harassed, and assaulted Gladys. As a result, on January 14, 2021, Philadelphia police sought a warrant to arrest Adriano.[562] But for six long days, Larry Krasner's office did nothing. As anyone involved in domestic violence cases will tell you, six days is an eternity, because the risk of severe violence is so high.

Finally, at 8:20 PM on January 20, 2021, Larry Krasner's office notified Philadelphia police they were declining to seek the arrest warrant. They wanted mundane additional information, such as the husband's email address, cell number, and DOB, before seeking the warrant from a judge. "The D.A.'s office also wanted to change some language in the arrest warrant,"[563] such as changing a reference to Coriano's "former wife of seven years" to "former wife of defendant."[564]

As an article explained, "There was only one problem—two hours earlier that day, Adriano Coriano drove over to his ex-wife's house and shot Gladys Coriano multiple times. An hour after the D.A. notified the police that they were declining to approve the arrest warrant for her husband, Gladys Coriano, 52, was pronounced dead at Jefferson Hospital."[565]

## FIRING THE TICKS

The fact that the warrant to arrest Adriano Coriano slipped through the cracks shouldn't come as a surprise to anyone. As mentioned in this book's introduction, immediately after taking office, Krasner fired thirty-one veteran prosecutors. Many of these firings had both short-term and long-term consequences.

For instance, "Andrew Notaristefano, a homicide prosecutor and District Attorney's Office employee for more than a decade, said he had a homicide trial scheduled to start on a Monday—and that he'd met with the victim's family the Thursday night before to prepare. He was at his desk working the Friday before his Monday trial when a human resources employee took him aside and told him he was fired…. He requested to leave after prosecuting his upcoming trial but was told no…."[566]

The following Monday, as Notaristefano sat in the back of the courtroom to support the victim's family, the judge overseeing the case took to the bench and harshly criticized Krasner's office. She said that Krasner placed the court, "because of the management decisions by the new district attorney, in an exceedingly difficult position today."[567] She said that Krasner's office had exhibited "bad management" by not having a better plan in place and noted that the almost three-month delay in the trial she ordered was "devastating" to both the victim's and the defendant's families.[568] She went on to say that her forced decision to delay the trial brought her "dissatisfaction and unhappiness."[569] The victim's family members echoed those sentiments. One family member said the delay made "it very hard to move on and grieve properly."[570] After Krasner and his new victim coordinator stopped by the courtroom, the victim's family members said they felt "re-victimized" by the entire process. They also said that Krasner never personally addressed them.[571]

Did Krasner regret this? Not in the least. In fact, when talking about the number of people he fired upon taking office, Krasner told Boston's rogue district attorney, Rachael Rollins, "I should have asked more to go. They dig in like ticks; they undermine you at every turn."[572]

Of course, Krasner could probably have used some advice from some of those ticks since he had never before been a prosecutor or even managed a large law office.

Even the lawyers Krasner hired abandoned him after working for him. More than seventy lawyers Krasner hired have left the office. The *Philadelphia Inquirer* reports that "the loss of 261 attorneys during Krasner's first term has thrown the office—already beset by conflict with the police and judiciary, and mired in pandemic-related backlogs—into what some describe as a state of chaos."[573]

Many prosecutors who remain in the office "say critical units are in disarray, such as Major Trials, which handles many of the office's most serious cases. Two-thirds of the lawyers in that unit, as of November [2021], were law-school graduates admitted to the Pennsylvania bar within the last five years. The same was true for the Family Violence and Sexual Assault Unit, and for about one-third of lawyers in the Homicide and Non-Fatal Shootings Unit."[574] One of Krasner's hires said that she initially "came to Philly to work for Krasner, because [she] believed in what he was trying to do" but was now looking for another job because she felt "betrayed" by the office and by what she "thought this job was going to be."[575] One sex crimes prosecutor said she reluctantly quit the office because of an "unsustainable" workload. She said, "I got to a point where I was afraid I was going to start missing things, and that for me was unacceptable…I was not going to have one of these cases slip through the cracks because of me."[576]

Others said morale is low because Krasner's office is "completely ill-equipped to prosecute serious cases outside of a handful of prosecutors. They don't have the experience. They don't have the talent, and they don't have the numbers to prosecute all the cases they need to…."[577] Other experienced prosecutors also left the office after realizing that Krasner "wasn't really trying to prosecute. He was trying to indoctrinate."[578] They said Krasner "would hire people that didn't think anybody belonged in jail at all…. He hired people who would cry after convicting someone."[579]

It's not surprising that neophyte district attorneys like Krasner, Baltimore's Marilyn Mosby, Chicago's Kim Foxx, and others plucked from obscurity and hoisted into office by the Soros machine are abysmal leaders. None of them had any management or leadership experience before assuming the office of the district attorney. None of them managed large or even medium-sized offices, or subdivisions, of any public or private entity. None had military experience. And for those who worked for a short time as a line prosecutor, none had any senior management experience where they oversaw policy or people, and none had any serious felony trial experience. But worst of all, they all have terrible judgment, as evidenced by their actions, policies, and statements while in office.

Upon taking office, Krasner selected two ideological allies to be his first assistants (essentially the number twos in the office): Carolyn Engel Temin, who was the first woman public defender in Philadelphia, was put in charge of training young prosecutors in the office. And Robert Listenbee, who served under President Barack Obama as the head of the US Justice Department's Office of Juvenile Justice and Delinquency Prevention.

Krasner's law firm, which he started in 1993 after serving as a state and federal public defender for over twenty years, was tiny, consisting of only a few attorneys. So, it's not a surprise that Uncle Larry has a hard time attracting and retaining qualified staff: if his procriminal, antipolice, and antiprosecutorial policies don't drive away employees (or prospective employees), his haphazard, slipshod, micromanager management style pushes away aspiring young lawyers, even ideologically aligned ones.

## PUTTING KRASNER'S REELECTION IN PERSPECTIVE

In 2021, Larry Krasner won his bid for reelection. Like the first time he won, his primary victory all but guaranteed his victory on election day given that Philadelphia overwhelmingly votes Democratic. In the primary, though, he ran against a relatively weak, underfunded opponent. His victory emboldened some supporters of the rogue prosecutor movement who hailed his victory in the Democratic primary as a watershed moment.

Some even crowed that his win "is a sign that communities understand that the failed tough on crime policies of the past don't work."[580] Others, such as the progressive magazine *The Nation*, said that Krasner's victory gives "a major boost to the national movement to stop police violence, end mass incarceration, and upend systemic racism."[581]

Of course, reality is much more complicated, and these statements reflect political posturing more than anything. After all, less than a year later, voters removed San Francisco's rogue DA, Chesa Boudin, and Baltimore's Marilyn Mosby from office. The cold, hard reality is that even though the surge in violent crime should have placed Krasner at a disadvantage going into the primary election, he still held many, many advantages. After all, his opponent didn't get an eight-part, fawning PBS docuseries airing for weeks leading up to the election, in which he was the titular hero.[582] And even though some have said that the Philadelphia police union invested in this race more heavily than others in recent years, Krasner still had about double the cash of his challenger.[583] Sadly, time has shown how this experiment ends for the citizens of Philadelphia—more violence and more crime.

## RADICAL POLICES PROMPT TALKS OF IMPEACHMENT

The increase in crime, Krasner's failure to accept any responsibility for his role in it, and his office's lack of candor before judges[584] all have contributed to the blowback against his policies—even after he won reelection—that he is now receiving. That's why some state lawmakers decided in the summer of 2022 to move to impeach Krasner and remove him from office.[585] The vote to begin the impeachment process passed the Pennsylvania House of Representatives on June 29, 2022, by a vote of 114–86 with bipartisan support. Four Democrats voted in favor of moving forward with establishing the committee that would investigate Krasner.[586]

And even though the full Pennsylvania House of Representatives did impeach Krasner, his removal from office faces long odds.[587] Two-thirds of the Pennsylvania Senate would have to vote to remove him from office, and it is unclear if enough legislators have the political courage to take this drastic step. There are currently twenty-eight Republicans (plus one independent who caucuses with the Republicans) and twenty-one Democrats in the Pennsylvania Senate—meaning every Republican would need to vote in favor of removing him from office and approximately five Democrats would need to cross the aisle too.[588]

That political decision may become more palatable if Krasner keeps making legally questionable decisions that draw sharp rebukes from the Pennsylvania Supreme Court. One of that court's justices recently wrote that Krasner's attempts to prosecute a police officer represent "a win-at-all cost office culture that treats police officers differently than other criminal defendants."[589] The justice went on to say that this "is the antithesis of what the law expects of a prosecutor."[590] The majority in that case said that doing as Krasner asked, to upend the state's use-of-force statute governing when police officers may use deadly force to protect themselves and others, "would essentially criminalize conduct the General Assembly [Pennsylvania's legislature] has deemed noncriminal."[591]

## A PUBLIC DEFENDER WITH POWER

Michael Kinsley is an American political journalist, commentator, and sometimes humorist. One of his more memorable expressions is, "a gaffe is when a politician tells the truth." The bespectacled Krasner, after he was elected in 2018, called himself "a public defender with power."[592]

To the ordinary citizen, this was a political gaffe. But the ever-calculating Krasner doesn't make mistakes; he said this on purpose. His statement crystalizes the problem, not only with Krasner, but the entire movement, as Krasner's vision of himself is shared by other Soros-funded or inspired prosecutors. They fully subscribe to Rachael Barkow's clarion call to "reverse engineer and dismantle the criminal justice infrastructure." When they are elected as the district attorney, they see themselves not as the minister of justice responsible for prosecuting criminals. They reject the American Bar Association's description of the function of the prosecutor—to protect the innocent and convict the guilty—and see themselves as warriors for the accused.

Imagine, for a moment, the opposite: a dyed-in-the-wool prosecutor placed into the role of head public defender who instructed his deputies to encourage all or most of their clients to accept responsibility for their crimes, to plead guilty in all cases (even those in which their clients had viable defenses and a more-than-colorable claim of innocence), and to not oppose the government's sentencing recommendation. This would be a radical departure from our adversarial system of justice where prosecutors prosecute and enforce the law, and defense attorneys defend the constitutional rights of those accused of crimes, and where both handle their respective duties zealously, ethically, and aggressively. Our criminal justice system—and really our system of government—requires each elected official to faithfully execute their duties. Unfortunately, Larry Krasner—and other rogue prosecutors—have undermined that, and the consequences have been deadly.

Unlike most of the other rogue prosecutors highlighted in this book, Krasner is exceptionally well educated, has had a long career fighting against the government, and is a smooth talking, articulate, slick politician. He obfuscates his policies with ease and effortlessly shifts the blame when it suits him. Unfortunately, Philadelphia's victims' rights community is not organized, has not been as successful at pushing back against many of his most egregious policies and failures, and, as a result, has been steamrolled or ignored by Krasner and the media. His deputy DAs cannot raise concerns about his policies or particular cases because they lack the civil service protections that deputy DAs in other cities, like Los Angeles, have. Because Krasner is a true believer in his policies and is a relatively sophisticated salesmen of them, he is one of, if not the, most dangerous rogue prosecutors still in power in the country. And people in the City of Brotherly Love are paying the price with their lives each day.

The silver haired, bespectacled, slick-talking Krasner stands in sharp contrast to St. Louis's Kim Gardner, who has a knack for saying (or not saying), the wrong thing at the wrong time as a matter of routine.

# CHAPTER 6

# KIMBERLY GARDNER: ST. LOUIS

## A POOR EXCUSE FOR A PROSECUTOR

*"I'm a city resident, and it's scary.... There's no assurance that if you're a victim of crime, that you or your cases are going to be treated well. I just feel like the prosecutor's office is just a mess."*[593]

**Terry Niehoff—Longtime St. Louis Defense Lawyer and Former Jefferson County Prosecutor**

*"She [Gardner] just has zero project management experience, and she has no willingness to trust people who do have that experience.... [Her office] was a system of micromanaging, but the managers didn't really know what they were doing on a technical level."*[594]

**Former High-Level Employee Who Resigned from Gardner's Office**

I t was like a scene from *My Cousin Vinny* unfolding in Judge Jason Sengheiser's St. Louis courtroom—except it wasn't funny because the stakes were so high. One man was dead, and another sat accused of killing him, having been charged with first-degree murder, armed criminal action, and unlawful possession of a firearm.[595] In late July 2021, the judge, the defendant, and the defense attorney all sat in their assigned seats at the assigned time for a scheduled hearing in Brandon Campbell's murder case. But the prosecutor from St. Louis Circuit Attorney Kimberly Gardner's office was nowhere to be found. It wasn't the first time no one from her office had shown up. It had happened at least two other times in this case, once at a May hearing and again at a June hearing.

As should be obvious, Campbell faced exceedingly serious charges. He sat accused of shooting and killing thirty-year-old Randy Moore, a father of three young children—twin boys and a girl—after the two had an argument on the night of April 9, 2020. A nearby security camera captured the entire incident.[596] After the shooting, Campbell fled to Arizona and then to Texas, where US Marshals tracked him, arrested him, and returned him to St. Louis to stand trial.[597] In April of 2021, a prosecutor in Gardner's office provided some information and items to Campbell's defense attorney, in response to her request, but this prosecutor stopped working for Gardner shortly after that. Gardner's office then reassigned the case to Assistant Circuit Attorney Kimberly Arshi.[598] Here's the problem: Arshi received the case on May 17, 2021. But she had started maternity leave a week earlier on May 10, 2021.

On the same day Gardner assigned the out-of-office Arshi to handle this case, Campbell's attorney filed a motion to compel additional discovery (information) from the office or to have Gardner's office sanctioned (penalized) if it did not produce it. The court set the motion for a hearing the following week on May 27, 2021. But no one from Gardner's office showed up because Arshi was still out of the office on maternity leave. So, the following day, Campbell's defense attorney emailed Gardner personally to ask who she should contact about the case. Campbell's attorney pointedly reminded Gardner that the assistant circuit attorney assigned to the case, Arshi, was out of the office on maternity leave. But neither Gardner, nor anyone from her office, ever responded to that email.

With the defendant's motion to compel still pending, and no response from Gardner or any prosecutor in her office, the court entered an order on June 4, 2021, setting the case for a hearing on June 15, 2021. When resetting the motion for another hearing, the court specifically noted that "[t]his [was] the second setting for this motion" because the "first time this motion was set no one from the State appeared."[599] The court then took the extremely unusual, but apparently necessary, step of making clear that with respect to the forthcoming hearing, "A representative from the Circuit Attorney's Office is ordered to appear and to be prepared to respond to Defendant's motion."[600] The court stated that if no one from Gardner's office appeared, "the allegations in the motion will be deemed admitted and the motion will be granted."[601] Needless to say, no one from Gardner's office appeared at the June 15, 2021, hearing. So, the court granted the motion and ordered Gardner's office to turn over all the information the defense attorney asked for by June 23, 2021. No one from Gardner's office ever responded to that order either, and no one from Gardner's office turned over additional discovery.

Seven days after the deadline for turning over the discovery had passed, Campbell's defense attorney filed a motion on June 30, 2021, to dismiss the case for willful violations of the discovery rules. On July 6, 2021, the court entered an order to show cause as to why the case should not be dismissed and set the hearing for July 12, 2021, at 1:30 PM. Because Gardner's office had missed the previous hearings, the judge took the highly unusual step of ordering his courtroom deputy sheriff to hand deliver a copy of the order to Gardner's office so that there would be no doubt the office had received it. When the day for the hearing came, after confirming that Gardner's office had, in fact, received the notice, Judge Sengheiser entered an order dismissing the case, essentially saying that he had no choice but to do so.

Perched on his bench, the judge intoned that the court "does not take this action without significant consideration for the implications it may have for public safety. Although presumed innocent, Defendant has been charged with the most serious of crimes. While the Court has a role to play in protecting public safety, that role must be balanced with adherence to the law and the protection of the rights of the Defendant."[602] Judge Sengheiser went on to say that Gardner's office "is ultimately the party responsible for protecting public safety by charging and then prosecuting those it believes commit crimes. [But in] a case like this where [Gardner's office] has essentially abandoned its duty to prosecute those it charges with crimes, the Court must impartially enforce the law and any resultant threat to public safety is the responsibility of [Gardner's office]."[603]

The dismissal of a murder charge is a serious and rare event. But Gardner was asleep at the switch. It took several days after the judge's order dismissing the charges against Campbell for Gardner to release a statement trying to explain and minimize this massive failure, saying, "Upon review of our internal policies and procedures regarding Family Medical Leave, we have determined that corrective measures are needed to further prevent any future repeat occurrence of the incident in question."[604] Gee, do you think? Never mind that those "corrective" measures should have, at the very least, been as simple as Gardner responding to her emails or responding to a hand-delivered notice to her office about the case. Gardner's official statement also said "that as the circuit attorney of the city of St. Louis, I am accountable to the public for the actions of the office and remain committed as ever to upholding the highest possible standards and practices of accountability at all levels of this office, particularly the public safety of the residents of the city of St. Louis. As a result, the individual in this case is (in) custody."[605]

Except he wasn't. Gardner had issued a false statement.

Her office later issued a revised statement confirming that the defendant remained at large after having been released from custody because of her office's screwup. Her revised statement also said that she had kept the victim's family informed about the status of the case.

Except that statement, too, was false.[606]

According to a local news station, "Family members said they [had] n't heard anything about the case from anyone other than homicide detectives."[607] The victim's sisters learned that Campbell had been released from custody from the local news station rather than from Gardner's office. The victim's oldest sister asked, "Why was it so hard to pick up the phone to call us to let us know what was going on?"[608] The victim's mother said that her family was living in fear while her son's alleged killer was on the loose. She said that to "think about somebody who took your son's life and he's out of jail. That's horrifying."[609] Even though Gardner's office refiled the charges after Campbell had been released from custody, the victim's sister said, "That's stressful because he can go out of town. He can hide, y'all have to find him, it ain't like he's going to turn himself in."[610] That assessment proved prescient. A US Marshal's task force had to again track him, arrest him, and return him back into custody.[611] One of the victim's sisters said, "Kim Gardner is a poor excuse for a prosecutor...It's not fair." She said, "I know she tries to give the [b]lack people chances, but on a murder? No. No."[612] Another of the victim's sisters said, "Why aren't they doing their job?"[613]

Gardner's office responded, saying that the "suggestion, however, that there have been additional instances that have occurred like the one in question have not been substantiated."[614] But, as the *St. Louis Post-Dispatch* reported at the time, the same prosecutor who had been assigned to prosecute Campbell's case had also been assigned to prosecute "about 30 [other] criminal cases—including 20 murders, one of them a death penalty case—after she began leave on May 10."[615] One defense attorney in St. Louis who had cases that were also assigned to that prosecutor said that the practice is "just a small reflection of what's going on in the office. Either they don't care or they're sloppy."

## GARDNER'S BACKGROUND

Gardner didn't always want to be St. Louis's chief prosecutor—or even a lawyer. She grew up in St. Louis's 21st Ward where her family owned a funeral home.[616] She ran track in high school and later attended Mississippi State University on a track and field scholarship. While there, she dated future NFL player Kevin Bouie and had their daughter before graduating. She later transferred to a college closer to home and graduated in 1999 with a degree in healthcare administration. Shortly after that, a court sentenced both her brother and her cousin to twenty years in prison for breaking into the home of a family friend where they "restrained her, threatened her with a knife, and stole electronics."[617] Gardner said this exposure to the legal system triggered her interest in the law.

Gardner attended Saint Louis University School of Law's part-time program. A profile piece on her says that during "law school, she worked as a sports agent on the side, representing several arena football players."[618] After graduating, she briefly worked in private practice before joining the St. Louis Circuit Attorney's Office as an assistant prosecutor. The Circuit Attorney's Office is the chief prosecutor, or district attorney, for St. Louis. One commentator noted that the then-circuit attorney Jennifer Joyce "had won a second term in 2004 and set out to overhaul what she calls a 'good-enough for government culture.' She instituted regular performance reviews and promoted attorneys on the basis of merit."[619] How did Gardner fare under this merit-based system? The reporter notes that "Gardner started in misdemeanors, then handled property crimes such as burglary; [but] she tried no serious violent crimes under Joyce."[620] She ultimately left the office and completed a master's degree in nursing in 2012.

Still, Gardner had long had her eye on elected office. She ran for a seat in the Missouri House of Representatives in 2008, but she lost that race by fifty points. Four years later, she ran again and won, ultimately serving two terms as a state legislator, though none of her filed bills passed the House.

In July 2016, when Gardner's former boss, Jennifer Joyce, announced she wouldn't seek reelection, Gardner filed to replace her as the St. Louis circuit attorney. She won the Democratic primary with slightly less than half of the vote. Her success stemmed in part from the fact that her "campaign received a huge boost of nearly $200,000 in donations from the Safety & Justice Political Action Committee, which is financed at least in part by the liberal billionaire philanthropist George Soros. That infusion of money came in mere weeks before the August 2016 primary...."[621] At least one of the internet and cable television ads supporting Gardner came from Soros' Safety and Justice PAC. It was a thirty-second video showing Gardner meeting people and walking around, and ended with her looking into the camera and saying, "Together we can make St. Louis safe by being smart and tough on crime by reforming a broken system."[622] Gardner took political heat from her opponents and others, as she was the only candidate who took money from the Soros super PAC.[623] Spread over at least five donations in direct or in-kind support, the super PAC gave Gardner at least $190,750.73.[624] The Soros money made a big impact. According to Gardner's July campaign filing report, she only had $63,000 on hand before the massive infusion of support.[625]

Gardner used the shooting of Michael Brown, a young black man who was shot and killed by a white police officer in the St. Louis suburb of Ferguson, Missouri, to justify her actions on the campaign trail. She said that her win was a chance to "heal our city."[626] The local paper said that her "campaign targeted those disillusioned by the criminal justice system...[after Brown's shooting] ripped the region apart..." two years earlier.[627] Gardner described herself as the "people's champ" who, among other actions, pledged to use special prosecutors to review police shootings. Of course, at least three investigations into Brown's shooting concluded that the officer should not be charged in that incident.[628]

Gardner admitted that the PAC "reached out and heard my platform and liked what I was saying about building trust.... They said they'd like to support me and get my message out."[629] It worked because she beat the three other Democrats running for the office. No Republican had filed to run for the office, so by winning the primary, Gardner became the next St. Louis circuit attorney on January 1, 2017.

## CRIME FLOURISHES UNDER GARDNER'S WATCH

In 2020, the City of St. Louis suffered through 264 homicides.[630] That was a 36.1 percent increase from the previous year and only three homicides shy of the highest total in the city's history, which topped out at 267 in 1993.[631]

But on a per capita basis, the 2020 murder rate was significantly higher because the City of St. Louis had about eighty-seven thousand fewer residents than it did in 1993—meaning that the per capita murder rate in 1993 was sixty-nine per one hundred thousand residents while in 2020 it was eighty-seven murders per one hundred thousand residents.[632] That's the highest per capita murder rate on record for the city in over fifty years.[633]

In 2021, the number dropped back down to the relatively low number of 195 homicides.[634] As of June 2022, the city had experienced eighty-six homicides.[635] One commentator noted that the "city, which saw just 74 homicides as recently as 2003, now rejoices when its homicide rate reverts to the levels of the 1990s crack cocaine epidemic."[636]

As a *City Journal* article said, "With a situation this grim, the city desperately needs competent and determined crime-fighters, but St. Louis Circuit Attorney (chief prosecutor) Kimberly Gardner remains focused not on law and order but on social justice—and on bizarre self-aggrandizement."[637] Despite her controversial tenure, Gardner won the Democratic primary for reelection in 2020—again relying on funding from George Soros-backed entities. The *St. Louis Post-Dispatch* reported that "Gardner's fundraising totaled about $200,000 including support from the Missouri Justice & Public Safety Political Action Committee, which on July 29 received a $116,000 donation from progressive New York mega donor George Soros."[638] She easily won reelection, securing a second four-year term as the City of St. Louis's top prosecutor.[639]

## PROSECUTIONS GO DOWN AND ACQUITTALS GO UP ON GARDNER'S WATCH

Gardner's reelection website touted that she "made several changes to the Office so that its resources would not be spent on petty offenses, but instead focused on serious, violent crime."[640] But as of July 2021, Gardner's office had dismissed 34 percent of all felony cases that it brought before the St. Louis Circuit Court. That was slightly down from 36 percent in 2020. The year before, in 2019, Gardner's office dismissed 32 percent of all the felony cases it brought before the court. In 2018, she dismissed 23 percent, and in 2017, she dismissed 15 percent of all felony cases she brought. The *St. Louis Post-Dispatch* reports that from "2008 through 2016, before Gardner took office, the yearly share of dismissed felony cases ranged from 10 percent to 15 percent."[641]

Gardner has said that the high dismissal rate is necessary "to reduce the number of cases unnecessarily charged [brought by prosecutors] in order to focus on the more difficult cases for trial."[642] But what do those statistics show? Has the gambit been successful? No. An investigation by a local television station "showed that in 2018, prosecutors got guilty verdicts in just 51% of cases. In 2019, the trial conviction rate was 54%."[643] In other words, Gardner's office was losing about half the cases it took to trial. According to the news station, "historical data…showed the Circuit Attorney's Office used to achieve guilty verdicts in approximately 72% of trials, on average."[644] Gardner's office, inexplicably, "claims a felony conviction rate of more than 90%, but has declined to explain its calculation."[645] A representative for the local St. Louis Association of Police noted that those numbers "are just the cases for which there have been charges or indictments."[646] The representative went on to say that "not only is she declining to prosecute a record number of cases that have already been filed, she is just filing less cases, so that's a double whammy."[647]

St. Louis University law professor Susan McGraugh, a criminal defense attorney and former Gardner supporter, said that Gardner's mismanagement of her office's caseload has essentially stopped many cases from moving forward. She said, "We've seen that trials can't go, pleas can't go and preliminary hearings can't go because of the inability of the circuit attorney to properly manage their caseload."[648] That's what happens when more than 470 years of criminal prosecutorial experience walks out the door. That's the combined total of years of experience of prosecutors who have left the office under Gardner's watch.

A local defense attorney in St. Louis said, "Quite honestly, the office is made up of rookies and that's why I think the win-rate is so bad.... Certainly, the results are better for the defense bar, but it's actually a lot more difficult to deal with them because there's not consistency in their office, and everybody's afraid to do things because they'll get fired on a whim."[649]

## A JET-SETTING PROSECUTOR LEAVES HER OFFICE IN DISARRAY

A large part of the reason Gardner's office has become so dysfunctional likely stems from the fact that she just isn't there as often as she needs to be. Questions have arisen about whether Gardner properly disclosed her activist-sponsored travel—much of which was sponsored and paid for by radical advocacy groups like Fair and Just Prosecution, which advocates procriminal, antivictim policies.

According to News 4 in St. Louis, Gardner "has often been gone from her office a couple of times every month, jetting around on someone else's dime."[650] Some of the people interviewed for that report said "that decisions delayed or made difficult by Gardner's travel were related to budgets, grants and personnel issues like hiring and firing." Some of those same individuals said that "Gardner's traveling was prolific and problematic... [and that] she was unreachable on trips, making it difficult to get decisions made."[651] Responsible leaders in positions of authority make themselves available to subordinates, superiors, and business associates 24/7 or leave a clear chain of command so that decisions can be made in his or her absence. But not Gardner. This is a basic failure of leadership on her part, and it has had devastating consequences.

Since taking office, Gardner has travelled to New York; Chicago; Seattle; Philadelphia; Cleveland; Atlanta; Washington, DC; New Haven, Connecticut; Selma, Alabama; and even outside the United States to Portugal, although it's unclear exactly how many trips she's been on since it is unclear whether she has been properly reporting her trips.[652] And what was the point of those trips? Was she there to learn how best to run a prosecutor's office or share best practices with others? We don't know. But from what we can tell, her overseas trips looked more like boondoggles with like-minded rogue prosecutors.

A local criminal defense attorney in St. Louis said, "I'm a city resident and it's scary.... There's no assurance that if you're the victim of crime, that you or your cases are going to be treated well. I just feel like the prosecutor's office is just a mess."[653] And no wonder, since Gardner took over, there has been more than 100 percent turnover in her office—meaning the office, in statistical terms, has completely turned over, plus some. Even some of her own hires have left. According to the *St. Louis Post-Dispatch*, the effect "is a state of dysfunction, low morale and dearth of legal wisdom necessary to safeguard the public from potentially dangerous criminals."[654]

And that dysfunction has real-world consequences. The *St. Louis Post-Dispatch* reported on "three dropped murder cases that [were] the consequence of continued turnover within the Circuit Attorney's Office, and its apparent failure to manage its caseload as the rollback of pandemic-era court restrictions allows more jury trials to take place."[655]

One of those was Campbell's case. Another involved Terrion L. Phillips. Authorities had accused Phillips of shooting and killing fifty-six-year-old Vincent Sanders while attempting to steal Sanders's truck and money. According to the *Post-Dispatch*, "The red Mitsubishi that Phillips drove to the park to rob Sanders had been taken in an armed carjacking in St. Louis County the previous day."[656] Shortly before Phillips's murder trial was set to begin, the recently assigned prosecutor moved to delay it, saying that "all previous assistant circuit attorneys assigned to this case have left the office and undersigned counsel is a new assistant circuit attorney who began employment with the St. Louis Circuit Attorney's Office on June 3, 2021."[657] He had only been assigned to the case on June 17, 2021, about a week prior to his request to delay the trial.[658] He had just completed another murder trial the previous week, where a jury acquitted the defendant.[659] The victim's sister in that case said that she had "lost all faith in the justice system."[660] You can see why she felt that way. Fortunately, in Phillips's case, Gardner's office refiled charges, which prevented his release from jail. But it started his case over "from scratch."[661]

One former high-level official who resigned from Gardner's office said that "she's an ideas person…. She just has zero project management experience, and she has no willingness to trust people who do have that experience."[662] One former high-level official in her office also said, "It was a system of micromanaging, but the managers didn't really know what they were doing on a technical level." At the end of the day, "Police are angry that Gardner isn't taking more cases. Defense attorneys are frustrated with delays. And some victims feel forgotten."[663]

## ETHICALLY CHALLENGED

So instead of focusing on doing the basic blocking and tackling of prosecuting cases and combatting the rise in violent crime in her city, what was Kim Gardner focused on? Gaining a high-profile political pelt. In late 2017 and early 2018, it was revealed that then-Missouri Governor Eric Greitens had engaged in an extramarital affair and had allegedly taken a photo of his mistress without her consent. Gardner opened a probe and eventually obtained an indictment against Greitens for invasion of privacy. She also opened another probe for alleged campaign finance violations by Greitens. Concerns about her handling of the case immediately began to emerge.

For starters, she attended an initial meeting with the potential victims without anyone else from her office present, such as an investigator or a police officer. That's a mistake, because as any rookie prosecutor would tell you, if any questions come up about what was said or done at that meeting, the prosecutor risks becoming a witness in her own case.

And guess what happened? Just that. Greitens's defense team raised questions about what Gardner had promised to the alleged victim, and a judge ordered her to testify about what was said at the meeting. Rather than testifying under oath, Gardner dismissed the charges. Why? Makes you wonder why she wasn't willing to testify under oath and set the record straight. And when Greitens later resigned from office, she also dropped the campaign finance investigation.

But that's not the end of the story. Rather than using police officers to investigate claims against Greitens, as is the usual protocol, Gardner hired an outside private investigator, William Don Tisaby, to work the case. Greitens's defense team deposed Tisaby about his work on the case and accused him of lying under oath during his deposition. A Missouri judge appointed a special prosecutor to investigate, and the special prosecutor presented the case to a grand jury, which indicted Tisaby on six counts of perjury for statements he made during the deposition, plus an additional count of tampering with physical evidence. Tisaby ultimately pled guilty to one count of misdemeanor evidence tampering, "thus avoiding a perjury trial that could have included testimony from St. Louis' top prosecutor," Kimberly Gardner.[664]

The whole thing is troubling, but here's where it gets particularly problematic for Gardner. As *St. Louis Magazine* reports, "Gardner sat by his side that day…[and] didn't correct his testimony."[665] Were Tisaby's false statements things she didn't know about? Unlikely, because as that same magazine article reports, one of the questions the defense team asked him was "whether he'd received any information from the circuit attorney [Gardner] before interacting with the [alleged victim]."[666] He said no, "[y] et in reality, the grand jury alleged, Gardner had sent him six pages of notes, plus they'd spoken for five hours on the phone, exchanged more than 100 texts, and even met in person in Louisiana."[667] Once the deposition resumed after a lunch break, the defense team asked Tisaby if he "had been in contact with Gardner during the break."[668] He said, "Not at all."[669] As the same article again reports, "In reality, the indictment alleges, they had spoken at least seven times on the phone for a total of 34 minutes."[670] Again, Gardner said nothing.

One of Gardner's former chief assistants said, "To say he's Inspector Clouseau would be a compliment."[671] Gardner, though, said that she didn't have an affirmative duty to correct the false statements because the private investigator wasn't technically her client, even though she hired him! Really? Is that the standard we want from our elected prosecutors (or any prosecutor, for that matter)? The special prosecutor said he wouldn't put himself in Gardner's shoes, but he said, "I can say I believe prosecutors have an ethical obligation to correct and make sure the record is clear as to what documents exist or don't exist and to correct a witness if you know that witness is not testifying appropriately or accurately as to what's going on."[672]

## MISSOURI BAR ACCUSES GARDNER OF BEING UNETHICAL

The Missouri Bar largely agreed with the special prosecutor's assessment of Gardner's actions. In fact, according to an article in the *St. Louis Post-Dispatch*, "[a]n ethics investigation resulted in allegations of professional misconduct against Gardner, alleging she concealed details about the Greitens investigation from her own team regarding interview notes with witnesses, failed to disclose potentially favorable evidence to Greitens' attorneys, and misrepresented facts about evidence to the court, defense lawyers and ethics investigators."[673] The article goes on to say that the "disciplinary complaint against Gardner says she failed to correct false and sworn statements by members of her team about the existence and disclosure of notes taken in interviews with Greitens' accuser."[674]

The charges against Gardner were very serious—so serious she faced disbarment as a possible punishment. It's not surprising that Gardner, through her lawyer, initially denied the allegations. Her lawyer said the allegations were "another attempt by Ms. Gardner's political enemies—largely from outside St. Louis—to remove Ms. Gardner and thwart the systemic reforms she champions."[675] On the eve of her disciplinary hearing, which could have lasted up to a week with numerous witnesses called and testimony received, Missouri's chief disciplinary counsel, Alan Pratzel, gave Gardner a sweetheart deal. He entered into a "joint stipulation" with her that recommended a simple reprimand and allowed her to avoid more severe punishments such as a suspension of her license, probation, or disbarment.[676] As part of the stipulation, Gardner admitted that her office "failed to maintain a comprehensive approach to collecting, producing and logging documents."[677] However, it allowed her to avoid stating that she intentionally failed to produce the documents. She also admitted that "she should have been more vigilant in ensuring the prosecution discovery obligations."[678] A three-person disciplinary panel also approved the deal, and the Missouri Supreme Court approved it, imposing a $750 fine.[679]

## GARDNER GOES ON OFFENSE WITH A LAWSUIT ABOUT PERSONAL SLIGHTS

Gardner, before admitting (some of) her errors, went on the offensive. She filed a federal lawsuit on January 13, 2020, against the City of St. Louis, local police unions, and the special prosecutor investigating the perjury allegations and her conduct, among others. Her complaint alleged violations of the Ku Klux Klan Act, claiming that their conduct amounted to a "racially motivated conspiracy to deny the civil rights of racial minorities."[680]

In September 2020, a federal judge, John A. Ross, appointed by former President Obama, dismissed her lawsuit writing that "[h]er 32-page complaint can best be described as a conglomeration of unrelated claims and conclusory statements supported by very few facts, which do not plead any recognizable cause of action."[681] He went on to say that "[h]er complaint is nothing more than a compilation of personal slights—none of which rise to a legal cause of action."[682] Those are strong words, especially coming from a federal judge.

## GARDNER DOESN'T WANT SUNSHINE IN HER OFFICE

Then there's Gardner's apparent defiance of a court order in litigation brought by a reporter under Missouri's Sunshine Law, which is its state-level equivalent of the federal Freedom of Information Act. The reporter wanted information about whom Gardner and her office had communicated with prior to and during her investigations of Greitens. When the reporter didn't receive the information, he filed a lawsuit and obtained a default judgment because Gardner's office refused to respond.[683] This is the same Kim Gardner who ran for office on a platform of restoring confidence in the criminal justice system.

The judge in the case didn't mince words. The fact that Gardner's office had been given an extra thirty days to respond but failed to do so surely contributed to his criticism of Gardner for her "reckless, dilatory and intentional refusal to timely file a responsive pleading."[684] Later that year, when Gardner's office tried to walk back her previous failure to comply, the judge again made clear that "this didn't just happen once. This is consistent behavior," and that he thought Gardner and her office were "attempting to obfuscate this process."[685]

## MCCLOSKEY FUNDRAISING

And then there's Gardner's mishandling of the Mark and Patricia McCloskey cases. Who can forget the images of the couple standing on their property, each wielding a gun, as Black Lives Matter protesters trespassed into their gated neighborhood and approached the McCloskeys' house on their way to the home of the St. Louis mayor? Gardner charged the couple with unlawful use of weapons as well as evidence tampering. But because she is Kim Gardner, she also sought to use the case for political gain and sent two fundraising emails touting her prosecution of the McCloskeys.

As a result, the judge handling Mark McCloskey's case disqualified her from handling his prosecution, saying that her fundraising emails gave the appearance that she had "initiated a criminal prosecution for political purposes."[686] She was later disqualified from Patricia McCloskey's case too.

For some inexplicable reason, Gardner appealed, but the Missouri Eastern District Court of Appeals affirmed Gardner's removal. Exhibiting a stunning lack of judgment, Gardner appealed to the Missouri Supreme Court, which also affirmed her removal from the cases.[687]

## CAUGHT IN A LIE ON VIDEO: THE TRAFFIC STOP

And then there's her bizarre encounter with a St. Louis police officer during a traffic stop. The officer says he pulled Gardner over—without knowing to whom the vehicle belonged or who was driving it at the time—because she was driving at dusk without her headlights on. Gardner later claimed that the stop was an intimidation tactic and that it lasted fifteen minutes without the officer telling her why she had been stopped. She even summoned her own investigator to the scene.[688]

Unfortunately for Gardner, the stop was captured on video, which told a different story. The video shows that the stop only lasted six minutes before the officer released her. It also showed her driving with her lights off. She acknowledged this was the reason she was stopped, although she later claimed that she didn't know why she was stopped.

This event was eerily similar to a bizarre encounter Boston's then-rogue prosecutor, Rachael Rollins, had with a news crew that was seeking information about a parking lot incident involving Rollins, which you can read about in Chapter 7. Again, the news crew's video called into question Rollins's version of events.

Trust in the criminal justice system starts with honest people. For the public to trust in the "system," prosecutors, defense attorneys, judges, police officers, and other stakeholders should tell the truth, even when it doesn't show them in the best light. But when elected district attorneys fudge the truth, or outright lie, that undermines the public's trust and confidence in the system. Yet in case after case, time after time, a defining characteristic of many of these rogue prosecutors is to lie, obfuscate, or shade the truth, not only about their personal behavior but also the impact of their dreadful policies on the public whom they are supposed to be protecting and serving.

## CITY OF ST. LOUIS HARMED BY HER POLICIES

Unfortunately, rather than acknowledging her mistakes and focusing on ways to combat the rising tide of violent crime in her city, Gardner seems to be doubling down. She attributes much of the opposition against her to racism and sexism—not to her failed and dangerous policies. Gardner's track record shows that she is more interested in grabbing headlines and placating the big money backers of the national rogue prosecutor movement than in doing the in-the-trenches work of enforcing the law and fighting violent crime in her city. And it's the citizens of St. Louis who suffer.

The only rogue prosecutor who has been elevated (so far) to become a United States Attorney in a state, Rachael Rollins, shares some of Gardner's penchant for odd and off-color remarks while in office. She is best known, however, for listing fifteen crimes you can commit in Boston on her official website.

# CHAPTER 7

# RACHAEL ROLLINS: BOSTON

## TEMPERAMENTALLY UNFIT FOR OFFICE

*"She has the politics of a public defender, street cred in poor and crime ridden communities, and truckloads of charisma."*[689]

**Catherine Elton—Boston Magazine**

*"[Rollins being DA] is a stepping-stone for some other political office."*[690]

**Anonymous Assistant District Attorney—**
**Suffolk County District Attorney's Office**

R achael Rollins is a different kind of rogue prosecutor, unlike each of the seven others featured in this book. During her tenure as the Suffolk County district attorney (which encompasses Boston), Rollins adopted the language of other rogue prosecutors but explicitly ramped up talk of racial recriminations and castigated the existing supposedly racist criminal justice system. But her policies, although controversial and violative of the separation of powers, were mild (though you would never know it from her language) compared to the policies of others featured in this book. But when you combine her policies, each of which rewards law breakers, with her vituperative race-infused language, she deservedly earned a chapter, albeit a short one.

None of her policies, from what we could tell, led directly to a horrific crime perpetrated under her watch. She didn't eliminate cash bail completely during her tenure as the Suffolk County district attorney, even though her announced policies suggested she would do just that.

She didn't pull a Krasner and go to war with the local United States Attorney. She routinely coordinated with the United States Attorney's Office for the District of Massachusetts on guns and gang cases. She worked closely with them through the federal-state partnership called Project Safe Neighborhoods, a Justice Department program designed "to identify the most pressing violent crime problems in a community and develop comprehensive solutions to address them."[691] As the district attorney, Rollins, to her credit, did not want to get crosswise with the US Attorney's Office, according to sources we interviewed for this book.

Unlike Krasner and Mosby and others, she didn't fire prosecutors upon taking office—although many left of their own accord.[692] By August 2019, thirty-one assistant district attorneys had left the office of around 160 prosecutors, and there was a general fear inside the office that due to low staffing, something could go wrong in a major case, which has been a recurring theme across many rogue prosecutors' offices.[693]

And unlike Gascón, Krasner, Mosby, Bragg, and Boudin, Rollins didn't have a policy that ordered her prosecutors to water down felonies to misdemeanors. Unlike, for example, Gascón, she didn't have a blanket policy prohibiting violent juvenile offenders from being tried as adults.

Rollins, who now serves as the United States Attorney for the District of Massachusetts, is best known for "The Rachael Rollins Policy Memo," which she published weeks after taking office in 2019. The most controversial and well-known part of that memo is in Appendix C, which lists fifteen crimes that "should be declined or dismissed pre-arraignment without conditions."[694] There are other controversial policies contained in her memo, discussed below, some of which she did not fully enforce during her tenure as Boston's top prosecutor. The prime example is this: she prosecuted criminals for assault and battery of police officers, unlike her fellow rogue prosecutors.

But her list of fifteen crimes you can commit in Boston enraged the police because they were forced to stand by and allow criminals to break the law. Morale in the police department plummeted during Rollins's tenure because of her policies and comments she made disrespecting police.

Her lax enforcement of the law showed up in more subtle ways, too, which we explore in this chapter, each of which will have a lasting impact on the ability of law enforcement to know the full extent of a criminal's history next time he is arrested.

Finally, one of Rollins's most distinguishing features is her lack of judgment, bizarre actions, and controversial statements she made as the district attorney. As you will see, she has a real knack for blurting out inflammatory, and at times racist, comments in public.

## ROLLINS'S BACKGROUND

Rollins grew up in Cambridge, Massachusetts. Her mother is an immigrant from the West Indies, and her father is an Irish American who served in the military and later as a corrections officer and then a public school teacher.[695] The oldest of five children, Rollins identifies as black, but says she is "fluent in white Irish male," a comment suggesting she sees everything and everyone through race-colored lenses.[696]

She earned a scholarship to attend high school at the Buckingham Browne & Nichols School in Cambridge, a prestigious private school that caters to the Boston elite; she graduated from there in 1989. A gifted lacrosse player, Rollins was selected to play for highly competitive lacrosse teams and earned a scholarship to play lacrosse at the University of Massachusetts at Amherst.[697] According to Rollins, at the end of her freshman year of college, three women's sports teams, including lacrosse, were eliminated due to budget cuts. Rollins got together with other female athletes and filed a Title IX lawsuit against the university, claiming discrimination. Rollins was successful in the lawsuit, and the university reinstated the three teams. That victory sparked her interest in the law.[698]

Rollins had another experience with the law as a college student. In 1991, when she was nineteen years old, she was charged with receiving stolen property under $200, a misdemeanor. She was arraigned in December 1991, pled not guilty, but later paid court costs of $200. Five months later the case was continued without a finding and was eventually dismissed.[699] There is no information in the public domain about what the property was or any details about the terms of any plea arrangement. Rollins has said, correctly, that she has passed state and federal background checks since the incident.[700]

Suffice it to say, many college students do dumb things. Many don't even get caught for doing dumb things, much less get in trouble. We all make mistakes, especially when we're young. Rollins is to be commended for paying the fine, which is a form of accepting responsibility. We only mention her minor brush with the law in college because years later, as the elected district attorney, she included receiving stolen property as one of the fifteen crimes where her prosecutors must decline to charge the offender. We are not suggesting, however, that the only reason she included that crime in her list of fifteen is because she was charged with committing that crime as a student. Rather, her list is essentially a copycat list from other rogue prosecutors who took office before her.

After graduating from the University of Massachusetts at Amherst, she attended Northeastern University Law School in Boston, graduated in 1997, and then attended Georgetown University Law Center and received a Master's of Law degree in labor and unemployment law.[701]

Rollins then worked as a field attorney for the National Labor Relations Board in Boston, and three years later moved to a law firm where she focused on matters involving the First Amendment, labor, and employment law.[702] In 2007, Rollins became an assistant United States Attorney in the Boston US Attorney's Office, where she focused on fraud, employment discrimination, and other matters.[703] She was in the Civil Division of the office. She did little criminal work while in the US Attorney's Office.

At the same time she joined the US Attorney's Office in 2007, the voters of Massachusetts elected Deval Patrick as the 71st Governor of Massachusetts; he was the first black man to occupy that office.[704] In 2011, Rollins was appointed by Patrick to be the general counsel of the Massachusetts Department of Transportation, and shortly thereafter, she became the general counsel of the Massachusetts Bay Transportation Authority. In 2013, she became the chief legal counsel of the Massachusetts Port Authority.[705]

In 2016, Rollins was diagnosed with breast cancer. Fortunately, she beat it, but that brush with her own mortality "combined with her increasing frustration with racial disparities in criminal justice inspired her initial thoughts about running for DA."[706]

In February 2018, the incumbent district attorney for Suffolk County, Dan Conley, announced that he was not going to run again for office in the upcoming fall election. At the time of the announcement, Rollins was in Florida visiting her sister. According to an interview Rollins did for *Boston Magazine*, on the day of Conley's announcement, she received dozens of voicemails, emails, and texts, all urging her to run for district attorney.[707]

By this time, the rogue prosecutor movement across the country had found its sea legs with the election of Kim Foxx in 2016, and Larry Krasner and Kim Gardner in 2017. Fair and Just Prosecution was also founded in 2017 to help elect and train rogue prosecutors.[708] The movement, as detailed in Chapter One, was well on its way to becoming a national movement and was looking for people to recruit and/or support for district attorney.

So, Rollins threw her name into the political ring. Outgoing District Attorney Conley had endorsed veteran Deputy District Attorney Greg Henning, who worked for him and had experience as the head of the office's gang prosecution unit. Henning also had the endorsement of the police union.[709] But in 2018, criminal justice reform was all the rage, and a white male running a traditional race based on law and order was not a recipe for victory, especially in a liberal city like Boston. As one veteran defense attorney said of Henning in 2018, "Greg continues to do the same old, same old. Prosecute, lock up, and then try to help them dig themselves out of a deeper hole."[710]

On September 14, 2018, voters went to the polls to vote in the Democratic primary. Rollins won the race with 39.3 percent of the vote, compared to runner-up Henning, who only received 23.1 percent of the vote.[711] On October 2, 2018, Massachusetts United States Senator Elizabeth Warren endorsed Rollins for Suffolk County district attorney.[712] She also got the endorsement of Philadelphia's Larry Krasner and said in an interview that when elected, she hoped to operate her office in the mold of Krasner and Chicago's Kim Foxx.[713]

L to R: Philadelphia DA Larry Krasner, newly elected Suffolk County DA Rachael Rollins. Photo taken shortly after Rollins was elected to office in 2018. Taken from Rollins' Twitter page, no longer available. See also https://www.dotnews.com/2018/after-primary-victory-rollins-hopes-give-da-office-another-voice

Not surprisingly, she won the general election against an Independent (no Republican even ran for DA) on November 6, 2018, by a vote of 72.6 percent to 17.4 percent.[714]

## THE ROLLINS POLICY MEMO

Before the primary, Rollins said, "I believe there are certain things we're just going to reject. I think there are certain charges that I don't want to prosecute any longer. Those are overwhelmingly the charges that fall on the mentally ill and those with substance abuse disorder."[715] She posted on her campaign website fifteen crimes for which the default of the office would be to decline prosecution unless supervisor permission was obtained by a line prosecutor.[716]

She was never, to our knowledge, asked to explain why she didn't think it was appropriate to prosecute those crimes, or, more importantly, what authority an elected district attorney in Massachusetts even had to refuse to prosecute entire categories of crimes. Like the other rogue prosecutors in this book, she just decided to do it because that's what the "reformers" were doing, and she could get away with it. She was following the prosecutorial nullification bandwagon.

A month after Rollins was elected, the National Police Association (NPA) filed a formal complaint with the Office of the Bar Counsel in Massachusetts against Rollins, claiming that her "reckless disregard for the laws enacted by the Massachusetts General Assembly mandate[d]" its decision to file such a claim.[717] The NPA asserted that her campaign promises not to prosecute entire classes of crimes, if implemented, would "adversely and will foreseeably impact the safety and well-being of those that she is soon charged to represent."[718] The NPA acknowledged in their complaint that it might not result in any formal action, finding, or adjudication, but they wanted to go on the record with their concerns.[719]

Rollins thumbed her nose at the bar complaint and published her policy memo on March 25, 2019.[720] To date, nothing has come of the bar complaint, so Rollins's cavalier gamble paid off.

The forty-three-page memo (plus attachments) opens with a "Message from the DA." Rollins stated that she wanted her office "to be data-driven in everything we do."[721] With the "help of some leading experts in the field," she claimed that a preliminary analysis of their data "has been completed" and a review "of other jurisdictions that have adopted similar policies shows that their experiences thus far have been positive."[722] The report does not list the leading experts, identify the data they analyzed, identify which jurisdictions have adopted similar policies, or show or explain the "experiences" they had that were positive, or explain what "positive" means. The memo did contain endnotes, which consisted of one page, listing twelve hyperlinked articles, which included six articles by news outlets or activists who advocated for criminal defendants. The policy memo was never updated, nor did Rollins or her office ever identify the experts they consulted.

Like all rogue prosecutors featured in this book, Rollins's written policies were dressed up as reasonable, thoughtful reforms based on proven programs that reduced crime and protected victims, when, in fact, they were just diktats from the front office. They come across, when you read them, as arrogant we-know-better-than-you orders rather than sober, vetted, peer-reviewed policy prescriptions.

Although the memo has fifteen substantive sections, ranging from appeals to witness protection, many of the sections are short, anodyne, and noncontroversial.

For example, the section on charging, which isn't even a page long, says that "criminal charges carry permanent, often irrevocable consequences"[723] and that assistant district attorneys may only bring charges when there is probable cause to believe that a crime was committed and there is sufficient evidence to present to a fact finder. This is common-sense stuff and applies in all traditional district attorney's offices.

The section on collateral consequences is equally short and routine stuff for any ordinary district attorney's office. The memo dictates that "going forward, staff in this office shall carefully consider, and factor into all decisions, potential collateral consequences and harms that may arise at any point along the spectrum of system involvement."[724] Again, this is not groundbreaking stuff, nor is it new to prosecutors' offices.

The section on community engagement is garden-variety stuff that district attorney's offices (and US Attorney's Offices) have been doing for a long time. The memo encourages "us to begin building stronger relationships with residents of neighborhoods that are victimized, prosecuted, and incarcerated at higher rates than others."[725] This is the bread and butter of what DA offices around the country have been doing for decades. In fact, many prosecutors' offices have community prosecutors who are assigned to work a particular district in a large city, attend community meetings in that district, work with community police officers, and work with and get to know members of the community, church leaders, educators, sports leaders, and the like. Rollins's policy memo fell well short of establishing any such program and consists of standard, old-school outreach to the community. It's certainly not cutting-edge reform stuff.

The crime survivors section is also nothing new in terms of policy. Less than a page in length, it, too, directs victim-witness advocates to "meet with survivors and other impacted parties to fully explain the range of potential outcomes and seek their input of how they would prefer to see the office proceed."[726] That, of course, is the job of any victim-witness advocate in every district attorney's office. It makes us wonder if victim-witness advocates in the office were not doing their job prior to

Rollins taking office. Nonetheless, this policy is basic blocking and tackling for any moderately competent and professional district attorney's office.

## FLOUTING THE LAW

The two most controversial sections of the Rollins policy memo relate to directing her staff to work against federal immigration officers and her list of fifteen crimes she wouldn't prosecute.

The first is the "Immigration Consequences" section of her memo. The memo notes that the city's "foreign-born" population has increased in the last decade to about two hundred thousand, which accounted for 29 percent of the general population in Suffolk County.[727] The memo does not distinguish between those born outside of the United States who lawfully immigrated to the United States and reside in Suffolk County, and those living in the United States illegally and residing in Suffolk County. But read in context, it seems clear that this section of the Rollins memo is aimed at protecting the latter.

This section lays out two basic rules that prosecutors must follow.

First, prosecutors must work with immigration counsel "to factor into all charging and sentencing decisions the potential of immigration consequences."[728] The memo does not specify whether immigration counsel will be in-house, new hires, or immigration counsel identified by Rollins or her chiefs to assist prosecutors. What the memo really required, despite careful wording, was assistant district attorneys to adjust their charging decisions, not to best reflect a fair assessment of the defendant's misconduct but to avoid drastic immigration consequences under federal law.

Moreover, this policy forced onto prosecutors the obligation of defense attorneys: it's the latter's job to advise clients of the immigration-related consequences of a guilty plea or finding of guilt. A criminal is a criminal, regardless of his immigration status. There are all sorts of collateral consequences when a person commits a crime, from imprisonment, loss of a driver's license, limiting employment opportunities, to having to register as a convicted sex offender, to other terms and conditions of probation. The best way to avoid those consequences is to remain a law-abiding citizen.

Under Rollins's policies, prosecutors were also required to help convicted illegal aliens by agreeing to any motion they file, including a motion for a new trial if the alien files the motion after a conviction and if the prosecutor finds out that the defense counsel did not "provide accurate advice about immigration consequences."[729]

Second, if any employee of the Suffolk County District Attorney's Office "observes Immigration and Customs Enforcement (ICE) officers, Department of Homeland Security (DHS) officers, or other civil immigration authorities apprehending or questioning parties scheduled to appear in court about residency status in or around the public areas" of the courthouse, they were required to notify Rollins, her number two in command, or her general counsel.[730]

Rollins's policy was clearly aimed at preventing immigration officers from doing their job. She later joined forces with Middlesex County District Attorney Marian Ryan and filed suit against ICE, claiming that its agents and officers did not have the statutory authority to arrest illegal aliens in state courthouses for violations of federal immigration law.[731] In the fall of 2020, the First Circuit Court of Appeals ruled against Rollins and others and found that ICE could arrest illegal aliens in state courthouses.[732]

The other highly controversial section of her memo is the one dealing with the fifteen crimes you can commit in Suffolk County. Despite the fact that those fifteen crimes were passed by the state legislature and signed into law by the governor, Rollins unilaterally decreed that those fifteen categories of crimes should either be "outright dismissed prior to arraignment" or "where appropriate," "diverted and treated as a civil infraction." A decision to prosecute someone for committing any of these crimes had to be approved by a supervisor.

The "Rollins 15" were:

1. Trespassing

2. Shoplifting, including offenses that are essentially shoplifting but charged as larceny

3. Larceny under $250

4. Disorderly conduct

5. Disturbing the peace

6. Receiving stolen property

7. Minor driving offenses, including operating with a suspended or revoked license

8. Breaking and entering where it is into a vacant property or is for the purpose of sleeping or seeking refuge from the cold and there is no actual damage to property

9. Wanton or malicious destruction of property

10. Threats (excluding domestic violence)

11. Minor in possession of alcohol

12. Drug possession

13. Drug possession with intent to distribute

14. Resisting arrest where the only charge is resisting arrest

15. Resisting arrest if the other charges include only charges that fall under the list of charges for which prosecution is declined

In other words, while Rollins was the DA in Boston, a violent career felon could break into your home, be in possession of cocaine, plan to distribute that cocaine to others, and resist arrest after you call the police, and all the charges would be "outright dismissed," especially if the reason he broke into your house—and terrified your family—was because he wanted "to sleep" or was "seeking refuge" from the cold.

Her nonprosecution policies also contributed to undermining public safety in a subtle, less obvious yet pernicious way. By not prosecuting criminals for crimes that they actually committed, countless individuals ended up not having criminal records, even though they had, in fact, committed criminal acts. That lack of a true criminal record benefitted criminals by creating the false impression to law enforcement, employers, universities, or others that the person did not violate the law, when, in fact, he did. It is impossible to tell how many thousands or tens of thousands of times criminals violated those fifteen crimes in Suffolk County during Rollins's tenure.

When these same individuals end up committing future crimes, and a prosecutor decides to file charges against that person, that prosecutor will not be able to use the prior conviction(s), or underlying conduct from previous cases, to help convict the person and/or seek a sentence enhancement because, simply put, thanks to Rollins's policies, those prior cases won't exist. This distortion also helped criminals avoid the more serious consequences of a federal prosecution, since federal prosecutors in Boston would not have known to single out a given criminal as an especially bad offender requiring additional deterrence that comes with a federal charge. In many instances, the police didn't even file a police report against the person who committed the crime because they knew that Rollins had prohibited her prosecutors from filing charges against these criminals.

## THE GROUNDED-IN-SCIENCE HOAX

In the introduction to her policy memo, Rollins vowed to craft "new policies that would dramatically change the way we approach criminal prosecution" and pledged that this new approach would be "data driven" and "grounded in science." The "data-driven" and "grounded-in-science" mantra is one used by rogue prosecutors to convince the unsuspecting listener that their approach is based on peer-reviewed, solid facts and experience, including rigorous studies. We suspect that most people who hear those dulcet phrases simply take them at face value.

But they shouldn't, because their lax approach is neither data driven nor grounded in science from what we can tell.

Rollins touted a study by the National Bureau of Economic Research published in March 2021 called "Misdemeanor Prosecution"[733] arguing that the findings of that study prove that her approach of not prosecuting misdemeanors does not lead to an increase in crime. But when you read the study, and understand what the researchers looked at, you realize that Rollins's claims are overbroad at best. This study has also been touted by other rogue prosecutors.

The researchers were given access to data provided by the Suffolk County District Attorney's Office on the prosecution of nonviolent misdemeanor criminal complaints between 2004 and 2018. Rollins took office in 2018 but didn't even release her policy memo until 2019, so the data set the researchers used had nothing to do with Rollins's policies of not prosecuting fifteen misdemeanors. Furthermore, when you dig into the data, it applies mostly to first-time offenders—those who are most likely to change their behavior if given a chance to make amends for their crime. On top of that, the study defines the word "prosecution" in a constrained manner, such that a person arrested and then permitted to enter into a diversion program is not deemed to have been "prosecuted" under the researchers' definition. Yet, anyone with experience in the criminal justice system will tell you that the most viable candidates for diversion are first-time offenders who commit misdemeanors.

Moreover, while people who, as part of a plea agreement, enter into diversion programs may be able to get the charges dismissed if they successfully complete the program, that does not mean that they were not prosecuted. It just means that the prosecutor gave them a break by allowing them to enter into a diversion program rather than forcing them to plead guilty or go to trial. If they do not successfully complete the program, the charges can be reinstated.

Furthermore, the study has not been peer-reviewed, and the researchers had to sign a non-disclosure agreement forbidding them from sharing the data. How do we know that? Because when we asked the researchers for the underlying data in order to test their conclusion—that by not prosecuting some misdemeanors in Suffolk County, crime did not go up—they told us they could not give us the data because of the nondisclosure agreement. When we talked to the Suffolk County District Attorney's Office itself (after Rollins had left) to get them to release the data, they generally agreed, though the process has been laborious and ongoing, and they have not yet released the data in a usable format.

This fact didn't stop Rollins from penning a law review article where she asserted that her office "operates with a high level of transparency and openness and with a commitment to progressive prosecution."[734] In the same article, Rollins claimed that there is no road map for progressive prosecutors, yet she cited *The Progressive Prosecutor's Handbook* by David Alan Sklansky, a veritable road map for progressive prosecutors. She also conveniently failed to mention the radical, rogue policies being pushed by Fair and Just Prosecution and other rogue prosecutors such as Krasner, Foxx, Mosby, and by the time she wrote this article, Gascón, who wrote the ultimate rogue rule book for others to emulate.[735]

Rollins included the standard obligatory, yet false, assertion that the "old strategies" of traditional prosecutors did little to improve public safety.[736] Yet as we discussed in Chapter One, and the statistics show, crime rates have been dramatically falling for the past thirty years, and incarceration rates have been also falling drastically since 2008. It was the hard work, creativity, and actual progressive and new ideas from "traditional" prosecutors who, working with others, were the drivers of those successes.

# ROLLINS'S ROTTEN RELATIONSHIP WITH POLICE

George Floyd died at the hands of a police officer in Minneapolis, Minnesota, on Wednesday, May 20, 2020. Protests broke out across the country, including on the afternoon of Sunday, May 31, in Boston. According to news report, thousands (at first) of peaceful protestors gathered in Roxbury, Chinatown, and the South End and began marching toward the State House in downtown Boston.[737] At 9:08 PM, people began throwing objects at police officers who were on guard in front of the State House.[738] At the same time, the Boston Police Department tweeted out that "dangerous projectiles" were being thrown at their officers near Washington and Winter Streets in downtown Boston.[739]

Mayhem broke out on a massive scale. According to the *Boston Globe*, criminals "smashed store windows, vandalized cars, stole merchandise, [and] burned trash barrels."[740] The city had not witnessed this scale of violence in decades.[741] As helicopters circled overhead, police officers showed up in riot gear to prevent further violence. Store windows were smashed, including at a jewelry store and a Walgreens. People smashed doors at a shopping center on Winter and Washington Streets. Stores were looted. Police were assaulted. Twenty-one police vehicles were damaged (including being set on fire), and at least seven officers were transported to the hospital.[742] On tony Newbury Street, the high-end retail corridor in the city, looters smashed windows and made off with armloads of expensive merchandise.[743] At least forty people were arrested, but many others who committed crimes were not arrested.[744] The riots and violence were so bad that the NAACP of Boston and Black Lives Matter Boston both issued statements that they did not help to organize the protests.[745]

While the riots were happening, at 10:20 PM, Rollins tweeted out the following:[746]

**DA Rachael Rollins** ✔
@DARollins

Ahmaud Arbery. George Floyd. Breonna Taylor. Tony McDade. Christian Cooper. While we are being *murdered at will by the police & their proxy, privileged racists like Amy Cooper play the victim.* No more apologies. No more words. Demand action. Radical change now. Nothing less. 🖤

10:20 PM · May 30, 2020

**272** Retweets **31** Quote Tweets **1,235** Likes

On June 1, 2020, the day after the riots, Rollins appeared at a public event with the Boston mayor and police commissioner. Instead of calming the waters, appealing to reason, and decrying the violence committed against police officers and property in Boston, Rollins took the opposite approach. Rollins started her remarks by saying that she was "exhausted" because police officers "shoot us in the street as if we were animals."[747]

She then said that her "heart certainly does go out to the officers and civilians that were harmed last night," but later said that "this burning rage that you are seeing when you turn your TV on or you hear in my voice is real. People are fed up, and to the white community that is now waking up to see this rage: we have been telling you this forever…you didn't care until you saw a video."[748]

Building to her crescendo, Rollins noted that it was ironic for police to tell protestors not to be violent and be compliant when it's the police who "murder us with impunity."[749]

She ended her diatribe by saying that "buildings can be fixed," and she hopes that the injured officers will "make it out of it," but there are "lives that were stolen, and people that were lynched and murdered, and they are never coming back."[750]

To call her comments incendiary would be an extreme understatement. But they were typical of Rollins, who has not shown the temperament or judgment one should expect and require of an elected district attorney. The Boston Police Patrolmen's Association (BPPA) denounced her remarks, sending Rollins a letter in which they called her comments "dangerous, divisive, and wholly unwarranted" and then tweeted out the letter.[751] BPPA President Larry Calderone and Vice President Richard Withington wrote, "While you quickly and cavalierly label all police officers murderers, the fact is that BPD officers responded to violent attacks against them with courage and restraint."[752] They said by calling officers "murderers" she "undoubtedly incited violence" against police and put the lives of police officers at risk as they patrolled the streets of Boston.[753]

Rollins didn't back down. After reading the letter from the BPA, Rollins fired off another tweet[754] saying:

**DA Rachael Rollins** ✓
@DARollins                                    •••

You mean Anti-Police BRUTALITY. And did I somehow miss BPPA's letter denouncing the murder of George Floyd and calling for the immediate termination and prosecution of the 4 police that murdered him and/or watched and did nothing while he died? White fragility is real people. 🐴

Her comments and distasteful, racist tweets after the George Floyd riots were not a one-off.

During a public event in the summer of 2020 (during COVID-19), with the Suffolk County sheriff, a congresswoman, and other local leaders, Rollins bragged about her list of fifteen crimes that can be committed with impunity and told a whopper of a tale: that after COVID-19 hit, "every police department in the nation used my list of 15."[755]

There are over eighteen thousand police departments across the United States. We doubt most police departments have ever heard of Rachael Rollins, and virtually no DA's offices subscribe to her lawless approach, except those featured in this book and perhaps a small handful of others also headed by rogue prosecutors. Yet that didn't stop Rollins from declaring it.

During that event, Rollins also claimed that even though "[p]olice actually carry guns and can harm us in the name of their job," there is "no oversight with respect to whether they have complaints against them, whether they have lawsuits filed."[756]

That, of course, is not true in Boston, nor anywhere else in the country. Complaints are filed against police officers every day, in virtually every jurisdiction across the country. Police departments have internal procedures they must follow when an officer fires his or her weapon in the line of duty. Furthermore, lawsuits are filed against police officers and police departments across the country. But to the rogue prosecutor, the police are the criminals, traditional prosecutors are to blame for "mass incarceration," and defendants are the victims. It's what they believe and explains why they say what they say and act how they act.

Their raison d'être was the supposed systemic racism of the criminal justice system. And Rollins was the perfect acolyte.

## ROLLINS'S RACE-COLORED GLASSES

The goal of prosecutors around the country is—or should be—to do justice, regardless of the race, color, nationality, religion, gender, or creed of anyone involved in the criminal justice process. That seems like it should be a fairly uncontroversial statement. Those same characteristics have no bearing on someone's ability to effectively enforce the laws as a district attorney.

Any time racially charged statements are made by a prosecutor, it's problematic and inappropriate because he or she is supposed to be impartially seeking justice. And when those statements come from an elected district attorney, a person charged with representing the interests of everyone in his or her jurisdiction, that's especially concerning.

Unfortunately, Rachael Rollins didn't get the memo, as she made a number of offensive, racist comments as district attorney that normally would have resulted in disciplinary action or at least public opprobrium. But Rollins suffered no negative blowback from her comments and instead has repeatedly used the race and gender cards to argue that any criticism of her policies or approach to her job is because she is black and female.[757]

For prosecutors like Rollins, hurling the race card does two things: it cuts off any further criticism for fear of being called a "racist," and it absolves Rollins from having to defend her policies on their merits.

One of the best examples of Rollins using the race card occurred on January 12, 2020, at a symposium at the University of California Hastings College of the Law entitled "Progressive Prosecution and the Carceral State." Rollins was one of four panelists on the first panel, along with Chesa Boudin, Marilyn Mosby, and McGregor Scott.

Scott was the US Attorney for the Eastern District of California in Sacramento and had served in the same position during the George W. Bush administration. An experienced prosecutor, Scott was previously the twice-elected district attorney for Shasta County, California, and was a deputy district attorney in Contra Costa County, California.

When it was his turn to speak, Scott said that he considered himself to be a "progressive prosecutor" because he gets "up every day and [tries] to make the criminal justice system a better place, a more just place, a more fair place for everybody in this country…."[758]

In a cordial tone, Scott agreed with his fellow panelists that the criminal justice system needed more mental health treatment options and more drug treatment options. He also agreed that work needed to be done to establish reentry courses, to reach out to the community, and to address hate crimes.

Scott then said that he "respectfully disagreed" with the progressive prosecutor movement for four reasons: (1) Progressive prosecutors usurp the constitutional role of the legislative branch; (2) they fundamentally misunderstand the role of the county prosecutor; (3) in many districts their policies have caused violent crime rates to increase; and (4) all too often, victims are forgotten.[759]

As to his first point, Scott noted that progressive prosecutors choose not to prosecute entire categories of crime, including, but not limited to, refusing to enforce the death penalty. Those decisions are for the legislature, not for prosecutors.[760]

To drive home his second point, Scott, said, "The District Attorney does not represent the defendant." Quoting from the California District Attorneys Association website, Scott said, "The primary goal of the District Attorney is to protect the community he or she is elected to serve. District Attorneys represent the public and endeavor to improve public safety by prosecuting those who threaten the well-being of the community and its citizens by breaking the law. Ultimately, the DA strives to improve the community he or she represents by making it a better place to live for everyone."[761]

To back up his third point, that crime increases in cities with rogue prosecutors, Scott noted that in the last two years there has been a "general decline in the homicide rate across the United States." But then he pointed to the very thing that is the Achilles heel of the movement: rising crime directly related to rogue prosecutors' policies.

He said: "In Philadelphia, in 2018, the first year of Mr. Krasner's term as district attorney, homicides went up 11 percent, the highest rate in more than a decade. In 2019, they were up again, and as of this morning, year to date over 2019, they are up again another 26 percent."[762]

Turning to fellow panelist Marilyn Mosby, Scott then said, "In Baltimore, homicides have risen yearly since 2015. In 2019, the highest number of per capita murders in Baltimore's history took place. In a 24-hour period in January of this year, there were eight separate shootings with 12 people wounded and five people dead in Baltimore."[763]

As his fellow panelists became visibly agitated, Scott pressed his fourth point. Scott opined that "sweetheart deals" between rogue prosecutors and defense attorneys left victims as an afterthought. He noted the irony of the fact that in 2018, 92 percent of homicide victims in Philadelphia were black or Hispanic and that 93 percent of homicide victims in Baltimore were black.

If this had been a normal, evenly balanced debate, Scott's comments would have been analyzed, discussed, and, if possible, explained in context. But in a symposium that featured Boudin, Mosby, Rollins, Krasner, and Contra Costa County DA Diana Becton, those were fighting words. Added to the one-sided lineup was the matriarch of the prison abolition movement, Angela J. Davis, and Miriam Krinsky of Fair and

Just Prosecution, both of whom were also speaking at the symposium. Contrarian viewpoints, however politely offered or fact based, were not to be tolerated.

Rather than substantively responding to Scott's criticisms, Rollins instead launched an ad hominem attack on Scott saying, "I really don't have much time for more white men telling me what communities of color need, because they don't know."[764]

She went on to say, "As a person who was actually elected to my job, rather than appointed to do my job, due respect sir (nodding at Scott), and I will say as a person of less than one percent of people with actual melanin that are actually in this role, I'm really tired, and as a person who has been at the US Attorney's office as well, when US Attorneys who hover up here in the good air, talking about the communities that they only touch with Project Safe Neighborhoods or other things. There is no diversity in those offices, number one, certainly in Massachusetts where I served."[765]

Never mind the fact that Scott spent roughly fourteen years in local California district attorney's offices both as a deputy district attorney in Contra Costa County and as the twice-elected district attorney in Shasta County. But why let facts get in the way of a personal attack unrelated to the impersonal, yet substantive, criticisms leveled against two fellow rogue prosecutors, both of whom Rollins had traveled with domestically and overseas on junkets paid for by Fair and Just Prosecution.

Rollins's comments are, unfortunately, typical of rogue prosecutors, who refuse to debate the consequences of their dangerous and reckless policies on the merits, and instead attack anyone who dares to question their abuse of office—even, and perhaps especially, if that someone is a fellow prosecutor.

## CONDUCT UNBECOMING A CHIEF PROSECUTOR

Rollins has a penchant for sticking her foot in her mouth. People in the public eye, who give lots of interviews, stumble sometimes. But Rollins has taken this to a new level, calling into question whether these are mere malapropisms or glimpses into who she really is and what she really thinks.

In early May 2020, during an appearance on the local NPR station, Boston's WGBH, Rollins once again created a firestorm when she advised a caller who complained that his public defender hadn't called him back to call her office. Shortly after that call, a defense attorney from the state's Committee for Public Counsel Services (CPCS) called the show to say that "a defendant shouldn't be advised to contact a district attorney's office for help."[766] Rollins responded to the defense attorney by telling him she was simply trying to help the man get in touch with his attorney and that she often hears from "black, brown and poor" defendants that they are "treated poorly" by their lawyers.[767]

Rollins, unable to control herself, then said, "When you hear in my voice disgust or outrage about CPCS [the public defender's office] not calling people back, it's their 'overwhelmingly privileged' staff that aren't calling back poor, black, and brown people," suggesting that the public defender's office lacked diversity.[768]

The defense bar, understandably, immediately reacted to Rollins's inappropriate remarks. One public defender tweeted, "Thank you for undermining my work."[769] Another tweeted, "That comment you made about CPCS and about me as a public defender were so incredibly offensive—I'm shocked."[770] The chief counsel for CPCS, Anthony Benedetti, sent a public letter to Rollins which said her "insults" hit "directly at the heart of our organization."[771]

Was Rollins referred to the state ethics committee of the Massachusetts Bar? No. Was she subjected to any disciplinary or administrative action for her attack on the defense bar? No. And while she explained away why she said what she said later, she never actually apologized.

But acting in a manner unbecoming of a district attorney, or any attorney, was par for the course for Rollins.

Later that year, on Christmas Eve at the South Bay Center mall in Dorchester, Rollins once again caused a controversy. As a woman named Katie Lawson was driving her car in the parking lot and trying to merge in front of Rollins, Rollins pulled her car within inches of Lawson's car, put on her sirens, put on the car's strobe light, and then said to Lawson, "Do you want me to write you a ticket? Because I'll write you a ticket."[772]

Lawson was so shaken that she called the police department because of Rollins's abusive tone and behavior.

After word got out that the person who accosted Lawson was Rachael Rollins (who, obviously, was not a police officer), a local news crew drove to the parking lot of Rollins's house to ask her about Lawson's claim. But instead of calmly saying it was a big misunderstanding or explaining in a reasonable tone her side of the story, Rollins instead launched into a tirade against the news crew, saying on video camera, "So the rantings of a white woman get you here and scare my children?"[773] She told the news crew "get off our private property, and I swear to God, I'm dead serious. I will find your name." When Rollins asked the news crew how they found out where she lived, and they responded that it was public record, Rollins again threw down the race card saying, "So as a black women, in this moment in this country, you're going to put my f-cking house on screen?"[774]

What "moment" is Rollins referring to? We have a black vice president of the United States. We've had a black female secretary of state. We have a black female associate justice on the United States Supreme Court. Women outnumber men in college. A black woman ran the largest district attorney's office in the country until Soros paid for George Gascón to run against and defeat Jackie Lacey.

As you can see from the video, there were no children in the video or near Rollins, and no apartment or identifiable address was visible in the video. Yet Rollins went off half-cocked, acting irrationally and unhinged.

Rollins threatened to call the police, saying to the news crew, "We'll see how that works for you," a not-so-subtle suggestion that she, as the district attorney, would make sure they were prosecuted. This was a profoundly unethical threat from a sitting district attorney. And imagine for a moment how this story would have become instant national news if Rollins were a white male, if Katie Lawson had a been black female, and the news crew had been black. It would have been on the front pages of the *New York Times*, *Washington Post*, *Newsweek*, and the video would have been shown repeatedly on CNN, MSNBC, ABC, CBS, and other liberal networks.

But they all ignored this story.

After President Joe Biden was elected, we wrote about the possibility that he would nominate a rogue prosecutor to become a United States Attorney.[775] We were correct. On July 26, 2021, President Biden nominated Rollins to be the United States Attorney for the District of Massachusetts.[776]

As one might have expected, Fair and Just Prosecution arranged for a letter of support for Rollins from other rogue prosecutors.[777] Signatories to the October 2021 letter included Chesa Boudin, Kim Foxx, Kim Gardner, George Gascón, Larry Krasner, and Marilyn Mosby. The list also included a Who's Who of Soros beneficiaries, including: Diana Becton, DA for Contra Costa County, CA; Wesley Bell, DA for St. Louis County, MO; Buta Biberaj, DA for Loudoun County, VA; Parisa Dehghani-Tafti, DA for Arlington County, VA; Steve Descano, DA for Fairfax County, VA; Jose Garza, DA for Travis County, TX; Mike Schmidt, DA for Multnomah County (Portland) OR; and Andrew Warren, DA for the 13th Judicial Circuit (Tampa), FL.

In their open letter, they touted that they "have served alongside" Rollins and seen her "steadfast commitment to serving every member of her community." In total, sixty-six elected district attorneys signed the letter, the vast majority of whom either received funding from George Soros, his PACs, or acted consistent with the policies espoused by the rogue prosecutor movement and Fair and Just Prosecution's suggested policies.

Only one out of the nine elected district attorneys from Massachusetts who had actually served "alongside" Rollins signed the letter.[778] That speaks volumes.

## THE IMPACT

In an odd sort of way, Rollins can do less damage to the cause of justice and law and order as the United States Attorney than she could as an elected district attorney. As the United States Attorney, she doesn't have the leeway she did as the elected district attorney.

That's because there are ninety-three Senate-confirmed United States Attorneys spread across the country, each of whom ultimately reports to the attorney general of the United States. Those ninety-three US Attorney's Offices, where we both had the privilege of working (in Florida and Washington, DC) as assistant United States Attorneys, have, for the most part, uniform policies and practices with respect to prosecution, sentencing, and investigations.

And while the attorney general is appointed by the president of the United States and carries out the policy priorities within that administration, the vast majority of the work at the US Attorneys' Offices changes little between administrations. Whether the president is a Democrat or Republican, the Justice Department and its ninety-three United States Attorneys will investigate and prosecute bank robberies, fraud, embezzlement, money laundering, narcotics trafficking, and other federal crimes.

Furthermore, public statements by employees of the Justice Department tend to be highly scripted, not off-the-cuff missives like Rollins was accustomed to making as the local elected district attorney. In each United States Attorney's Office, there is a public affairs officer who knows the department's policies regarding what employees, including the United States Attorney, can or should say publicly.

Overall, Rollins has done an unremarkable job as the United States Attorney for the District of Massachusetts from what we have observed. Unlike her predecessor, Andrew Lelling, who uncovered the college admissions scandal and consistently indicted those who violated the law (including police officers), Rollins hasn't had any high-profile cases of note during her tenure, at least not so far.

That's not to say that Rollins hasn't made it into the press. In July 2022, she drove a government-issued vehicle with official plates to a Democratic National Committee fundraiser that featured First Lady Dr. Jill Biden, arguably a clear violation of the federal act that forbids federal government employees from using government equipment to engage in partisan political activity.[779] Soon after, Senator Tom Cotton publicly called on the DOJ inspector general to investigate this apparent misconduct.[780]

Rollins has also kept her habit of accusing law enforcement officers of racism. In July 2022, members of the Patriot Front, a far-right group, marched through downtown Boston. The march was mostly peaceful, though witnesses allege that the group got into a scuffle with a black onlooker along the route (this appears to still be under investigation). Following the event, local news sources questioned why local law enforcement authorities were not aware of the march in advance or present when it occurred. Rollins commented publicly after the march, "If this were a Black Lives Matter protest, would the response have been different?"[781] That is, she implied that if the marchers had been black instead of white, they would have been closely monitored by law enforcement from the start. There is, of course, no evidence to support this racist slander of local and federal law enforcement, which actively investigates radical movements of all races and creeds. But that did not stop Rollins from scoring points for herself at the expense of the police and agents who work with her.

Rollins has also abused her position to intimidate local municipalities and raise her own personal profile. In May 2022, Rollins sent a threatening letter to the Massachusetts town of Quincy, which at that time was in a dispute with the City of Boston over whether to reopen a bridge from Quincy to an island in Boston Harbor that, years earlier (but not now), had featured a drug rehabilitation center.[782] Rollins declared that she would open a federal investigation of Quincy's reluctance to reopen the bridge and to re-establish the center, accusing Quincy of violating the Americans with Disabilities Act. But there was no legally viable theory under that act, and Rollins identified none, nor did she identify a legal basis for the information and documents she demanded from the city.

Similarly, in June 2022, Rollins fired off a letter to the local town of Everett after local citizens publicly complained of racism in the city council.[783] There are obviously federal civil rights laws applicable to state government but, based on information that is currently public, there is no apparent federal violation in Everett, and again, Rollins has demanded documents and information from the town without any apparent legal basis for doing so. Rollins appears to be under the mistaken impression that any public accusation of racism, or other discrimination, by anyone, is sufficient to threaten the full weight of federal enforcement.

Rollins isn't the worst rogue prosecutor to have served as district attorney, especially compared to the seven others featured in this book. But her policies of not enforcing the law with respect to misdemeanors and immigration seem to be a thing of the past in Boston.

Massachusetts Governor Charlie Baker appointed Kevin Hayden to succeed Rollins and serve out the remainder of her term. A former assistant district attorney in the Suffolk County District Attorney's Office from 1997 to 2008, and chairman of the State's Sex Offender Registry Board, Hayden had the experience to run the medium-sized office.[784] When he was appointed, he said he would maintain Rollins's commitment to reducing the prison population, "not criminalizing poverty and drug addiction and not prosecuting low-level offenses."[785] But it quickly became clear that he didn't buy into many of the policies espoused by rogue prosecutors like Rollins.

A month after being appointed, Hayden announced that he would run for Suffolk County district attorney in the fall and said that although he is a reformer, he would not create a "decline to prosecute" list like Rollins but would look to alternatives to prosecution when warranted.[786]

Sounds like Hayden is on the right track to us.

Somebody who has never been on the right track when it comes to holding criminals accountable and protecting victims is the son of two domestic terrorists, Chesa Boudin.

# CHAPTER 8

# CHESA BOUDIN: SAN FRANCISCO

## A SON OF A RADICAL MOVEMENT WHO WAS RIGHTLY REJECTED BY VOTERS

*"It's either the mayor, it's the police, it's the pandemic, it's poverty, it's a host of other issues or agencies who are the issue and not Chesa," according to him.*

**Brooke Jenkins—Former San Francisco Deputy DA and Boudin's Successor as DA**[787]

*"I hope that people in the District Attorney's Office will shift their focus from some of the bigger issues and concern themselves with the unglamorous yet necessary work of public prosecution.... It's time to really take care of business at home instead of thinking about the national or state stage."*

**Bruce Chan—California Superior Court Judge**[788]

It's a tale of one city and of two calendar dates. On Tuesday, June 8, 2022, the voters of San Francisco kicked their rogue, radical district attorney, Chesa Boudin, out of office after only a little over two years on the job. But the wave of dissatisfaction with Boudin began in earnest at the end of his first year on the job, on New Year's Eve 2020 at the intersection of San Francisco's Mission and 2nd Streets. It was there that forty-five-year-old felon Troy McAlister, armed with a 9mm handgun with an extended magazine, high on meth and drunk, fresh off a robbery, driving a stolen car, ran a red light, T-boned another car, and hit and killed sixty-year-old Elizabeth Platt and twenty-seven-year-old Hanako Abe as they were trying to safely cross the street in a crosswalk.[789] Did McAlister try to help them? Of course not. Instead, he jumped out of the car, removed his shirt to make identifying him harder, and attempted to flee until a group of San Francisco citizens chased him down and detained him until police could arrive. His actions, though, shouldn't have come as a surprise.[790]

## BOUDIN'S SWEETHEART DEAL ENABLED MCALISTER

In fact, when Boudin first took office, McAlister sat in jail awaiting trial for a 2015 robbery, facing a potential life sentence under California's "Three Strikes Law" if convicted. As the *San Francisco Chronicle* noted, the "District Attorney's Office, then led by George Gascón, alleged three prior strikes for violent crimes,"[791] even with Gascón's well-known antipathy to the Three Strikes Law. The *Chronicle* went on to explain that his "prior strikes were for a robbery in 1995, an attempted carjacking in 2005 and another robbery in 2010. His record shows additional serious convictions in 2006 and 2007."[792] But that's really just a drop in the bucket when compared to his overall criminal record.

When arguing against McAlister's release from jail pending trial, one commentator noted that the "District Attorney's Office (then helmed by George Gascón) pointed out that McAlister was in possession of methamphetamine and committed a robbery as well as battery on a police officer, all while on parole. 'The defendant has a history of violent felony convictions dating back to 1995 and has sustained many misdemeanor convictions,' said the DA['s office]....."[793]

But after only two months on the job, Chesa Boudin dismissed the strikes, agreed to let McAlister plead guilty to second-degree robbery with a sentence of time served and to get out of jail on parole.[794] Not a bad deal for McAlister, whom Boudin once represented as his criminal defense attorney while serving as a public defender.[795]

Rather than staying on the straight-and-narrow following this sweetheart deal from Boudin, McAlister quickly fell into familiar patterns and engaged in an epic crime spree over the next several months. A little over two months after being released, San Francisco police officers arrested him on June 28, 2020, for burglary, possession of burglary tools, giving a false name to a peace officer, and a parole violation.[796]

On August 20, 2020, police officers arrested McAlister for vehicle theft, possession of stolen property, possession of narcotics for sale, and possession of narcotics paraphernalia.[797] On October 15, 2020, officers arrested McAlister for vehicle theft, possession of stolen property, possession of narcotics, cell phone theft, and a parole violation.[798] Less than a month later, San Francisco State University police arrested him for felony auto burglary and possession of burglary tools. One journalist who reviewed the records said that "[o]fficers ask[ed] why he [was] limping, and McAlister [said] he was shot during an argument a few months ago near his home…."[799] He was wearing a GPS ankle monitor when officers arrived. The shocked officers noted in their arrest report that "[t]his suspect is dangerous. He has 73 felonies and 34 misdemeanors in S.F. alone."[800] Still, only the next month on December 20, 2020, he was already out of jail and back on the streets when officers arrested him for possession of a stolen vehicle, two counts of possession of stolen property, possession of suspected methamphetamine, and possession of drug paraphernalia.[801]

For this laundry list of serious crimes, McAlister spent only a combined eleven days in jail![802] And Chesa Boudin did *not* charge him for *any* of these new crimes. Instead, he simply notified the state parole office.[803]

We know the rest of the story: less than eleven days later, another car theft, another armed robbery, and this time, two dead innocent victims. Hanako Abe's mother said that "I know in my heart Hanako would be alive today if Chesa Boudin properly handled the Troy McAlister case."[804] According to the *San Francisco Chronicle*, "Boudin said his agency, along with others, missed opportunities to intervene in ways that could have prevented the tragedy."[805] How many other "missed opportunities" by Boudin's office resulted in death or injury, misery and heartache? It's impossible to know.

## SON OF DOMESTIC TERRORISTS: BOUDIN'S BACKGROUND

To say that Boudin did not have the background of a typical prosecutor would be an understatement. In 1981, when Boudin was a baby, his parents, Kathy Boudin and David Gilbert, both members of the Weather Underground, a radical, militant Marxist organization, drove the getaway car following an armed robbery of a Brinks truck in New York in which a Brinks guard and two police officers were shot and killed.

His mother, Kathy, pled guilty to murder and robbery and spent nearly two decades in prison as a result of those charges. A jury convicted his father, David, of those same charges, and a judge imposed three consecutive terms of life imprisonment on him. Under the terms of the sentence, he wasn't supposed to be eligible for parole until he had served a minimum of seventy-five years behind bars. The sentencing judge said that the would-be robbers "hold society in contempt and have no respect for human life." He continued, saying that they "anticipated resistance and went about their task armed to the teeth." Gilbert showed no remorse, though, at sentencing. He read a statement denouncing the United States.[806]

While his parents were serving long prison sentences, Boudin was raised in Chicago by Bill Ayers and Bernardine Dohrn, co-founders of the Weather Underground who organized a series of bombings of public buildings to protest US involvement in the Vietnam War and who lived underground as fugitives for many years. Ayers has infamously said that "a lot of great people have been on [the FBI's 10 Most Wanted] list."[807] Boudin's mother was released from prison in 2003, while disgraced former New York governor, Andrew Cuomo, released Boudin's father from prison in late 2021 in one of his final acts in office.[808]

While condemning his parents' crime, Boudin initially embarked down a more predictable professional career path.[809] Before attending law school, Boudin lived in Venezuela and served as a translator to its then-dictator President Hugo Chavez.[810] After graduating from Yale Law School, Boudin served as a law clerk to two federal judges and then worked for several years in the San Francisco Public Defender's Office where, among other things, he argued on behalf of his clients that the California bail system is unconstitutional.[811]

In 2019, armed with feel-good talking points, Boudin ran for district attorney promising to end "mass incarceration," to end cash bail, to establish a unit to review alleged wrongful convictions, to aggressively prosecute police misconduct, and to refuse to provide any assistance to Immigration and Customs Enforcement officials.[812]

When Boudin first ran for office, and again shortly after he won, he pledged to end pretextual traffic stops, to stop charging gang enhancements, and to end the use of California's Three Strikes Law.[813] While Boudin said exceptions to these polices could be made for "extraordinary circumstances," apparently those didn't exist in Troy McAlister's case until after he had killed two people and incited a public backlash against Boudin's soft-on-crime policies that were emblematic of his administration from its very beginning. In November 2019, after winning his race to serve as the district attorney of San Francisco, Chesa Boudin said, "The people of San Francisco have sent a powerful and clear message: It's time for radical change to how we envision justice."[814] Well, if radical change is what the voters of San Francisco wanted, they certainly got it but experienced a severe case of buyer's remorse.

Declaring the death penalty to be "racist" and "immoral,"[815] Boudin agreed to resentence the one person on death row in his jurisdiction and pledged that his office would not seek the death penalty in any future cases.[816] He also signed a letter urging President Biden to end the death penalty in federal cases.[817]

Boudin announced when he was elected that he was going to deemphasize the prosecution of drug cases, so-called "quality of life" cases, and property offenses—the very opposite of the effective, proactive "broken windows" approach to law enforcement that worked so successfully in cities like New York.[818]

## DISASTROUS CONSEQUENCES OF BOUDIN'S POLICIES

What have the results been? Disastrous. Regarding drug offenses, the Tenderloin, which Boudin has described as "one of the most diverse" neighborhoods in San Francisco, is awash with human misery.[819] Drug dealers—mostly gang members—openly hawk their wares, usually with impunity. Drug addicts shoot up and collapse in the streets. First responders crisscross the neighborhood trying to revive overdosing individuals—sometimes they're too late. Children and families have to step over used needles and mounds of human feces. Shootings are not uncommon occurrences.

Things got so bad in the Tenderloin District that San Francisco's mayor, London Breed, declared a state of emergency.[820] One local newspaper said that the "neighborhood, just steps from City Hall, has been ground zero for drug dealing, overdose deaths and homelessness for years."[821] But rather than supporting Breed's "plan to flood San Francisco's Tenderloin neighborhood with police and crack down on drug dealers as well as people who use drugs in the open,"[822] Boudin opposed it, saying, "We can't arrest and prosecute our way out of problems that are afflicting the Tenderloin."[823] He even joined a press conference criticizing the plan, saying, "The last thing we need is to clog up every available court with a misdemeanor possession-of-a-pipe charge."[824] He went on to say that "arresting people who are addicted to drugs, jailing people who have mental health struggles, putting folks who are vending hot dogs or other food on the streets in cages will not solve these problems, and they are certainly not the only tools available...."[825] He criticized Mayor Breed's approach, saying that because the "chances of people [with addiction] even showing up to court is very small," in his view it wasn't a "useful approach" to the problem.[826]

It's odd—to say the least—for a prosecutor to oppose prosecuting criminals and to de facto legalize crime. But that's exactly what Chesa Boudin did, which puts him in good company with the other rogues in this book.

CBS News reported in late May 2021, that in 2020, Boudin's first year in office, "284 different individuals were arrested for selling drugs more than once. Of those, 89 were arrested three times, one individual was arrested seven times last year. Of the 30 or so individuals who make up the most repeat arrests, not a single one of them is currently in custody."[827]

Boudin took office on January 8, 2020. The year before he took office (2019), San Francisco had 441 drug overdose deaths. By the end of his first year in office, 711 San Franciscans had died from drug overdoses. And approximately 640 died in 2021.[828] Many of these deaths were concentrated in the Tenderloin District.[829] And in a sad twist of irony given that Boudin sold many of his radical policies as an effort to help members of the black and other minority communities, black San Franciscans have disproportionately borne the brunt of these increased overdose deaths.[830] In late 2021, a *San Francisco Chronicle* headline blared that "San Francisco's Overdose Epidemic Disproportionately Affects Black People, Data Shows."[831] In 2020, black San Franciscans had an accidental overdose death rate of 241.8 per one hundred thousand people compared to white San Franciscans who had an accidental overdose death rate of "only" 60.4 per one hundred thousand people.[832] In 2021, the overall overdose death rate among all San Franciscans increased, but the disparity between black San Franciscans and others became even more stark. In 2021, black San Franciscans overdosed at a rate of 418.2 per one hundred thousand people, while white San Franciscans overdosed at a rate of "only" 91.4 per one hundred thousand people. In other words, the overdose death rate among black San Franciscans almost, but not quite, doubled over the course of a single year.[833]

Fentanyl, a deadly synthetic opioid, which is fifty times more potent than heroin,[834] played a role in many of San Francisco's overdose deaths. That is understandable since a mere two milligrams can kill someone.[835]

In 2020, 73 percent of overdose deaths in the City of San Francisco involved fentanyl,[836] and in 2021, about 74 percent of overdose deaths in the city involved fentanyl.[837] Yet in all of 2021, local media reported that "the Office of District Attorney Chesa Boudin did not secure a single conviction for dealing the deadly opioid [fentanyl] for cases filed during 2021...."[838] In fact, in all of 2021, Boudin's office secured just three convictions for "possession with intent to sell" drugs.[839] Three—at a time when overdose deaths and misery were surging.

Boudin's feckless actions make George Gascón look good. Gascón was Boudin's immediate predecessor in San Francisco. In 2018, while he was the San Francisco DA, Gascón obtained ninety convictions for dealing drugs.[840] But Gascón's prosecutorial zeal for prosecuting possession with intent to distribute drugs waned when he became the Los Angeles County district attorney, as that crime is on Gascón's nonprosecution list.

## BOUDIN IS BFF WITH ILLEGAL ALIENS

The actual explanation for why Boudin's drug-dealing convictions were so low is more complicated and nefarious. Boudin allowed defendants involved in many cases in 2021 to plead to "accessory after the fact" charges instead of the possession with intent to distribute charges.[841] Importantly for Boudin—and the criminal defendants and their associates—the accessory after the fact conviction doesn't carry the same immigration-related consequences—likely deportation—as a possession with intent to distribute conviction[842]—meaning someone in the United States illegally can be convicted of accessory after the fact and still have a potential pathway to legal status.[843] One news outlet reporting on this legal sleight of hand move by Boudin wrote:

> The data show Boudin has aggressively expanded the deportation-conscious conviction process. When looking at a subset of narcotics cases that encompass dealing of fentanyl, heroin, cocaine and other narcotics, about 80% of Boudin's convicted cases were convicted of "accessory after the fact," compared to about a third under Gascon. The 56 cases that led to a conviction under Boudin represented about a quarter of Gascon's convictions in 2018 for the same category of crime.

The outlet went on to explain:

> The deportation-safe convictions are not just going to first-time offenders. In one example of using the "accessory after the fact" conviction for fentanyl dealing, a defendant was arrested and charged five different times from July 2020 through December 2021 for dealing fentanyl, heroin, meth and crack cocaine. According to court documents, evidence included a backpack with cash and "numerous" colorful plastic baggies of drugs. All five cases were consolidated for a January 2022 sentencing where he received two "accessory after the fact" felonies and served several months in jail.
>
> Another example in San Francisco involved a man with four separate drug dealing arrests [in 2021]

between June and December. He was charged with selling fentanyl, crack, more than an ounce of meth and over 14 grams of heroin. His ultimate conviction was for two misdemeanors for "accessory after the fact," and his sentence was two days in county jail, which he had already served.

If you are bothered by that, you should be. It's outrageous, especially since "taking office, Boudin [had] repeatedly cited Honduran nationals as a key group contributing to the organized drug trafficking taking place in the Tenderloin."[844] He even admitted that "a significant percentage of people selling drugs in San Francisco, perhaps as many as half, are here from Honduras."[845]

But similar to the way Larry Krasner speaks, Boudin prevaricated, opining that many of those individuals might have been victims of trafficking or crimes themselves.[846] A spokesperson for his office offered the excuse that "we're not talking about folks that are dealing in kilos, we're talking about folks that are dealing in grams...,"[847] which is of little comfort since only two *milligrams* can kill someone—meaning that someone possessing a single gram of fentanyl potentially has enough to provide a deadly dose to five hundred people.

## NO ONE'S PROPERTY IS SAFE IN BOUDIN'S SAN FRANCISCO

One of the more iconic and representative images people have when they think of crime in San Francisco is the myriad videos of brazen criminals smashing store windows and hauling away armloads of goods in broad daylight. San Francisco's well-documented problem has been shared via viral clips of vandalized cars, smash-and-grab robberies, and theft from local retailers.

Furthermore, car break-ins are so ubiquitous in San Francisco that some residents have taken to leaving notes in the cars informing would-be robbers that there's nothing of value inside. Others roll down their windows, unlock their doors, or even leave their trunks open.[848] The *San Francisco Chronicle* maintains a close-to-real-time Car Break-In Tracker to keep citizens informed.[849]

By the end of 2021, citizens of San Francisco had reported 20,663 thefts from vehicles to the San Francisco Police Department.[850] That's a 39 percent increase in the number of reported thefts from vehicles from the previous year (2020).[851] What's even more shocking is that the available numbers for 2022 look even worse. As of March 31, 2022, San Franciscans had reported 4,724 thefts from vehicles. That's a 36 percent increase in the number of those thefts as of the same date in 2021, which was already an extremely high number.

"Smash-and-grabs" at retail stores became commonplace, too, with a number of them filmed by incredulous shoppers.[852] These thefts have prompted some stores to put all their items behind locked display cases, a mere annoyance to many thieves who have no problem breaking the glass enclosures. National drugstore chain Walgreens reports that at one point it had spent thirty-five times more on security guards at its San Francisco stores than in other cities where it operates[853] and recently announced that it was closing seventeen stores in the city.[854]

Target stores are now closing early because of rampant shoplifting at certain locations.[855] Boudin's response? It happens in other cities too.[856]

In a softball *New York Times* interview, the reporter pushed back against some of Boudin's claims. The reporter said, "I brought up property theft in San Francisco and you made a comparison with Manhattan. But Target *is* limiting its hours in your city, and Walgreens *is* closing stores explicitly because of too much theft. There's also those viral videos of flash-mob robberies."[857]

Boudin responded, "Sorry, David [the reporter], you're saying you didn't see videos of flash-mob burglaries in other cities?" to which the reporter responded, "I haven't, no."[858] Boudin, like Mosby and Foxx, when confronted with inconvenient facts, block and bridge and blame anyone but themselves or their policies.

Regarding the tsunami of retail thefts in San Francisco, which Boudin did nothing about because he refused to prosecute misdemeanor theft cases, Boudin proceeded to blame companies like Walgreens or Target for the thefts in their own stores. Boudin said that:

> "When it comes to retail theft in particular is that stores like Walgreens have decided it's not in their

interest to have their security detain shoplifters. The reason is that the police almost never make it to the stores in response to a shoplifting call in time to effectuate an arrest. They rely on store security to hold people long enough for the police to arrive. If Walgreens or Target or any other store decides that it's too risky, in terms of people getting injured or racial-profiling lawsuits or disturbing other customers—if those costs outweigh the benefit of having their staff make arrests, how do they expect me to prosecute? If the police can't make arrests, to then say it's the district attorney's fault simply doesn't add up."[859]

So what happened to one of those cases that Boudin did prosecute, the case of Jean Lugo Romero? Few people may know his name, but it's very likely many people have seen the viral video of him riding his bicycle through a Walgreens, stuffing black trash bags full of merchandise, and then casually rolling out of the store as shocked—and disgusted—bystanders look on.[860] His punishment for pleading guilty to his crimes? Time served.[861]

As of October 2021, his charging rates, and conviction rates, for theft and petty theft were lower than George Gascón's when he served as San Francisco's DA.[862] As one commentator noted, "There's a pretty clear answer to why police aren't rushing out to arrest shoplifters in these cases. It's probably because they a) don't have the manpower for it and b) know it's a given that anyone they arrest will be released within hours and probably only charged about 1/3 of the time. Why waste their time on cases they know the DA won't prosecute?"[863]

The police in San Francisco have little to no incentive to arrest people for theft. Not only will the DA not file charges in most cases, but also if the suspect resists arrest, the DA won't charge the suspect for resisting arrest. Why put your life on the line for Boudin who, like Uncle Larry, is really more of a "public defender with power" than a real DA?

# OTHER EXAMPLES WHERE BOUDIN'S POLICIES HAVE WREAKED HAVOC

Boudin spoke at a Columbia University conference only a few months after taking office. He said that career prosecutors "don't want to believe that for their entire life, their entire career, they've been doing harm." He continued that they "don't want to believe that an outsider like me, a career public defender, knows better than they do how to be a prosecutor, or how to be a prosecutor that helps to promote public safety."[864] Of course, Boudin could not point to any of his own experiences to support his statement that he knew better than the career prosecutors who had much more experience than him. After all, he had never before served as a prosecutor. He wanted people in his office, like former public defenders, who, in his words, know "that the person they're prosecuting is a three-dimensional person."[865] He wanted people in his office who understood the harms of racial profiling and the harms of wrongful convictions. He believed it was hard for experienced prosecutors to do this since he believed they had been using their power wrongfully or for bad purposes. While he claimed his approach could accomplish his goals while still protecting public safety, he obviously didn't promote public safety with his handling of the Troy McAlister case. Sadly, there are other examples, like the case of Jerry Lyons.

Lyons had a record dating back to 2007, including charges of attempted robbery, burglary, evading police, driving a stolen vehicle, weapons charges, shoplifting, trespassing, and drug charges.[866] In December 2020, Lyons, driving a stolen car, was observed running a red light, making an illegal U-turn, driving over a traffic median, and weaving between two lanes. He was on supervised release for a theft case at that time. He was arrested for driving a stolen car and driving without a license and on suspicion of driving while under the influence of drugs and alcohol. Boudin's office insisted on getting the positive lab results back before charging Lyons, who had been released by the time those lab results were returned. But the office had more than sufficient evidence of Lyon's criminality, especially given his prior record and the fact that he was driving a stolen vehicle. The latter charge alone was sufficient to hold Lyons in jail pending trial. But that kind of commonsense appeal to safety of the community did not exist in Boudin's office while he was the DA.

On January 22, 2021, an intoxicated Lyons, driving a stolen truck, ran a red light and plowed into eight cars, killing twenty-six-year-old Sheria Musyoka and severely injuring three others. That's not promotion of public safety. Musyoka, a married father of a three-year-old son, had moved to San Francisco only ten days prior to his death.[867] His wife said they had "saved up every penny [they] could for" the move so that they could "find a nice neighborhood that was safe."[868] Musyoka had legally immigrated to the United States from Kenya and had graduated in the top 3 percent of his class at Dartmouth College. His company described him as "brilliant, thoughtful, and kind," and as someone who "brought such a positive influence to the world."[869] His wife, Hannah, made clear who she blamed for his death. When asked, she answered with a "strong and clear" voice, simply, "The DA."[870]

Then there's the case of James McGee.[871] McGee bludgeoned sixty-two-year-old cab driver Arif Mohammed Qasim to death with a pipe.[872] When officers arrived, they "located Qasim lying on the sidewalk in a pool of blood with massive blunt force trauma injuries to his head [and] face…. On a nearby wall, they also discovered a white piece of matter that appeared to be from 'either the brain or skull' of Qasim, who had been beaten beyond recognition, his face caved in and his teeth lodged in his brain."[873]

Originally charged with murder and resisting a police officer, McGee faced a minimum sentence of twenty-five years in prison.[874] But Boudin allowed him to plead out to involuntary manslaughter—unintentionally killing someone. He ended up serving only a little over a year in jail for this crime and was released the day of his sentencing with time served.[875] Why? There was no explanation from Boudin's office. How is this remotely close to justice? It's not.

Boudin's office has also entered into other indefensible plea bargain agreements. For example, it was recently reported that an individual who robbed thousands of dollars of camera equipment from a professional photographer at gunpoint was allowed to plead guilty to a misdemeanor noise violation.[876] The prosecutor in that case was a recent Boudin recruit, having spent the previous seven years working as a public defender. Other criminals clearly got the message because robberies of film crews in the area continued.

In March 2021, a local news crew was out working on a report of recent brazen car break-ins when around 12:37 in the afternoon a car pulled up next to them, three criminals hopped out, and one put a gun in the cameraman's face telling him, "We're taking the camera."[877] A year later, in March 2022, criminals robbed a Canadian film crew in broad daylight in a local park.[878] The suspects were caught after committing a robbery in Oakland, and both cases will be prosecuted by the Alameda County district attorney.

Like all the Soros-financed or inspired rogue prosecutors, Boudin pledged not to prosecute "quality-of-life" crimes[879] and instead focus on prosecuting more serious offenses. But that promise is illusory. And it should be evident that the only persons whose "quality of life" is improving are criminals. Criminals don't worry a bit about being arrested, much less about going to jail for their crimes. Victims, including small and large business owners, people who own cars, homeowners, apartment dwellers, and law-abiding residents of the city, are suffering and in danger because of Boudin's reckless and irresponsible abrogation of his duty to faithfully enforce the criminal laws on the books.

## BOUDIN'S REFUSAL TO DO THE BASIC BLOCKING AND TACKLING OF PROSECUTION

But in addition to pushing his rogue, radical policies, Boudin showed an inability, or unwillingness, to do the basic blocking and tackling of prosecuting cases.

Two days after taking office, Boudin fired seven of the most seasoned prosecutors in his office.[880] According to reports, he said that "the actions were necessary to carry out the progressive policies he campaigned on."[881] As of October 2021, San Francisco's local NBC affiliate reported that there are "at least 51 lawyers at the San Francisco District Attorney's Office who have either left or been fired since Boudin took office in January 2020... that's about a third of the department's attorneys now gone."[882]

The *San Francisco Chronicle* reported that one "of San Francisco's recent departures [was] Xochitl Carrion, an out queer Latina who left the general felonies unit…after six years in the office. She said cases changed hands so often because of high turnover that she worried about inheriting troubled cases: She might assume responsibility for previous mistakes and potentially even be disbarred."[883]

Her worries were well-founded.

In one case, Boudin's office lost a binder full of evidence and grand jury records. The result? A twenty-nine-count indictment against three individuals who had caused tens of thousands of dollars of damage to businesses in San Francisco had to be dismissed.[884]

It was this frustration that led Superior Court Judge Bruce Chan to openly criticize Boudin and his office from the bench for their handling of cases.[885] Though Chan later apologized, his criticisms about the office's disorganization were blistering.[886] He said, "I cannot express in any more certain terms my disapproval of the manner in which the Office of the District Attorney is being managed…Not to make light of the situation, but you can't run an airline this way."[887] He continued, "I hope that people in the District Attorney's Office will shift their focus from some of the bigger issues and concern themselves with the unglamorous yet necessary work of public prosecution…. It's time to really take care of business at home instead of thinking about the national or state stage."[888]

If one sitting Superior Court judge was brave enough to say that on the record, you can be sure that other judges, his colleagues, felt the same way but were unwilling to say any such thing on the record. And unlike the DA's office in Los Angeles, where deputy district attorneys are protected under county civil service rules and thus free not only to speak out publicly against their boss, or even sue their boss—like the Association of Deputy District Attorneys for Los Angeles County (ADDA) did to their boss George Gascón—deputy district attorneys in Boudin's office are all at-will employees. At-will employees in DA offices can be fired for any reason whatsoever, cannot speak out publicly about their boss, and are not members of a union.

# RECALL CAMPAIGN AND ITS IMPLICATIONS

The entire rogue prosecutor movement is built on at least two fundamentally flawed premises: (1) that the entire criminal justice system is systemically racist and (2) that to fix the system, you have to reverse-engineer and dismantle the criminal justice infrastructure. Many of the rogue radical policies of not prosecuting crimes, of not holding criminals accountable, and of not seeking justice for victims is supposedly designed to help black and minority members of the community. Boudin believed that charging certain sentencing enhancements—such as gang related ones—unfairly punished black and Latino community members.[889] But one of the former prosecutors who left his office, herself black and Latina, said that "Boudin's blanket policy bothers her because he touts it as benefiting Black and Latino communities when the victims of gang crimes are usually Black and Latino...."[890]

San Franciscans recognized that Boudin's policies failed them, too, and acknowledged as much by recalling him from office. While Boudin sought to blame the bipartisan recall on Republicans,[891] which is ironic because 62.9 percent of San Francisco's voters are registered Democrats while only 6.7 percent are registered Republicans,[892] the truth is that average San Franciscans saw that his radical policies of non-prosecution did not work.[893] It turned out that San Franciscans not only want to live in a city that is safe and compassionate but also a city where criminals are held accountable for their crimes, where drug addicts receive treatment, and where store owners, shoppers, millennials, and city dwellers can live without the constant fear of being a crime victim.

And like rats fleeing a sinking ship, his original left-leaning billionaire backers are now trying to put distance between themselves and Boudin. An operative from the public relations firm BerlinRosen, which represents George Soros, contacted a news outlet, the *Washington Free Beacon*, shortly after Boudin's recall to object to their characterization of him as a "George Soros darling" or a "Soros prosecutor."[894] As the *Free Beacon* noted, while it's true that Soros never directly contributed to Boudin's campaign, Boudin was intimately connected with many third-party groups that were funded by Soros directly or indirectly. To say that

Boudin is not affiliated with him, or at the least, inspired by his policies toward rogue prosecutors is just not true.

But as we wrote in our first major research paper on the subject, the Achilles heel of the movement is rising crime rates.[895] Soros, his supporters, and the larger progressive prosecutor movement must realize that if San Francisco voters can recall Chesa Boudin, voters in any city can potentially recall that city's rogue prosecutor.

They must also recognize that Boudin's recall could be a major impediment to their efforts to reverse engineer the criminal justice system and build a new one based on their warped view of justice.

Even though it was his policies that sunk him with the voters, Boudin initially refused to rule out running again in the future to reclaim his position as San Francisco's district attorney,[896] though he seems to have later backed off that position. Regardless, Boudin's recall shows that the movement itself, although well-funded, is on rocky ground with voters across the country.

Voters in Baltimore also had enough of their rogue prosecutor, Marilyn Mosby. Like Kim Gardner, she was a horrible leader, ethically challenged, and pursued policies that led to a massive spike in violent crime that took the "C" out of "Charm City."

# CHAPTER 9

# MARILYN MOSBY: BALTIMORE

## IN WAY OVER HER HEAD

*"The City of Baltimore is a poster child for the basic failure to stop lawlessness. There's a prosecutor who refuses to prosecute crime and there's a revolving door of repeat offenders who are being let right back onto the streets to shoot people again and again."*[897]

**Larry Hogan (R)—Then-Governor of Maryland**

*"Baltimore's crime problem stinks.
Marilyn Mosby is the stinkee."*[898]

**Stephen J. K. Walters—Chief Economist,
Maryland Public Policy Institute**

*"Right now people do not feel safe in the communities that they live and work."*[899]

**Eric Costello (D), Baltimore City Council**

Usually when you break up with someone, you lick your wounds, regroup, seek solace from your friends, and then get back out on the market and start dating again. It's not fun, but it's part of life. We've all been there.

But not Luther Trent. If he couldn't have Alexis, then no one was going to have her. Alexis had enough of his abuse, his demeaning comments and texts, and his behavior, which was becoming more and more concerning, bordering on violent.

No doubt, her girlfriends had told her to break up with him many times, but she didn't listen at first. He would change, right? But he didn't.

Finally, in March 2021, she called the Baltimore Police on Trent. She had a video of him this time, and things had gone too far. Alexis petitioned the local court, which issued an Order of Protection for her against Trent.

Alexis and her two roommates lived in the Bolton Hill section of the City of Baltimore, about a ten-minute drive north from Baltimore's famous Inner Harbor and ten minutes south of the Baltimore Zoo. The protection order forbade Trent from coming into close contact with her and forbade him from entering her residence in the 1900 block of Linden Avenue.

Around 1:30 AM on May 21, 2021, two months after the Order of Protection was issued, Trent decided to take matters into his own hands. Trent, armed with a can of gasoline, went to the house where Alexis and her roommates lived, sneaked around the back of the townhouse, poured the gasoline on the side of the house and under the wooden deck, and lit it. Alexis and her roommates fortunately escaped the burning house before it was engulfed in flames.

Like a lot of arsonists, Trent hung around to see his handiwork. He didn't leave the scene for good but instead showed up after the fire department and arson detectives arrived.

Trent was shirtless and wore jeans and was acting nervous. He spoke to a detective at the scene of the arson and identified himself to the detective as "Trey Johnson." He told the detective that his cousin lived in the residence. After speaking to the detective, "Trey Johnson" drove off in a two-door black Honda Accord.

The detective, who later interviewed Alexis and watched the video she took of Trent two months earlier, realized that "Trey Johnson" was actually Luther Trent. Alexis confirmed that Luther Trent drove a two-door black Honda Accord.

Law enforcement found video surveillance that showed a man walking up the street toward the residence at approximately 1:30 AM, just prior to the fire. A couple of minutes later, just after the fire was set, an individual, who appeared to be shirtless, was seen running down the street, away from the residence. Other video surveillance footage showed a black two-door Honda circling the area after the fire.

Trent was arrested and charged by Marilyn Mosby's office—the Baltimore City State's Attorney's Office—with eighteen felonies, including three counts of attempted murder and arson.

Then, seemingly out of nowhere, rogue prosecutor Marilyn Mosby authorized a plea deal with Trent. In exchange for a plea of guilty to the arson charge, Mosby okayed a ten-year suspended sentence and time served—which meant that Trent was let out of jail after a mere six months of incarceration.

On January 11, 2022, Trent, then out of jail and ever the criminal mastermind, was interviewed by Mikenzie Frost, a politics reporter for Fox 45 Baltimore.[900] In the interview, Trent expressed surprise at the overly lenient plea deal he received and the slap on the wrist, saying, "I was just charged with 18 different counts, that was dropped to 10, that was dropped to one. When I shouldn't be out right now. I disrupted somebody's life. I traumatized somebody because of how I felt in a situation. Personally, yes, I want to be out but principally, no I shouldn't be out because I could have done a lot more damage than I did. I was expecting to get time. People who were in that situation, they should expect to get time."[901]

In that same interview, Trent admitted that he poured gasoline on the side of his ex-girlfriend's house in an attempt to kill her, saying, "The love of my life is in Baltimore. I know where she lives at and I can't even talk to her. Can't say nothing to her. In my head, it was some Romeo and Juliet type of thing—if I can't have you, no one can have you, at least in Baltimore."[902]

In what should have gotten Mosby's attention, Trent said that his plea deal sends the wrong message to criminals in Baltimore, noting, "That tells…anybody that 'I can go shoot somebody or I can attempt to shoot somebody, and I'll be completely fine.' It would empower me because I would be like, okay, this man just shot somebody, just blew his head off and he's just out walking free. I can do anything I want. I can rob somebody, I can shoot somebody, I can do anything I want."[903]

When Alexis heard about the sweetheart deal Mosby gave to Trent, she told the media, "I was in shock. I didn't really know what to feel. It doesn't seem like justice was served, it feels like a political game, but not my justice."[904] Alexis said that a prosecutor from Mosby's office called her right before the plea deal was finalized "as a professional courtesy," but that her objections to the deal didn't matter to the prosecutor.[905]

This is an all-too-common occurrence and feature of the rogue prosecutor movement: the blatant trampling of victims' voices and rights in the judicial process. All of their policies and actions inure to the benefit of criminals and revictimize the real victims in the criminal justice system. Alexis's case is just one of countless examples.

The problem for Mosby in this particular case was that when the victims found out about the plea deal, and the judge presiding over Trent's case found out that the victims hadn't been afforded the right of providing their victim impact statements, the entire scheme fell apart.

Alexis and her roommates filed a motion with the judge to withdraw Trent's guilty plea. The judge granted their motion, ordered Trent back into custody, and reinstated the original charges against Trent.

On February 3, 2022, the United States Attorney's Office for the District of Maryland filed a criminal complaint against Trent in federal district court, alleging one count of malicious destruction of property used in and affecting interstate commerce by fire, in connection with the arson at Alexis's rental home. If convicted of the federal charge, Trent would receive between five to twenty years in federal prison.

This is the same United States Attorney's Office that has indicted Marilyn Mosby for committing several federal crimes, discussed later in this chapter. Mosby, through her attorneys, filed a motion in federal district court to get the US Attorney and the assistant United States Attorney kicked off the case, claiming that the charges against her are racially motivated. The federal district court judge handling Mosby's case denied the motion.

The United States Attorney for the District of Maryland is Erek L. Barron, the first black man to serve in that position in the history of the state. Barron had served as local prosecutor in Prince George's County, Maryland, and in Baltimore City, and in the United States Department of Justice's Criminal Division. He was also a former counsel and policy advisor to then-Senator Joseph R. Biden Jr. on the United States Senate Judiciary Committee's Subcommittee on Crime and Drugs, where he focused on law enforcement, crime policy, and oversight of the United States Department of Justice. Barron was nominated by President Biden to serve as the US Attorney for Maryland and was confirmed unanimously to that position on July 26, 2021.[906]

It's rare for a federal prosecutor to step in and bring charges against a local criminal. In order for a federal prosecutor to bring charges against anyone, they have to find a violation of federal law. But since the dawn of the rogue prosecutor movement, it is becoming increasingly common for United States Attorney's Offices to bring federal charges, if they can, against local criminals when their local rogue prosecutor is failing to keep the community safe.

As one local Baltimore defense attorney remarked after the feds charged Trent with arson, "I think what's obvious in the Luther Trent case is that the federal government stepped in to do what the Baltimore City State's Attorney's Office did not."[907]

On June 30, 2022, Trent pled guilty to one count of malicious destruction of property by fire in federal district court.

## AN AVOIDABLE MURDER OF A POLICE OFFICER

Sadly, another victim of Mosby's policies suffered his fate not in the inner city of Baltimore but instead in the picturesque town of Pittsville, which is nestled on Maryland's flat Eastern Shore, just outside of Salisbury, Maryland, only a twenty-minute drive to the Atlantic Ocean.

In June 2022, the word got out quickly that a stranger was in town. That stranger was twenty-year-old Austin Jacob Allen Davidson, a fugitive and convicted felon wanted by law enforcement across several counties in Maryland.

Davidson's life of crime started early. He has twenty juvenile arrests alone, starting in November 2016. That's on top of his ten adult arrests.

In 2019, he was charged at seventeen years old as an adult for armed robbery. On that occasion, Davidson put on a face mask, drove up to the drive-through window of a McDonald's restaurant in Northeast Baltimore, where he used to work. He pointed a semi-automatic handgun at the drive-through worker, who handed Davidson the entire cash register drawer, which contained over $1,100.

Two weeks later, Davidson went back to the same restaurant to rob it again. The same employee was there, recognized Davidson, and asked him why he pointed a gun at her two weeks ago. Davidson replied, "Because I can." She alerted her coworkers, and together they grabbed Davidson and restrained him until the police arrived.

A subsequent search of Davidson's residence turned up McDonald's receipts from the day of the robbery, as well as a mask and gloves he allegedly wore that day.

Armed robbery is generally considered a crime of violence, including in Maryland. Conviction for armed robbery carries a maximum possible penalty of twenty years under Maryland law, and use of a handgun during the commission of a robbery carries a minimum of five years in state prison.

But since armed robbery involving the use of a handgun was not apparently considered a serious offense in Marilyn Mosby's office, she allowed Davidson to plead guilty to one count of armed robbery, dropped the attempted robbery, somehow avoided the mandatory minimum, and made sure he got probation before judgment (PBJ). Why he wasn't sentenced to the mandatory minimum five-year sentence for using a handgun during the robbery is not known. Mosby's office was silent at the time of the sentencing, and only later, after Davidson killed a law enforcement officer, did Mosby try to blame the judge for the overly lenient sentence.

PBJs, also referred to by local practitioners in Maryland as "peanut butter and jelly sandwiches" because they are so childish and forgiving, are common plea offers in Mosby's office, even for serious crimes. Typically, to get a sentence of PBJ, the defendant agrees to plead guilty to one or more charges. In exchange, the prosecutor agrees not to ask for jail time, the judge sentences the defendant to a period of time in jail or prison, but then suspends the sentence for a period of months or years. As long as the defendant does not commit any crimes during that period of the suspended sentence (essentially a probationary period), then at the end of that time, the defendant's record with respect to that crime is wiped clean. However, if a defendant who gets a PBJ commits a criminal offense during the period of the suspended sentence, then the government may ask the judge to revoke the defendant's suspended sentence and impose the maximum period of incarceration.

Offering a PBJ is an easy way for a prosecutor to get rid of (give away) a case, and a no-brainer for a defense attorney and defendant, as there are rarely any negative consequences in the future, even if the defendant commits further violations of the law.

Over the next two years, after receiving a PBJ plea deal from Mosby, Davidson committed numerous other crimes and suffered several convictions in various counties in Maryland. Each arrest and conviction are entered into the state database, which is available to law enforcement personnel, including prosecutors in Mosby's office. It was only after Davidson had repeatedly violated the terms of his probation that Mosby's office requested a warrant for Davidson's arrest. But by then, it was too late.

On September 16, 2021, while on probation for the armed robbery, Davidson was arrested in Worcester County, Maryland, and charged with possession with intent to distribute marijuana, possession of marijuana, and possession of forged currency. Lenwood Wright, his parole and probation officer, notified Mosby's office of the new charges the next day.

Mosby's office could have asked the court to revoke Davidson's probation but did nothing.

On February 11, 2022, Davidson, pursuant to a plea bargain, pled guilty to possession of marijuana in Worcester County Circuit Court and was sentenced to six months—all of which was suspended but for one day—and one year of probation. Five days later, Lenwood Wright notified Mosby's office of this development. Mosby did nothing.

Less than a month later, on March 7, 2022, Davidson was arrested in Maryland for driving without a license, failure to attend a required driver improvement class, and other driving infractions. On March 16, 2022, Wright notified Mosby's office about this. Mosby did nothing.

Ten days later, on March 16, 2022, Davidson was arrested and charged with second-degree assault in Worcester County. Before Wright could even update Mosby's office, Davidson was charged with malicious destruction of property and petty theft for another incident on April 18, 2022, in Wicomico County. Wright once again notified Mosby's office.

In April 2022, Davidson, still on the loose, was arrested in Ocean City, Maryland, a beach town, for assault. His case was set for trial on May 18, 2022, but he failed to appear.

ZACK SMITH AND CHARLES D. STIMSON

In May 2022, in Salisbury, Maryland, Davidson was charged with second-degree burglary and possession of a firearm by a convicted felon. He was in possession of a rifle and ammunition. Second-degree burglary under Maryland law is where a person breaks and enters into a building that is not his home with the intent to commit theft, arson, or a violent crime. It is a fifteen-year felony. Possession of a firearm by a convicted felon in Maryland disqualifies that person from ever owning a gun again, and carries a minimum prison sentence of five years and a maximum sentence of fifteen years. Mosby's office finally took action and requested a warrant for Davidson's arrest, which was issued.

By June 2022, Davidson had outstanding arrest warrants from Baltimore City, Wicomico County, Worcester County, and Somerset County—all in Maryland.

On Sunday, June 12, 2022, the Wicomico County Sheriff's Office heard from a tipster that Davidson was in an apartment complex in the small town of Pittsville. The county sheriff, Mike Lewis, dispatched two of his officers to the complex, including Wicomico County Sheriff Deputy First Class Glenn Hilliard, a black forty-one-year-old married man with three children.

Hilliard, originally from New Jersey, attended the University of Maryland Eastern Shore and then joined law enforcement immediately out of college.

The two deputies searched the area in their police cruisers. They did not find Davidson, but they decided to remain in the area.

Eventually, Hilliard saw Davidson peeking out from under a stairwell. Davidson saw Hilliard and started walking away from the officer at a quick pace. Hilliard put his vehicle in park, exited the vehicle, and started chasing him on foot.

While chasing Davidson, Hilliard repeatedly told him to halt and yelled that he would deploy his taser. But Davidson kept running. Hilliard yelled, "Taser, taser." Davidson, who had a backpack over his shoulder, stopped, reached into the backpack with his right hand, produced a semi-automatic 9mm handgun with a thirty-round, fully loaded magazine, and turned. Davidson applied a two-handed grip to the gun, pointed the red-dot, laser-sighted gun at Hilliard, and squeezed off three rounds.

One round hit Hilliard in the shoulder, and another smashed into his forehead, dropping him instantly. He died later that day in a local hospital.

The entire episode was caught on Hilliard's body camera.

Dozens of law enforcement officers fanned out to locate Davidson, who eventually was captured without incident later that day. He is now facing first-degree murder charges, among others.

Typically, law enforcement officers in Hilliard's situation would pull their weapons during a foot pursuit of a known and dangerous suspect like Davidson. But Hilliard did not because of a recent change in the law. That change was arguably the difference between life and death for Deputy Hilliard.

On April 11, 2021, during the last minute of the legislative session for the year, the Maryland legislature passed the "Maryland Police Accountability Act of 2021."[908] The controversial and sweeping law repealed the Law Enforcement Officers' Bill of Rights, a decades-old police accountability and officer rights act.

Maryland Governor Larry Hogan vetoed the bill, but a week later the legislature overrode his veto.

The most controversial portion of the law was the new police use of force rule, which would make it much more difficult for officers to use force even in appropriate circumstances, thereby jeopardizing their safety and the safety of their communities. Under the new law, a police officer may not use force against a person unless, given the totality of the circumstances, such force is "necessary and proportional to prevent an imminent threat of physical injury to a person or effectuate a legitimate law enforcement objective."

Two weeks after the new law was passed, Mosby heaped praise on the Maryland Police Accountability Act, saying that the law was a "testament to the hard work of advocates…who have been fighting for the substantive transformation of our country's law enforcement."[909] Mosby bemoaned "that dismantling the status quo does not happen overnight," that there is more work to be done to "rectify Maryland's police infrastructure," but that "these bills are only the beginning."[910]

That statement, like many from Mosby, was odd and ill-informed. That's because police officers in the City of Baltimore—Mosby's turf—

had been operating under essentially the same use of force standards since 2019.

Even though the new law didn't go into effect until July 1, 2022, law enforcement agencies in Maryland started training to the new standard in 2021.

In practice, that meant that Sheriff Mike Lewis's deputies (and law enforcement officers across the state) were training to use less than lethal force, such as using a taser, instead of pulling their guns, as they came closer to the July 1, 2022, implementation date.

Ironically, three weeks before he was murdered, Hilliard had been trained on and issued the taser he was carrying when Davidson shot and killed him.

Sheriff Mike Lewis told us, "I can't help but think my deputy died because of this new law enforcement 'reform' and antilaw enforcement rhetoric that is being spewed from Annapolis, Maryland"[911] and cheered on by Marilyn Mosby.

Immediately after Davidson murdered Hilliard, the political recriminations began.

Then-Maryland Governor Larry Hogan and Wicomico County Sheriff Mike Lewis held a press conference the day after Officer Hilliard was murdered. Sheriff Lewis, who was clearly upset and unnerved that one of his deputies was murdered by a career criminal, said that Davidson "should have been in prison at the time of the fatal shooting."[912]

Turning toward Governor Hogan, Sheriff Lewis said, "This suspect is not only a convicted felon. He was just convicted in 2019 in Baltimore City for armed robbery with a handgun of which he received—Governor—probation before judgment."[913]

Governor Hogan, in response to Sheriff Lewis's comments, said that it was "just unacceptable" that Davidson was out and "not serving any jail time for armed robbery."[914]

Like all rogue prosecutors, Mosby wasn't willing to accept responsibility for her reckless policy of giving a slap on the wrist to an armed robber and instead tried to blame the judge for the light sentence. Blaming the judge is a favorite tactic of this new breed of prosecutor.

A spokesman for Mosby's office told the press: "After securing a conviction, prosecutors make a sentence recommendation to a judge, who is responsible for imposing a sentence. In this case, the prosecutor secured a conviction and made a sentence recommendation of jail time. The court imposed a sentence of probation before judgment."[915]

Notice what Mosby did not say. She didn't say, "We asked the court to impose the maximum sentence allowed under the law, fifteen years, but the court disagreed." Nor did Mosby's office say, "The State implored the court to impose the mandatory five-year minimum sentence in this case because the defendant used a loaded firearm during the commission of a violent crime," or, "The court refused to sentence the defendant to the mandatory five-year period of incarceration despite the fact that our office argued forcefully for that sentence." Notice also that the spokesman used the word "jail" and not prison. Jail is for people serving one year or less; prison is where felons who must serve a year or more are housed.

The explanation from Mosby didn't pass the smell test. Anyone who has practiced criminal law in Maryland for any period of time can read between the lines and can guess what happened here: Mosby authorized a plea deal with the defense attorney, and that deal included a PBJ, a suspended sentence, and, for some reason, she agreed not to ask for the mandatory minimum sentence of five years. The defendant would get time served (he had served several months in jail, pending the disposition of the case), and everyone would move on to the next case.

Even members of Baltimore's criminal defense bar were skeptical of the flimsy excuse and blatant rear end covering by Mosby's office. Kurt Nachtman, a former prosecutor in Mosby's office and current criminal defense attorney, told ABC News that it was "highly unlikely that the judge in the case, Melissa Phinn, did what Mosby's office is suggesting without the prosecutor's approval...Phinn does not make sentencing recommendations; she wants binding pleas from prosecutors and defense attorneys."[916]

Judge Phinn is the same judge in Baltimore City who withdrew the plea deal from the amorous arsonist and attempted murderer, Luther Trent.

Baltimore City Fraternal Order of Police Lodge #3—Baltimore's police union—didn't buy Mosby's excuse either, tweeting out, "The irresponsible plea bargains and violent crime policies of Marilyn Mosby have now gotten a Deputy Sheriff killed. She is a plague on our city and region. This tragedy should never have occurred."[917]

Ivan Bates, one of three Democratic nominees to unseat Mosby in the July 2022 Democratic primary, said, "The problem that I have is the state's attorney's office had the ability to call [ask for] a mandatory minimum sentence of five years without the possibility of parole if they wanted to and this would have never been the issue. They did not; they failed to do their job, and unfortunately, now we have a deputy sheriff that's murdered."[918]

On June 21, 2022, hundreds of members of the Maryland law enforcement community gathered in Salisbury to pay their respects to and bury Officer Glenn Hilliard. His wife, Tashica, daughters De'Aijah (22), Jersi (16), and his son Trenton (12), sat numbly through the solemn memorial service at Emmanuel Wesleyan Church.

Davidson is in jail awaiting his trial in Wicomico County at the time this book went to print. Marilyn Mosby never asked for his suspended sentence to be reinstated for his crimes in Baltimore City.

## IN OVER HER HEAD FROM DAY ONE

Dorchester, Massachusetts, may only be five miles south of downtown Boston, but back in 1980, when Marilyn James was born there, it was a world apart from its historical and cosmopolitan cousin to the north. It was a gritty, poor, diverse area of Boston, and crime was ever present.

Born into a family of police officers, Marilyn James was raised by her grandparents. At the age of fourteen, her closest friend and cousin, Diron Spence, who was seventeen, was mistaken for a drug dealer and killed by a criminal outside her house. Another cousin was convicted of attempted murder in a separate case. These two incidents affected young Marilyn, who, after graduating from Dover-Sherborn High School and Tuskegee University, attended Boston College Law School where she earned her JD in 2005. While in law school, she took a clinical class for future public defenders but also interned in the local DA's office and the US Attorney's Office in Boston.

After graduating law school, she was admitted to the Maryland Bar in December 2006. There is no information in the public record as to why it took Mosby a year and a half to be admitted to the Maryland Bar. She could have failed the bar exam (potentially a couple of times), or there could be other explanations for the delay in being admitted to the bar, such as a family obligation, an emergency, or the like.

She joined the Baltimore City State's Attorney's Office after she passed the Maryland Bar. That office is the largest state's attorney's office in the small state of Maryland, with approximately 160 prosecutors and additional support staff. The Baltimore City State's Attorney's Office is the third smallest office of the eight featured in this book. The LA DA's office is the largest, with approximately 1,000 attorneys, followed by Chicago (900), Manhattan (500), Philly (300), Boston (160), San Francisco (150), and the City of St. Louis (60).

Like all recent law school graduates, Mosby was assigned to handle misdemeanor bench trials in district court. Mosby handled misdemeanors for years, which to us is a red flag because she should have graduated from misdemeanors to low-level felonies in a year or maybe two at the most. She claims that after only five months prosecuting misdemeanors, she was promoted to a supervisory position. But according to a former prosecutor in the office who was familiar with Mosby's work at the time, Mosby barely supervised anyone while in district court, occupying a position with only one subordinate—a placeholder position for a poor performer.

After toiling for years in Maryland District Court (where only misdemeanors are tried), Mosby eventually moved up to circuit court, which handles all felonies. According to her biography on the Baltimore City State's Attorney's Office website when she was the State's Attorney, Mosby claims to have "successfully prosecuted hundreds of cases and some of the most heinous felonies in the State of Maryland."[919] But "prosecuting" is different from "trying" cases. According to former senior prosecutors who were familiar with Mosby's tenure in the office during this time, Mosby actually tried very few felonies in front of a jury. One former senior prosecutor told us that Mosby only conducted four felony jury trials, which is a shockingly low number for a state prosecutor. He went on to say that Mosby was not a "standout or extraordinary." The *Baltimore Sun*, the paper of record in Baltimore, in a 2014 editorial after she won her primary race for state's attorney, wrote that Mosby "never prosecuted a rape or murder case."[920]

Larry Doane served as one of her supervisors while she was in general felonies. During her performance reviews at that time, he told her that she needed more trial experience.

She left the State's Attorney's Office in 2011 because she "didn't necessarily agree with the priorities of the office"[921] after Gregg Bernstein won the election in 2010 to become Baltimore City's new chief prosecutor. Mosby went to work for Liberty Mutual Insurance as a field counsel, which is a relatively low-level attorney position charged with reviewing and defending the company against suspicious insurance claims.

In 2014, at the age of thirty-four, Marilyn Mosby decided to run against her old boss Gregg Bernstein for Baltimore state's attorney. That she even ran in the first place was not a surprise to those who knew her when she worked in the office as a young prosecutor. As one former colleague of Mosby put it, "She has an ego the size of Montezuma."

During the race she consistently hammered Bernstein for the crime rate in Baltimore City at that time, although today she refuses to accept any blame for the massive spike in crime, including homicides, since she took office or even acknowledge that the chief prosecutor's policies have an impact on crime rates. Her campaign ads were organized "around crime victims and their realities."[922]

Her campaign platform and goals included:[923]

- Strategic violent repeat offender coordination: within the first one hundred days of office, she promised to have a comprehensive process to manage the violent repeat offender list that is mutually agreed upon by the State's Attorney's Office and Baltimore Police Department.

- Truth in sentencing: she promised to continue to push for strengthening the total percentage of actual time served for violent crimes.

- Sexual assault legislation: she touted her work on Maryland House Bill 1528, which, according to Mosby, "Would bring Maryland law in line with federal statutes so that sexual assault victims have a fair opportunity to receive justice."

- Victim/witness services unit: she pledged to create a victim/ witness services unit that would transform the way the State's Attorney's Office interacts with victims, witnesses, and the general public.

- Transparency and innovation: she promised to make case dispositions publicly available and easily searchable and accessible.

- "Back on Track" pilot program: she promised to create a new program to introduce young drug offenders to the possibilities of engaging in a "legitimate" line of work in an effort to reduce recidivism rates and strengthen communities by increasing access to education and employment.

It won't surprise you that Mosby hasn't lived up to any of her original campaign promises. But the one that stands out to us was contained in a flyer she mailed to potential voters.

One of Mosby's campaign mailers, ironically, said: "We need a prosecutor who can win the tough cases."[924] Little did she know that within eleven months, with the death of Freddie Gray, she would lose the tough cases against the police whom she accused of killing Gray, and would, in fact, be accused of prosecutorial misconduct and malicious prosecution.

## LOSING THE FREDDIE GRAY CASES

By now, many people know the story about what happened to Freddie Gray on April 12, 2015. There have been numerous books written about Gray's death and the subsequent trials and acquittals of the officers involved in the incident.[925]

In summary, Gray, a career criminal, was arrested on April 12, 2015, for illegal possession of a knife. While being transported in a police van to the police station, he sustained severe injuries and was taken to a hospital, where, after falling into a coma for a week, he died. Various witnesses opined that the six police officers involved used excess force in subduing Gray. Those six officers were suspended on April 21, 2015, pending an internal investigation. The medical examiner concluded that Gray's death was not accidental and characterized it as a homicide.

Major protests across Baltimore broke out after the public learned of Gray's arrest, injury, and death. These protests resulted in violence, multiple arrests, and injury to officers. After Gray's funeral on April 27th, more riots broke out, including the looting of stores and burning of businesses. Ultimately, Maryland Governor Larry Hogan declared a state of emergency and called out the Maryland National Guard.[926]

On the day the medical examiner's report was delivered to Mosby's office, she held a press conference where she announced that there was probable cause to believe that the "Baltimore Six," the six police officers involved in the case, committed criminal acts against Freddie Gray. In a long-winded speech, Mosby announced the charges, including second-degree depraved heart murder, involuntary manslaughter, and varying degrees of assault charges.[927]

Wicomico County Sheriff Mike Lewis was one of dozens of law enforcement officers deployed to Baltimore City during the riots following Gray's death. Lewis told us, "I watched Marilyn Mosby handle the indictments of the 'Baltimore Six.' I was blown away at her inexperience and her juvenile actions that are consistent with a young prosecutor, quite honestly. Then I watched that whole case implode before my eyes."[928]

Implode is the right word indeed.

The first trial was against Officer William Porter, who was charged with involuntary manslaughter, second-degree assault, and misconduct in office. The jury could not reach a verdict, and a mistrial was declared in December 2015.

Officer Edward Nero was the second officer to go on trial. He chose to forego his right to a jury trial and consented to be tried before a judge; no doubt because his attorney advised him that the facts were on his side so a jury trial would be too risky since the jury was likely to decide based solely on emotion. This is a common practice in criminal law. A criminal defendant has the final say on whether to be tried before a jury or judge.

Nero was charged with second-degree intentional assault, assault in the second degree negligent, misconduct in office, and false imprisonment. Circuit Court Judge Barry Williams found Nero not guilty in May 2016.

After essentially losing two high-profile police misconduct cases, an experienced prosecutor would reconsider whether to move forward with any other cases. But not Mosby, who had no meaningful management or serious prosecutorial experience.

A month later, the police van driver, Officer Caesar Goodson, who was charged with depraved heart second-degree murder (among other charges), was also acquitted following a bench trial before Judge Williams.

At this point after suffering humiliating losses like the Porter, Nero, and Goodson cases, a competent prosecutor would have dropped the remaining cases altogether, or at least paused, consulted with experts, regrouped, and revised her trial strategy. But not Mosby, who, by now, was proving to the public that she was in way over her head. In fact, she was just getting started.

Lieutenant Brian Rice was the fourth (and last) officer to go on trial. He was astride a bicycle when he saw Gray with the knife and was charged with involuntary manslaughter (among other charges). Once again, after a bench trial, Rice was acquitted by Judge Williams in July 2016.

Mosby finally wised up and dropped the charges against Porter, Sgt. Alicia White, and Officer Garrett E. Miller in July 2016.

On September 12, 2017, the United States Department of Justice, after a thorough independent federal investigation into the death of Freddie Gray Jr., found insufficient evidence to support federal criminal civil rights charges against the six Baltimore Police Department officers.[929]

Most elected DAs who lose high-profile cases suffer politically, like Gil Garcetti, the Los Angeles County district attorney during the O. J. Simpson murder trial. But not Mosby, whose political star only rose after flubbing the Gray cases.

## JUVENILE, MALICIOUS, AND VINDICTIVE

One of the common features of the elected prosecutors featured in this book is that all of them, except George Gascón, fired employees from their office whom they either didn't like or saw as threats to their rogue approach.[930] The only reason Gascón didn't fire any of the one thousand prosecutors in his office was because he couldn't, as the line prosecutors in his office—unlike all the other line prosecutors in the other seven offices—were protected under county civil service rules.

When Mosby assumed office, she fired six employees immediately, including four prosecutors and two support staff. Whom she fired and how she did it set the stage for a mass exodus from the office of other prosecutors who didn't trust her, refused to put up with her mercurial outbursts, and refused to abide by her radical policies, which all inured to the benefit of criminals and caused a massive spike in crime.

The six employees who Mosby fired in her first week were Nancy Olin, Larry Doane, Grant McDaniel, Keri Borzilleri, support staffer Cristie Cole, and one other support staffer.

Nancy Olin was a senior prosecutor in the office, where she had worked for over twenty years. She was in trial the week Mosby was sworn into office. Over her career, she had been assigned some of the most high-profile cases in the office and was the lead prosecutor in a case against Demetrius Carter, the nephew of Bernard "Jack" Young, who was the president of the city council at the time. Young later became the mayor. Mosby's husband, Nick, also on the Baltimore City Council, was friends with Young.

After Olin had selected a jury and made her opening statement, and was on a short lunch break during trial, she got an email from Stu Beckham, the head of human resources in Mosby's office. He wanted to see her at 3 PM that day. Knowing that she would be in court at 3 PM, Olin decided to drop by Beckham's office during her lunch break instead.

According to witnesses to the event, Olin was standing in the vestibule of Beckham's office when he emerged from his office. Olin asked Beckham what the purpose of the meeting was, and he said it was about a personnel issue. Olin asked, "Are you firing me?" Beckham demurred. Olin asked again, "Are you firing me?"

Beckham answered, saying, "Miss Mosby is going in a different direction."

Olin, clearly dumbfounded, said, "What direction is that?" Beckham refused to answer. Upset, Olin asked Beckham if he even knew that she was in a trial. He didn't but shockingly asked Olin if she would finish the trial. Olin, now crying, refused.

Olin left the office immediately, and another prosecutor jumped in to finish the case. It turns out that Mosby never told Olin's supervisors that she was firing Olin. They found out after the fact.

Mosby also fired Larry Doane, who had been Mosby's boss when she worked in circuit court trying felonies and who was responsible for her performance evaluations at that time. Grant McDaniel, whom Mosby interned for when she was a law clerk in the office, was also fired.

Keri Borzilleri was fired when the word got out that Borzilleri had attended a "meet and greet" with Gregg Bernstein, the then-incumbent and the person Mosby beat in the primary.

Borzilleri filed suit against Mosby in the federal District Court of Maryland on December 9, 2015, seeking damages under 42 U.S.C. § 1983 for violations of her First Amendment rights to free speech and free association and other claims under state law. Mosby filed a motion to dismiss the case for failure to state a claim upon which relief could be granted.

On May 31, 2016, the district court granted Mosby's motion and dismissed with prejudice Borzilleri's state and federal free association claims and her federal free speech claim and dismissed without prejudice her remaining state law claims, which means that she can file an amended complaint reasserting the latter claims but not the former. Borzilleri appealed these dismissals to the United States Court of Appeals for the Fourth Circuit and lost.[931]

Borzilleri then filed an amended complaint in Baltimore Circuit Court, and the case eventually went to a jury trial in 2019, where Mosby had to testify under oath. Mosby claimed, under oath, that she did not know Borzilleri had supported Bernstein and instead claimed that she fired her because she did not show enough sympathy for victims and witnesses.

During the trial, Syeetah Hampton-EL, a former assistant state's attorney in the Baltimore office, testified that Mosby made a "throat-slitting motion" toward her when she attended an event—the Alliance of Black Women Attorneys—with the then-State's Attorney Bernstein. Mosby denied the allegation, saying that she would never make such a gesture, suggesting that any animosity between the two stemmed from the time when Mosby was Hampton-EL's supervisor in misdemeanor court. The jury returned a verdict for Mosby.

After the verdict, Michelle Wilson, a talented former homicide prosecutor in Mosby's office and current assistant attorney general for the State of Maryland, took to Facebook and wrote that Mosby lied under oath, which is a serious allegation. As discussed later in the chapter, Biden's

Justice Department later indicted her for lying under oath in a different circumstance. Wilson later wrote out an affidavit explaining why she believed Mosby lied under oath. In turn, Borzilleri's attorneys filed a motion for a new trial based on new evidence. At the time this book went to print, the motion hadn't been resolved by the judge.

Meanwhile, on May 21, 2019, Baltimore Police Commissioner Michael Harrison named Michelle Wilson to be a deputy police commissioner in charge of overseeing police misconduct investigations. But two days later, that job offer was rescinded. Wilson sued, claiming that she was being punished for exercising her First Amendment rights for the Facebook post and affidavit saying Mosby lied in court. In November 2019, the City of Baltimore settled the case with Wilson for $75,000.[932]

**Mikenzie Frost** ✔
@MikenzieFrost
⋯

NEW | I just got these photos sent to me: if you just saw my story on @FOXBaltimore, these photos are even clearer.

From the video it was difficult to tell if Baltimore City SA Marilyn Mosby flipped the person off. Her office said it was a thumbs up.

These photos clear it up.

4:44 PM · May 20, 2021 from Annapolis, MD

**7** Retweets   **2** Quote Tweets   **19** Likes

In 2021, Mosby was photographed and videotaped giving the middle finger to a bicyclist in Baltimore who yelled at her for her repeated prosecutions of a murder suspect. Mosby, through a spokesman, said that she did not extend her middle finger but her thumb. This is the same Mosby who claimed, under oath, that she did not make a throat-slitting gesture.

Baltimore City State's Attorney Marilyn Mosby makes an obscene gesture toward Sean Gearhart after he pushed her at a restaurant while recording. Images taken from video shot by Sean Gearhart.

## TOP HEAVY WITH PUBLIC DEFENDERS AND LIGHT ON PROSECUTING CRIMINALS

After he was elected to be Philadelphia's district attorney, Larry Krasner described his new role as a "public defender with power." Krasner was a career criminal defense attorney before he became the DA. Similarly, Chesa Boudin, the disgraced, recalled San Francisco district attorney, was a career public defender before he was the top prosecutor in the city by the bay.

It wouldn't surprise you that, once elected, they hired criminal defense attorneys and public defenders to "reimagine prosecution" and help them enact their policies.

But hiring public defenders and criminal defense attorneys into district attorney offices is not unique to Krasner and Boudin. Even though most were not criminal defense attorneys, each of the other prosecutors we cover in this book have done the same thing, with predicable results.

At the outset, we want to make something very clear: as we have written elsewhere, the criminal justice system needs, and indeed relies on, intelligent, zealous, hard-charging criminal defense attorneys.[933] One of us was a criminal defense attorney in the Navy. Anyone charged with a crime is presumed innocent, and that presumption of innocence remains with the accused unless and until the government can prove, by legal and competent evidence, each and every element of each crime charged beyond a reasonable doubt, which is the highest burden known in American law.

But for our system of criminal justice to function properly, it must remain an adversarial system of justice. Prosecutors must prosecute; defense attorneys must defend. And while there are myriad ways in which each side can carry out their duties, it should be a given that prosecutors should, at the very least, enforce the law and protect victims, and defense counsel should represent the interests of their clients and put the government to the test in each case.

And as we have written elsewhere, there are plenty of examples of brilliant criminal defense attorneys who have started their careers as prosecutors, and talented defense attorneys who have gone on to become extraordinary prosecutors.[934]

The rogue prosecutor movement, whose goal is to "fundamentally reverse engineer and dismantle" the criminal justice system, counts, in part, on newly elected prosecutors hiring criminal defense attorneys, who perpetuate their roles as a criminal defense attorney while in the office of the prosecutor. Their mindset, actions, and policies benefit criminals— their old clients. They see the criminal justice system as racist, rigged, and retrograde, and one where past, present, and future prosecutions are tainted and must be fixed or made right.

So, it's not surprising that Mosby hired numerous criminal defense attorneys and elevated them into positions of authority in her office. And unlike Gascón's office, where hiring must be done according to county civil service rules and requisite qualifications, Mosby could hire and fire at will and was not required to adhere to any city or county civil service rules.

One of her first hires was Jan Bledsoe to be deputy state's attorney for criminal justice. A criminal defense attorney, Bledsoe had previously worked in the city State's Attorney's Office and had been in charge of the police integrity unit but was fired by Bernstein. Mosby tasked Bledsoe with charging the officers in the Freddie Gray cases.

Mosby also hired Michael Schatzow away from a partnership at a prestigious national law firm. A defense attorney who focused on white collar criminal cases, Schatzow, a graduate of University of Chicago Law School, had served as a federal prosecutor earlier in his career and was known in Maryland as an aggressive, smart attorney. He was Bledsoe's co-counsel in the Gray cases and Mosby's chief deputy—the number two in the office—until he retired from the office in October 2021. He was succeeded by Bledsoe.

In 2016, Mosby hired Valda Ricks to be a deputy state's attorney in the office. Ricks was a career criminal defense attorney and had worked in the Baltimore Public Defender's Office since 1991. Another hire was Deborah Warner-Dennis, who also came from the Baltimore Public Defender's Office. Mosby appointed Warner-Dennis as head of the crime control and prevention unit, even though she had never prosecuted a case in her life. And rounding out the influx of criminal defense attorneys, Mosby hired Dennis Laye, who went on to try felony violent crimes.

According to a veteran prosecutor in the office, "It was like the Public Defender's Office was running the State's Attorney's Office."[935]

At the same time Mosby was firing experienced prosecutors and hiring public defenders, she abandoned her campaign promises (listed earlier) and stopped prosecuting so-called quality of life crimes including drug possession, prostitution, and most misdemeanors. However, due to ego or inexperience, she didn't think through, or worse, did not care about, the implications of her prosecutorial nullification or the impact it would have on the police or crime rates.

Unlike Rachael Rollins and George Gascón, who each assembled teams to draft policies to announce after they won their elections, Mosby did no such thing. Unlike Rollins and Gascón, who had been an assistant United States Attorney, and chief of police in two major cities and the DA of San Francisco, respectively, Mosby didn't have the experience or savvy to plan out her tenure. Rollins and Gascón, after they were elected, published various policy memos, including memos explaining to their employees which crimes they refused to prosecute.

Mosby, despite running on a transparency and accountability platform, simply announced that she would no longer prosecute most misdemeanors. She didn't consult with the Baltimore police commissioner at the time, Anthony W. Batts, much less work with any of the next four Baltimore police commissioners to coordinate her hands-off approach to crime in the city.

The current commissioner of police, Michael Harrison, criticized Mosby's ham-handed implementation of misdemeanor nullification, saying that Mosby "can plan for months and create a policy, spring it on me and now I have to train 3,000 people to create a new policy and then train all those people on what to do now."[936]

Harrison is no Alex Villanueva, the bold and plainspoken former sheriff of Los Angeles County, who has consistently lambasted LA DA George Gascón for implementing many of the same policies as Mosby, including refusing to prosecute most misdemeanors. Instead, like many in Baltimore's ruling elite, Harrison is a weak leader, more focused on keeping his job than causing political waves in the incestuous City of Baltimore politics. When asked if Mosby's policies are making it more difficult for law enforcement to do their jobs, he meekly said, "Listen, it's not my job to decide that…it's really not my place to say who's doing a good job or bad job."[937]

Someone needs to tell Harrison that it is his job to tell the truth about Mosby and the effect her hands-off approach has on crime in the city and the devastating effect it has had on police morale, recruitment, and retention. The Baltimore Police Department is in dire straits, morale is terrible, and they are short at least four hundred officers.[938] They are so short staffed that they are considering hiring civilians to investigate low-level crimes, internal affairs complaints, and, believe it or not, cold cases.[939]

## INVESTIGATED, INDICTED, AND INCOMPETENT

Mosby is in a class by herself when it comes to missteps while in office, both professionally and personally. No other prosecutor in this book has been investigated by the inspector general of her city for fiscal irregularities and lying about travel, indicted for fraud by the Biden Justice Department, and excoriated by judges for incompetence and potentially violating a gag order—though some others like St. Louis's Kim Gardner have come excruciatingly close. Each of these incidents, which we describe briefly below, happened because of Mosby's lack of attention to detail, utter dearth of legal or political sophistication, and her capacious ego.

## IG FINDINGS AND REPORT

Believe it or not, despite the Freddie Gray prosecution fiasco and a massive spike in violent crime after she took office (see below), Mosby became a much sought-after speaker for the progressive prosecutor movement. In part, that's because those behind the movement, like Fair and Just Prosecution, the Vera Institute, and other Soros-funded, affiliated, or inspired groups, simply cannot afford to abandon any of their anointed social justice warriors—until absolutely necessary. And Mosby, as you'll see, quickly became a darling of the movement and benefitted from their support. The problem for Mosby, however, was that she was less than accurate in her yearly reports to the Maryland Ethics Commission—the state commission that monitors elected officials' performance in office.

It all started when a local news outlet, the *Baltimore Brew*, started looking into Mosby's ethics reports. They noticed that Mosby was gallivanting around Europe and Africa at posh resorts, ostensibly for work. On July 16, 2020, the *Brew* wrote a special report entitled "The Peripatetic Prosecutor: Marilyn Mosby Took 23 Trips in 2018 and 2019, Accepting $30,000 in Reimbursements."[940] They alleged that Mosby spent two weeks in Europe in 2019, staying in five-star hotels in Germany and Portugal learning about their prison systems. She also traveled to the Great Rift Valley Lodge and

Golf Resort in Kenya, ostensibly for work to talk about government graft with Kenyan officials. And she traveled to the luxurious Balmoral Hotel in Edinburgh, Scotland, to talk about drug-sentencing laws.

Fair and Just Prosecution, the sponsor for the trips to Europe and Africa, posted pictures on their Instagram account of Mosby and her fellow attendees, including Larry Krasner, Rachael Rollins, and other lesser-known rogue prosecutors.

Photo taken May 8, 2019 in Berlin, Germany, during Fair & Just Prosecution junket to Europe. Front row, L to R: Brian Middleton, District Attorney, Fort Bend County, TX; Rachael Rollins, District Attorney, Suffolk County, MA; Unknown; Unknown; Miriam Krinksy, Executive Director, Fair & Just Prosecution; Unknown; George Gascon, District Attorney, Los Angeles County, CA; Back row, L to R: Unknown; Mark Gonzalez, District Attorney, Nueces County, TX; Larry Krasner, District Attorney, Philadelphia, PA; Marilyn Mosby, State's Attorney, City of Baltimore, MD; Eric Gonzalez, District Attorney, Kings County, NY; Satana DeBerry, District Attorney, Durham County, NC; Wesley Bell, District Attorney, St. Louis County, MO; Beth McCann, District Attorney, Denver, CO; Third row, unknown male.

**marilynmosbyesq** • Follow    ···

**marilynmosbyesq** 🇰🇪🇰🇪 I had the amazing opportunity to go to Kenya to represent 21st Century Prosecutors and I am still in awe at the majestic beauty of our Motherland. #Africa #Blessed #ForThePeople #GlobalChange #LetsGo

45w

**cjxb80** Super Awesome!

45w    Reply

**paulacampbell** ▾▾▾▾

Photo taken November 9, 2017 at New York University School of Law at Fair & Just Prosecution event.
L to R: Anthony C. Thompson, Marilyn Mosby, Larry Krasner, Miriam Krinksy.

Photo taken November 9, 2017 at New York University School of Law at Fair & Just Prosecution event.
L to R: Miriam Krinksy; Anthony C. Thompson, Marilyn Mosby and Larry Krasner.  Krinsky is the Executive Director of
Fair & Just Prosecution. Thompson is the NYU Professor of Clinical Law Emeritus and the founding faculty Director of the
Center on Race, Inequality and the Law at NYU.  He is the author of several books, including, *"Releasing Prisoners, Redeeming
Communities"* and *"A Perilous Path"* with co-authors Sherrilyn Ifill, Loretta Lynch and Bryan Stevenson. A graduate of Harvard
Law School, Thompson served for nine years as a Deputy Public Defender in Contra Costa, California.

Finally, the *Brew* noted that in 2019, Mosby formed a private company named Mahogany Elite Enterprises, listing herself as the resident agent and owner. The "enterprises" consisted of Mahogany Elite Travel company, whose purpose was to offer "traveling hospitality services" and Mahogany Elite Consulting, whose purpose was to provide "consulting and legal services."

The *Brew*'s article, the first of many, accused Mosby of going on twenty-three out-of-town trips sponsored by nonprofits and other groups in 2018 and 2019, accepting at least $30,672 in airfare, hotel rooms, and per diem, more than any other elected official in Maryland. The *Brew* also reported that Mosby accepted more than $1,500 in free items and forty-one gifts, including a Tiffany bracelet.

Shockingly, the *Brew* noted that Mosby was absent from the city State's Attorney's Office for at least eighty-five days in 2018 and 2019. Mosby attended conferences in Alabama, Arizona, California, Georgia, Louisiana, Massachusetts, Minnesota, New York, Tennessee, Texas, and Wisconsin. Homicides, which averaged 229 per year in the five years before she took office, rocketed north to over three hundred each year she was in office and averaged 331 per year for her first five years in office.

As press inquiries mounted about her ethics reports, the purposes for her trips, and what she did with the gifts she received in the past few years, Mosby, to her credit, wrote the Office of the Inspector General (OIG) for the City of Baltimore on July 20, 2020, to request an investigation into the information she had disclosed to the State Ethics Commission.

On February 9, 2021, the OIG issued its official report, which confirmed much of what the *Baltimore Brew* first reported, but also found additional misinformation provided by Mosby.

The OIG found that Mosby had reported that the twenty-three trips she had taken during 2018–2019 were sponsored or paid for by outside organizations or the city. In her travel disclosure reports, Mosby separated travel and gifts, but the OIG said it was "unclear which expenses were paid for by sponsoring organizations, which by the city, and which by SA Mosby herself."

The OIG noted that Mosby failed to include another official sponsored trip on her financial disclosure document. That trip, paid for by the Vera

Institute of Justice (a Soros-funded organization), was to the Salamander Resort and Spa in Middleburg, Virginia, and took place immediately after Mosby arrived back in the United States from Kenya. The agenda for the three-day retreat, which took place from August 28–30, 2019, included "spa and individual wellness coaching sessions." When questioned why this boondoggle was left off her official report, Mosby said it was an "error on [the] ethics form."

The OIG also noted other slight discrepancies in the costs reported by Mosby for her sponsored trips.

The OIG's investigation found that the out-of-town trips did not comply with the relevant travel policies and procedures as required by the City of Baltimore. The rules required that city employees must submit travel requests for approval to either the agency head or the Board of Estimates (BOE) and include cost of the trip, length of absence, location of travel, the source or type of funds, and the like. Travel that costs more than $800, as well as any travel outside of the continental United States regardless of source of funds or cost of trip, must be approved by the BOE. Additionally, BOE approval is required if the official's absence exceeds five workdays or involves one or both weekend days. The OIG found that Mosby did not request BOE approval for any of her twenty-four trips.

In addition to the sponsored trips discussed above, the OIG found that Mosby traveled out of town on an additional fifty-nine workdays during 2018 and 2019 for a total of 144 days out of the office, an average of one workday a week.

Finally, the OIG took issue with Mosby's candor with respect to the value of the gifts she received, what she did with them, and whether her businesses served any real business purpose, since neither reported any income.

While the OIG concluded that "it is not within the purview of the OIG to make a determination as to whether SA Mosby fully complied with the State Public Ethics Law, including the State's disclosure requirements," the facts speak for themselves.

It's disturbing when any public official is less than candid, or just sloppy, on yearly ethics or compliance reports. Public service is a privilege, not a right. Public officials have an obligation to be forthright, honest, direct, and accurate with the public they serve. But it's even more disturbing when that public official is not only a lawyer but the chief prosecutor of a district who voters would assume pays attention to details and is scrupulously accurate when it comes to following the law.

Mosby's lack of attention to detail and cavalier attitude about complying with the rules would come back to bite her when she decided to prematurely take money out of a government retirement account during the pandemic.

## BIDEN JUSTICE DEPARTMENT INDICTS MOSBY

On January 13, 2022, the United States Attorney for the District of Maryland unveiled a four-count indictment against Mosby for two counts of perjury and two counts of false statements on a loan application. Two months later, on March 10, 2022, the same office announced a superseding indictment against Mosby with the same charges and additional factual allegations.

Mosby, like all defendants, is presumed innocent unless and until proven guilty beyond a reasonable doubt. The information below was obtained from publicly available documents, including the superseding indictment.[941]

The first count (charge) of the indictment stems from the fact that Mosby withdrew $40,000 from the deferred compensation plan offered by her employer, the Baltimore City State's Attorney's Office. Typically, retirement money you earn as a government employee in this type of plan is not taxed until it is withdrawn. Under her IRS § 457 plan, she could withdraw the money after she left her government job or for unforeseen emergencies that meet certain criteria if all her other financial resources were exhausted.

According to the indictment, Congress passed the CARES Act on March 27, 2020, which permitted qualifying members to receive a COVID-related financial distribution. On May 26, 2020, Mosby emailed Nationwide Insurance, which administered the 457 plan for Baltimore, and requested a one-time withdrawal of $40,000 from her employee retirement account. She signed a form, under penalty of perjury, stating that she had experienced "adverse financial consequences stemming from"

COVID-19 as a result of "being quarantined, furloughed or laid off; having reduced work hours; being unable to work due to lack of childcare, or the closing or reduction of business hours." Mosby signed the form, and the "additional acknowledgements" section of the form that reiterated that she was signing under penalty of perjury.

On May 29, 2020, Mosby received $36,000 from her retirement account and used the money for the down payment for a vacation home in Kissimmee, Florida, that she purchased in September 2020.

Marilyn Mosby's gross salary in 2020 was $247,955.58.

The indictment alleges that Mosby did not experience any adverse financial consequences stemming from COVID-19 even though she represented—under oath—that she did.

The second count alleges that Mosby made a false statement on her loan application. The allegations stem from the government's assertion that Mosby and her husband, Nick, who filed joint tax returns for tax years 2014 through 2018, were delinquent in paying their taxes, had been given official notice by the IRS that they were delinquent, yet in 2020, when applying for a mortgage for the second home in Florida, denied being delinquent or in default on any federal debt. This was not true, according to the government, because at the time she signed that loan application, she was aware of an IRS tax lien against her in the amount of $45,022.

The third count alleges that Mosby committed perjury for conduct that was similar to the allegations in count one. The government alleges that on December 29, 2020, she submitted a second form to Nationwide requesting to withdraw $50,000 from her deferred compensation plan account, and again, swore under oath that she was qualified to do so under the "adverse financial circumstances" carve-out from the CARES Act. On December 31, 2020, she received $45,000 from her retirement account and used that money toward a down payment for a second vacation home in Longboat Key, Florida.

The fourth count is similar to the second count: false statement on a loan application. Here, the government alleges that Mosby, on January 14, 2021, when signing the loan application for the Longboat Key vacation home, perjured herself when she said that she was not delinquent or in default on any federal debt. Again, the IRS had filed a $45,022 tax lien against her on March 3, 2020, which, according to the government, she knew at the time she signed the loan application documents under perjury. Furthermore, to close on the Longboat Key home, Mosby needed $35,699 in liquid assets, but she only had $31,043 in her checking account. But instead of waiting for her next paycheck ($9,183.54 bi-weekly) to hit her checking account, Mosby submitted a false gift letter to the mortgage company on February 10, 2021, saying that her husband had made her a gift of $5,000 "to be transferred at closing." Her letter said the $5,000 came from Nick's credit union checking account. That wasn't true, according to the government. In reality, Mosby wired her husband the $5,000 two days later, on February 12, and later Nick moved the money from his checking account to his savings account and back to his checking account before wiring the money to the escrow agent before closing. The reason Mosby lied in the false gift letter on February 10 was to lock in a lower interest rate than she would have received had she waited for her next paycheck, according to the government.

The government disclosed during pretrial motions that they have audio recordings of the phone calls between Mosby and Nationwide, the company that manages the city's retirement plans.

Mosby, through her attorneys, denies that she committed any crimes. During pretrial motions, her attorneys moved to dismiss the indictments against her, claiming that US Attorney for the District of Maryland Erek Barron and Assistant United States Attorney Leo Wise harbor animosity toward Mosby, are vindictive, and have a racial bias against her.

US Attorney Barron, who is black, was having none of it. He filed a scathing response in court to Mosby's claims, writing, "Name-calling is not facts and that is all the defendant offers...the defendant has invented a tale of victimhood in an attempt to deflect attention from her own behavior. As the evidence at trial will show, the only thing the defendant is a victim of is her own lies and choices."[942]

Mosby's federal trial has faced repeated delays. In January 2023, her entire defense team from the law firm of Reed Smith asked to be recused from representing Mosby. The federal district court judge approved their request. As of February 2023, Mosby is represented by a federal public defender, who informed the trial judge on February 3, 2023, that the defense would not be ready for trial until at least June 6, 2023. If she is convicted in her federal trial, even if she had won the primary on July 19, 2022, Mosby would not have been eligible to serve as the city state's attorney under Maryland law. She would have had to resign if convicted.

## VINDICTIVE PROSECUTION AND CONTEMPT OF COURT

Besides the Freddie Gray cases, one of the most high-profile homicide cases prosecuted by Mosby's office since she was first elected was the *State of Maryland v. Keith Davis Jr.* Her critics say that her deportment, public comments, and handling of this seven-year ongoing saga show Mosby at her worst: mean, vindictive, unsophisticated, and lacking in common sense.

Keith Davis Jr. has been prosecuted by Mosby's office four times for second-degree murder for the alleged killing of Kevin Jones on June 7, 2015. Davis is now awaiting his fifth trial for the same killing and has been in jail since 2015. He was tried twice in 2017. The first jury hung; the second jury convicted him, but the case was overturned when the trial judge found that Mosby's office violated discovery rules relating to a key government witness. Davis's third trial resulted in a hung jury. He was convicted at his fourth trial, but his conviction was overturned on appeal because the trial judge didn't allow the defense to ask appropriate questions at trial.

From 2016 through 2022, Mosby made comments in the public that call into question whether she has engaged in vindictive prosecution. Davis's defense attorneys eventually filed a motion to dismiss the case for vindictive prosecution in 2022, based on Mosby's public comments about the case and also a late filing in another murder case.

The day before Judge John S. Nugent, a Baltimore City Circuit Court judge, held the hearing on Davis's motion to dismiss on June 7, 2022, Mosby appeared before the Baltimore City Council for an oversight hearing about her office. When asked about the Davis case, Mosby said that Davis had been convicted three times, failing to acknowledge that under the law, Davis, whose retrial was pending, is presumed to be innocent.

On June 30, 2022, Judge Nugent issued a scathing opinion and order finding Mosby's actions "established a presumption of vindictiveness" in one of two cases pending before the court.

In denying the motion to dismiss the charges against Davis in the Jones murder case for vindictive prosecution, the judge found that the defense did establish a presumption of vindictiveness in another case in which Mosby's office belatedly filed murder charges against Davis—after having initially declined to file them. The court wrote that "it is evidence that the State has been frustrated in its efforts to prove the [Jones] murder case against Mr. Davis in a constitutionally sufficient forum." Judge Nugent called out Mosby by name, finding that "the State's Attorney and her staff engaged in conduct establishing personal animosity towards Mr. Davis outside the bounds of legitimate prosecutorial conduct." He noted that the state waited to pursue the attempted murder charge against Davis in the other case for almost one year after the incident and only after Davis was granted the right to a fifth trial.

In conclusion, the court held that "the temporal proximity between the new indictment and the grant of a new trial coupled with the words and actions of the State's Attorney and her staff, including the actions of homicide prosecutors, establish a presumption of vindictiveness." As a result, the judge will force Mosby and her prosecutors to give him communications, correspondence, and other potentially embarrassing or damaging information related to this case. He will review that information in his chambers and then decide what to do next, up to including a motion in open court in which he allows that information to be given to the defense counsel and aired out for the public to see.

As if that's not bad enough, on June 7, 2022, Judge Nugent issued a gag order to all the parties in the Davis case, including against Mosby herself. It prohibited any party to the case from speaking about the case whatsoever. Within an hour of the gag order taking effect, Mosby appeared on a local radio show and when asked about the Davis case, said the following: "Let me just be clear; I can't talk about the specifics of that case, but I can tell you that we are going to fight, and if a case has nothing substantively to do with the fact that we believe this is the individual who committed the offense, we're going to fight for justice for that family, and that's what I'll continue to do for every family in the City of Baltimore."[943]

In response, Davis's lawyers filed a petition for contempt against Mosby, alleging that she had not complied with the judge's gag order. On June 22, 2022, Judge Nugent found the defense petition "not frivolous on its face" and issued a Show Cause Order, ordering Mosby to appear in his court on August 12, 2022, to explain to him why he shouldn't hold her in contempt of court.[944] At the hearing, Judge Nugent found that Mosby had committed a "willful violation" of the gag order, held her in contempt of court, and fined her $1,500—though he said she wouldn't have to pay the fine if she followed an even stricter gag order for the next ninety days.[945]

## SLOW MOTION CAR CRASH

The cumulative effect of Mosby's prosecutorial nullification, sweetheart deals for career criminals, failure to fully enforce gun laws, lack of transparency and attention to detail, and hiring of public defenders won't come as a surprise. Prosecutors from her office have left in droves, community leaders are outraged, and crime has exploded.

Tony Foreman, a native of Baltimore and owner of several top restaurants there, summed it up best, saying that Mosby has been a "slow motion car crash" for "quality of life, economic life, development life, business life, employment life, protection of life in our city."[946]

It is difficult to tell how many prosecutors have left Mosby's office during her years as the state's attorney. The *Baltimore Sun*, the *Baltimore Brew*, Fox Baltimore, and other news outlets have reported over the years that the office is suffering from a massive shortage of prosecutors, anywhere from an eighty-prosecutor to over a one-hundred-prosecutor shortfall. That is significant, especially in an office of around 160 prosecutors.

Michael Turiello, the former deputy chief of the narcotics unit in the office until he left in June 2022, said that the lack of staffing in the office has "been a threat to public safety for years."[947] The *Baltimore Sun* interviewed more than two dozen current and former prosecutors from Mosby's office, most of whom spoke to the paper on the condition of anonymity out of fear of retribution by the thin-skinned Mosby. They confirmed that under Mosby, there was a severe lack of staffing, grueling hours, and huge caseloads resulting in prosecutors not being able to prepare for trial.[948]

During an oversight hearing before the city council in the spring of 2022, where she was questioned by City Councilman Eric Costello about staff departures and low morale, Mosby said her office was down forty-two assistant state's attorneys and that she had 144 prosecutors on staff. But internal staffing records showed that there were only 133 prosecutors on her staff, down from 206 prosecutors in 2018. Not only had prosecutors left the office in droves under Mosby's tenure, but also their departure lowered the median experience level of prosecutors in the office from 8.9 years (under Gregg Bernstein) to 5.3 years under Mosby.[949]

Mosby started her presentation blaming the attrition in her office on the COVID-19 pandemic, large caseloads, noncompetitive salaries, and uncooperative judges.[950] But her response rang hollow with the council, as her office (like all prosecutors' offices and courts) prosecuted fewer cases during the COVID-19 shutdowns, caseloads dropped, and the salaries in her office were in the middle of the pack for prosecutors' offices in Maryland.[951]

Her comments about judges contributing to the attrition in her office were odd and belied by at least one judge's recent ruling, wherein he took Mosby to task for failing to provide prosecutors on a high-profile case involving twenty-six defendants. On June 28, 2022, Judge Jeffrey M. Geller excoriated the Baltimore City State's Attorney's Office, in a conspiracy case against twenty-six correctional officers, for not replacing a prosecutor who resigned from the office, who had been on the case for more than a year, and not replacing the remaining prosecutor on the case who resigned two weeks before the trial. Judge Geller wrote, "The Court is deeply troubled by the manner in which the Officer of the State's Attorney for Baltimore City has handled this matter."[952]

According to one established attorney in Baltimore who is familiar with the attrition and morale problems in the office, "She [Mosby] has lost more prosecutors than you can count, frankly. People just don't like working for her. And she's got a terrible reputation as someone who is impossible to work for. And I personally know a few prosecutors that left her office because they said she's just mercurial; you just don't know when she is going to blow up at you. And she's unreasonable."[953]

And even though Mosby ran on a campaign of transparency, to this day, her office's website does not list the number of prosecutors currently working in her office.

In 2019, after Baltimore experienced more than three hundred homicides, as it had every year since Mosby was elected in 2015, Maryland Governor Larry Hogan announced a host of plans to target increased violence in Baltimore City. Hogan requested data from Mosby's office, including the number of homicide cases dropped, the reasons for dropping those cases, the number of cases pled down to lesser charges, and the number of repeat violent offenders who were offered plea deals. Mosby refused to comply and instead insisted that Hogan had "used Baltimore as a punching bag."[954] So much for transparency.

Hogan responded to Mosby's punching-bag comment, saying, "I thought it was silly; she threw kind of a temper tantrum…. It was like 'a dog ate my homework [excuse].' She doesn't want to provide the information."[955] Hogan noted that if Mosby didn't provide the information, he would work to cut off funding to her office, later saying that "Baltimore needs a prosecutor who will actually prosecute violent criminals."

A few weeks before this incident, Mosby's office tweeted out that they had held a press conference to announce that they just secured two homicide convictions. The problem was that no press was at the press conference, causing Dr. Richard Vatz, a rhetoric professor at Towson University, to comment, "It seems she's strategically avoiding questions from the press…. It's not the first time this month it appears no press was invited to her press conferences posted to social media."[956]

Community leaders across Baltimore, most of whom self-identify as Democrats, have decried Mosby's policies.

Art Estopinan, who served on Capitol Hill for twenty-seven years and is an influential real estate investor in Baltimore said, "The residents of Baltimore do not feel safe under [Mosby's] new policies [of] not prosecuting prostitution or drug events…it's a disgrace."[957]

Ron Furman, who owns Max's Taphouse, a popular bar and restaurant near Baltimore's famous inner harbor and the Fells Point section of town, is frustrated with what he sees as Mosby's anything-goes attitude, saying, "I'm fed up with what's going on in this city…we've seen business decline, we've seen crime go up, we've seen quality-of-life issues that keep getting worse. It's the definition of insanity; you keep doing the same thing and expect different results."[958]

The Reverend P. M. Smith is a native of Baltimore and a product of its public schools. A black pastor of the Huber Memorial Church in Baltimore, Smith has a law degree from the University of Michigan Law School and practiced criminal law for a decade until he was called to the church. A married father of two grown children, Smith has been outspoken about Mosby's lax policies, their impact, and the kind of prosecutor Baltimore needs. "There are a couple of things that I don't need. I don't need a politician in that office. I don't need a civil rights advocate in that office. I don't need a social worker; I need a prosecutor. I need a street fighter."[959]

When asked by the reporter what a good prosecutor for Baltimore would look like, Pastor Smith laid out a commonsense, three-point plan. "Get guns. If you commit a crime with a water gun or a ghost gun, you go to jail. Clear the corners. He who controls the corners controls that whole community. Get them off the corners. Number three: nuisances. Nip the nuisance in the bud, otherwise it's going to grow. Our young folks will go and graduate to more serious crimes, so let's get them while they are dealing with the lesser crimes."[960]

Tony Foreman, the restaurant owner mentioned earlier, who describes himself as the "most socialist entrepreneur you'll ever meet," attended a community forum in Roland Park with Mosby and concerned citizens on April 6, 2022. That meeting, which was videotaped, showcases Mosby as the defensive, inarticulate, and thin-skinned person that she is. Foreman asked Mosby if she saw any connection between her lax policies and the rise in crime, including homicides. Mosby, in a snitty tone, quipped, "Am I responsible? Am I responsible for the number of high homicides? You understand the role of a prosecutor, right? I do. And so, to attribute the number of homicides to my prosecutors, I think...it's illogical."[961]

This is the same Marilyn Mosby who in 2015 accused then-State's Attorney Gregg Bernstein of being responsible for crime in Baltimore and who promised to lower crime rates if she was elected.

When another attendee asked Mosby about her upcoming federal trial, Mosby said that she was not at the meeting to defend herself and added, "I'm being racially and politically and personally, they're being attacked by an individual who has combed every aspect of my life for the past two years...."[962]

Richard Vatz, a local commentator and media analyst mentioned earlier, asked Mosby about prematurely withdrawing money from her retirement account. Mosby snapped, "It's my money."

Befuddled by the comment, Vatz retorted, "No it's not." Vatz, commenting on Mosby's demeanor and performance at the Roland Park meeting, said, "This is not the way to seriously answer questions if you are a public servant. You look self-pitying, you look like you're uninterested in solving problems of your venue, and instead, you look like you are only interested in protecting yourself."[963]

Christine McSherry, a Democrat who lives in Roland Park, said, "It's up to her office to prosecute cases and I do feel like they haven't been prosecuting enough of the minor crimes, which eventually lead to the larger crimes."[964] McSherry formerly worked in the Office of the Attorney General for the State of Maryland.

After the tense meeting, Foreman told the media that Mosby "was professionally immature. She wasn't taking responsibility for her core functionality in her position and her office."[965]

When we spoke with Foreman, he added, "The thing that shocked me with the conversation with Marilyn was I was laying out simple questions; I was surprised she was so unsavvy, surprised that she was so out of control, and I was surprised that she so quickly played the race card."[966] In the same conversation, Foreman said he wasn't surprised with Mosby's inability to answer the city council's questions about staffing shortages in her office, saying, "She doesn't know the answers. She is not a competent person."[967]

And when you look at the carnage that has taken place in Baltimore since Mosby became the city state's attorney, you can see why the residents of the city are gravely concerned.

# CRIME EXPLODED IN BALTIMORE UNDER MOSBY'S WATCH

## Homicides

In the eight years before Mosby was elected, there were fewer than three hundred murders per year in Baltimore City, averaging 229 per year. Every year since Mosby has been in office, there have been well more than three hundred murders.[968]

Between 2015 and 2021, there was an average of 333 murders per year, a whopping increase of 104 murders per year. The vast majority of those killed are African Americans.

From 2009 to 2014, the murder rate in Baltimore City fell from fewer than eight per one hundred thousand to six per one hundred thousand, but in 2015 the murder rate shot up and has remained well above eight per one hundred thousand ever since. Put another way, from 2015–2021, there were 2,332 homicides in Baltimore City, meaning that about one out of every 350 residents was murdered during that time frame.

As of July 20, 2022, Baltimore had 198 homicides, which put it on track to have another three hundred-plus homicides this year.

## Rape Numbers Up

Rapes have shot up as well. The five-year average of rapes per year before Mosby was elected was 292 per year. After Mosby was elected, the five-year average has been 330 per year. In other words, there were 190 more people raped in the first five years of Mosby's tenure, compared to the five years before she assumed office.

## Aggravated Assault Numbers Up

Aggravated assaults, which could include the use of a gun, have predictably shot up under Mosby's tenure as well. In the five years before Mosby was elected, there were 23,707 aggravated assaults. In the five years since she was elected, there have been 26,519 aggravated assaults, representing an additional 2,812 aggravated assaults in total or 562 additional aggravated assaults per year.

## Burglary Numbers Down

Burglaries have gone down under Mosby's watch. In the five years from 2010 through 2014, there were 38,275 burglaries in the city, averaging 7,655 per year. After Mosby showed up, between 2015 through 2019, there have been 34,635 burglaries, averaging 6,927 per year.

## Number-One Robbery City in the USA

Under Mosby's hands-off approach to enforcing the law, Baltimore City has become the most dangerous city in the country for robberies. In the five years from 2010 through 2014, there were 17,809 robberies in the city, averaging 3,562 per year. After Mosby was elected, between 2015 through 2019, there have been a staggering 25,350 robberies in the city, averaging 5,070 robberies per year. Put another way, 7,541 additional people were robbed, many at gunpoint, while Mosby acted as Baltimore's gatekeeper to the criminal justice system.

Robberies are so commonplace in Baltimore now that even Daniel Mitchell, the deputy police commissioner, and his wife, were robbed at gunpoint in 2019. In fact, in 2019, Baltimore City was the number-one city in America for robberies, topping out at ninety-five robberies for every one hundred thousand residents.[969]

Mosby refuses to talk about the rising crime rate in Baltimore, even though everyone else in Baltimore, from the defense bar, judges, business owners, residents, and even the criminals, knows crime has exploded in Charm City since 2015.

The reason she won't talk about rising crime rates is because rising crime rates is the Achilles heel of the rogue prosecutor movement. Even Mosby knows this but will not take any responsibility for her role in the carnage that is taking place in Baltimore.

But as the saying goes, actions have consequences. Inaction, or failure to act, also has consequences.

On July 19, 2022, the voters of Baltimore City went to the polls and voted in the primary for the next city state's attorney of Baltimore. The three candidates were Mosby, Ivan Bates, and Thiru Vignarajah. Mosby lost the primary to Ivan Bates, a former prosecutor-turned criminal defense attorney who campaigned on restoring law and order to the streets of Baltimore and repairing the relationship between the City State's Attorney's Office, the Baltimore Police Department, and the residents of Charm City.

It seems the residents of Baltimore, just like those in San Francisco, had enough of their "progressive" prosecutor.

And it didn't take long for the residents of Gotham City to realize that their newly elected district attorney was nothing to brag about either.

# CHAPTER 10

# ALVIN BRAGG: NEW YORK CITY

## GOTHAM'S WORST NIGHTMARE

*"The fact that a district attorney had to send out a
new memo stating that armed robbery will NOW
be charged as a felony is almost as scary as the
crime crisis he's supposed to [be] fighting."*[970]

**Paul DiGiacomo—President of the
Detectives' Endowment Association**

*"My son is dead, and nobody cares."*[971]

**Madeline Brame—Murder Victim's Mother**

Hason Correa, a thirty-five-year-old married father of three young
children, survived a combat tour in Afghanistan.[972] But on October
19, 2018, four assailants—two brothers, their sister, and a family friend—
attacked Correa and his father in front of a Harlem apartment building.
Some of the assailants stabbed both men in their chests multiple times.
While Correa's father survived, the army veteran did not, and Harlem
Hospital staff pronounced him dead shortly after arrival.[973]

Fast forward almost four years, and Correa's mother, Madeline Brame,
sat in a Manhattan courtroom, beside herself with outrage and emotion,
as she watched prosecutors from recently elected District Attorney Alvin
Bragg's office cut a sweetheart deal with one of the people involved in her
son's murder. Bragg permitted Travis Stewart to plead guilty to attempted
gang assault and to be sentenced to only seven years' imprisonment.[974]
Brame said, "In the four years that I sat through this I never missed a

court date…. I never once saw one ounce of remorse from Mr. Stewart. I saw smiles, waiving, blowing kisses like he's a rock star. Not one drop [of remorse]!"[975] Outraged, she yelled at Bragg's deputy, "Take that restorative justice bulls—t and shove it up your asses…. Not for murder."[976]

Her outrage is more understandable given that shortly before Stewart's sentencing, Bragg had allowed Mary Saunders, the woman involved in the assault, to plead guilty to the relatively minor charge of second-degree assault with a sentence of only one year in jail, meaning authorities immediately freed her with time served.[977] Bragg's deputy DA said that Saunders was "not a determining factor in causing the fatal injuries to Mr. Correa."[978] Never mind the fact that at a minimum she kicked and tried to hit him while her brothers stabbed him. Prosecutors under Bragg's predecessor had originally charged her with murder in the second degree and gang assault and had alleged that Saunders tried to hold down Correa while her brothers repeatedly stabbed him.[979]

Not only was Brame outraged by the lenient terms of this deal but also with how it came about. In an open letter addressed to both Bragg and New York Governor Kathy Hochul, Brame said that Bragg "violated my rights as a crime victim to be fully informed, and to be heard."[980] She told him that "you and your office chose to not meaningfully consult our family that you were going to dismiss the murder charges against two of the people…until after you agreed to that deal with the attorneys representing the defendants."[981] She went on to ask him, "Why did you not want the public to hear what our family thought about the dismissal of murder charges against two individuals who, the prior administration and homicide prosecutors said, were clearly responsible?"[982] According to reports, Bragg's team met with Brame only days before the deals were finalized in court, but they did not consult with her before they made the decision to offer and accept the deals.[983]

## BRAGG'S BACKGROUND

Bragg's ascent to the top prosecutor's job in Manhattan did not come as a surprise to many who knew him. As far back as his undergraduate days at Harvard, observers said that given his gregarious nature and his keen intellect, he would be a natural choice to pursue elective politics.[984] Though neither of his parents was a native New Yorker, he grew up in Harlem on a tree-lined street of brownstones. His mother worked for the Borough of Manhattan Community College, and his father worked as the director of the New York Urban League and later as an assistant superintendent for welfare in the New York City Human Resources Administration.[985] Bragg attended the tony Trinity School from the age of four through high school. This private Episcopalian school, which was founded in 1709, is regarded as one of the country's best schools and has a price tag to reflect that status. Tuition for the 2022–2023 school year currently runs $58,385, plus additional fees, though students can apply for financial aid.[986]

After graduating from Trinity, Bragg attended Harvard where he received his undergraduate degree in government. He then continued his education by attending Harvard Law School where he "was on the first-place team in the Ames Moot Court Competition and was an editor for the *Harvard Civil Rights-Civil Liberties Law Review*."[987] After law school, he clerked for federal district court judge Robert Patterson Jr.[988] It was during this time that Bragg first began considering a career as a prosecutor because "he saw how influential those in the role could be."[989] After briefly working in private practice, Bragg joined the New York Attorney General's Office under Eliot Spitzer. He then left that position to become the chief of litigation and investigations for the New York City Council.[990]

In 2009, Bragg joined the US Attorney's Office for the Southern District of New York until he rejoined the New York Attorney General's Office in 2013 where he eventually was promoted to chief deputy attorney general.[991] In December 2018, he left the Attorney General's Office to become a visiting professor and the codirector of the Racial Justice Project at New York Law School.[992] Six months later, he was running to be Manhattan's new DA with a million dollars in support from George Soros.[993] Six months after that, after successfully winning the Democratic primary and the general election, he took office as Manhattan's new DA on January 1, 2022.

## RADICAL POLICIES

In addition to his professional experience and his personal charisma, his friends have long said that "Bragg is also a smooth and convincing talker."[994] On the campaign trail, Bragg said that he was running for the office "to make the District Attorney's office the progressive leader it should be. One that proves we can keep neighborhoods safe and end the racial disparities that are still deeply ingrained in the system."[995] He said the "most important responsibilities [of an elected DA] are to keep people safe and deliver justice for all." He went on to say that the "District Attorney must enact policies and make decisions that keep Manhattanites safe. The DA must also promote fairness and justice for all. …you can't have one without the other."[996]

Following in the footsteps of Los Angeles's rogue prosecutor, George Gascón, Bragg sent a memo to his entire staff shortly after taking office detailing "key principles" and policies that took effect that same day.[997] Bragg actually issued his "Day One Memo," as it is colloquially known, on his third day in office. Even reporters friendly to him noted, it "sparked an immediate firestorm."[998] While Bragg officially titled the memo "Achieving Fairness and Safety," it quickly became apparent his policies furthered neither goal. Like Boston's former rogue district attorney, Rachael Rollins, whom the Biden administration elevated to be the US Attorney for Massachusetts, Bragg announced crimes that his office would no longer prosecute, even though they remain criminal offenses in the state of New York.

## DO NOT PROSECUTE LIST

Some of the crimes you can now commit with impunity under Bragg's watch include:

- Possessing marijuana
- Refusing to pay the fare for public transportation
- Trespassing
- Failing to pay fines for unlicensed operation of a motor vehicle
- Committing any traffic infraction
- Resisting arrest
- Obstructing governmental administration

- Engaging in prostitution
- Committing most other misdemeanor offenses

In other words, Bragg unilaterally appointed himself as a one-man legislative committee with the power to ignore—and override—the laws New York's legislature passed and New York's governor duly signed into law. At one point Bragg even bragged that "the only misdemeanor I ever prosecuted were two people who were blocking access to a Planned Parenthood facility."[999]

## WATERING DOWN FELONIES TO MISDEMEANORS

Although Bragg's "won't prosecute" list was bad, even more disturbing was his decision to require his deputies to water down (undercharge) serious criminal offenses from felonies to misdemeanors. When you combine this policy with Bragg's new directive requiring a presumption of pretrial nonincarceration for every case, except for those charged with homicide and a few other heinous crimes, there is no doubt that his policies favor criminals at the expense of the New Yorkers he was elected to protect. Under Bragg's initially issued policies, he ordered his deputies to water down the following crimes:

- First-degree robbery must be charged as petty larceny. That's required even in cases where force or threat of force is used, and the criminal displays a dangerous weapon. As long as the criminal "does not create a genuine risk of physical harm," the charge must be watered down to petty larceny. This means that the majority of robberies in commercial settings like stores and gas stations will be reduced to misdemeanors. And how will Bragg define "genuine risk of physical harm"? That terminology is not in the penal law. Or another possible scenario: someone commits a robbery while brandishing a gun that, unbeknownst to the victim, is not loaded. Since the gun is not actually loaded, under Bragg's policy, there would be no "genuine risk of physical harm," even though the victim would be scared for her life. Robbery is a Class B violent felony, meaning that, if convicted, a felon would receive a minimum of five years in prison and a maximum of twenty-five years. Petty larceny is a Class A misdemeanor, with a maximum punishment of one year in jail and up to three years' probation.

- Residential burglary watered down: theft of property from a storage area or a portion of a home that is "not accessible to the living area" must not be charged as a first-degree felony but rather should be charged as a second- or third-degree felony. Under this scheme, if a person breaks into an enclosed attic from the roof and steals property, and the attic is not accessible from a living area, he can only be charged with third-degree burglary.

- Commercial burglary watered down: a criminal who commits second-degree burglary (knowingly entering a building with intent to commit a crime therein) shall only be charged with a third-degree burglary. That's the difference between a possible prison sentence of three and a half years to fifteen years under second-degree burglary to a sentence of probation for up to seven years. This effectively means that almost all commercial burglaries will only be charged as a third-degree burglary, even if someone lives in an apartment in the commercial establishment.

- Drug dealers get off easy. A so-called low-level agent of a seller shall be charged with misdemeanor possession in the seventh degree, instead of possession with the intent to distribute illegal drugs, which is a Class D felony. That's the difference between a possible sentence of probation of one year for simple possession versus up to seven years' imprisonment for the felony.

This makes all suspected low-level drug dealers subject only to misdemeanor prosecution. "Low-level" is not defined in the penal law. This also ignores the many existing opportunities for treatment and diversion. In other words, drug dealers are getting a good deal from Bragg.

## BRAGG'S GET-OUT-OF-JAIL-FREE ZONE

One of the more dangerous aspects of the rogue prosecutor movement is the effort to eliminate cash bail. According to Bragg's Day One Memo, there is a "presumption of pretrial non-incarceration" for the following cases:

- Robbery
- Burglary
- Breaking and entering
- Carjacking
- Possession with intent to distribute any drug
- Witness tampering
- Domestic violence
- Arson
- Bribery
- Kidnapping
- Larceny
- Use of child in a sexual performance
- Criminal possession of a firearm
- Child endangerment
- Elder abuse
- Unlawful surveillance
- And others

There's a narrow class of cases where there is a presumption of pretrial incarceration, including:

- Homicide
- Class B violent felonies where a weapon causes an injury
- Sex offenses (presumably other than offenses involving "use of a child in a sexual performance")
- Domestic violence felonies

## VIRTUALLY NO PRISON SENTENCES ALLOWED

Under Bragg's Day One Memo, which has since been slightly modified—though most of its policies remain in place—prosecutors were not allowed to ask for pretrial detention and weren't allowed to seek a sentence of imprisonment for most cases. Bragg's prosecutors could only ask for prison where defendants are convicted of the following offenses:

- Homicide
- A Class B felony where the victim suffered serious physical injury from a deadly weapon
- Domestic violence felonies
- Sex offenses, such as rape and child sexual abuse
- Public corruption
- Rackets
- Major economic crimes

On top of that, prosecutors in Bragg's office could not request a sentence of more than twenty years in most circumstances.

## BLOWBACK AGAINST RADICAL POLICIES

These policies immediately had real-world consequences. One judge told a knife-wielding robber that he got "lucky." If his case had been prosecuted two weeks earlier, before Bragg took office, the judge told the defendant, "Based on your record, you would have faced a long period of time in jail if convicted."[1000] But now, he was only charged with a misdemeanor.

A New York Police detective's widow, delivering the eulogy for her husband who was killed in the line of duty, said that "we are not safe anymore. Not even members of the service."[1001] She said that the "system continues to fail us" and that her husband was "tired of these laws, especially the ones from the new D.A.," Alvin Bragg.[1002] New York's recently appointed police commissioner, Keechant Sewell, issued a statement to all the members of her department saying that she was "very concerned about the implications to your safety as police officers, the safety of the public and justice for victims" as a result of the policies Bragg announced in his Day One Memo.[1003]

Bragg, though, quickly tried to spin concerns about his nonprosecution policies as simply misunderstandings or messaging issues. Friendly media outlets said that "Bragg is by no means a newcomer to New York law enforcement, but he has virtually no prior experience with the gauntlet of New York City politics or media."[1004] Shortly afterward, "In a series of public appearances, Bragg apologized for 'confusion' created by the memo. The document, he said, 'left many New Yorkers justifiably concerned for how we will keep them safe.'"[1005]

"I've got a lot to learn about comms and messaging...Lesson learned."[1006] His office also said that Bragg looked "forward to the opportunity to clear up some misunderstandings" with Commissioner Sewell.[1007]

On February 4, 2022, Bragg issued a second memo.[1008] He said that his original memo had been "a source of confusion, rather than clarity."[1009] The *New York Times* summarized the changes like this:

- He said that commercial robberies that involved the use of guns—or even convincing-looking fake guns—would be charged as felonies, as would some robberies committed with other weapons. Mr. Bragg had said earlier that he would only charge robberies as felonies if a defendant had created "a genuine risk of physical harm."

- He said that gun possession would be taken seriously and that those "walking the streets with guns" would be prosecuted. "The default in gun cases is felony prosecution," he said. Gun possession had not been among the crimes Mr. Bragg previously said he would seek incarceration for.

- He reiterated that violence against police officers would not be tolerated and that anyone who harmed an officer, or tried to, would be prosecuted—a clarification to his earlier announcement that he would not prosecute the stand-alone charge of resisting arrest.[1010]

Still, as the *Times* reported at the time, "Much of the original memo—often called the Day One memo, though it was released several days into Mr. Bragg's tenure—remains in place."[1011] The president of the Detectives' Endowment Association said that "the fact that a district attorney had to send out a new memo stating that armed robbery will NOW be charged as a felony is almost as scary as the crime crisis he's supposed to [be] fighting."[1012] Bragg said that he "was surprised by the intensity and pro-longed nature of the reaction" to his policies.[1013] But he shouldn't have been given what's happened in New York City since they were enacted.

## OPEN SEASON ON POLICE IN NYC

Despite his pledge to work with NYPD Commissioner Sewell to keep both community members and police officers safe, what's happened since has shown that Bragg's policies have contributed to a mentality that NYPD officers can be attacked with impunity. For instance, the *New York Post* reported in June 2022 that Bragg "cut a break for two women who allegedly attacked NYPD cops in a wild caught-on-video assault—letting one of them off the hook and downgrading the charges for the other."[1014] The one woman whom Bragg still moved forward with prosecuting had "her felony assault charges dropped to third-degree attempted assault, a misdemeanor" despite the fact that the *Post* reports she was "allegedly seen on video coming up behind the cops and appears to try to hit and spit on the officers."[1015] Bragg says the charges against the other woman were dropped because her conduct constituted a "summonsable, non-criminal offense," even though his office admits that at "one point during her arrest, she momentarily put her feet up against the police car to prevent police from placing her in the vehicle...."[1016] One NYPD officer said this was another example of a situation where "the district attorney blocks the cops and protects the criminals."[1017]

Then there's the viral video from July 2022 of a teenager rampaging against NYPD officers who had the temerity to stop him for turnstile jumping. The fifty-four-second clip showed the towering teen "throwing more than 20 punches at an NYPD officer, slamming him into a metal gate and putting him in a chokehold at a subway station in Harlem."[1018] The officer finally gained control of the situation and arrested the six-teen-year-old assailant. At his first court appearance for this conduct, though, Bragg's office "recommended the teen's release without bail and diversion to family court—where [they said] he'll be tried as a child and face rehabilitation rather than prison."[1019] Here's the problem: according to reports, this was "the teen's third felony arrest in less than four months."[1020] In fact, just "three days earlier, the same troubled teen was arrested and released without bail for allegedly beating and robbing a stranger near Madison Avenue…."[1021] Bragg's office was both aware of and handling that case! The office, though, apparently was not aware of an earlier arrest of this defendant for "possessing a .40 caliber handgun and a crossbow in Brooklyn…."[1022]

When explaining Bragg's decision not to keep the case involving the violent assault on an NYPD officer in adult criminal court, Bragg's spokesperson said, "Our system must respond to children as children."[1023] Bragg's office could have lobbied to keep the case against the sixteen-year-old offender in adult criminal court "if the crime involves significant physical injury, the display of a firearm, a sexual offense or 'extraordinary circumstances.'"[1024] A former Manhattan prosecutor and current criminal defense attorney said that "if [the prior violent robbery only days earlier] is not an extraordinary circumstance, what is?"[1025] He went on to say that if "violence against police officers is unacceptable, why ignore the violent robbery arrest. This isn't accountability. This is lunacy."[1026] New York Mayor Eric Adams largely agreed. He said, "When I say we're the laughingstock of the country, this is what I'm talking about."[1027] He said, "We're not talking about someone that steals an apple…We're talking about someone that has repeatedly used violence in our city."[1028] The Patrolmen's Benevolent Association (PBA) president, Pat Lynch, said, "Every perp knows they can fight a cop and get away with it…. No one is going to jail. We are releasing these criminals to the streets literally within hours, before the paperwork is processed. And we're not being dramatic when we say it literally is a revolving door at this juncture."[1029] Even NY Governor Kathy Hochul said that "no one has a right to assault a police officer, and in a case where there is a prior offense and someone is already out pending trial under our bail laws, they should be held."[1030]

But in Alvin Bragg's New York, they are not.

## GOTHAM SUFFERS THE CONSEQUENCES

And these stories go on and on—from the petty to the extremely serious. Like all rogue prosecutors, Alvin Bragg's policies promote a culture of lawlessness and undermine the rule of law. In another *New York Post* story, an "alleged NYC gym thief got a slap on the wrist despite a lengthy rap sheet that includes 17 larceny arrests, including multiple fitness-center thefts."[1031] Under her plea deal with Bragg's office, she didn't have to serve any jail time and didn't have to make restitution to the victims. One of the victims of that theft certainly disputed the rogue prosecutors' contention that so-called quality-of-life crimes, like petty theft, have no impact on victims and the community. The infuriated victim said, "I am beyond outraged. …She stole personal stuff of mine: Cash, bank card, state ID. I had to get my $1,500 iPhone replaced and new glasses.… She impacted my life majorly. It makes me very disgusted the way the justice system is working."[1032]

Bragg gave another serial shoplifter a sweet deal too. NYPD arrested Nolan Gonzalez at Macy's flagship-Herald-Square store on May 29, 2022, after he allegedly tried to steal three hundred and fifty dollars' worth of merchandise.[1033] Because he was [a] repeat offender who had already been arrested five other times that year, including at both the Manhattan and Queens Macy's locations, Macy's had him "trespassed." This means that Gonzalez was instructed not to enter any Macy's and that if he did and stole goods, he essentially committed burglary. That's why after the March 29, 2022, incident, police initially charged him with grand larceny, burglary, and possession of stolen property. "But once the accused thief got to court, District Attorney Alvin Bragg's office reduced the charges to possession of stolen property and petty larceny, a misdemeanor—and [he] walked out without bail."[1034] A former Bronx prosecutor and current criminal defense attorney said that it "sounds like the DA is being soft on shoplifting again."[1035] One NYPD official said that "everything property-related gets downgraded. …The DA's office just doesn't care."[1036]

Though these property offenses are serious—and seriously impact the quality of life for everyone in Manhattan and NYC, not just merchants—Bragg's laissez-faire approach to prosecution has led to more serious offenses too. For instance, Bragg reduced the charges for a man who, according to reports, had "36 busts on his rap sheet."[1037] After receiving a break from Bragg, he walked up to a random woman on New York's streets and hit her in the face. Then there's the allegation that Bragg's prosecutors failed to secure a warrant sought by NYPD detectives for a gun used in a robbery that the same suspect later allegedly used to kill someone.[1038]

Paul DiGiacomo, the Detectives' Endowment Association president asked, "Why didn't DA Bragg's office act?…Why did another New Yorker have to die?"[1039]

## BOTCHED BODEGA PROSECUTION

Then there's Alvin Bragg's perplexing decision to prosecute Jose Alba, a sixty-one-year-old bodega worker who fatally stabbed thirty-five-year-old Austin Simon as Simon attacked him at the bodega where he worked.[1040] Bragg's office initially charged Alba with second-degree murder and sought to have him held on $250,000 bail until they eventually negotiated a lower bail and home confinement after video of the incident began circulating. Video even appeared to show Alba trying to de-escalate the confrontation before he had no choice but to defend himself.[1041] Bragg's perplexing prosecution even led the *New York Post*'s editorial board to ask whether it's only "*actual* criminals the DA wants to protect…."[1042] Under pressure and video evidence that strongly supported Alba's self-defense claim, Bragg belatedly dismissed the murder charges against him.[1043]

His charging decisions look even more perplexing considering that Bragg's office declined to prosecute Simon's girlfriend who pulled out a knife during the altercation and stabbed Alba. Bragg's office said she was just defending her boyfriend—the one who was the aggressor and attacked Alba.[1044] The decision not to charge her perplexed former prosecutors. The woman claimed she never stabbed Alba, though the video footage and Alba's wounds suggest otherwise.[1045] In a follow-up editorial about the incident, the *Post*'s editorial board asked, "How many times can Manhattan District Attorney Alvin Bragg get it wrong when it comes to criminals and crime victims?"[1046] Apparently, the answer is a lot.

## CRIME STATISTICS PAINT A GRIM PICTURE

Manhattan's crime statistics also support the increased crime and real-world impact that many Manhattanites are experiencing. In August 2022, New York's local CBS affiliate published a story saying that Manhattan's 6th Precinct, "which includes the West Village and Greenwich Village" has received a "distinction no neighborhood wants in New York City."[1047] It had experienced "the largest spike in crime in the five boroughs."[1048] The numbers are staggering. Compared to the same period the previous year, burglaries increased 119 percent, grand larcenies 100 percent, car thefts 39 percent, robberies 45 percent, and rapes 43 percent.

NYPD divides the borough of Manhattan into two overarching administrative divisions, Patrol Borough Manhattan South and Patrol Borough Manhattan North. The 6th Precinct is in Manhattan South.[1049] Overall, in Manhattan South, as of August 14, 2022, compared to the same period the previous year, murders are up 12.5 percent.[1050] Rapes are up 4.8 percent. Robberies are up 45.5 percent. Felony assaults are up 7.6 percent. Burglaries are up 57.5 percent. Grand larcenies are up 66.5 percent. And grand larceny automobile thefts (GLA) are up 25.8 percent. The year-to-date increase from the same time period two years earlier is even more shocking. Murders are up 100 percent. Rapes are up 35.8 percent. Robberies are up 85.8 percent. Felony assaults are up 41.9 percent. Burglaries are up 13.2 percent. Grand larcenies are up 70.6 percent. And GLAs are up 51.9 percent.

Manhattan North fairs slightly better in some categories but as bad or worse in others.[1051] Murders are down 20 percent compared to the same time the previous year, but every other crime category reported has increased. Rapes have increased by 33 percent. Robberies have increased by 24.1 percent. Felony assaults have increased by 13.7 percent. Burglaries have increased by 33.3 percent. Grand larcenies have increased by 33.9 percent. And GLAs have increased by 44 percent. From the same time period two years earlier, murders are down 20 percent. But rapes are up 36 percent. Robberies are up 23.2 percent. Felony assaults are up 35.9 percent. Burglaries are down 7.4 percent. Still, grand larcenies are up 46.1 percent. And shockingly, GLAs are up 112.8 percent.

## NOTHING TO BRAGG ABOUT

Unlike some elected rogue prosecutors, like Philadelphia's Larry Krasner, Bragg was a prosecutor before he was elected. As a former line prosecutor, Bragg should know better than most that the job of the district attorney is to enforce the laws as written and to exercise appropriate prosecutorial discretion in individual cases. But once Bragg ran for office, he publicly bought into the rogue prosecutor mantra and pursued policies that harm the citizens of Manhattan and New York City.

Is it any wonder that veteran prosecutors are fleeing his office?[1052] One former prosecutor said that Bragg "wants to get rid of all the senior people who prosecuted high-profile cases and replace them with young inexperienced people who think like him and don't want to uphold the law."[1053]

Is it any wonder that the district attorneys in New York City's four other boroughs—some of whom would not consider themselves to be law-and-order prosecutors—are trying to distance themselves from Bragg's policies?[1054]

One former NYPD detective succinctly summed up the problem, stating that Bragg's policies "send the wrong message to criminals."[1055] He said that "Bragg seems to be more concerned for the welfare of the criminal rather than the victims or our society. When a crime is committed, the punishment must be swift...If the DA is only looking to incarcerate for the most serious crimes, then the criminal will be released and free to commit more crimes. Yes, because that's what criminals do!"[1056] That sentiment perfectly encapsulates the problems not only with Bragg's policies but with the rogue prosecutor movement generally.

# CHAPTER 11

# THE WAY FORWARD

After reading this book, we hope that we have convinced you that our observation—there is nothing "progressive" about the progressive prosecutor movement—is true.

These individuals haven't created anything new that improves public safety, incentivizes lawbreakers to change their behavior and become productive members of society, or honors and protects victims of crime. Quite the opposite: their radical policies harm public safety, incentivize more lawbreaking, and ignore and/or harm victims. There is nothing positive or laudatory about the movement whatsoever, as it is an abomination that is, quite frankly, a cancer on the body politic.

Furthermore, the movement is built on a fundamentally false and disingenuous narrative: that the entire criminal justice system is systemically racist, which has resulted in a mass incarceration problem.

That's why we call progressive prosecutors "rogue prosecutors," because they (and the movement behind them) bastardize and contort the role of the prosecutor into a macabre creature that is a prosecutor in name only.

Fortunately, the tide is slowly turning. The movement is showing some signs of weakness. Poster children for the movement, like Boudin and Mosby, are no longer in office. Gascón's policies have weakened him politically, even though he survived two attempts to recall him. Foxx and Gardner are vulnerable in their next election. Bragg is being attacked by all sides. Only Larry Krasner is comfortably well off, politically speaking. But that, too, can change in an instant.

It's our hope that our book, and others like Barry Latzer's *The Myth of Overpunishment* and *The Rise and Fall of Violent Crime in America*, and Rafael Mangual's *Criminal (In)Justice: What the Push for Decarceration and Depolicing Gets Wrong and Who It Hurts Most*, and other scholarship, will expose the truth behind the rise and fall of violent crime, crime policies that work, the myths of mass incarceration, and the fallacy of systemic racism in the criminal justice system.

In this final chapter, we take head-on the dual myths of the criminal justice system being systemically racist and its cousin, the myth of mass incarceration. We explain in broad terms the role and duties of a real prosecutor. And we end with an optimistic road map on how to identify and defeat a Soros-backed or inspired rogue prosecutor candidate for district attorney, show you how it has been done, and how it can be repeated.

## THE CRIMINAL JUSTICE SYSTEM IS NOT SYSTEMICALLY RACIST

The viability of the rogue prosecutor movement depends on the belief that the American criminal justice system is "systemically racist" and inevitably subjugates black Americans through police violence and "mass incarceration." A public convinced that the tools of criminal justice are used to harm black Americans is primed to view prosecutors' decisions ignoring or underenforcing laws as humane, even necessary correctives.

Yet the accusation that systemic racism afflicts the whole criminal justice enterprise does not withstand scrutiny, and the persistence of the belief comes from the term's frequent, imprecise use in popular discourse, not from its merit.

Assessing the accusation requires some grasp of what structural racism means. Racism is "a belief that race is a fundamental determinant of human traits and capacities and that racial differences produce an inherent superiority of a particular race."[1057] Thus, to be a racist structure, the criminal justice system must implement the belief that blacks are by their very nature inferior and confine them to lower social and economic orders.[1058]

Human systems cannot autogenerate their own beliefs. If racist beliefs suffuse the criminal justice system, they must be held or adopted by those persons charged with creating, maintaining, and applying our laws and policies, namely legislators, attorneys general, prosecutors, and law enforcement officers. While it is common to speak of the criminal justice system as a single, unitary entity, it is in fact comprised of multiple separate systems operating at the local, state, and federal levels. So, to indict the entire criminal justice apparatus as racist, critics should give an account covering the wide variety of actors, motives, and situations involved. In practice, most critics dispense with nuance when inveighing against the "system." Instead, they deploy "racist" or "racism" to describe any outcome that blacks experience with greater statistical frequency than nonblacks.[1059]

The laws and policies comprising the criminal justice system are facially neutral—they make *no* distinctions based on race.[1060] The Constitution flatly forbids legislators, whether state or federal, from enacting laws that make race-based distinctions except in the rarest of cases where they can identify a compelling government interest and demonstrate that the racial considerations are the most narrowly tailored means of achieving that interest, though even those are on shaky grounds.[1061] In practice, legislators have made such distinctions not in criminal law but in areas like education in a belief racial distinctions should be used to increase the representation of black and other non-white and non-Asian Americans.[1062]

Our race-blind system of neutral laws is the product of a conscientious, if sometimes halting, effort to move American society away from prior regimes that enshrined racial hierarchies in law, such as the system of chattel slavery predating the Thirteenth Amendment and the era of supposedly separate-but-equal segregation typified by the Supreme Court's 1896 decision in *Plessy v. Ferguson*.[1063] Because the letter of the law no longer relegates blacks to a lower social caste, evidence of racism must be found elsewhere in the criminal justice system.

Legislators could hide racist intent beneath neutral language, knowing that a given law's operation will target blacks for exclusion or subordination. Or law enforcement might apply otherwise well-intentioned laws in a discriminatory fashion by pursuing and prosecuting only black offenders while allowing nonblacks to offend at will. But the march of American society away from *Plessy* and Jim Crow segregation has resulted in a "criminal justice system [that] works hard to identify, root out, and remedy racial discrimination."[1064] Thus, we have mechanisms like *Batson* challenges, named from the Supreme Court case establishing the rule that prevents prosecutors from using race to disqualify potential jurors from serving in a particular case.[1065] There is no evidence that racist attitudes pervade the actors working at the various levels of law enforcement, and even in the rare cases where that might be the case, the justice system has guardrails to prevent such invidious motives from taking free rein.

Instead, critics take two avenues to sidestep the difficulty of generalizing about the often-unknowable motives of so many actors across a variety of circumstances: disparate impact and implicit bias.

The disparate impact argument is premised on the assertion that racially unequal outcomes evidence racist motivations or that unequal outcomes suffice to show racism regardless of intent.[1066] In criminal law, advocates point to high rates of arrest and incarceration within black communities, particularly among black men, as evidence that the justice system is racist.

From a legal standpoint, the argument is a nonstarter.[1067] The Supreme Court has turned aside many attempts to incorporate disparate impact into its review of criminal laws, explaining that "even if a neutral law has a disproportionately adverse effect upon a racial minority, it is unconstitutional under the Equal Protection Clause only if that impact can be traced to a discriminatory purpose."[1068] Disparate impact is, at most, a form of circumstantial evidence about possible intentions; it does not do the necessary work of identifying the actual motives behind a given policy or piece of legislation.

One criminal law often cited as a quintessential example of racism based on its disparate impact is the Anti-Drug Abuse Act of 1986, a centerpiece in the ongoing "War on Drugs," which targeted the sale and use of crack cocaine by imposing stringent mandatory minimum sentences for possession of relatively small amounts of crack.[1069] The act contained no express racial considerations, but its enforcement resulted in many black offenders being arrested, convicted, and given lengthy sentences for drug-related crimes.[1070] Thus, the law's impact fell heavily on black communities with many fathers, brothers, and sons being removed for years to penal facilities. For critics, the point is not that these offenders were innocent or that crack isn't dangerous, but that the act targeted wrongs black Americans were prone to committing for enforcement and harsh punishment,[1071] while the sentences for powder cocaine, which was seen as less prevalent in—though not absent from—many predominantly black communities were less severe.

Yet even for the Anti-Drug Abuse Act, the case that the law was enacted based on racist motivations is not compelling. Often ignored is the fact that the law passed with nearly unanimous support from the Congressional Black Caucus.[1072] Those representatives were not deceived by mendacious white lawmakers—concerns from their own districts for black victims of crack-driven crime and underenforcement in black communities prompted their support of the legislation.[1073] Black legislators saw the act as a means of protecting black communities.

The efficacy of the act can fairly be questioned, but the accusation of racism is unfounded. Subsequent congressional actions, such as reducing the sentencing ratio for crack cocaine and making that more lenient sentencing standard retroactive, do not validate assertions that the act itself was racist rather than perhaps ill-conceived as some might argue. But the fact that Congress has acted to lessen the effects on black communities is further evidence undercutting the assertion that our lawmakers are maintaining a racist criminal justice system.

From the standpoint of enforcement, disparate impact's focus on arrest and incarceration rates shorn of broader context presents a misleading picture. It is true that on a per capita basis, black individuals are a higher percentage of the prison population than they are in the national population. But these individuals also comprise a higher percentage of criminal offenders than other racial demographic groups.[1074] Critics argue that the higher arrest rate is a direct product of overpolicing in black neighborhoods. But that rejoinder is question-begging. Police make most effective use of their limited resources when they concentrate their efforts in high-crime areas. Predominantly black neighborhoods not only have higher frequency of crimes and higher concentrations of criminals, they are also theaters for so-called street crime, e.g. corner drug sales, theft, mugging, murder, and so on, that are more readily detectable and subject to enforcement than subtler offenses like white collar crime.[1075] Routinely, police departments receive calls about criminal activity from predominately black neighborhoods; police officers, of course, respond to those calls.[1076]

Phrases like "mass incarceration" evoke thoughts of innocent men imprisoned without justification. But American prisons are not filled with inmates oversentenced for simple drug possession.[1077] The stubborn fact remains that most black inmates are incarcerated for violent offenses.[1078] Nor is it true that black offenders routinely get longer sentences than nonblack offenders for comparable crimes; sentencing data indicate that any disparity between black and nonblack offenders is "relatively small."[1079]

The other route fashionable among critics for grappling with the difficulty of proving racist intent is to cite so-called implicit bias studies. These social-scientific experiments aim to show that white Americans, including those who explicitly reject racism, are predisposed to demonstrate racist reactions toward nonwhites at a subconscious level.[1080] By extension, most everything whites do, including the legislation they write and the interactions they have, is pervaded by a subconscious belief in the inferiority of black Americans.[1081]

The problems with these experiments and their foundational assumptions are myriad. We canvass only a few here. The implicit bias experiments record reaction times to the pairings of photo images with select racial stereotypes, some of the latter are simply disfavored political views such as disapproval of affirmative action.[1082] The difference between a so-called neutral reaction and a so-called racist one is a matter of milliseconds.[1083] Moreover, the experiments fail to control for nonracial considerations that can slow reaction times, making the alleged correlation between reaction times and racial bias even weaker.[1084] Needless to say, implicit bias experiments provide no firm answers regarding the extent to which supposed subconscious animus actually affects legislative or enforcement choices in the criminal justice system.

When all else fails, critics contend that the supposed indifference of policymakers and the public to the lingering effects of past laws or the burdens of current laws is itself racism.[1085] But here, critics have it backward. Their critique focuses on the small segment of the black community that commits criminal offenses. Often discounted in their assessment is the much larger portion of the black community that desperately needs protection from the violent, destabilizing crime that has afflicted black communities for decades.

A system of criminal justice is necessary "to punish offenders [and] to deter or incapacitate them from harming others."[1086] It protects individuals, families, and the stability and integrity of the communities in which they live. When black offenders find themselves subject to the restraints and sanctions of the criminal justice system, it is often because of wrongs they have committed against other members of the black community. Black Americans suffer from violent crime at much higher rates than white Americans. They are murdered at higher rates and even in greater absolute numbers than whites even though blacks are only 13.4 percent of the population.[1087] The violence comes overwhelmingly at the hands of other black Americans.[1088]

Given these facts, the true mark of indifference would be to withhold law enforcement resources from black communities and to abandon their populations to the permanent insecurity that arises wherever violent crime is both pervasive and undeterred. There would be no simpler way of assuring that black Americans were permanently confined to a lower social caste. Crime acts as a regressive form of taxation on black communities, forcing the constituent businesses and families to incur crime-preventing costs and forego productive activities out of fear.[1089] Thus, nowhere are the rationales of criminal law better served than when those laws are enforced in communities ravaged by criminality—indeed, there may be no way toward a more stable future for black communities absent such enforcement.[1090]

## THE MYTH OF MASS INCARCERATION

It has become a commonly accepted fact that there is "mass incarceration" in the United States. Everyone "knows" it. Movies, books, law review articles, and popular culture all accept it as a fact.

The problem is that it's not true.

In fact, there is a strong argument that we don't send enough people to prison given the amount of violent crimes committed in this country that aren't solved.

In Ava DuVernay's Emmy Award-winning documentary called *13th*, former President Barack Obama opens the Netflix documentary saying, "So let's look at the statistics. The United States is home to five percent of the world's population, but twenty-five percent of the world's prisoners. Think about that."[1091]

The next voice is that of Van Jones, the controversial Obama administration "Special Advisor for Green Jobs" who was fired shortly after joining the administration. Prior to joining the administration, Jones advocated for convicted cop killer and former Black Panther Mumia Abu-Jamal.[1092] By 2016, when the documentary had been released, Jones had rehabilitated his career, first joining the liberal Center for American Progress, then working as a Distinguished Visiting Fellow at Princeton University, and eventually landed a gig at CNN, where he had been featured on several talk shows.[1093] In 2014, Jones launched #cut50, a communications campaign to cut the US prison population by half in ten years.[1094] Today, #cut50 is a project of Change.org.[1095]

In the documentary, Jones says in a disquieting tone, "A little country with five percent of the world's population, having twenty-five percent of the world's prisoners? One out of four? One out of four human beings with their hands on bars, shackled, in the world are locked up here, in the land of the free."

Next comes Bryan Stevenson, founder and executive director of the Equal Justice Initiative, and author of *Just Mercy*, a *New York Times* bestselling book about justice and mercy. Stevenson says, "We had a prison population of 300,000 in 1972. Today, we have a prison population of 2.3 million. The United States now has the highest rate of incarceration in the world." Bryan Stevenson was the lead counsel in a series of cases argued before the Supreme Court involving the constitutionality of life-without-out-parole sentences for juvenile offenders, including murderers. In general, he is a well-known advocate for individuals who have received the death penalty.

Next to speak to the camera is Michelle Alexander, author of *The New Jim Crow: Mass Incarceration in the Age of Colorblindness*. She says, "So, you see, now suddenly there is an awakening that, 'Oh, perhaps we need to downsize our prison system.' It's gotten too expensive. It's gotten too out of hand. But the very folks who often express so much concern about the cost and the expense of the system are often very unwilling to talk in any serious way about remedying the harm that has been done."

Kevin Gannon, then a professor at Grand View University in Des Moines, Iowa, is next. He says, "History is not just stuff that happens by accident. We are the products of the history that our ancestors chose, if we're white. If we are black, we are product of the history that our ancestors most likely did not choose. Yet here we are all together, the products of that set of choices. And we have to understand that in order to escape from it."

Gannon sets the stage for the theme of the rest of the documentary, saying, "The Thirteenth Amendment to the Constitution, makes it unconstitutional for someone to be held as a slave. In other words, it grants freedom to all Americans. There are exceptions, including criminals."

Khalil G. Muhammad, professor of History, Race, and Public Policy at Harvard University, takes over, saying, "There's a clause, a loophole."

Back to Gannon, who says, "If you have that in the structure, in this constitutional language, then it's there to be used as a tool, for whichever purposes one wants to use it."

Still photos of black men in prisoner uniforms and chain gangs follow, made all the more impactful with ominous music blaring in the soundtrack.

The documentary is an homage to the following notion: ever since slavery was abolished, and especially today, white people have used criminal law to enslave black people, and prisons are modern-day slave plantations.

The Netflix documentary also features (not surprisingly) Angela Davis and Senator Cory Booker, but also criminal justice reform advocates like former Republican Speaker of the House, Newt Gingrich.

When you type "mass incarceration" into Google, you get 19,100,000 results (as of August 22, 2022). Those pushing the narrative that mass incarceration exists pop up in your Google search, including the Prison Policy Initiative, the Brennan Center, the ACLU, The Sentencing Project, Vera Institute of Justice, Vox.com, and the Fair Fight Initiative, just to name a few entries.

Similarly, there is an entire genre of books dedicated to the subject, some of which are best sellers. They include, in no particular order: *The New Jim Crow* by Michelle Alexander; *Policing the Black Man: Arrest, Prosecution, and Imprisonment* by Angela Davis; *Just Mercy* by Bryan Stevenson; *Prisoners of Politics: Breaking the Cycle of Mass Incarceration* by Rachel Elise Barkow; *Locking Up Our Own: Crime and Punishment in Black America* by James Forman Jr.; *Charged: Overzealous Prosecutors, The Quest for Mercy, and the Fight to Transform Criminal Justice in America* by Emily Bazelon; and *Understanding Mass Incarceration: A People's Guide to the Key Civil Rights Struggle of Our Time* by James Kilgore, just to name a few of the more widely read books on the subject.

And not surprisingly, given the tilt of the legal academy, there are scores of law review articles about mass incarceration.

If you read this entire genre of books and law review articles, watched the movies, listened to the pundits, visited the websites of the organizations listed above, and listened to rogue prosecutors, you couldn't be blamed for believing that our society is racist, unfair, the system is rigged against black men, and that police and prosecutors stop black men and send them to jail simply for being black. Not all of them come right out and say that, but that's exactly what they want you to believe. Or, as Rafael Mangual summarized their narrative, "The United States can aptly be described as an oppressive carceral state that has expelled justice from every corner and crevice of its law enforcement apparatus."[1096]

Barry Latzer, the renowned criminologist, sums up the decarcerationists' opinion of the American prison system as an "unrelieved horror."[1097]

## UNCOMFORTABLE FACTS

Open up any dictionary and look up the word *incarceration*. The definition is the same. The word *incarceration* means "confinement in a jail or prison.[1098] Similarly, the word *mass*, as in "mass incarceration," means "a large body of persons in a group."[1099]

Based on those definitions, you would think that those subjected to "mass incarceration" are people in prison or jail. That makes sense, because words have meaning, or at least they should. Whether you subscribe to the idea that words should have their original public meaning when interpreting them, or, you believe that words evolve over time, there is little wiggle room to the definition of the word *incarceration*.

But not to leading decarcerationists. In fact, Michelle Alexander, perhaps the leading voice in the movement, equates "mass incarceration" with "correctional control," even though "the overwhelming majority of people under such 'control' are at large in the community."[1100] As Barry Latzer notes in *The Myth of Overpunishment*, "Alexander adopts an inflated, and essentially dishonest, definition of mass incarceration."[1101] As Latzer points out, citing Justice Department statistics, "Only one-third of criminal defendants in the United States are incarcerated in prison or jail; two-thirds are free on probation or parole."[1102]

To put it more bluntly, "Incarceration, mass or otherwise, should not be inflated to include its very opposite, non-incarceration. This is especially true when the non-incarcerative controls imposed by the criminal justice system are minimal."[1103]

So, when Bryan Stevenson and others assert that the United States has a prison population of 2.3 million people, they are conflating the number of people in actual prison with the number of people at any given time on parole or probation. There are not 2.3 million people in prison, at least if you define the word *prison* the way it is used and defined by regular people.

According to the United States Department of Justice, Bureau of Justice Statistics (BJS), in 2019, there were 1,430,800 state and federal prisoners in the United States and 878,900 parolees.[1104] Federal prisoners only account for 11 percent of all prisoners.[1105]

There is no doubt that 1.4 million prisoners is a large number. It represents a rate of 419 prisoners per one hundred thousand persons.[1106] But it isn't 2.3 million.

# CRIME-WAVE AMNESIA

Besides inflating the number of criminals actually in prison, decarcerationists rarely analyze the why. Why are there are 1.4 million people in prison or so many people on parole, probation, or in local jails?

They don't want to talk about it because it undercuts their political narrative. But it's rather simple.

Crime. And lots of it.

So, when Bryan Stevenson whines that the United States only had three hundred thousand people in prison in 1972 but points out that we have 2.3 million people in prison (not true) today, he intentionally neglects to point out the massive crime wave that hit the United States in the 1960s.

In *The Myth of Overpunishment*, Latzer writes, "The crime tsunami went on for nearly three decades. From the low point in 1961—158 violent crimes for every 100,000 Americans—to the high point in 1991—an eye popping 758 violent crimes per 100,000—the rise was 380 percent."[1107] As the crime rate came down, the imprisonment rate followed. In fact, the 2019 rate is the lowest in twenty-four years, dating back to 1995.[1108]

The crime tsunami was not some media-generated moral panic or a by-product of fake statistics; nor was it a Republican plot to undo civil rights or the war on poverty.[1109] To put this into perspective, more Americans were murdered in the crime boom than perished in World War II, the Korean War, the Vietnam War, and the conflicts in Iraq and Afghanistan combined. Between 1970 and 1995, a staggering 540,019 Americans were slain. War fatalities totaled 507,340.[1110]

And the carnage didn't just result in deaths. Whereas fewer than one million service personnel suffered nonfatal injuries in the foreign conflicts mentioned above, around 2.2 million Americans—per year—were injured by violent crime.[1111]

The response to this crime wave was predictable. The public wanted politicians to beef up the criminal justice system to stem the tide of violence. Since the states, not the federal government, handle the vast majority of crimes, it took time for politicians to strengthen their criminal codes and attach harsher penalties for violent crime.

As Barry Latzer notes in his book, complete with accompanying graphs to prove his point, there were two lags or delays that happened in America that took place when the crime tsunami took place. The first lag was when crime began its meteoric rise in the late 1960s. Imprisonment remained low at first, then started to rise a decade later by the mid-1970s.[1112] Why? Because states and the federal government started toughening up their laws to address the wave. But it took time for those laws that were passed to be put to use against the worst of the worst. Eventually, incarceration increased.

The second lag occurred in the mid-1990s, when the crime tsunami started to roll back. At the same time, however, incarceration was reaching new heights. And that lag "fed the great anti-incarceration crusade," according to Latzer.[1113]

The results of the great toughening were positive: crime began to drop in the mid-1990s, and it kept dropping.[1114] Several empirical analyses found a strong relationship between the incarceration buildup and the fall in violent crime.[1115]

## IT'S THE VIOLENT CRIME, STUPID

In her *New York Times* bestselling book, *The New Jim Crow*, Michelle Alexander writes in no uncertain terms: "Violent crime is not responsible for mass incarceration."[1116] According to her, mass incarceration, especially of black men, is due to convictions for drug offenses. But when you look at the actual data, you see that violent crime caused the spike in the prison population and that the vast majority of black men serving time in state and federal prison are there for nondrug offenses.

According to the most recent report from the US Justice Department's Bureau of Justice Statistics, in state prisons there are 409,600 black inmates, 394,800 non-Hispanic whites, and 274,300 Hispanics, for a total of 1,078,700 inmates.[1117] Blacks make up 37.97 percent of the state prison population. Among those inmates, the following were sentenced to drug offenses: 52,100 blacks, 64,500 whites, and 28,000 Hispanics.[1118] If you removed all the drug inmates, that would reduce the black prisoner count to 357,500, the white to 330,300, and the Hispanic to 245,500, for a total of 933,300.[1119] By removing all drug offenders, blacks would make up 38.30

percent of the inmate population, an increase of .33 percentage points over the actual distribution.[1120]

And if you combine all black drug offenders, state and federal, drug sentences account for only 5.5 percent of black Americans in prison. As Latzer writes, "In other words, contrary to Alexander, more than ninety-four out of one hundred African American prisoners, state and federal, are serving time for non-drug offenses."[1121]

That's why law professor John Pfaff has called Alexander's claim that drug crimes are responsible for the growth in imprisonment and for so-called mass incarceration "blatantly false."[1122]

## THE UNSOLVED CRIME PROBLEM

Each year since 1973, the United States Census Bureau has been conducting the National Crime Victimization Survey (NCVS). Now housed in the US Justice Department's Bureau of Justice Statistics, the latest survey of 249,000 people in 2019 showed that there is a very high percentage of serious crimes that are not reported to the police or never solved even if they are reported to the police.[1123]

According to the interviews of victims and other available data, while nearly half of murderers were caught and imprisoned, less than 6 percent of those who committed rape, robbery, or aggravated assault met a similar fate.[1124]

## CRIMES RESULTING
## IN IMPRISONMENT, 2019

| Crime | Claimed by Victims | Known to Police | Arrests | Admitted to Prison | |
|---|---|---|---|---|---|
| Murder | — | 16,425 | 9,352 | 8,033 | 48.9% |
| Rape | 459,310 | 139,815 | 19,592 | 22,583 | 4.9% |
| Robbery | 534,420 | 267,988 | 65,560 | 30,385 | 5.7% |
| Aggravated Assault | 1,019,490 | 821,182 | 317,632 | 55,268 | 5.4% |

Notes: Murder includes non-negligent manslaughter. Prison admissions for rape include other sexual offenses. Prison admissions for assault include aggravated and simple assault. Prison admissions in 2019 include some crimes and arrests made in previous years.

SOURCES: *THE MYTH OF OVERPUNISHMENT: A DEFENSE OF THE AMERICAN JUSTICE SYSTEM AND A PROPOSAL TO REDUCE INCARCERATION WHILE PROTECTING THE PUBLIC* BY BARRY LATZER, J.D., PH.D. (2022), P. 107; VICTIMS: U.S. DEPARTMENT OF JUSTICE, BUREAU OF JUSTICE STATISTICS, CRIMINAL VICTIMIZATION, 2019 (2020), TABLE 1 (SEE INTRO., N. 3). KNOWN CRIMES: FBI, UNIFORM CRIME REPORTS 2019, TABLE 1 (SEE INTRO., N. 4). ARRESTS: FBI, CRIME DATA EXPLORER, ARREST DATA, CRIME-DATA-EXPLORER.APR.CLOUD.GOV/PAGES/EXPLORER/CRIME/ARREST. PRISON ADMISSIONS: NATIONAL CORRECTIONS REPORTING PROGRAM, 1991-2019: SELECTED VARIABLES, ICPSR 38048, JULY 15, 2021, WWW.ICPSR.UMICH.EDU/WEB/NACJD/STUDIES/38048/VARIABLES#.　　🗲 heritage.org

As you can see from the table above, there were 459,301 claims of rape by victims in 2019. That number fell to 139,815 that were known to police, which resulted in 19,592 arrests, and a mere 22,583 offenders were sentenced to prison.1125 We know that many rape victims, especially male victims, fail to report the crime to the police. So the people who committed those crimes were not held criminally accountable for those rapes.

The same grim statistics hold true for robbery and aggravated assault, according to the chart above.

And of the 16,425 murders (which includes nonnegligent homicide) in 2019, there were only 9,352 arrests, and of those, only 8,033 went to prison.[1126] What happened to the other murderers? Did they get away with the ultimate crime? With advances in DNA technology and other forensic testing, some of them may be caught in another year. But there is no doubt that some people are getting away with murder, literally, and, as you will see, scores of other crimes every year.

And when you look at the actual reasons people are sent to prison, it's clear that the vast majority of them are there because they committed violent crimes and that they deserve to be right where they are.

Fifty-six percent of state prisoners are serving time for nasty, violent crimes, including murder, rape, robbery, or assault.[1127] Sixteen percent are serving prison sentences for property crimes, to include burglary, theft, motor vehicle theft, fraud, and other property crimes.[1128] Fourteen percent are serving time in state prison for drug related crimes, only 3.7 percent of which is for possession. And many of these may be individuals who were originally charged with possession with intent to distribute but who pled down to a mere possession charge. Public disorder offenses make up the rest of the prison population or 12 percent, and include weapons offenses, driving while intoxicated, and other public order offenses.[1129]

Another argument advanced by the decarceration crowd is that our prison sentences are way too long, especially compared to other countries. Again, the numbers show a different story.

In the year 2000, only 19.6 percent of state prisoners who were released had completed their full terms.[1130] When you add in parole and "good time" credit, you see that only about 20 percent of state prisoners actually serve their full sentence in prison.

What may surprise you more is the following statistic: on average, released prisoners only serve 2.6 years, and the median time served is a mere one year and four months.[1131] For violent crimes, the time served is slightly higher, as you would expect, at 4.7 years.[1132]

The other major argument decarcerationists make is that compared to Europe, Canada, and Australia, criminals in the United States serve more time in prison than comparable criminals in those countries. As is clear from the chart below, that is true.

## AVERAGE TIME SERVED IN MONTHS BY COUNTRY AND CRIME TYPE, 1980-1999

| Country | Homicide | Rape | Robbery | Assault |
|---|---|---|---|---|
| England and Wales | 88.33 | 34.05 | 18.00 | 6.66 |
| United States | 113.63 | 59.78 | 41.60 | 23.40 |
| Sweden | 86.95 | 15.41 | 15.20 | 3.07 |
| Australia | 120.33 | 50.91 | 36.20 | 23.08 |
| Scotland | 94.70 | 36.40 | 17.60 | 7.00 |
| Canada | 72.39 | — | 25.90 | 27.95 |
| Switzerland | 46.16 | 25.14 | 20.50 | 10.13 |
| Netherlands | 69.20 | 15.880 | 12.14 | 4.91 |
| Mean of all Eight Average | 82.58 | 29.62 | 20.79 | 11.83 |

SOURCE: *CROSS-NATIONAL MEASURES OF PUNITIVENESS* BY ALFRED BLUMSTEIN, MICHAL TONRY, AND ASHELEY VAN NESS, 33 CRIME & JUSTICE 347, P. 370, TABLE 13.

☎ heritage.org

As Latzer notes, however, there are three main reasons why sentences in the United States are roughly double those in Europe, Canada, and Australia. When you take those three key influences into account, the "United States doesn't look nearly as punitive."[1133]

The three factors, according to Latzer are: recidivism, guns, and murder.

Before the 1990s, western Europe, Canada, and Australia had far lower crime rates than the United States, far fewer offenders, and thus far fewer recidivists.[1134] In the United States, however, starting with the crime wave in the 1960s, recidivism rates went sky high, and states passed increased sentencing for those who recidivated.[1135]

As for guns, Western Europe, Canada, and Australia have far fewer guns, and compared to the United States, far fewer crimes committed by firearms.[1136] Many crimes in the United States have increased punishments when the criminal uses a firearm. From 2000 to 2012 there were an estimated 1,500 gun homicides per year in all of Europe. But in the United States, during a comparable period, there were nearly twelve thousand annual gun homicides, or eight times as many as in Europe. Is it any surprise then that there would be increased periods of incarceration imposed? We think not.

Unlike countries in Western Europe, Canada, or Australia, the United States has a constitutional right to keep and bear arms, guaranteed by the Second Amendment to the Constitution. That right has been upheld by the United States Supreme Court. There are thousands of rules and regulations related to guns in the United States. Many, if not most, gun homicides in the United States are not committed by people who lawfully purchased a gun and then unlawfully murdered someone.[1137] Rather, they are committed by armed felons or gang members who use unlawfully obtained handguns to murder other individuals.[1138] Therefore, additional gun control measures and attempts to repeal or alter the Second Amendment will have little effect and limit the ability of Americans of any race to defend themselves.

Murder and manslaughter account for only 2.2 percent of serious violent crime arrests in the United States but 14 percent of state prisoners.[1139] Think about this: the United States' average for the three decades that began with 1970 was nine homicides for every one hundred thousand of the population. That is roughly seven times more than the average in the UK, Holland, France, Germany, Italy, Spain, Sweden, Canada, and Australia.[1140]

Given the fact that we have a violent crime problem in the United States and the fact that smart-on-crime initiatives and creative solutions by real prosecutors have reduced the prison population dramatically in the last twenty-five-plus years, what is the solution offered by rogue prosecutors and those backing them?

In 2016, right after the rogue prosecutor movement got its start, the Brennan Center released a report that called for a 39 percent reduction in our prison and jail population.[1141] They claim that "nearly 40 percent of the U.S. prison population—576,000—are behind bars with no compelling public safety reason."[1142]

Not to be outdone, the ACLU launched its "Smart Justice" initiative, announcing "an unprecedented, multiyear effort to reduce jail and prison population by 50% and to challenge racism in the criminal legal system."[1143]

Jails are different than prisons in that jails house those serving sentences shorter than one year, those who could not make bail and have pending charges or are awaiting trial, and those awaiting a hearing to determine if they pose a flight risk or the like. In 2019, there were 10.3 million jail admissions. That sounds like a lot of people, and it is. But the average daily jail population that year was under 742,000. And the average jail stay was only twenty-six days.[1144] So while there is a large number of people per year who go to jail as a result of contact with the criminal justice system, they spend virtually no time in jail compared to those who go to prison.

The solutions offered by rogue prosecutors, and the decarceration lobby, are unrealistic now that you see who makes up the US prison population. Given the relatively short sentences many prisoners actually serve, and the amount of violent crime they commit, and the amount of crimes that are unsolved in this country, it is difficult to take them seriously when they propose to cut prison populations in half, refuse to prosecute criminals for entire categories of crime, or take other actions, all of which undoubtedly would lead to another crime tsunami.

That's why we need real prosecutors to be elected to office, not procriminal zealots.

## THE PROPER ROLE OF A REAL PROSECUTOR

As the gatekeeper to the criminal justice system, the American prosecutor occupies a unique role among lawyers. The prosecutor has a higher duty than other attorneys. His or her duty is to seek justice, not simply to obtain convictions. As the American Bar Association notes, "The prosecutor should seek to protect the innocent and convict the guilty, consider the interests of victims and witnesses, and respect the constitutional and legal rights of all persons, including suspects and defendants."[1145]

As you have seen time and time again throughout this book, the notion of holding the guilty fully accountable for their crimes is anathema to rogue prosecutors.

Real prosecutors play a vital and indispensable role in the fair and just administration of criminal law. As members of the executive branch at the local, state, or federal level, they, like all other members of the executive branch, take an oath to support and defend the Constitution and faithfully execute the law as written. They do not make laws. That is the duty of the legislative branch.

On one level, prosecutors carry out the intent of the people by enforcing the laws their representatives passed and the governor or president signed. On another level, they work with the other two branches of government by sharing their views with legislators about bills up for consideration and with judges about the proper application of those laws in particular cases. In doing so, they occupy a unique, distinct role as key members of the executive branch with immense power and even greater responsibility.

As we mentioned in Chapter One, nationally, crime rates were the lowest they had been in decades. Crime rates have gone up recently in cities with rogue prosecutors. Incarceration rates are also the lowest they have been in decades. This did not happen by accident, nor did it happen because of the policies of rogue prosecutors. Instead, it happened because independent traditional prosecutors, who follow the law and believe in protecting victims' rights and the right to be safe from crime and violence, created alternatives to incarceration, specialty courts, community outreach programs, and more.

The rogue prosecutor movement's success depends in large part on the public's historical ignorance of these and other facts.

At the federal level, the two parties to a criminal case are the United States and a defendant or defendants. At the state level, the state is represented by a prosecuting attorney who represents the people of the state. Regardless of whether the prosecutor is called the district attorney, the state's attorney, or the commonwealth's attorney, criminal cases pit the state against a defendant or defendants.

The criminal justice system in the United States is designed, like those in most common law countries, to be an adversarial system.[1146] Under that system, the prosecution and defense compete against each other, representing their respective clients. The people are represented by the prosecutor; the defendant is represented by the defense counsel. The judge serves as a referee to ensure that the trial is conducted in a fair and orderly manner and that the rules of evidence and criminal procedure are followed.[1147] Rogue prosecutors' policies often blur the line, if not outright erase it, between the prosecutor and defense counsel, thus eliminating the adversarial nature of the system and turning it into a system with two defense attorneys. That benefits the defendant, leaving the people, particularly victims of crime, with no advocate. That's unjust and not the way the system is designed to work.

At the federal level, and in all fifty states and the District of Columbia, we utilize the adversarial system rather than the inquisitorial system[1148] because we believe that it is the best way to get to the truth of the matter through a competitive, zealous process within the bounds of rules designed to ensure fairness to both sides.

The American prosecutor has unique ethical duties because of the awesome responsibilities that he or she has. A prosecutor must avoid conflicts of interest, one of the most obvious of which is spelled out by the American Bar Association: "The prosecutor should not represent a defendant in criminal proceedings in the prosecutor's jurisdiction."[1149] While prosecutors owe a duty of candor to courts and must respect the constitutional and legal rights of everyone, including defendants, it is their job to enforce the law zealously and represent the people, not defendants.

To accomplish their legal, ethical, and moral responsibilities, prosecutors must be and are independent. They work closely with victims of crimes, but they do not form an attorney-client relationship with them. Prosecutors are not the lawyers for victims of rape, child abuse, or robbery in the sense of establishing an attorney-client relationship with them. They represent the people and their interests, and since legislators have passed laws making rape, child abuse, and robbery criminal offenses, prosecutors prosecute on behalf of the people, not any particular person.

Prosecutors are also independent from the police. Police investigate crimes, make arrests, and in some jurisdictions file charges. Prosecutors, who are lawyers subject to state bar ethics rules and other rules, must be able to evaluate the evidence independently and decide on their own whether the evidence was gathered lawfully, whether the witness statements make sense, whether there are credibility problems with the police officers, or whether there are other flaws in a case before deciding whether or not to file charges. Every day, prosecutors reject cases brought to them by police officers because those cases have some sort of problems.

Police officers are not only investigators in cases; they often are witnesses in criminal cases. Prosecutors must be able to evaluate the credibility of all witnesses and are required under the discovery rules to turn over to the defense *Brady*,[1150] Jencks,[1151] or *Giglio*[1152] material that may be in the possession of the police. Prosecutors do not represent the police any more than they represent rape, child abuse, or robbery victims. Each is a witness, and prosecutors are required to maintain professional distance from all witnesses in order to fulfill their professional and ethical responsibilities.

One of the major criticisms the rogue prosecutor movement levies against traditional prosecutors is that because they are, in the words of one critic, "heavily dependent on police officers to make out their cases," prosecutors are "often reluctant to pursue charges against them."[1153] According to another critic, "Traditional prosecutors tend to abandon their zealous investigation and prosecution tendencies when the perpetrator of a crime is a police officer."[1154] Neither author cites empirical data to support this charge, as no reliable data exist to verify their claims. On the other hand, there are scores of articles in which prosecutors have taken police shooting cases to grand juries, and grand juries, which are composed of everyday members of the community, have decided not to return indictments.

There are over 2,300 separate felony prosecutor offices in the United States. On top of that, there are ninety-three United States Attorneys spread across the country. The vast majority of criminal cases, however, are handled at the state and local levels.

As a result, the state prison systems have substantially more prisoners than the federal system, and because most crimes are committed at the state and local levels, more individuals are involved in the criminal justice system of the states than are involved in the federal system. In essence, prosecutors are the gatekeepers to the criminal justice system. Without independent traditional prosecutors, sworn to uphold the law as written, there is no guarantee that the law will be enforced or that charges will be filed in appropriate cases.

According to Merriam-Webster's dictionary, the word *progressive* means "making use of or interested in new ideas, findings, or opportunities."[1155] There is nothing "progressive" about the rogue prosecutor movement, and the only thing that is "new" about this dangerous movement is its members' approach, which has caused crime to explode in the cities where rogue prosecutors rein, harming the very people about whom they profess to care the most.[1156]

The *real* progressives are the independent progressive and traditional prosecutors who have created thousands of new diversionary programs across the country; have started conviction integrity units in their offices; and have created drug courts, domestic violence courts, and teen/peer courts,[1157] prostitution diversion courts,[1158] veterans courts, mental health courts,[1159] family justice centers,[1160] community prosecutors,[1161] and more. They started these new initiatives because they are charged with keeping the community safe and are constantly trying new ways to tackle old problems in a better, more cost-effective way within the bounds of the law. Given these welcome developments, it is no surprise that crime rates in their jurisdictions have gone down along with incarceration rates.

Prosecutors at the state and federal levels are required to be members of their state's bar, in compliance with that state's bar ethics rules, and to follow the written internal guidelines of their office and local court rules. They exercise professional judgment and discretion each day, from misdemeanor cases to the most serious felonies. Valid and proper prosecutorial discretion takes myriad forms: from telling police officers that they do not have probable cause to refusing to file charges in cases where the evidence is weak; telling a victim that the case cannot be proven beyond a reasonable doubt; refusing to file charges where the accused's Fourth, Fifth, and/or Sixth Amendment rights were violated; dropping prior convictions at sentencing to lower the overall exposure of a convicted criminal; agreeing to a plea to a lesser included offense; deferring on a sentence recommendation; limiting the number of charges despite the fact that the accused committed other crimes; providing discovery to the defense beyond what is legally required; and more. Independent progressive and traditional prosecutors engage in this type of prosecutorial discretion thousands of times a day.

Misdemeanor prosecutors, given the volume of cases they have, exercise discretion every day by dropping cases, holding them in abeyance, or offering a multitude of diversionary programs to those who are accused of minor crimes. The rogue prosecutor movement, by contrast, ignores the everyday use of proper prosecutorial discretion, painting independent progressive and traditional prosecutors as racists intent on notching convictions on their belt above all else: justice be damned.

Elected rogue prosecutors assert arrogantly that they, and they alone, know what is best for the districts they represent and that they have the power to ignore the laws passed by the people's representatives in state capitals. Rogue prosecutors have followed through on their campaign promises not to enforce the law, but when they claim that their policies will reduce and have reduced crime rates and help underprivileged communities, the facts demonstrate otherwise.

As we have made clear throughout this book, the Achilles heel of the rogue prosecutor movement is rising crime rates and disregard and disrespect of victims. Citizens and legislatures are starting to clue into the fact that their policies, despite claims to the contrary, directly lead to higher crime rates and harm minorities at astounding rates. That's the primary reason that Marilyn Mosby lost her primary, Chesa Boudin was recalled, the Pennsylvania House of Representatives has impeached Larry Krasner, why thirty-one city councils in Los Angeles County voted "no confidence" in George Gascón, and the GOP nominee for governor in New York vowed if elected to fire Alvin Bragg from office.

The concern is so severe that George Soros himself took to writing an op-ed in the *Wall Street Journal* explaining why he supports "reform prosecutors."[1162]

In his piece, he sets up the tired old straw man argument that as a society, we should not have to "choose between justice and safety."[1163] He urges everyone to "trust the justice system," and if you do, "it will work." And if the "system works, public safety will improve."

Of course, no one is asking people to choose between justice and safety. And the "system" is a composed of millions of actors, spread across the federal government and fifty state governments. Imploring people to trust the "system" is just ludicrous.

He next argues that "reform-minded prosecutors…have been coalescing around an agenda that promises to be more effective and just…[and it]…includes prioritizing the resources of the criminal justice system to protect people against violent crime."[1164] The statement is baffling, because it implies that before his rogue prosecutors came into being, prosecutors across the country did not prioritize resources to protect people against violent crime. That's exactly what real prosecutors have been doing for decades. If they hadn't been doing that, how do you explain the precipitous drop in crime, including violent crime, in the last three decades?

His next argument is even more vacuous. He writes that even though "some politicians and pundits" (perhaps he is referring to us!) have "tried to blame recent spikes in crime on the policies of reform-minded prosecutors," that the "most rigorous academic study…shows no connection between the election of reform-minded prosecutors and local crime rates." Does he name the study? No. Does he hyperlink to the study? No.

He then adds that the recent increase in crime is because of the rise in mental illness caused by COVID-19 lockdowns, the "pullback in policing in the wake of public criminal justice reform protests, and increases in gun trafficking."[1165] The problem with this argument is that the rise in crime rates started happening in cities with rogue prosecutors starting in 2016, four years before COVID-19. He is correct that the violent protests after the murder of George Floyd produced a spike in crime in large cities across the country. But in the cities with his rogue prosecutors, very few of those criminals were brought to justice, thanks in large part to him installing rogue prosecutors into office. Guns are trafficked by people; they don't traffic themselves. They are inanimate objects. And when the rogue prosecutors featured in this book, and the other lesser-known ones, refuse to prosecute criminals to the fullest extent of the law for gun possession, or refuse to add gun enhancements to other charges, they contribute to the violent crime in their cities.

The fact that he (or someone on his behalf) felt the need to write this op-ed in the first place is a sign that Soros and the movement itself is feeling the heat of rising crime rates and the connection between those sky-high rates and his paid-for or inspired prosecutors. It smacks of desperation. Coming on the heels of the Boudin and Mosby losses, and the violent crime news emanating from large inner cities, the movement is on the defensive.

But Soros said at the end of his op-ed, "I have no intention of stopping."[1166]

## THE REAL PROGRESSIVES: INDEPENDENT TRADITIONAL PROSECUTORS

Independent traditional prosecutors who believe in protecting victims' rights and the right to be safe from crime and violence and who exercise proper discretion are the real progressive prosecutors. They have been at the forefront of keeping communities safe. Crime rates and incarceration rates have fallen dramatically on their watch.

They have worked hard with the bench and bar to create alternatives to incarceration and have been the primary drivers behind specialty courts. Those courts, started decades ago, combined with thousands of alternatives to incarceration and diversionary programs, work to benefit those accused of crime, those addicted to drugs, and others, and this in turn benefits society. They have been tremendously successful in reducing crime and providing necessary resources and incentives to those charged with crimes.

## DOMESTIC VIOLENCE COURTS

Until domestic violence courts were created decades ago, assault cases involving intimate partners were often difficult, if not impossible, to prosecute. Back then, a typical domestic violence case would involve a man assaulting a woman. The woman would call 911, the police would arrive on the scene, she would give the police a statement, and charges would be filed. By the time the case came up for trial, however, the woman would refuse to testify, and the prosecutor would have no choice but to dismiss the case. In many cases, the same defendant would later do the same thing to the same or a different woman—and with the same results.

Independent progressive and traditional prosecutors, working with social workers, judges, academics, and the defense bar, realized that there had to be a better way to break the cycle of violence and get those who were inclined to abuse their intimate partners the help they need while at the same time holding them accountable and providing a safe place for the victims of these crimes.

Domestic violence courts were the result of this new "progressive" thinking. Traditional prosecutors worked with police to gather evidence and contemporaneous statements from victims of domestic violence at or near the time of the assaults. Charges were funneled to domestic violence courts where trained judges, learned in the cycle of violence, presided over cases. Victim services, including temporary housing, shelter, financial support, and emotional or psychological support, were made available to victims immediately so that they had the option of not going back to their abusers. Waiting times for trials were shortened, lessening the chance that the victim would recant her statement that she was beaten.

Prosecutors listen to and work with defense attorneys to find out about the defendant and his issues. In most cases where the charges are misdemeanors, the defendant is offered a pretrial diversion program, which usually consists of going to therapy and domestic violence counseling. Successful completion of the program results in dismissal of the charges.

In cases where the accused chooses to go to trial, and the victim refuses to testify, the prosecutor can still proceed utilizing a recording of the victim's 911 call, photos, the victim's excited utterance to the police officer, and other evidence. If the accused is found guilty, he is usually given some jail time, which is suspended as long as he completes the domestic violence recovery programs described in the preceding paragraph.

These courts, which have existed for decades, are in operation in many jurisdictions around the country. These courts work not only for the victims but also for the defendants if they take advantage of the recovery programs that are offered.

## DRUG COURTS

Until drug courts were created decades ago, minor drug crimes, like simple possession or use, were processed in regular misdemeanor courts. Offenders, many of whom were young and in need of treatment, were not offered the services they needed, and many continued to use drugs and build up criminal records. It was a vicious cycle.

Drug courts, like domestic violence courts, were created by independent progressive and traditional prosecutors with input from defense attorneys, judges, healthcare professionals, and others to give those who are addicted to marijuana and other illegal drugs the substance abuse help they needed. They are like no other specialty courts in the country.

When a person is caught using or possessing illegal drugs like cocaine, heroin, methamphetamines, LSD, marijuana, or other illicit substances, and when a drug court exists and that individual otherwise qualifies, that person's case is diverted to drug court. In drug court, the defense attorney, prosecutor, judge, and drug court specialist work together.

As a predicate, the defendant must agree to plead guilty and be willing to enter drug treatment. The judge imposes a jail sentence on the accused and then suspends the sentence pending successful completion of a set number of weeks (usually one year) of drug treatment sessions. Most drug courts require defendants to look for a job, prove it, and be subjected to random urinalysis tests.

It is common for defendants, especially early into treatment, to test positive. When that happens, they are brought back into court, and the lawyers work with the defendant to find out why he or she relapsed. In some cases, the judge imposes a few nights of jail; in others, the judge simply resets the clock to zero, requiring the accused to begin treatment again. The goal, as with all diversionary courts, is to help the offender succeed in addressing the underlying issue (be it substance abuse, a mental health issue, an anger management issue, or the like), not to hope that the offender fails and ends up in prison.

When a defendant successfully completes drug treatment, many drug courts hold a graduation ceremony for the defendant. Studies have shown that those who complete long-term drug treatment programs through drug courts have a much higher chance of not relapsing than do those who did not undergo drug treatment.

Drug courts have been a smashing success. There are not enough of them, and more need to be created and funded. But where they exist, they are a benefit to everyone, and the rogue prosecutor movement had nothing to do with their creation.

# OTHER COURTS AND PROGRAMS

Other specialty courts and programs are flourishing across the country.

In teen and peer courts, for example, prosecutors and defense attorneys bring high school students to a courthouse, teach them over a day how to present a case, and then allow the students themselves to play the part of the judge, jury, prosecutor, and defense counsel in a hypothetical case. Traditional prosecutors helped to create teen and peer courts years ago as a way to educate high school students about the criminal justice system and the rule of law.

Traditional prosecutors also created the community prosecutor movement decades ago. Community prosecutors work with members of the community, attend community meetings, go to town halls, attend events, and go to schools, churches, mosques, and other houses of worship to listen and explain the criminal justice system. They act as ambassadors from the district attorney's office to the community, providing a valuable information loop from the office to the community and from the community to the leadership of the office.

Traditional prosecutors engage with thousands of other professionals across a broad spectrum of diversion and treatment programs. Some of those programs support victims, and others support defendants. Independent progressive prosecutors have also created better choice courts, mental health courts, elder abuse units, and other specialty units in their offices.

The rogue prosecutor movement is a failed social experiment. They have failed by any traditional measure of success. They have caused death and misery everywhere they have been elected. But the movement is still committed to identifying, recruiting, funding, and supporting candidates who will follow their playbook if elected.

Their playbook and tactics are well known. But because they are well known, we can identify the best practices of how best to defeat a rogue candidate.

# LESSONS LEARNED FROM THE SUCCESSFUL DEFEAT OF A ROGUE PROSECUTOR

Only one large city elected district attorney has defeated a Soros-backed rogue prosecutor, and then the next election cycle, fended off anyone running against her, even though her city was one of the top prospects for the Soros machine: her name is Summer Stephan, the elected district attorney of San Diego County. In multiple conversations with her and others we interviewed for this book, we have identified several lessons learned from her campaign and other races against rogue candidates.

Generally, a successful strategy hewed closely to the admonitions offered in the classic war strategy book *The Art of War*,[1167] Chinese military general Sun Tzu implores fellow warfighters to know thy enemy, writing:

"If you know the enemy and know yourself, you need not fear the result of a hundred battles. If you know yourself but not the enemy, for every victory gained you will also suffer a defeat. If you know neither the enemy or yourself, you will succumb in every battle."

And while the election for district attorney was not (thankfully) a military battle, Stephan and others found wisdom in General Tzu's advice that is applicable to anyone running against a Soros-backed or inspired candidate: know yourself and your enemy.

Here are nine lessons learned from successful campaigns.

1. They read our book, so to speak. They understood the origins and beliefs of the rogue prosecutor movement. They learned their language, and what it actually means. They were aware of their goals and how they plan to "reverse engineer and dismantle" the criminal justice system in your county.

2. They were prepared well before the primary and knew how they would run against their opponents. They observed that this has nothing to do with political party, party loyalty, or, for that matter, public safety. Their opponents didn't care about any of that whatsoever. They simply wanted to win. They flooded the zone with

money for their candidate, arming their candidate with poll-tested happy talk and language, and promising the voters that it's time to "reform" and "reimagine" the criminal justice system. The opposition took no account of party labels, but they realized that if the opponent was backed by Fair and Just Prosecution, Color of Change, received money from George Soros, Cari Tuna, or any of the persons we mentioned in this book, that they were likely a Soros-backed or inspired prosecutor.

3.   They know who they are and what their messages were going to be. They did not wait for the opposition to find a candidate. They did not wait for election season.

4.   They went on offense from day one. They knew the three-part mission of being a great district attorney: honoring the Constitution and following the rule of law by (1) protecting the rights of victims, (2) protecting the rights of defendants, and (3) protecting the rights of people in the community where you serve and their right to be safe. They advertised their strengths as a DA and what their office has done to further the three-part mission. They were open and transparent by sharing data as a matter of routine. They do justice.

5.   They attracted support from a wide base. They explained why they were raising money and told voters about how the person selected as the district attorney will make a huge difference in their lives and those of their neighbors, the community, and small and large businesses. They gave examples of other cities that have elected rogue prosecutors and how badly that has turned out. They understood that you don't have to outraise the rogue prosecutor candidates, because that may be impossible, but they also understood that they had to raise enough to get their story out there.

6.   They developed organic natural allies with very strong voices in the community to ensure they stood with them when the time came. They worked with victims' orga-

nizations, local small and large businesses, and other community leaders to make the community safer. They planned strategically way before the race to leverage those voices to stand with their reforms. When the race began, they were on the lookout for the opposition to create fake or faux-sounding victims' groups. They stayed on offense with their message. They never acted defensively. They did not make promises as a reaction to their Soros-backed or inspired opponents. They deliberately decided not to adopt their language. They did not use words or phrases like *mass incarceration, corrections-free lunch, systemically racist, reimagine,* or other blather that rogue prosecutors and their supporters have made up and have pushed, with some success, in elections across the country. As Ms. Stephan told us, "The race for DA is much bigger than any other office. We have seen the impact of the election of one DA can make. For good or for bad. It's a fight worth having, but you have to be willing to fight."[1168]

7. They planned to outwork the other side, and then went out every day and outworked them.

8. They remembered that they were in charge of making sure the community is safe. Unlike the rogue prosecutors featured in this book, and lesser-known ones, they did not rely on excuses. Unlike the rogue candidates, they did not let anyone tell them what to do. Rogue prosecutors have a playbook that they must follow once elected. The only voices that they listened to were the voices of the people they served. No billionaire or billionaire-funded organization was going to tell them what to do as the district attorney, unlike their opponent.

9. They were very clear on one very simple fact: the definition of reform is actually making something better. Unfortunately, that is not the definition that rogue prosecutors use. They stood up and leveraged the reforms that they had accomplished in their communities, with the help of others, to make the communities safer, help vic-

tims and defendants. They embraced reform and did not run away from it. They called out the so-called "reforms" of Soros-backed and inspired candidates and showed how their "reforms" had a proven track record of failure.

Given the devastation caused by the rogue prosecutors featured in this book, and others less well known except to their local communities, we are confident that, in time, this movement can and will be defeated. Our safety, and the safety of millions who live in our communities, depends on it.

# Endnotes

1    Amanda Woods, Joe Marino, & Gabrielle Fonrouge, "'I Need Help':
     Good Samaritan Comes to Aid of Woman Raped by Stranger on Morning
     Jog," *New York Post* (Nov. 3, 2022), https://nypost.com/2022/11/03/
     jogger-43-raped-by-total-stranger-in-nyc-cops/.

2    Of course, like all criminal defendants, he remains innocent of any crimes unless
     proven guilty beyond a reasonable doubt.

3    Chelsea Edwards, "Torrance Woman Brutally Beaten, Raped by
     Homeless Man Released from Jail Hours Earlier," FOX 11 Los
     Angeles (updated Oct. 21, 2022), https://www.foxla.com/news/
     torrance-woman-beaten-raped-homeless-man-released-jail.

4    *Ibid.*

5    *Ibid.*

6    *Ibid.*

7    Yaron Steinbuch, "Calif. Woman Recalls Attack, Rape by Homeless Man—
     Released from Jail Hours Earlier," *New York Post* (Oct. 25, 2022), https://nypost.
     com/2022/10/25/California-woman-recounts-horrifying-attack-by-homeless-man/.

8    *Ibid.*

9    *Ibid.*

10   Charles Stimson, Zack Smith, & Kevin Dayaratna, "The Blue City Murder Problem,"
     Heritage Foundation. Legal Memorandum No. 315 (Nov. 4, 2022), https://www.
     heritage.org/crime-and-justice/report/the-blue-city-murder-problem.

11   "Justice for Sale: How George Soros Put Radical Prosecutors in Power," Law
     Enforcement Legal Defense Fund (June 2022), http://www.policedefense.org/wp-con-
     tent/uploads/2022/06/Justice_For_Sale_LELDF_report.pdf.

12   *Ibid.*

13   Some cities, like Chicago and Philadelphia, did not submit crime data for certain
     crimes to the FBI's Uniform Crime Reporting system. In those cases, we relied on
     other published crime statistics, such as from the relevant police department, state
     police, state comptroller, and/or paper of record in that city.

14   Gavin Newsom @GavinNewsom, Twitter, Oct. 18, 2022, 10:16 AM, https://
     twitter.com/gavinnewsom/status/1582375031278927872 (last accessed Nov. 29,
     2022); Snejana Farberov, "Lefty Philadelphia DA Larry Krasner Says Crime Worse
     in 'Trump States' in Fiery Interview," *New York Post* (Sept. 30, 2022), https://nypost.
     com/2022/09/30/philly-da-larry-krasner-says-crime-worse-in-trump-states/.

15   Robert S. Redmount, "Psychological Views in Jurisprudential Theories," 107
     University of Pennsylvania Law Review 472, 501 (1959); B.F. Skinner, *Science and
     Human Behavior* (New York: Simon and Schuster, 1953), 138–39.

16  *Ibid.*

17  Dakin Andone, "Baltimore's Deputy Police Commissioner Was Robbed at Gunpoint, Police Say," CNN (July 20, 2019), https://www.cnn.com/2019/07/20/us/baltimore-deputy-police-commissioner-robbed/index.html.

18  Elizabeth Janney, "Robbery Rate in Baltimore Is Highest in U.S.: Report," PATCH (Apr. 5, 2019), https://patch.com/maryland/baltimore/robbery-rate-baltimore-highest-us-study.

19  Television interview of Philadelphia District Attorney Larry Krasner by Fox29 on September 28, 2022, https://www.fox29.com/news/da-larry-krasner-good-day-philadelphia-city-violence-impeachment-efforts.

20  Numbers for 2022 as of November 13, 2022.

21  Mike D'Onofrio, "Philadelphia Homicides Hit Historic Level in 2021," AXIOS (Jan. 10, 2022), https://www.axios.com/local/philadelphia/2022/01/10/philadelphia-record-homicides-2021-police.

22  Fair and Just Prosecution website (last visited November 29, 2022), https://fairandjustprosecution.org/.

23  Fair and Just Prosecution, "Issues, Addressing the Poverty Penalty and Bail Reform," https://fairandjustprosecution.org/issues/addressing-the-poverty-penalty-and-bail-reform/ (last accessed Nov.18, 2022).

24  *Ibid.*

25  Michelle Alexander, *The New Jim Crow: Mass Incarceration in the Age of Colorblindness* (New York: The New Press, 2010). The Index at the back of her book does not list "recidivism," nor is there any serious discussion of it in her book. Bryan Stevenson, *Just Mercy: A Story of Justice and Redemption* (United Kingdom: One World Publisher, 2014). Angela J. Davis, *Policing the Black Man: Arrest, Prosecution, and Imprisonment* (New York: Pantheon, 2017). Rachel Elise Barkow, *Prisoners of Politics: Breaking the Cycle of Mass Incarceration* (Boston, MA: Belknap Press: An Imprint of Harvard University Press, 2019).

26  Emily Hoerner, "Cook County Chief Judge Orders Sweeping Reform of Bail System," Injustice Watch (July 17, 2017), https://www.injusticewatch.org/news/2017/cook-county-chief-judge-orders-sweeping-refrm-of-bail-system/.

27  An example of this can be found in Illinois's recently enacted—and disastrously misnamed—SAFE-T Act. Under this act, dangerousness is defined so narrowly that it will be difficult, if not impossible, to apply it to the overwhelming majority of defendants. There's also a dispute over whether the poorly drafted statute includes a category of offenses under which dangerousness cannot be considered at all—thus making the claim that judges can still consider a suspect's dangerousness during the bail determination doubly misleading. Paul Mauro, "Illinois' UN-Safe-T Act," *City Journal* (Oct. 17, 2022), https://www.city-journal.org/illinois-un-safe-t-act.

28  *Ibid.*

29  Bail Reform in Cook County: An Examination of General Order 18.8A and Bail in Felony Cases, State of Illinois Circuit Court of Cook County, Office of the Chief Judge (May 2019), https://www.cookcountycourt.org/Portals/0/Statistics/Bail%20Reform/Bail%20Reform%20Report%20FINAL%20-%20%20Published%2005.9.19.pdf.

30  Paul G. Cassell and Richard Fowles, "Does Bail Reform Increase Crime? An Empirical Assessment of the Public Safety Implications of Bail Reform in Cook

County, Illinois," 55 Wake Forest Law Review 933 (disputing the data and conclusions of a study commissioned by the Chief Judge of the Cook County Circuit Court, which asserted that new, more generous pretrial release policies did not lead to an increase in overall crime or to an increase in violent crime and instead concluding that the "[s]tudy's methodology and data significantly undercount the number of defendants who committed violent crimes after the changes").

31  David Jackson, Todd Lightly, and Gary Marx, "Bail Reform Analysis by Cook County Chief Judge Based on Flawed Data, Undercounts New Murder Charges," *Chicago Tribune* (Feb. 13, 2020), https://www.chicagotribune.com/investigations/ct-cook-county-bail-bond-reform-tim-evans-20200213-tkodxevlyvcp7k66q2v2ahboi4-story.html.

32  *Ibid.*

33  Fair and Just Prosecution, Issues, Addressing the Poverty Penalty and Bail Reform, https://fairandjustprosecution.org/issues/addressing-the-poverty-penalty-and-bail-reform/ (last accessed Nov.18, 2022).

34  See Black's Law Dictionary, 9th ed. 160 (St. Paul; West, 2009).

35  See Rafael A. Mangual, "Reforming New York's Bail Reform: A Public-Safety Minded Proposal," Issue Brief, Manhattan Institute, 4 (March 2020), https://www.manhattan-institute.org/reforming-new-yorks-bail-reform.

36  *Ibid.*

37  New York State Senate, Criminal Procedure Law, Article 530.40 et seq. (2019).

38  Exceptions include felony witness intimidation, witness tampering, felony criminal contempt, money laundering to further terrorism, or operating as a major drug trafficker.

39  Mangual, *supra* note 35 at 6–8.

40  Bernadette Hogan, Larry Celona, Tina Moore, Bruce Golding, "Recidivism Rates for New York City Burglars and Thieves Soar Amid Bail Reform: NYPD Data," *New York Post* (July 28, 2022), https://nypost.com/2022/07/28/recidivism-rates-for-burglars-and-thieves-soar-nypd-data/.

41  *Ibid.*

42  *Ibid.*

43  *Ibid.*

44  *Ibid.*

45  *Ibid.*

46  Chae Mamayek, Ray Paternoster, Thomas A. Loughran, "Temporal Discounting, Present Orientation, and Criminal Deterrance, in The Oxford Handbook of Offender Decision Making," ed. Wim Bernasco, Jean-Louis van Belder, and Henk Elffers (New York: Oxford University Press, 2017), p. 223: "[T]he clerity principle concludes that there is higher deterrent value in more immediate punishments," and "punishments delivered further into the future will be decreased in value," which supports "increase[ing] the immediacy of sanction in order to increase the cost associated with crime."

47  Hogan, *supra note* 40.

48  Greg B. Smith and Suhail Bhat, "Four in 10 Bail Reform Release Program Participants Rearrested, State Stats Show," The City (Jan. 11, 2022), https://www.thecity.nyc/2022/1/9/22875181/bail-reform-release-program-participants-rearrested.

49  *Ibid.*

50    Yolo County Emergency Bail Analysis (Aug. 5, 2022), https://yoloda.org/wp-content/uploads/2022/08/Emergency-Bail-Analysis.pdf.
51    Length of Incarceration, United States Sentencing Commission (June 2022), https://www.ussc.gov/research/research-reports/length-incarceration-and-recidivism-2022.
52    Angela Davis, *Are Prisons Obsolete?* (Canada: Publishers Group Canada, 2003), 8.
53    Patrisse Cullors, *What Is Abolition and Am I an Abolitionist?*, YouTube (Feb. 22, 2021), https://web.archive.org/web/20220522035018/https://www.youtube.com/watch?v=-RbFhM32YNI.
54    Mark Levin, *American Marxism* (Threshold Editions, July 13, 2021), 42.
55    *Ibid.*, 58.
56    Davis, *supra* note 1, at 8. We can imagine such a world, and it's not one we want our families to live in.
57    *Ibid.*, 16.
58    *Ibid.*, 25.
59    *Ibid.*, 113.
60    Mike Gonzalez, *BLM: The Making of a New Marxist Revolution* (Encounter Books, September 7, 2021), 86.
61    Eric Mann, "Growing Activism: Labor/Community Strategy Center," YouTube (Feb. 8, 2008), https://www.youtube.com/watch?v=BO6MR2s4a0s.
62    Dignity & Power Now, https://dignityandpowernow.org/about-us/# (last visited Mar. 3, 2022).
63    *Ibid.*
64    Patrisse Cullors, "Abolition and Reparations: Histories of Resistance, Transformative Justice, and Accountability," 132 Harvard Law Review, 1684, 1685–86 (2019), https://harvardlawreview.org/2019/04/abolition-and-reparations-histories-of-resistance-transformative-justice-and-accountability/.
65    Left Forum 2015, "Saturday Evening Event," YouTube (May 30, 2015), https://www.youtube.com/watch?v=ETdStVAXwgk.
66    *Ibid.*, 29:06.
67    "Democracy Now: Angela Davis & BLM Co-Founder Alicia Garza in Conversation Across Generations" (PBS television broadcast Jan. 23, 2017), https://www.youtube.com/watch?v=_gqGVni8Oec.
68    Emily Bazelon, *Charged: The New Movement to Transform American Prosecution and End Mass Incarceration*, (Random House: New York, 2019), 78.
69    Just Impact website, https://justimpactadvisors.org/ (last visited Aug. 29, 2022).
70    *Ibid.*
71    *Ibid.*
72    Scott Bland, "George Soros' Quiet Overhaul of the U.S. Justice System," *Politico* (Aug. 30, 2016), https://www.politico.com/story/2016/08/george-soros-criminal-justice-reform-227519.
73    Bazelon, *supra* note 17, 79.
74    *Ibid.*
75    *Ibid.*, xvii.
76    *Ibid.*, xxxi.
77    *Ibid.*, 83.
78    Barry Latzer, "The Myth of Mass Incarceration," *Wall Street Journal*, Feb. 22, 2016, https://www.wsj.com/articles/the-myth-of-mass-incarceration-1456184736.

79  *Ibid.*

80  *Ibid.*

81  Michael Shellenberger, *San Fransicko: Why Progressives Ruin Cities*, (Harper: New York, 2021), 40.

82  *Ibid.*, 41.

83  Jeffrey Bellin, "Defending Progressive Prosecution: A Review of Charged by Emily Bazelon" (Yale Law & Policy Review [Faculty Publication], 2020), 218, 225.

84  *Ibid.*

85  Shellenberger, *supra* note 30, 40.

86  *Ibid.*

87  *Ibid.*

88  *Ibid.* at 39; E. Ann Carson, "Prisoners in 2019," Bureau of Justice Statistics (Oct. 2020), www.bjs.gov.

89  Heather MacDonald, "Testimony before the United States Senate Committee on the Judiciary, Hearing on the Sentencing Reform and Corrections Act of 2015," October 19, 2015, https://www.judiciary.senate.gov/download/10-19-15-mac-donald-testimony.

90  Shellenberger, *supra* note 30, 262.

91  Rachel Elise Barkow, *Prisoners of Politics: Breaking the Cycle of Mass* Incarceration (Cambridge, MA: Harvard University Press, 2019), 1–16.

92  Bazelon, *supra* note 17, xxv.

93  *Kevin A. Sabet, PhD, Reefer Sanity: Seven Great Myths About Marijuana (Beaufort Books, 2013).*

94  Margery Eagan, "Time to End Smoke and Mirrors on Pot," *Boston Herald* (Sept. 18, 1994).

95  Eric Schlosser, "Reefer Madness," *The Atlantic Monthly* (Aug. 1, 1994), https://www.theatlantic.com/magazine/archive/1994/08/reefer-madness/303476/.

96  Sabet, *supra* note 42, 90.

97  *Ibid.*

98  *Ibid.*, 92.

99  *Ibid.*

100  Cheech and Chong are fictional characters in the 1978 comedy movie *Up in Smoke*. A classic movie of the 1970s, the characters smoke pot throughout the story line and bounce from one sketch to the next.

101  *Fast Times at Ridgemont High* is a 1982 American coming-of-age comedy featuring Southern California high school students engaged in sex, drugs, and all the pleasures of the teenage years. Jeff Spicoli, played by actor Sean Penn, plays the part of the stoner.

102  Rachel E. Barkow, "Three Lessons for Criminal Law Reformers from Locking up Our Own," California Law Review 1967, 1968 (2019), 107.

103  Miriam Aroni Krinsky, *Change from Within: Reimagining the 21st Century Prosecutor* (The New Press: New York, 2022), xvi.

104  David Alan Sklansky, *The Progressive Prosecutor's Handbook*, 50 *U.C. Davis Law Review Online* Volume 25 (2017); David Alan Sklansky, Commentary, *The Changing Political Landscape for Elected Prosecutors*, 14 Ohio State Journal of Criminal Law Volume 647 (2017).

105 James Forman Jr., *Locking up Our Own, Crime and Punishment in Black America (New York: MacMillan Publishers, 2017); Rachel Elise Barkow, Prisoners of Politics: Breaking the Cycle of Mass Incarceration (Boston:* Belknap Press: An Imprint of Harvard University Press, *2019); Paul Butler, Chokehold: Policing Black Men* (New York: The New Press, 2017); Angela J. Davis, "The Progressive Prosecutor: An Imperative for Criminal Justice Reform," *Fordham Law Review* 1 (2018), 87.

106 55George Gascón, "Transformative Justice: Prosecution Strategies to Reform the Justice System and Enhance Community Safety," https://www.georgegascon.org/wp-content/uploads/2020/09/SFDA_Transformative-Justice_George-Gascon_2019.pdf (last visited Oct. 19, 2020).

107 Scott Bland, "George Soros' Quiet Overhaul of the U.S. Justice System," *Politico* (Aug. 30, 2016), https://www.politico.com/story/2016/08/george-soros-criminal-justice-reform-227519; Paige St. John and Abbie Vansickle, "Here's Why George Soros, Liberal Groups Are Spending Big to Help Decide Who's Your Next D.A.," *Los Angeles Times* (May 23, 2018), https://www.latimes.com/local/california/la-me-prosecutor-campaign-20180523-story.html (detailing the tens of millions of dollars Soros and other like-minded individuals have poured into various DA races and PACs in order to back rogue prosecutor candidates).

108 57Definition, *Merriam-Webster* Dictionary online, https://www.merriam-webster.cictionary/progressive.

109 Law Enforcement Legal Defense Fund, "Prosecutorial Malpractice: Progressive Prosecutors, Public Safety, and Felony Outcomes (2020)," http://www.policedefense.org/wp-content/uploads/2020/06/Prosecutorial-Malpractice.pdf (showing that in six cities where rogue prosecutors were elected, guilty verdicts decreased substantially, and those same offices dropped or lost cases by substantial percentages compared to when the offices were headed by independent, traditional law-and-order prosecutors); Paul G. Cassell, "Explaining the Recent Homicide Spikes in U.S. Cities: The 'Minneapolis Effect' and the Decline in Proactive Policing," Federal Sentencing Reporter (forthcoming 2020), https://papers.ssrn.com/sol3/papers.cfm?abstract_id=3690473.

110 "Teen Courts: A Focus on Research," Juvenile Justice Bulletin, Office of Juvenile Justice and Delinquency Prevention, U.S. Department of Justice (Oct. 2000) (describing teen courts "as a voluntary alternative in lieu of more formal handling by the traditional juvenile justice system" where other "young people rather than adults determine the disposition, given a broad array of sentencing options"), *available at* https://www.ncjrs.gov/pdffiles1/ojjdp/183472.pdf; Teen Court, Montgomery County, Maryland state's attorney's office, https://www.montgomerycountymd.gov/SAO/other/teencourt.html (last visited Oct. 23, 2020).

111 Sarah Schweig, Danielle Malangone, and Miriam Goodman, "Treatment Courts and Court-Affiliated Diversion Projects for Prostitution in the United States" (2012); stating that "People arrested for prostitution tend to cycle through the justice system again and again. Recognizing this, some justice practitioners are trying new approaches—rather than fines and jail time—to address the problems, such as trauma, abuse, and drug addiction, that keep many women and girls in 'the life' of prostitution," https://www.courtinnovation.org/sites/default/files/documents/CI_Prostitution% 207.5.12%20PDF.pdf; Ana Ley, "The Impact of Specialty Courts: 'I've Seen Girls Go from Prostitution to College,'" *Las Vegas Sun* (June 8, 2014);

describing Nevada's specialty courts, https://lasvegassun.com/news/2014/jun/08/
impact-specialty-courts-ive-seen-girls-go-prostitu/.

112  Mental Health Courts Program, Bureau of Justice Assistance, U.S. Department of
Justice, https://bja.ojp.gov/program/mental-health-courts-program/overview (stating
that the "Mental Health Courts Program funds projects that seek to mobilize communities to implement innovative, collaborative efforts that bring systemwide improvements to the way the needs of adult offenders with mental disabilities or illnesses are
addressed"), (last visited Oct. 23, 2020); Treatment Court Locators, Substance Abuse
and Mental Health Services Administration, U.S. Department of Health & Human
Services, https://www.samhsa.gov/gains-center/treatment-court-locators (stating that
"Mental health courts for adults and juveniles work with people with mental illnesses
who are involved in the justice system. These courts connect people to effective treatment and support after they undergo screening and assessments"), (last visited Oct.
23, 2020).

113  Family Justice Center Alliance, https://www.familyjusticecenter.org/ (last visited Oct.
23, 2020) (stating that they "develop and support Family Justice Centers that help
survivors and their children find the services they need in ONE place"); San Diego
Family Justice Center, https://www.sandiego.gov/sandiegofamilyjusticecenter/fjcinfo/
(last visited Oct. 23, 2020) (stating that it is "dedicated to transitioning victims of
domestic violence, sexual assault, and sex trafficking into survivors" and that it "is a
team of professionals including therapists, nurses, attorneys, prosecutors, advocates,
immigration attorneys, police, and other social service providers").

114  John S. Goldkamp, Cheryl Irons-Guynn, and Doris Weiland, "Community
Prosecution Strategies: Measuring Impact, Bureau of Justice Assistance," U.S.
Department of Justice (Nov. 2002) (stating that "community prosecution initiatives
deploy prosecutors or, in some jurisdictions, nonlegal staff in the community to identify the public safety concerns of residents and to seek their participation in developing and implementing strategies to address the problems that are the community's
highest priorities"), https://www.ncjrs.gov/pdffiles1/bja/192826.pdf.

115  Madison McWithey, "Taking a Deeper Dive into Progressive Prosecution:
Evaluating the Trend Through the Lens of Geography," *Boston College
Law Review* E-Supp. I.-32, I.-49–50 (2020), 61, *https://lira.bc.edu/work/
ns/29f83b28-fc20-41ab-880c-ccd5e4a9ad88.*

116  Olwyn Conway, "How Can I Reconcile with You When Your Foot Is on My Neck?
The Role of Justice in the Pursuit of Truth and Reconciliation," 2018 *Michigan State
Law Review* 1349, 1353 (2018).

117  *Ibid.*

118  Michelle Alexander, *The New Jim Crow*, 11–19, 20–58; Note, *The Paradox of
"Progressive Prosecution,"* 1 *Harvard Law Review* 748, 756 (2018), 32.

119  *The Paradox of "Progressive Prosecution," Harvard Law Review* 748, 750 (2018), 132.

120  *Ibid.*

121  McWithey, *supra* note 63.

122  *Ibid.*; Open Society–U.S., https://www.opensocietyfoundations.org/who-we-are/
programs/open-society-us (last visited Oct. 19, 2020) (listing goals such as ending
"mass incarceration," holding police departments accountable, decriminalizing drugs,
ending the death penalty, and more).

123 Carissa Byrne Hessick and Michael Morse, "Picking Prosecutors," 105 Iowa L. Rev. 1537, 1544 (2020).

124 *Ibid.*

125 *Ibid.*

126 *Supra* note 52.

127 Chris Brennan, "$1.45 Million Soros Investment in Philly DA's Race Draws Heat for Krasner," *Philadelphia Inquirer* (May 5, 2017), https://www.inquirer.com/philly/news/politics/Soros-145-million-investment-in-DAs-race-draws-heat-for-Krasner.html.

128 Chris Palmer, Julie Shaw, and Mensah M. Dean, "Krasner Dismisses 31 from Philly DA's Office in Dramatic First-Week Shakeup," *Philadelphia Inquirer* (Jan. 5, 2018), https://www.inquirer.com/philly/news/crime/larry-krasner-philly-da-firing-prosecutors-20180105.html-2.

129 *Supra* note 67 at 760–63, where the author suggests that there is "significant potential for noncompliance from those on the lower rungs of the hierarchy due to a lack of buy-in to the goals of the head prosecutor." He suggests that this defiance exists across a spectrum and can be subtle but that such defiance "can undermine a chief prosecutor's progressive agenda." He suggests that the most "brazenly defiant" will be fired. Paul Butler, *Let's Get Free Help: A Hip-Hop Theory of Justice* (New York: The New Press, 2009).

130 Hessick and Morse, *supra* note 71, 1546.

131 *Ibid.*

132 Bazelon, *supra* note 17, 290.

133 "Justice for Sale: How George Soros Put Radical Prosecutors in Power," Law Enforcement Legal Defense Fund (June 2022), http://www.policedefense.org/wp-content/uploads/2022/06/Justice_For_Sale_LELDF_report.pdf.

134 Andrew C. McCarthy, "How Progressive Prosecutors Are Betraying the Constitution," *National Review* (Jan. 22, 2022), https://www.nationalreview.com/2022/01/how-progressive-prosecutors-are-betraying-the-constitution/.

135 *Ibid.*

136 *Ibid.*

137 *Ibid.*

138 *Supra* note 67, 752.

139 Bellin, *supra* note 32, 226.

140 John E. Foster, "Charges to Be Declined: Legal Challenges and Policy Debates Surrounding Non-Prosecution Initiatives in Massachusetts," *Boston College Law Review* 2511, 2534 (2019), 60.

141 *Ibid.*, 2534–35.

142 *Ibid.*

143 Shellenberger, *supra* note 30, 262.

144 *Ibid.*, 263.

145 McCarthy, *supra* note 82.

146 *Ibid.*

147 Lea Hunter, "What You Need to Know About Ending Cash Bail," Center for American Progress (March16, 2020), https://www.americanprogress.org/issues/criminal-justice/reports/2020/03/16/481543/ending-cash-bail/; Tana Ganeva, "The Fight to End Cash Bail," *Stanford Social Innovation Review* (Spring 2019), https://ssir.org/articles/entry/the_fight_to_end_cash_bail.

148 Adureh Onyekwere, "How Cash Bail Works," The Brennan Center (Jun. 2, 2020), https://www.brennancenter.org/our-work/research-reports/how-cash-bail-works.

149 "The Truth About Bail: It Doesn't Work," ACLU, https://www.aclu.org/video/truth-about-bail-it-doesnt-work (last visited Oct. 19, 2020).

150 "Pretrial Release Advocacy," National Association of Criminal Defense Attorneys, https://www.nacdl.org/Landing/PretrialReleaseAdvocacy (last visited Oct. 19, 2020).

151 "No Cash Bail," San Francisco District Attorney, https://www.sfdistrictattorney.org/policy/no-cash-bail/ (last visited Oct. 19, 2020).

152 *Ibid.*

153 *Ibid.*

154 *Ibid.*

155 "The Rachael Rollins Policy Memo," 15, http://files.suffolkdistrictattorney.com/The-Rachael-Rollins-Policy-Memo.pdf (last visited Oct. 13, 2020).

156 *Ibid.*

157 Jesse Kinley, Alan Feuer, and Luis Ferre-Saduri, "Why Abolishing Jail for Some Crimes Has Law Enforcement on Edge," *New York Times* (Dec. 31, 2019), https://www.nytimes.com/2019/12/31/nyregion/cash-bail-reform-new-york.html; National District Attorney's Association, National Prosecution Standards, Third Edition, Part IV, 4-4.2 Bail Amount Request, https://ndaa.org/wp-content/uploads/NDAA-NPS-3rd-Ed.-w-Revised-Commentary.pdf (last visited Oct. 19, 2020).

158 Christian M. Wade, "State Panel Rejects Dropping Cash Bail," *Salem News* (Jan. 12, 2020), https://www.salemnews.com/news/state_news/state-panel-rejects-dropping-cash-bail/article_90d166a5-e81a-543a-857f-89ca123c601b.html.

159 Scott Bland, "George Soros' Quiet Overhaul of the U.S. Justice System," Politico (Aug. 30, 2016), https://www.politico.com/story/2016/08/george-soros-criminal-justice-reform-227519.

160 *Ibid.*

161 "Justice for Sale: How George Soros Put Radical Prosecutors in Power. " (Law Enforcement Legal Defense Fund, June 2022), 3, http://www.policedefense.org/wp-content/uploads/2022/06/Justice_For_Sale_LELDF_report.pdf.

162 *Ibid.*, 8–9.

163 *Ibid.*, 3.

164 *Ibid.*, 6.

165 Theodore Schleifer, "Mark Zuckerberg is Creating a New Criminal Justice Reform Group in Overhaul of His Operation," VOX (Jan. 27, 2021), https://www.vox.com/recode/2021/1/27/22251211/mark-zuckerberg-priscilla-chan-czi-criminal-justice-im-migration-overhaul; Joe Schoffstall, "Mark Zuckerberg Cash Discreetly Leaked into Far-Left Prosecutor Races," Fox News (Aug. 2, 2021), (quoting Capital Research Center's Parker Thayer about how Zuckerberg's cash quietly influenced the race).

166 "Criminal Justice Reform Strategy," Open Philanthropy, https://www.openphilan-thropy.org/focus/us-policy/criminal-justice-reform/criminal-justice-reform-strategy (last visited Apr. 2, 2022).

167 Paige St. John and Abbie Vansickle, "Here's Why George Soros, Liberal Groups Are Spending Big to Help Decide Who's Your Next D.A.," *Los Angeles Times* (May 23, 2018), https://www.latimes.com/local/california/la-me-prosecutor-cam-paign-20180523-story.html (detailing the tens of millions of dollars Soros and other

like-minded individuals have poured into various DA races and PACs in order to back rogue prosecutor candidates).

168 "Grants Database," Open Philanthropy, https://www.openphilanthropy.org/giving/grants (last visited Oct. 15, 2020); $170,000 of those grants was earmarked for Run, George, Run to support George Gascón's bid to become the Los Angeles County DA. *See Run, George, Run—General Support (September 2020)*, Open Philanthropy, https://www.openphilanthropy.org/grants/run-george-run-general-support-september-2020/ (last visited Oct. 15, 2020); "Run, George, Run—General Support (February 2020)," Open Philanthropy, https://www.openphilanthropy.org/focus/us-policy/criminal-justice-reform/run-george-run-general-support-2 (last visited Oct. 26, 2020; "Run, George, Run—Los Angeles District Attorney Recruitment (Sept. 2019)," Open Philanthropy, https://www.openphilanthropy.org/focus/us-policy/criminal-justice-reform/run-george-run-los-angeles-district-attorney-recruitment (last visited Oct. 15, 2020). This also included $4.3 million in grants to the Texas Organizing Project, with $4.2 million earmarked for broad criminal justice work and $100,000 earmarked "to hire canvassers to engage with community members to elect a reform-minded candidate for Houston district attorney." Texas Organizing Project PAC—General Support (Feb. 2020), Open Philanthropy, https://www.openphilanthropy.org/focus/us-policy/criminal-justice-reform/texas-organizing-project-pac-general-support (last visited Oct. 15, 2020); "Texas Organizing Project—Criminal Justice Reform (2019)," Open Philanthropy, https://www.openphilanthropy.org/focus/us-policy/criminal-justice-reform/texas-organizing-project-criminal-justice-reform-2019 (last visited Oct. 15, 2020).

169 Home page, Just Impact website, https://justimpactadvisors.org/ (last visited Apr. 2, 2022).

170 About Us, Our Team, Just Impact, https://justimpactadvisors.org/aboutus (last visited Apr. 2, 2022).

171 "Grants Database," Open Philanthropy, https://www.openphilanthropy.org/giving/grants (last visited Apr. 2, 2022).

172 Fair and Just Prosecution, https://fairandjustprosecution.org/ (last visited Apr. 2, 2022).

173 "Joint Statement from Elected Prosecutors," Fair and Just Prosecution (June 24, 2022), https://fairandjustprosecution.org/wp-content/uploads/2022/06/FJP-Post-Dobbs-Abortion-Joint-Statement.pdf; Joint Statement from Elected Prosecutors and Law Enforcement Leaders Condemning the Criminalization of Transgender People and Gender-Affirming Healthcare, Fair and Just Prosecution (June 2021), https://www.glad.org/wp-content/uploads/2021/06/20210701_Curb-v-Lee_Joint-Statement-From-Elected-Prosecutors-and-Law-Enforcement-Leaders-Condemning-the-Criminalization-of-Transgender-People-and-Gender-Affirming-Healthcare.pdf.

174 "Florida Senate Pauses Review of Andrew Warrant's Suspension," WESH 2 (updated Aug. 18, 2022), https://www.wesh.com/article/florida-senate-warren-suspension-review-pause/40930590.

175 *Justice for Sale, supra* note 3, 7.

176 Some have raised concerns that Mosby continued to receive substantial outside free travel and travel expenses from Fair and Just Prosecution. A local Baltimore news station reported that Marilyn Mosby "has received roughly $30,000 in free travel and travel expenses over the past two years" and that "30% of the trips Mosby listed

[in her financial disclosures] were sponsored by Fair and Just Prosecution." Someone from the Maryland Public Policy Institution went so far as to say that "even if they're implicit and there's not legal consequences Marilyn Mosby is no longer a free agent to do the will of the people of Baltimore. She is in the thrall of someone else, and that's why public servants can't take gifts...cash...and....trips...." Joy Lepola, "The Political Ties to Travel," Fox 5 News Baltimore (July 23, 2020), https://foxbaltimore.com/features/operation-crime-justice/the-political-ties-to-trave

177 Tides Foundation, Influence Watch, https://www.influencewatch.org/non-profit/tides-foundation/ (last visited Aug. 23, 2022).

178 "Our Work and Vision," Fair and Just Prosecution, https://fairandjustprosecution.org/about-fjp/our-work-and-vision/ (last visited Apr. 2, 2022).

179 Mark Egan and Michelle Nichols, "Soros: Not a Funder of Wall Street Protests," Reuters (Oct. 13, 2011,), https://www.reuters.com/article/us-wallstreet-protests-funding/soros-not-a-funder-of-wall-street-protests-idUSTRE79D01Q20111014.

180 St. John and Vansickle, *supra* note, 9; Color of Change advocates for "holding prosecutors accountable and accelerating prosecutor reform" and "decriminalizing poverty ad stopping unnecessary prosecutions," among other initiatives. "About Color of Change," ColorofChange.org, https://colorofchange.org/about/ (last visited Apr. 2, 2022).

181 Letter from Jean L. Tom, Davis Wright Tremaine LLP, to California Department of Justice, Office of the Attorney General, Charitable Trusts Section (July 10, 2020), https://capitalresearch.org/app/uploads/Black-Lives-Matter-Thousand-Currents-Tides-Center-Handoff.-07.28.20.pdf.

182 Erik Eckholm, "A.C.L.U. in $50 Million Push to Reduce Jail Sentences," *New York Times* (Nov. 6, 2014), https://www.nytimes.com/2014/11/07/us/aclu-in-dollar50-million-push-to-reduce-jail-sentences.html?_r=0.

183 St. John and Vansickle, *supra* note, 9. In fact, the Democracy Alliance, founded in 2005, describes itself as "the largest network of donors dedicated to building the progressive movement in the United States." "About the DA," Democracy Alliance, https://democracyalliance.org/about/ (last visited Oct. 15, 2020). It has since revised its website to call itself a "preeminent network" instead of "the largest network." "About the DA," Democracy Alliance, https://democracyalliance.org/about/ (last visited Apr. 2, 2022).

184 "Color of Change," Influence Watch, https://www.influencewatch.org/non-profit/color-of-change/ (last visited Aug. 23, 2022).

185 "Color of Change PAC," Influence Watch, https://www.influencewatch.org/political-party/color-of-change-pac/ (last visited Aug. 23, 2022).

186 Accountable Justice Action Fund, https://accountablejusticeaction.org/ (last visited Apr. 2, 2022).

187 *Ibid.*

188 "The Strategy," Real Justice PAC, https://realjusticepac.org/#the-strategy (last visited Oct. 15, 2020).

189 "Endorsement," Real Justice PAC, https://realjusticepac.org/endorsements/ (last visited Oct. 15, 2020).

190 "The Team," Real Justice PAC, https://realjusticepac.org/team/ (last visited Oct. 15, 2020); Collin Jones, "Activist Shaun King Calls for the Doxxing of the Officer

Who Shot Jacob Blake," *The Post Millennial* (Aug. 29, 2020), https://thepostmillennial.com/activist-shaun-king-calls-for-the-doxxing-of-the-officer-who-shot-jacob-blake; Kali Holloway, "Shaun King Keeps Raising Money, and Questions About Where It Goes," *The Daily Beast* (May 26, 2020), https://www.thedailybeast.com/shaun-king-keeps-raising-money-and-questions-about-where-it-goes-3.

191 "Justice for Sale: How George Soros Put Radical Prosecutors in Power," PoliceDefense.org (June 2022), 3, http://www.policedefense.org/wp-content/uploads/2022/06/Justice_For_Sale_LELDF_report.pdf.

192 St. John and Vansickle, *supra* note, 9.

193 *Ibid.*

194 Bland, "George Soros' Quiet Overhaul of the U.S. Justice System," *Politico* (Aug. 30, 2016), https://www.politico.com/story/2016/08/george-soros-criminal-justice-reform-227519; Zusha Elinson and Joe Palazzolo, "Billionaire Soros Funds Local Prosecutor Races," *Wall Street Journal* (Nov. 3, 2016), https://www.wsj.com/articles/billionaire-soros-funds-local-prosecutor-races-1478194109.

195 *Justice for Sale, supra* note, 3.

196 *Ibid.*

197 *Ibid.,* 11.

198 Soros also contributes to Safety & Justice, one of those 527 organizations. Center for Responsive Politics, OpenSecrets.org, https://www.opensecrets.org/527s/lookup.php?cycle=2014&donor=George%20Soros&type=donor&page=2 (last visited Apr. 2, 2022).

199 *Justice for Sale, supra* note 3, 11.

200 *Ibid.*

201 *Ibid.*

202 *Ibid.*

203 CA Justice & Public Safety: Committee to Support George Gascón for Los Angeles District Attorney 2020, Cal-Acess (last visited Apr. 2, 2022), https://cal-access.sos.ca.gov/Campaign/Committees/Detail.aspx?id=1402586&session=2019&view=contributions; Jeffrey Cawood, "George Soros Intervenes Again, This Time Pumping $1.5 Million into Los Angeles County D.A. Race," *The Daily Wire* (Sept. 29, 2020), https://www.dailywire.com/news/george-soros-intervenes-again-this-time-pumping-1-5-million-into-los-angeles-county-d-a-race; Maloy Moore, Ryan Menezes, and James Queally, "Here Are the Mega-Donors and Police Unions Pouring Millions into the L.A. County District Attorney Race," *Los Angeles Times* (Nov. 3, 2020), https://www.latimes.com/projects/la-district-attorney-race-top-donors/.

204 CA Justice & Public Safety: Committee to Support George Gascon for Los Angeles District Attorney 2020, Cal-Acess (last visited Apr. 2, 2022), https://cal-access.sos.ca.gov/Campaign/Committees/Detail.aspx?id=1402586&session=2019&view=contributions.

205 *Ibid.*

206 "Run, George, Run: George Gascon for LA DA 2020, Independent Expenditure Report," California Form 496 (Feb. 1, 2020), https://apps1.lavote.net/camp/Schedules/5253.pdf; Jeffrey Cawood, "Wife of Netflix CEO Pumps $1 Million into L.A. County D.A. Race," *The Daily Wire* (Feb. 11, 2020), https://www.dailywire.com/news/wife-of-netflix-ceo-pumps-1-million-into-l-a-county-d-a-race.

207 Moore, Menezes, and Queally, "Here are the Mega-Donors," *supra* note 45.

208 Rachel Hinton, "Another Billionaire Weighs in on State's Attorney's Race: George Soros Gives $2M to Group Backing Foxx," *Chicago Sun-Times* (Feb. 20, 2020), https://George.suntimes.com/politics/2020/2/20/21146269/ George-soros-kim-foxx-bill-conway-states-attorney.

209 *Justice for Sale, supra* note 3, 12.

210 *Ibid.*

211 *Ibid.*

212 *Ibid.*

213 Parker Thayer, "Living Room Pundits Guide to Soros District Attorneys," Capital Research Center (Jan. 18, 2022), https://capitalresearch.org/article/living-room-pun-dits-guide-to-soros-district-attorneys/; *Justice for Sale, supra* note 1, 13.

214 "Liberal Billionaire George Soros Has Entered Delco Politics. It's More Momentum for Democrats Who Now Outnumber Republicans," NBC10 Philadelphia (Oct. 29, 2019), https://www.nbcphiladelphia.com/news/local/left-turn-in-delaware-county-dis-trict-attorney-political-race-billionaire-george-soros-backs-democrat/2089717/.

215 Jason Garcia, "Group with Ties to Billionaire George Soros Spends $1.5 Million on Last-Minute Ads in Orange-Osceola State Attorney Race," *Orlando Sentinel* (Aug. 16, 2020), https://www.orlandosentinel.com/news/os-ne-monique-worrell-george-so-ros-state-attorney-20200816-xgstfmgnlnbzrek5bbja4ykm6u-story.html.

216 *Ibid.*

217 Monivette Cordeiro, "Orange-Osceola State Attorney Aramis Ayala to Leave Office When Term Ends but Says 'I'm Not out of the Fight,'" *Orlando Sentinel* (Oct. 31, 2019), https://www.orlandosentinel.com/news/crime/os-ne-aramis-aya-la-leaves-state-attorney-20191031-uz25n7oiv5bhpn7cvcmmojafaa-story.html; "Gov. Ron DeSantis Removes State Attorney Aramis Ayala from Murder Case," *Orlando Weekly* (Jan. 31, 2020), https://www.orlandoweekly.com/Blogs/archives/2020/01/31/ gov-ron-desantis-removes-state-attorney-aramis-ayala-from-murder-case.

218 Rafael Olmeda, "Secret Money Shakes up Broward State Attorney Race. And Even Billionaire George Soros Has Pitched in," *South Florida Sun-Sentinel* (Aug. 14, 2020), https://www.sun-sentinel.com/news/politics/fl-ne-broward-sao-pac-money-20200814-phgj6qytuzevhmths3w2drsul4-story.html.

219 *Ibid.*

220 *Justice for Sale, supra* note 3, 13.

221 Greg Moran, "DA Race: Stephan Easily Defeats Challenger Jones-Wright, Earns Full Term," *The San Diego Union-Tribune* (Jun. 6, 2018), https://www.sandi-egouniontribune.com/news/public-safety/sd-me-elex-da-20180531-story.html; Jill Castellano, "Breaking Down the Outside Spending in the District Attorney's Race," INEWSOURCE (May 18, 2018), https://inewsource.org/2018/05/18/ outside-spending-san-diego-district-attorney/.

222 George Soros, "Why I Support Reform Prosecutors," *Wall Street Journal* (Jul. 31, 2022), https://www.wsj.com/articles/why-i-support-reform-prosecutors-law-enforces-jail-prison-crime-rate-justice-police-funding-11659277441.

223 *Justice for Sale, supra* note 3, 3.

224 Interview with Andrew Lara, Council Member City of Pico Rivera, in Pico Rivera, Calif. (Apr. 6, 2022) (conducted by co-author Charles Stimson. Authors have copy of the recorded interview and transcript.).

225 Comments by Sheriff Alex Villanueva, Heritage Foundation Rogue Prosecutor in Los Angeles, Calif. (Apr. 7, 2022), https://www.youtube.com/watch?v=zAaZwevC8yk (relevant comment at the 6:10 minute mark).

226 Sara is a pseudonym we created to protect the victim from further public scrutiny.

227 Email from Shawn Randolph, Deputy District Attorney, to Maria Ramierz, Deputy District Attorney (Jan. 4, 2021, 1:39 PM) (on file with authors). Randolph copied Andre Holmes and Flora Podratz, both Los Angeles County DDAs, on this message. Ramirez's reply, also on file, was sent roughly twenty minutes later at 2:01 PM. Of note, the subject line of the email was "James Tubbs – Filing Tomorrow."

228 Sophia is a pseudonym we have used to protect the victim's identity.

229 The authors have a copy of the Bakersfield Police Department police report on file. The incident, which took place on Friday, August 30, 2013, occurred at the public library located at 3725 Columbus Street in North Bakersfield, California.

230 The authors spoke on the record with several deputy district attorneys from the Los Angeles Deputy District Attorney's Office for this book. Unlike the prosecutors in the seven other offices featured in this book, prosecutors in the Los Angeles District Attorney's Office are protected by Los Angeles County civil service rules. As a result, they do not work at the will of the district attorney and cannot be summarily fired by the district attorney without cause or a prolonged civil service process. For this reason, the deputy district attorneys in the LA office have been more vocal about their boss, have sued him, have participated in the recall efforts, have spoken to the media about his disastrous policies, and have lambasted him on social media. The prosecutors employed in all the other offices featured in this book can be fired at will, for no reason. Many of the rogue prosecutors in this book have fired career attorneys in their office when they were first elected, purging the ranks of dedicated law-and-order prosecutors and replacing them with public defenders, criminal defense attorneys, or soft-on-crime attorneys who were aligned with their bosses' Soros-inspired ideas.

231 Charles D. Stimson and Zack Smith, "'Progressive' Prosecutors Sabotage the Rule of Law, Raise Crime Rates, and Ignore Victims," Heritage Foundation Legal Memorandum No. 275 (Oct. 29, 2020), https://www.heritage.org/crime-and-justice/report/progressive-prosecutors-sabotage-the-rule-law-raise-crime-rates-and-ignore.

232 Karen Ocamb, "L.A. County Democratic Party Endorses Gascón in DA Race," *The L.A. Blade* (Dec. 11, 2019), https://www.losangelesblade.com/2019/12/11/l-a-county-democratic-party-endorses-Gascón-in-da-race/.

233 Evan Sernoffsky, "*SF District Attorney George Gascón Decides Not to Seek Re-Election*," *San Francisco CHRONICLE* (Oct. 1, 2018), https://www.sfchronicle.com/bayarea/article/San-Francisco-District-Attorney-George-Gasc-n-13276393.php.

234 Jason McGahan, "*Why Do Officials Who Worked with George Gascón in S.F. Appear to Be Snubbing Him Now?*," *L.A. MAGAZINE* (Nov. 23, 2019) (noting that the San Francisco Mayor's and elected City Attorney's endorsement of Gascón's opponent in Los Angeles served as a tacit rebuke of his positions and performance as San Francisco's District Attorney), https://www.lamag.com/citythink-blog/george-gascon-london-breed-snub/; Erin Stone, "*SF District Attorney Hosts Symposium on Drug-Facilitated Sexual Assault*," *San Francisco CHRONICLE* (Aug. 2, 2018) (noting that "Advocates and victims have criticized the district attorney's office handling of sexual assault cases"), https://www.sfchronicle.com/crime/article/SF-district-attorney-hosts-symposium-on-13127817.php; Jonah Owen

Lamb, "*SF Prosecutor Dedicated Solely to Stalking Cases Reassigned*," *San Francisco Examiner* (Jun. 9, 2016) (noting that while he was San Francisco district attorney, Gascón reassigned his office's only assistant dedicated to handling stalking cases, a move which caused police officials concern), https://www.sfexaminer.com/news/sf-prosecutor-dedicated-solely-to-stalking-cases-reassigned/.

235 Federal Bureau of Investigation, "Crime in the U.S., 2010," https://ucr.fbi.gov/crime-in-the-u.s/2010/crime-in-the-u.s.-2010/tables/10tbl05.xls (last visited Jan. 11, 2021); Federal Bureau of Investigation, Crime in the U.S., 2009, https://ucr.fbi.gov/crime-in-the-u.s/2009 (last visited Jan. 11, 2021); Federal Bureau of Investigation, Crime in the U.S., 2008, https://ucr.fbi.gov/crime-in-the-u.s/2008 (last visited Jan. 11, 2021); Federal Bureau of Investigation, Crime in the U.S., 2007, https://ucr.fbi.gov/crime-in-the-u.s/2007 (last visited Jan. 11, 2021); Federal Bureau of Investigation, "Crime in the U.S., 2006," https://ucr.fbi.gov/crime-in-the-u.s/2006 (last visited Jan. 11, 2021).

236 Federal Bureau of Investigation, "Crime in the United States, 2019," https://ucr.fbi.gov/crime-in-the-u.s/2019/crime-in-the-u.s.-2019/tables/table-5 (last visited Jan. 11, 2021); Federal Bureau of Investigation, Crime in the United States, 2018, https://ucr.fbi.gov/crime-in-the-u.s/2018/crime-in-the-u.s.-2018/tables/table-8/table-8-state-cuts/california.xls (last visited Jan. 11, 2021); Federal Bureau of Investigation, *Crime in the United States, 2017*, https://ucr.fbi.gov/crime-in-the-u.s/2017/crime-in-the-u.s.-2017/tables/table-6 (last visited Jan. 11, 2021); Federal Bureau of Investigation, *Crime in the United States, 2016*, https://ucr.fbi.gov/crime-in-the-u.s/2016/crime-in-the-u.s.-2016/tables/table-6/table-6-state-cuts/california.xls (last visited Jan. 11, 2021); Federal Bureau of Investigation, "Crime in the United States, 2015," https://ucr.fbi.gov/crime-in-the-u.s/2015/crime-in-the-u.s.-2015/tables/table-8/table-8-state-pieces/table_8_offenses_known_to_law_enforcement_california_by_city_2015.xls (last visited Jan. 11, 2021); Federal Bureau of Investigation, "Crime in the United States, 2014," https://ucr.fbi.gov/crime-in-the-u.s/2014/crime-in-the-u.s.-2014/tables/table-6 (last visited Jan. 11, 2021); Federal Bureau of Investigation, "Crime in the United States, 2013," https://ucr.fbi.gov/crime-in-the-u.s/2013/crime-in-the-u.s.-2013/tables/table-8/table-8-state-cuts/table_8_offenses_known_to_law_enforcement_california_by_city_2013.xls (last visited Jan. 11, 2021); Federal Bureau of Investigation, "Crime in the United States, 2012," https://ucr.fbi.gov/crime-in-the-u.s/2012/crime-in-the-u.s.-2012/tables/8tabledatadecpdf/table-8-state-cuts/table_8_offenses_known_to_law_enforcement_by_california_by_city_2012.xls (last visited Jan. 11, 2021); Federal Bureau of Investigation, "Crime in the United States, 2011," https://ucr.fbi.gov/crime-in-the-u.s/2011/crime-in-the-u.s.-2011/tables/table8statecuts/table_8_offenses_known_to_law_enforcement_california_by_city_2011.xls (last visited Jan. 11, 2021).

237 John Gramlich, "*What the Data Says (and Doesn't Say) About Crime in the United States*," Pew Research Center (Nov. 20, 2020), https://www.pewresearch.org/fact-tank/2020/11/20/facts-about-crime-in-the-u-s/ (last visited Jan. 11, 2021); Press Release, Office of Public Affairs, Dept. of Justice, "*FBI Report on Crime Shows Decline in Violent Crime Rate for Third Consecutive Year*" (Sept. 28, 2020), https://www.justice.gov/opa/pr/fbi-report-crime-shows-decline-violent-crime-rate-third-consecutive-year.

238 *Supra* notes 13 and 14.

239 Los Angeles County District Attorney's Office, Justice System Integrity Division, "Officer Involved Shooting of Kenneth Ross" (May 28, 2019).

240 Melina Reimann was born in Oakland California. Her father, John Reimann, was a Trotskyite and union organizer, who writes about Marxist ideology on a blog called the Oakland Socialist. Melina's grandfather was Guenter Reimann, a member of Germany's Communist Party in the 1920s and 1930s. She is a third-generation Marxist. She took her last name from her ex-husband.

241 Eunice G. Pollack, "Before BLM: Anti-Semitic Black Activists' Identification with Palestinian Arabs," Jewish News Syndicate (June 10, 2021).

242 "Gun Pointed at Black Lives Matter Protestors Visiting LA DA Jackie Lacey's Home," CBS Los Angeles (May 3, 2020) (showing the video of Jackie Lacey's husband David demanding Abdullah get off of his porch and pointing the gun), *available at* https://www.youtube.com/watch?v=zm246U1ZipI.

243 Lara Interview, *supra* note 1.

244 McGahan, *"Why Do Officials Who Worked with George Gascón in S.F. Appear to Be Snubbing Him Now?" supra* note 11; Stephanie Elam and Jason Kravarik, *"Black Lives Matter's Surprising Target: Los Angeles County's First Black District Attorney,"* CNN (Jul. 15, 2020), https://www.cnn.com/2020/07/10/us/jackie-lacey-la-da-black-lives-matter/index.html; Jason McGahan, *L.A.'s Controversial DA Jackie Lacey Takes on Her Critics: 'I Think Prosecutor Is an Honorable Job,'* LOS ANGELES MAGAZINE (Jan. 6, 2020), https://www.lamag.com/mag-features/jackie-lacey-interview/; Jessica Pishko, *"How District Attorney Jackie Lacey Failed Los Angeles,"* APPEAL (Nov. 12, 2019), https://the-appeal.org/how-district-attorney-jackie-lacey-failed-los-angeles/.

245 Maloy Moore, Ryan Menezes, and James Queally, *"Here Are the Mega-Donors and Police Unions Pouring Millions into the L.A. County District Attorney Race,"* Los Angeles TIMES (Nov. 3, 2020), https://www.latimes.com/projects/la-district-attorney-race-top-donors/.

246 Priya Krishnakumar and Iris Less, *"How George Gascón Unseated L.A. County Dist. Atty. Jackie Lacey,"* Los Angeles TIMES (Nov. 6, 2020), https://www.latimes.com/projects/2020-la-da-race-gascon-lacey-vote-analysis/.

247 *"George Gascón Announces Transition Team"* (Nov. 19, 2020), https://www.georgegascon.org/campaign-news/george-gascon-announces-transition-team /.

248 *California District Attorneys Association (CDAA)*, https://www.cdaa.org/ (last visited Jan. 11, 2021).

249 *National District Attorneys Association (NDAA)*, https://ndaa.org/ (last visited Jan. 11, 2021).

250 *Association of Prosecuting Attorneys*, https://www.apainc.org/ (last visited Jan. 11, 2021).

251 Zero Abuse Project (a 501©(3) "committed to transforming institutions in order to effectively prevent, recognize, and respond to child sexual abuse"), https://www.zeroabuseproject.org/about/ (last visited Jan. 11, 2021); International Association of Prosecutors (IAP) (an organization "committed to setting and raising standards of professional conduct and ethics for Prosecutors worldwide"), https://www.iap-association.org/About (last visited Jan. 11, 2021).

252 Stimson and Smith, *"'Progressive' Prosecutors Sabotage the Rule of Law," supra* note 8, 23 (citations omitted).

253 *George Gascón Announces Transition Team, supra* note 25.

254 Prosecutors Alliance of California, About Prosecutors Alliance, https://prosecutorsalliance.org/about/ (last visited Jan. 11, 2021).

255 About, JKH Consulting Services, https://jkhconsultingservices.com/about/ (last visited Jan. 11, 2021).

256 James Queally, "Deputy D.A. Becomes Latest to Challenge Jackie Lacey," Los Angeles Times (April 10, 2019), https://www.latimes.com/local/lanow/la-me-ln-joseph-iniguez-district-attorney-20190410-story.html.

257 Max Szabo, Szaboa and Associates, https://szaboandassociates.com/#max (last visited Jan. 11, 2021).

258 Dolores Canales, The Bail Project, https://bailproject.org/team/dolores-canales/ (last visited Jan. 11, 2021).

259 Robin Steinberg, The Bail Project, https://bailproject.org/team/robin-steinberg/ (last visited Jan. 11, 2021).

260 Special Directive 20-06, Pretrial Release Policy, from Los Angeles District Attorney George Gascón to All Deputy District Attorneys (Dec. 7, 2020), https://da.lacounty.gov/sites/default/files/pdf/SPECIAL-DIRECTIVE-20-06.pdf.

261 Ibid., 1.

262 Ibid.

263 Ibid., 2.

264 Ibid.

265 Ibid.

266 Ibid., 4.

267 Ibid., 4, § I. F; Ibid,. 4, n. 4.

268 Charles D. Stimson, "The First Step Act's Risk and Needs Assessment Program: A Work in Progress," Heritage Foundation Legal Memorandum No. 265 (June 8, 2020), https://www.heritage.org/sites/default/files/2020-06/LM265_0.pdf.

269 Special Directive 20–06, Pretrial Release Policy, supra note 38.

270 Ibid., 5.

271 Ibid.

272 Ibid.

273 Ibid.

274 2022 Felony Bail Schedule for the Superior Court of Los Angeles County (last visited May 17, 2022), https://www.lacourt.org/division/criminal/pdf/felony.pdf.

275 Kathleen Cady, "A Preventable Murder," Association of Deputy District Attorneys Blog (undated), https://www.laadda.com/a-preventable-murder/.

276 Ibid., 3.

277 Ibid.

278 This story is taken in large part from the blog post by Kathleen Cady. Cady, supra note 52.

279 Michael Romano, Stanford Law School, https://law.stanford.edu/directory/michael-romano/ (last visited Jan. 12, 2021).

280 Special Directive 20-08, Sentencing Enhancements/Allegations, from Los Angeles District Attorney George Gascón, to All Deputy District Attorneys (Dec. 7, 2020), https://da.lacounty.gov/sites/default/files/pdf/SPECIAL-DIRECTIVE-20-08.pdf.

281 Cal. Penal Code § 1170.12 (West).

282 Cal. Penal Code § 190.2 (West).

283 Special Directive 20–08, Sentencing Enhancements/Allegations, supra note 58, 1.

284 *Ibid.*

285 *Ibid.*; Michael Mueller-Smith, "*The Criminal and Labor Market Impacts of Incarceration*" (Aug. 18, 2015), https://sites.lsa.umich.edu/mgms/wp-content/uploads/sites/283/2015/09/incar.pdf.

286 Daniel Kessler and Steven D. Levitt, "*Using Sentence Enhancements to Distinguish Between Deterrence and Incapacitation*," NATIONAL BUREAU OF ECONOMIC RESEARCH, WORKING PAPER 6484 (March 1998), https://www.nber.org/papers/w6484; David S. Abrams, "*Estimating the Deterrent Effect of Incarceration Using Sentencing Enhancements*," INSTITUTE FOR LAW AND ECONOMICS, UNIV. OF PENN. LAW SCHOOL, RESEARCH PAPER NO. 11–13 (Jan. 2011) (taking a "similar methodological approach to Kessler and Levitt" and finding "evidence for a deterrent effect of sentence enhancement in the form of add-on gun laws"), https://scholarship.law.upenn.edu/cgi/viewcontent.cgi?article=1360&context=faculty_scholarship.

287 Kessler and Levitt, *supra* note 62.

288 *Ibid.*

289 *Ibid.*

290 Special Directive 20–08, Sentencing Enhancements/Allegations, *supra* note 58, 2.

291 COUNTY OF LOS ANGELES DISTRICT ATTORNEY'S LEGAL POLICIES MANUAL at 40 (Nov. 12, 2020) (on file with authors).

292 *Ibid.*, 51.

293 *Ibid.*, 232.

294 Special Directive 20–08.2, Amendment to Special Directive 20-08 (Dec. 18, 2020), https://da.lacounty.gov/sites/default/files/policies/SD-20-08-2.pdf.

295 *Ibid.*, 2.

296 *Ibid.*

297 Verified Petition for Writ of Mandate and/or Prohibition and Complaint for Declaratory and Injunctive Relief at 2, The Association of Deputy District Attorneys for Los Angeles Cnty. v. Gascón, et al. (Dec. 30, 2020), https://www.laadda.com/wp-content/uploads/2020/12/2020.12.29-Writ-Petition.pdf.

298 *Ibid.*, 8.

299 Decision on Application for Preliminary Injunction, Hon. James C. Chalfant of the Superior Court for the County of Los Angeles (February 8, 2021), https://www.tentativerulings.org/search/?location=222&judge=257&zpage=&zresults=50.

300 Bill Melugin, "Gascon Planning to Dissolve or Severely Downsize LA County DA Hardcore Gang Unit, Sources Say," FOX LA (Mar. 16, 2021) https://www.foxla.com/news/gascon-planning-to-dissolve-or-severely-downsize-la-county-hardcore-gang-unit-sources-say.

301 Lara Interview, *supra* note 1.

302 Kathy Cady, "Gascon's Ignorance on Allegations and Enhancements Leads to Injustice and Endangers Public Safety, for the Association of Deputy District Attorneys," Association of Deputy District Attorneys Blog (undated), https://www.laadda.com/gascons-ignorance-on-allegations-and-enhancements-leads-to-injustice-and-endangers-public-safety/.

303 California Penal Code § 3055, which makes a person eligible.

304 Los Angeles County District Attorney Special Directive 21-01, Revised Policies Pursuant to Preliminary Injunction (Feb.10, 2021), https://da.lacounty.gov/sites/default/files/policies/Special-Directive-21-01.pdf.

305 Neal Kumar Katyal, "The Appalling Damage of Dropping the Michael Flynn Case," *New York Times*, (May 8, 2020), https://www.nytimes.com/2020/05/08/opinion/michael-flynn-trump-barr.html. Some of the DDAs who attended the oral argument in the spring of 2022 urged the lawyer representing the Association to mention Katyal's op-ed to the appeals court, but counsel declined, no doubt, as the op-ed was not a part of the record in the case.

306 Katyal may have been influenced or inspired to use the "Presidents are not kings" line by his friend and fellow liberal Katanji Brown Jackson, who, while she was a United States District Court judge, used the expression in a high-visibility case she ruled upon during the Trump administration. See "Committee on the Judiciary, United States House of Representatives v. Donald F. McGahn II, Civ. No. 19-cv-2379," at 114 (Nov. 25, 2019), https://ecf.dcd.uscourts.gov/cgi-bin/show_public_doc?2019cv2379-46.

307 Matthew Ormseth, "Gascon Appeals Order that Knocked Down Prior Strikes Directive to California Supreme Court," *Los Angeles Times* (Jul. 15, 2022, 5:54 PM PT), https://www.latimes.com/california/story/2022-07-15/gascon-appeals-order-that-knocked-down-prior-strikes-directive-to-california-supreme-court-to.

308 About, 8th Amendment Project, http://www.8thamendment.org/about/ (last visited Jan. 11, 2021).

309 *Ibid.*; Dan Gainor, *"A Day in the Life of the Soros Empire,"* Wall Street Journal (Mar. 8, 2011) (noting the funding provided by George Soros to MoveOn.org), https://www.wsj.com/articles/SB10001424052748703386704576186624219408298.

310 Sean Kennedy, Loyola Law School, https://www.lls.edu/faculty/facultylisth-k/seankennedy/ (last visited Jan. 11, 2021).

311 Natasha Minsker, LinkedIn, https://www.linkedin.com/in/natasha-minsker-77427019/ (last visited Jan. 11, 2021).

312 Special Directive 20-11, Death Penalty Policy, from Los Angeles District Attorney George Gascón, to All Deputy District Attorneys (Dec. 7, 2020), https://da.lacounty.gov/sites/default/files/pdf/SPECIAL-DIRECTIVE-20-11.pdf.

313 *Ibid.*, 1.

314 *Ibid.*; "Facts About the Death Penalty," Death Penalty Information Center (Jan. 8, 2021), https://documents.deathpenaltyinfo.org/pdf/FactSheet.pdf.

315 Special Directive 20–11, Death Penalty Policy, from Los Angeles District Attorney George Gascón, to All Deputy District Attorneys (Dec. 7, 2020), https://da.lacounty.gov/sites/default/files/pdf/SPECIAL-DIRECTIVE-20-11.pdf.

316 *Ibid.*

317 *Ibid.*

318 *"California High Court Upholds Death Penalty for Man Convicted of Raping, Strangling 10 Women in L.A.,"* KTLA 5 (updated Nov. 30, 2020, 9:24 PM PST), https://ktla.com/news/local-news/california-high-court-upholds-death-penalty-for-man-convicted-of-raping-strangling-10-women-in-l-a/.

319 Special Directive 20–11, Death Penalty Policy, *supra* note 93, 4.

320 The Glasgow Coma Scale (GCS) is a commonly used measure of an individual's level of impairment. The lower the number, the more impaired a person is. A GCS score of three is highly impaired, bordering on death. For more information about the GCS, read: https://www.glasgowcomascale.org/.

321 HILLARY BLOUT, "FOR THE PEOPLE," HTTPS://WWW.FORTHEPPL.ORG/HILLARY-BLOUT (last visited Jan. 12, 2021).

322 CURRENT FELLOWS, "LEADERSHIP IN GOVERNMENT FELLOWSHIP," OPEN SOCIETY FOUNDATIONS, HTTPS://WWW.OPENSOCIETYFOUNDATIONS.ORG/GRANTS/LEADER-SHIP-IN-GOVERNMENT-FELLOWSHIP (last visited Jan. 12, 2021).

323 About Us, Who We Are, *The Appeal*, https://theappeal.org/about-us/.

324 KATE CHATFIELD, *THE APPEAL*, HTTPS://THEAPPEAL.ORG/AUTHORS/KATE-CHATFIELD/ (last visited Jan. 12, 2021).

325 CHRISTOPHER HAWTHORNE, LOYOLA LAW SCHOOL, HTTPS://WWW.LLS.EDU/FACULTY/ FACULTYLISTH-K/CHRISTOPHERHAWTHORNE/ (last visited Jan. 12, 2021).

326 ATTORNEYS & STAFF, CALIFORNIA APPELLATE PROJECT, LOS ANGELES, HTTP://CAP-LA.ORG/CONTACT (last visited Jan. 12, 2021).

327 Special Directive 20–14, Resentencing, from Los Angeles District Attorney George Gascón, to All Deputy District Attorneys (Dec. 7, 2020), https://da.lacounty.gov/sites/default/files/pdf/SPECIAL-DIRECTIVE-20-14.pdf.

328 *Ibid.*, 3.

329 *Ibid.*

330 *Ibid.*, 4; CAL. PENAL CODE § 1170(d) (providing for recall of sentence, which essentially allows a judge to resentence a defendant within a specified time period if specified conditions are met).

331 *"Felony Murder Doctrine,"* LEGAL INFORMATION INSTITUTE (explaining that this rule allows someone to be charged with murder for a death, even an accidental death, that occurs during the course of a dangerous felony, even if the felon is not the killer), https://www.law.cornell.edu/wex/felony_murder_doctrine (last visited Jan. 19, 2021); *see also People v. Chun*, 203 P.3d 425 (Cal. 2009) (discussing California's interpretation and adaptation of the felony murder rule).

332 CAL. PENAL CODE § 1170.95 (allowing a "person convicted of felony murder or murder under a natural and probable consequences theory" to "file a petition with the court that sentenced the petitioner to have the petitioner's murder conviction vacated and to be resentenced on any remaining counts" when certain conditions are met).

333 Special Directive 20–14, Resentencing, *supra* note 105, https://da.lacounty.gov/sites/default/files/pdf/SPECIAL-DIRECTIVE-20-14.pdf.

334 *Ibid.*, 7.

335 *Ibid.*

336 *Ibid.*

337 Kathleen Cady, "Hundreds of Murder Victim's Families Are Abandoned by Gascon at Parole Hearings," Association of Deputy District Attorneys, undated https://www.laadda.com/hundreds-of-murder-victims-families-are-%ef%bb%bfabandoned-by-gascon-at-parole-hearings/.

338 California Constitution, Article I, Section 28. https://leginfo.legislature.ca.gov/faces/codes_displaySection.xhtml?lawCode=CONS&sectionNum=SEC.% 2028.&article=I

339 Letter from Alex Villanueva, L.A. Cnty. Sherriff, to George Gascon, L.A. Cnty. Dist. Atty., (Feb. 3, 2021), https://lasd.org/wp-content/uploads/2021/02/Transparency_Response_Gascon_Letter_Parole_Hearings_020321.pdf.

340 *Ibid.*

341 *Ibid.*

342 *Ibid.*

343 *Ibid.*, 7–8.

344 *Ibid.*, 8.

345 *Ibid.*

346 Frankie Guzman, National Center for Youth Law, https://youthlaw.org/staff-biographies/#Guzman (last visited Jan. 12, 2021).

347 Meet the ARC Team, Anti-Recidivism Coalition (ARC), https://antirecidivism.org/meet-the-arc-team/ (last visited Jan. 12, 2021).

348 Maureen Pacheco, Pacific Juvenile Defender Center, https://www.pjdc.org/board-member/maureen-pacheco/ (last visited Jan. 12, 2021).

349 Patricia Soung, Pacific Juvenile Defender Center, https://www.pjdc.org/board-member/patricia-soung/ (last visited Jan. 12, 2021).

350 Special Directive 20–09, Youth Justice, from Los Angeles District Attorney George Gascón, to all Deputy District Attorneys (Dec. 7, 2020), https://da.lacounty.gov/sites/default/files/pdf/SPECIAL-DIRECTIVE-20-09.pdf.

351 *"Youth Counselor Beaten to Death by Teens at Los Angeles Group Home, Officials Say,"* ABC 7 (Jan. 5, 2021), https://abc7.com/wayfinder-family-services-david-mck-night-hillman-youth-counselor-beaten-to-death-fatal-attack/9356808/.

352 Villanueva Comments, *supra* note 2.

353 The Dru Sjodin National Sex Offender Public Website (NSOPW), U.S. Department of Justice, https://www.nsopw.gov/ (last visited Jan. 11, 2021).

354 Special Directive 20–09, Youth Justice, *supra* note 128, 4.

355 *Ibid.*

356 *Ibid.*

357 *Ibid.*, 5.

358 Special Directive 20–07, Misdemeanor Case Management, from Los Angeles District Attorney George Gascón, to All Deputy District Attorneys (Dec. 7, 2020), https://da.lacounty.gov/sites/default/files/pdf/SPECIAL-DIRECTIVE-20-07.pdf.

359 *Ibid.*, 1.

360 Stimson and Smith, *"'Progressive' Prosecutors Sabotage the Rule of Law,"* *supra* note 8.

361 Special Directive 20–07, Misdemeanor Case Management, *supra* note 136, 1.

362 Stimson and Smith, *"'Progressive' Prosecutors Sabotage the Rule of Law,"* *supra* note 8 at 21–26 (citations omitted) (discussing the increase in violent crimes in Philadelphia, San Francisco, Boston, Chicago, and other cities where rogue prosecutors have been elected).

363 Paul G. Cassell and Richard Fowles, *"Does Bail Reform Increase Crime? An Empirical Assessment of the Public Safety Implications of Bail Reform in Cook County, Illinois,"* Wake Forest L. Rev. 933, 55, (disputing the data and conclusions of a study commissioned by the chief judge of the Cook County Circuit Court, which asserted that new, more generous pretrial release policies did not lead to an increase in overall crime or to an increase in violent crime and instead concluding that the "[s]tudy's methodology and data significantly undercount the number of defendants who committed violent crimes after the changes").

364 *"The Rachael Rollins Policy Memo,"* Appendix D (D-1), http://files.suffolkdistrictattorney.com/The-Rachael-Rollins-Policy-Memo.pdf (last visited Jan. 11, 2021); *Zack* Smith and Cully Stimson, *"Meet Steve Descano,* the Rogue Prosecutor Whose Policies Are Wreaking Havoc in Fairfax County, Virginia," Daily Signal (Dec. 14, 2020), https://www.dailysignal.com/2020/12/14/meet-steve-descano-the-rogue-prosecutor-whose-policies-are-wreaking-havoc-in-fairfax-county-virginia/ (discussing Descano's

refusal to prosecute most misdemeanors in Fairfax County, Virginia, though he offers the excuse that his office is not staffed to handle misdemeanors and that he is not statutorily obligated to prosecute them—though the local prosecutors before him did so).

365 Stimson and Smith, " *Progressive' Prosecutors Sabotage the Rule of Law*," *supra* note 8, 24 (citations omitted) (noting that "[a]s of August 2020, the number of shootings in Boston was up 29 percent compared to the same time last year. More tragically, 'Deadly shootings [were] up 34 [percent], jumping from 23 victims in 2019 to 31 victims in 2020.'").

366 Special Directive 20–07, Misdemeanor Case Management, *supra* note 136, 2.

367 *Ibid.*

368 *Ibid.*

369 *Ibid.*, 2–4.

370 *Ibid.*, 4.

371 *Ibid.*, 5.

372 *Ibid.*

373 *Ibid.*

374 Cindy Carcamo, "715,833 Signatures Turned in to Recall L.A. County D.A. Gascon, Election Officials Say," *Los Angeles Times* (Jul. 9, 2022, 2:36 PM PT), https://www.latimes.com/california/story/2022-07-09/715-833-signatures-turned-in-to-recall-los-angeles-county-da-gascon-election-officials-say.

375 David Lauter, "George Gascon Recall Effort Had Good Chance to Win Had It Made the Ballot, Poll Finds," *Los Angeles Times* (Aug. 26, 2022, 9:57 AM PT), https://www.latimes.com/california/story/2022-08-26/failed-effort-to-recall-george-gascon-had-a-good-chance-of-winning-new-poll-shows.

376 *Ibid.*

377 Editorial Board, "Lightfoot's Budget: Pain from the Pandemic, Salve from Nearly $2 Billion in Federal Aid," *Chicago Tribune* (Sept. 20, 2021), https://www.chicagotribune.com/opinion/editorials/ct-editorial-lightfoot-budget-address-tax-increases-20210920-dfekha2dz5exzn4r5cr3xb33wy-story.html.

378 "Kim Foxx Is Stupid, Crooked and a Joke': Foxx Compared to Smollett After Calling His Case 'Mob Justice,'" *Chicago City Wire* (May 14, 2022), https://chicagocitywire.com/stories/621827371-kim-foxx-is-stupid-crooked-and-a-joke-foxx-compared-to-smollett-after-calling-his-case-mob-justice.

379 Special Prosecutor Dan K. Webb, The Office of the Special Prosecutor's Summary of Its Final Conclusions, Supporting Findings and Evidence Relating to the Cook County State's Attorney's Office's and the Chicago Police Department's Involvement in the Initial Smollett Case 3-6 (Aug. 17, 2020), https://dig.abclocal.go.com/wls/documents/2021/122021-wls-smollett-report.pdf; Cully Stimson, "Unanswered Questions in the Jussie Smollett Case," *The Daily Signal* (Mar. 28, 2019), https://www.dailysignal.com/2019/03/28/unanswered-questions-in-the-jussie-smollett-case/; Cully Stimson, "Answers May Be Coming in the Jussie Smollett Case," *The Daily Signal* (Apr. 30, 2019), https://www.dailysignal.com/2019/04/30/answers-may-be-coming-in-the-jussie-smollett-case/.

380 Katie Galiato, "Trump Condemns 'Horrible' Attack on Actor Jussie Smollett," *Politico* (Jan. 31, 2019), https://www.politico.com/story/2019/01/31/trump-condemns-attack-jussie-smollett-1140398.

381 Brian Pascus, "Jussie Smollett Asked to Pay City of Chicago $130,000 for Cost of Investigation," CBS News (Mar. 28, 2019), https://www.cbsnews.com/news/jussie-smollett-pay-city-of-chicago-130000-cost-investigation-today-live-updates-2019-03-28/.

382 Michael Blackmon, "Smollett and the Prosecutors Who Dropped Charges Against Him," *Buzzfeed* (Mar. 26, 2019), https://www.buzzfeednews.com/article/michaelblackmon/rahm-emanuel-jussie-smollett-prosecutors-chsrhes-dropped.

383 "Chicago FOP Want Kim Foxx Out, Order Federal Investigation Against Cook County State Attorney," *Ark Republic* (Apr. 5, 2019), https://www.arkrepublic.com/2019/04/05/chicago-fop-want-kim-foxx-out-order-federal-investigation-against-cook-county-state-attorney/.

384 National District Attorneys Association Statement on Prosecutorial Best Practices in High Profile Cases (Mar. 27, 2019), https://ndaa.org/wp-content/uploads/NDAA-Press-Release-on-Prosecutorial-Best-Practices-in-High-Profile-Cases.pdf.

385 Order from Cook County Circuit Court Judge Michael P. Toomin, IN RE APPOINTMENT OF SPECIAL PROSECUTOR, No. 19 MR 0014 (Jun. 21, 2019), https://s3.documentcloud.org/documents/6164963/Judge-s-order-for-a-special-prosecutor-in.pdf.

386 Webb, The Office of the Special Prosecutor's Summary of Its Final Conclusions, *supra* note 3.

387 *Ibid.*, 1.

388 *Ibid.*, 1–4.

389 Order from Cook County Circuit Court Judge Michael P. Toomin, In Re Appointment of Special Prosecutor, *supra* note 9, 3.

390 Maria Luisa Paul, "Actor Jussie Smollett Was Sentenced to 150 Days In Jail. After Serving Six, He's Been Released While He Appeals," *Washington Post* (Mar. 17, 2022), https://www.washingtonpost.com/nation/2022/03/17/jussie-smollett-actor-released-jail-false-hate-crime/.

391 *Ibid.*

392 Stephanie Pagones, "Jussie Smollett Sentencing: Kim Foxx Says 'Kangaroo Prosecution' Led to Actor's Punishment," Foxnews.com (Mar. 11, 2022), https://www.foxnews.com/us/kim-foxx-jussie-smollett-sentencing-justice-system-kangaroo-prosecution.

393 Prior to joining Mayor Lightfoot, Johnson worked for BerlinRosen, the same public relations firm used by George Soros, and whose clients included George Gascón, Pennsylvania Justice & Safety PAC, and other Democratic candidates for office.

394 Ryan Johnson (@Ryan_Johnson), Twitter (Mar. 10, 2022, 8:39 PM) (issuing Statement of Chicago Mayor Lori Lightfoot), https://twitter.com/Ryan_Johnson/status/1502096881110986757?ref_src=twsrc%5Etfw%7Ctwcamp%5Etweetembed%7Ctwterm%5E1502096881110986757%7Ctwgr%5E%7Ctwcon%5Es1_&ref_url=https%3A%2F%2Fwww.foxnews.com%2Fus%2Fkim-foxx-jussie-smollett-sentencing-justice-system-kangaroo-prosecution.

395 Emily Bazelon, "Charged: The New Movement to Transform American Prosecution and End Mass Incarceration," 27.

396 *Ibid.*, 31.

397 MDatcher, "Toni Preckwinkle: The Iron Fist in the Velvet Glove," *Chicago Defender* (Mar. 23, 2016), https://chicagodefender.com/toni-preckwinkle-the-iron-fist-in-the-velvet-glove/.

398 *Ibid.*

399 *Ibid.*

400 Press Release, Open Society Foundations, "Patrick Gaspard Named President of the Open Society Foundations," (Dec. 13, 2017), https://www.opensocietyfoundations.org/newsroom/patrick-gaspard-named-president-open-society-foundations.

401 Patrick Gaspard, Center for American Progress, https://www.americanprogress.org/people/gaspard-patrick/ (last accessed Aug. 8, 2022).

402 John Chase, "Foxx Parlays Personal Story, Message of Change to Big Win," *Chicago Tribune* (Mar. 16, 2016), https://www.chicagotribune.com/politics/ct-kim-foxx-cook-county-states-attorney-met-20160315-story.html.

403 Brandon E. Patterson, "This Chicago Election Hinges on a 'Black Lives' Case—And It's Not the Only One," *Mother Jones* (Feb. 17, 2016), https://www.motherjones.com/politics/2016/02/chicago-cook-county-states-attorney-race-anita-alvarez-kim-foxx-black-lives-matter/.

404 Bazelon, *supra* note 19, 83.

405 Influence Watch, Civic Participation Action Fund (CPAF), https://www.influence-watch.org/non-profit/civic-participation-action-fund/ (last accessed August 8, 2022).

406 Gara LaMarche, Senior Advisor, The Raben Group, https://rabengroup.com/people/gara-lamarche/.

407 Mick Dumke, "The Trials of Anita Alvarez," Chicago Reader (Sept. 16, 2015), https://chicagoreader.com/news-politics/the-trials-of-anita-alvarez/.

408 *Ibid.*

409 *Ibid.*

410 Max Greenwood, "Foxx Wins Key Endorsement from Cook County Dems, Tightening Race," *Medill Reports Chicago* (Jan. 14, 2016), https://news.medill.northwestern.edu/chicago/foxx-wins-key-endorsement-from-cook-county-dems-tightening-states-attorney-race/.

411 Shawn Jones, "Kim Foxx Launches State's Attorney Campaign in Evanston," *Evanston RoundTable* (Dec. 16, 2015), https://evanstonroundtable.com/2015/12/16/kim-foxx-launch"es-states-attorney-campaign-in-evanston/.

412 *Ibid.*

413 *Ibid.*

414 Greenwood, *supra* note 34.

415 *Ibid.*

416 Anne Li, "A Race to Claim Justice," *South Side Weekly* (Feb. 23, 2016), https://southsideweekly.com/a-race-to-claim-justice/.

417 Chase, "Foxx Parlays Personal Story," *supra* note 26.

418 *Ibid.*

419 *Ibid.*

420 Tom Schuba, "Cook County State's Attorney Candidate Fined After Violating Campaign Finance Law," NBCChicago.com (Mar. 1, 2016), https://www.nbcchicago.com/news/local/cook-county-states-attorney-candidate-kim-foxx-fined-after-violating-campaign-finance-law/102027/.

421 *Ibid.*

422 *Ibid.*

423 Yasmin Nair, "Angela Davis on Guns, Violence and History," *Windy City Times* (Sept. 9, 2013), https://www.windycitytimes.com/lgbt/-Angela-Davis-on-Guns-Violence-and-History/44313.html.

424 *Ibid.*

425 *Ibid.*

426 *Ibid.*

427 Steve Schmadeke, "Cook County Jail Exits Oversight of More Than 40 Years," *Chicago Tribune* (Jun. 12, 2017), https://www.chicagotribune.com/news/breaking/ct-cook-county-jail-consent-decree-20170612-story.html.

428 Rebecca Hendrick, "The Great Recession's Impact on the City of Chicago," Great Cities Institute, Publication Number GCP-10-7 (2010), https://greatcities.uic.edu/wp-content/uploads/2013/08/2010_Hendrick_The-Great-Recession.pdf.

429 "Cook County President, State's Attorney Battle Over 10 Percent Cuts," ABC7 News (Feb. 8, 2011), https://abc7chicago.com/archive/7946905/.

430 *Ibid.*

431 Dumke, "The Trials of Anita Alvarez" *supra* note 31, 16.

432 *Ibid.*

433 "Fight Brews Between Cook County's Top Female Politicians," ABC7 News (May 7, 2015), https://abc7chicago.com/toni-preckwinkle-anita-alvarez-cook-county-states-attorney/703933/.

434 *Ibid.*

435 *Ibid.*

436 *Ibid.*

437 Carol Felsenthal, "Why Kim Foxx Is Challenging Anita Alvarez for State's Attorney," *Chicago Magazine* (Oct. 28, 2015), https://www.chicagomag.com/Chicago-Magazine/Felsenthal-Files/October-2015/Kim-Foxx/.

438 *Ibid.*

439 Hunter Clauss, "Kimberly Foxx Shares Vision for Cook County State's Attorney's Office," WTTW (Nov. 17, 2015), https://news.wttw.com/2015/11/17/kimberly-foxx-shares-vision-for-cook-county-state-s-attorney-s-office.

440 *Ibid.*

441 Evan F. Moore, "Q & A with Kim Foxx," *Citizen Weekly* (Nov. 18, 2015), https://citizennewspapergroup.com/news/2015/nov/18/q-kim-foxx/.

442 *Ibid.*

443 *Ibid.*

444 Toni Preckwinkle and Jesus "Chuy" Garcia, "Why Anita Alvarez Should Resign," *Chicago Tribune* (Dec. 2, 2015), https://www.chicagotribune.com/opinion/commentary/ct-anita-alvarez-resign-preckwinkle-garcia-perspec-20151202-story.html.

445 *Ibid.*

446 Mark Konkol, "Toni Preckwinkle Didn't Think Anita Alvarez Would Lose THAT Badly," *My Chicago* (Mar. 17, 2016), https://www.dnainfo.com/chicago/20160317/hyde-park/toni-preckwinkle-didnt-think-anita-alvarez-would-lose-that-badly/.

447 Chase, "Foxx Parlays Personal Story," *supra* note 26.

448 *Ibid.*

449 Patterson, "This Chicago Election Hinges on a "Black Lives" Case," *supra* note 27.

450 *Ibid.*

451 "Kim Foxx, Cook County State's Attorney," Transition Report (Dec. 5, 2016), https://www.ccachicago.org/wp-content/uploads/2016/12/Cook-County-States-Attorney-Transition-Report.pdf.

452 *Ibid.*

453 Steve Schmadeke, "Foxx Raises Threshold for Felony Shoplifting: State's Attorney Seeks Less Jail for Nonviolent Suspects," *Chicago Tribune* (Dec. 15, 2016), https://digitaledition.chicagotribune.com/tribune/article_popover.aspx-?guid=9ac9f3b1-0978-4ba4-a81b-bca34e82a2fa#:~:text=Foxx%20raises%20threshold%20for%20felony%20shoplifting%20%2D%20City&text=In%20her%20first%20major%20policy,shoplifters%20with%20a%20felony%20crime.

454 *Ibid.*

455 The Appleseed Network was created by members of Harvard Law School's Class of 1958. In 1994, the Appleseed Foundation was created and today includes sixteen centers across the United States and Mexico. The Chicago Appleseed Center for Fair Courts, one of the sixteen centers, works to "find anti-racist solutions to systemic injustices," and works "on safe and cost-effective alternatives to incarceration." Chicago Appleseed Center for Fair Courts, https://www.chicagoappleseed.org/ (last accessed Aug. 8, 2022).

456 Erica Demarest, "Shoplifting Under $1,000 Will No Longer Be A Felony, Kim Foxx Says," DNA Info (Dec. 15, 2016), https://www.dnainfo.com/chicago/20161215/little-village/kim-foxx-raises-bar-for-retail-theft-felonies/.

457 "Shoplifting Soars as Prosecutors Back Off," CWBChicago (Oct. 16, 2019), https://cwbchicago.com/2019/10/shoplifting-soars-as-prosecutors-back-off.html.

458 Ted Slowik, "Money Buys Influence, Preckwinkle Tells Business Owner During Lunch In South Holland," *Chicago Tribune* (Aug. 30, 2019), https://www.chicagotribune.com/suburbs/daily-southtown/opinion/ct-sta-slowik-preckwinkle-sixth-district-st-0830-20190829-swd7v7eozbajhaeaejpumsa4sy-story.html.

459 *Ibid.*

460 *Ibid.*

461 Emily Hoerner, "Cook County Chief Judge Orders Sweeping Reform of Bail System," *Injustice Watch* (Jul. 17, 2017), https://www.injusticewatch.org/news/2017/cook-county-chief-judge-orders-sweeping-reform-of-bail-system/.

462 *Ibid.*

463 "Bail Reform in Cook County: An Examination of General Order 18.8A and Bail in Felony Cases, State of Illinois Circuit Court of Cook County," Office of the Chief Judge (May 2019), https://www.cookcountycourt.org/Portals/0/Statistics/Bail%20Reform/Bail%20Reform%20Report%20FINAL%20-%20%20Published%2005.9.19.pdf.

464 Paul G. Cassell and Richard Fowles, "*Does Bail Reform Increase Crime? An Empirical Assessment of the Public Safety Implications of Bail Reform in Cook County, Illinois,*" WAKE FOREST L. REV. 933, 55 (disputing the data and conclusions of a study commissioned by the chief judge of the Cook County Circuit Court, which asserted that new, more generous pretrial release policies did not lead to an increase in overall crime or to an increase in violent crime and instead concluding that the "[s]tudy's methodology and data significantly undercount the number of defendants who committed violent crimes after the changes").

ROGUE PROSECUTORS

465 David Jackson, Todd Lightly, and Gary Marx, "Bail Reform Analysis by Cook County Chief Judge Based on Flawed Data, Undercounts New Murder Charges," *Chicago Tribune* (Feb. 13, 2020), https://www.chicagotribune.com/investigations/ct-cook-county-bail-bond-reform-tim-evans-20200213-tkodxevlyvcp7k66q2v2ahboi4-story.html.

466 *Ibid.*

467 "In Pursuit of Justice for All: An Evaluation of Kim Foxx's First Year in Office," A Report from Community Partners by Reclaim Chicago, The People's Lobby, and Chicago Appleseed Fund for Justice, https://thepeopleslobbyusa.org/wp-content/uploads/2017/12/Equal-Justice-for-All-A-Report-on-Kim-Foxxs-First-Year-ForPrint.pdf.

468 Annie Sweeney, "Chicago Reached at Least 800 Homicides in 2021, A Level Not Seen in 25 Years," *Chicago Tribune* (Jan. 3, 2022), https://www.chicagotribune.com/news/criminal-justice/ct-2021-homicides-final-20220103-lrpzuh5nsjhspmos3edrzx-u2ei-story.html.

469 *Ibid.*

470 Rafael A. Mangual, *Criminal [In]Justice: What the Push for Decarceration and Depolicing Gets Wrong and Who It Hurts the Most* (Hachette Nashville: Center Street Press, 2022), 28.

471 *Ibid.*, 29.

472 *Ibid.*, 25.

473 Frank Main, "As Murders Soar in Chicago, Judges are Freeing More Violent-Crime Suspects on Electronic Monitoring," *Chicago Sun Times* (Aug. 21, 2020), https://chicago.suntimes.com/2020/8/21/21373707/electronic-monitoring-violent-crime-cook-county-chicago-police-department-david-brown-kim-foxx.

474 *Ibid.*

475 "45 Shot, 10 Fatally, Across Chicago This Weekend," *Chicago Sun-Times* (Sept. 21, 2020), https://chicago.suntimes.com/crime/2020/9/20/21446469/chicago-weekend-shootings-gun-violence-sept-18-19-20-21.

476 "50 Shot, 9 Fatally, In Chicago Weekend Violence," *Chicago Sun-Times* (Sept. 28, 2020), https://chicago.suntimes.com/crime/2020/9/27/21458287/chicago-weekend-shooting-gun-violence-homicide-september-25-28.

477 "Man Fired Gun Into Restaurant Ceiling While On Electronic Monitoring For More Than 27 Felonies Including Home Invasion, Carjacking, and Kidnapping: Prosecutors," *CWBChicago* (Mar. 15, 2022), https://cwbchicago.com/2022/03/man-fired-gun-restaurant-ceiling-electronic-monitoring-27-felonies-home-invasion-carjacking-kidnapping-prosecutors.html.

478 *Ibid.*

479 *Ibid.*

480 *Ibid.*

481 Craig Wall, "Chicago Violence: Prosecutors Reject Charges In Deadly Gang-Related Austin Shooting," ABC7 Chicago (Oct. 4, 2021), https://abc7chicago.com/chicago-shooting-violence-austin-police/11079879/.

482 *Ibid.*

483 David Jackson, Todd Lighty, Gary Marx, and Alex Richards, "Kim Foxx Drops More Felony Cases as Cook County State's Attorney Than Her Predecessor, Tribune Analysis Shows," *Chicago Tribune* (Aug. 10, 2020), https://www.chicagotribune.

com/investigations/ct-kim-foxx-felony-charges-cook-county-20200810-ldvrmqv-v6bd3hpsuqha4duehmu-story.html.
484 *Ibid.*
485 *Ibid.*
486 *Ibid.*
487 *Ibid.*
488 Matthew Hendrickson and Manny Ramos, "Foxx Moves to Release 3 Long-Serving Inmates Early Under New Initiative," *Chicago Sun-Times* (Mar. 18, 2022), https://chicago.suntimes.com/crime/2022/3/18/22984820/kim-foxx-resentence-cook-county-victims-larry-frazier-roland-reyes-charles-miles-crime.
489 *Ibid.*
490 For the People website, https://www.fortheppl.org/hillary-blout (last accessed Aug. 14, 2022).
491 Megan Crepeau, "Questions Remain As Resentencing Initiative Championed By Kim Foxx Is Slow Out of the Gate in Cook County," *Chicago Tribune* (Mar. 25, 2022), https://www.chicagotribune.com/news/criminal-justice/ct-cook-county-prosecutors-resentencing-analysis-20220325-7j4lqzl7ebgjhcs5v4hzbegdgm-story.html
492 *Ibid.*
493 *Ibid.*
494 *Ibid.*
495 Matthew Hendrickson, "Judge Denies Kim Foxx's Bid to Let Inmate Out Early Under New State Law," *Chicago Sun-Times* (May 6, 2022), https://chicago.suntimes.com/crime/2022/5/6/23060521/kim-foxx-cook-county-resentence-charles-miles-illinois-criminal-justice-reform.
496 John O. McGinnis, "Chicago's Toxic Trio," *City Journal* (Jan. 26, 2022), https://www.city-journal.org/crime-and-chicago-toxic-leadership.
497 Greg Hinz, "Lightfoot Goes on Attack on City Crime," *Crain's Chicago Business* (Dec. 20, 2021), https://www.chicagobusiness.com/greg-hinz-politics/chicago-crime-lori-lightfoot-agenda-west-side-speech.
498 *Ibid.*
499 *Ibid.*
500 *Ibid.*
501 Mitchell Armentrout and Michael Sneed, "Veteran Prosecutor Slams Kim Foxx in Blistering Resignation Letter: 'Zero Confidence' in Her Leadership," *Chicago Sun-Times* (Jul 30., 2022, 3:19 EDT), https://chicago.suntimes.com/politics/2022/7/30/23285184/james-murphy-resignation-letter-kim-foxx-states-attorney.
502 Adam Manno, "Two Asian Children, Aged 10 and 15, Are Stabbed in the Back of the Head While Defending Their Mother, 37, 'From a Co-Worker Who Knifed Her in the Back' Before Turning Himself in to Police in Philadelphia," DailyMail.com (updated March, 7, 2022, 10:19 EDT), https://www.dailymail.co.uk/news/article-10584145/Two-Asian-children-10-15-woman-37-stabbed-Philadelphia-Suspect-turned-in.html.
503 *Ibid.*
504 Chris Brennan and Aubrey Whelan, "Larry Krasner Wins Race for Philly DA," *Philadelphia Inquirer* (Nov. 7, 2017), https://www.inquirer.com/philly/news/politics/city/larry-krasner-wins-race-for-philly-da-20171107.html#loaded.

505 Chris Palmer, Julie Shaw, and Mensah M. Dean, "Philly SWAT Officer, 46, Is Fatally Shot While Trying to Serve a Warrant in Frankford," *Philadelphia Inquirer* (Mar. 14, 2020), https://www.inquirer.com/news/cop-shot-philadelphia-police-officer-20200313.html.

506 *Ibid.*

507 Statement of U.S. Attorney William M. McSwain Regarding the Murder of Philadelphia Police Corporal James O'Connor, U.S. Dept. of Just. (Mar. 16, 2020), https://www.justice.gov/usao-edpa/pr/statement-us-attorney-william-m-mcswain-regarding-murder-philadelphia-police-corporal. (Much of the summary of Hassan's criminal activities and his case is taken from this statement).

508 *Ibid.*

509 Stephanie Farr, "FOP Prez Calls Vulgar Changers at Krasner Victory Party 'Parasites of the City,'" *Philadelphia Inquirer* (May 17, 2017), https://www.inquirer.com/philly/news/crime/FOP-pres-Those-who-chanted-F----the-FOP-at-Krasner-victory-party-are-.html.

510 Chris Brennan, "Krasner and FOP Make Peace over DA Race Victory-Party Chants," *Philadelphia Inquirer* (May 31, 2017), https://www.inquirer.com/philly/news/politics/city/Krasner-and-FOP-make-peace-over-DA-race-victory-party-chants.html.

511 *Ibid.*

512 Statement by United States Attorney William M. McSwain on the Shooting of Six Philadelphia Police Officers, U.S. Department of Justice (Aug. 15, 2019), https://www.justice.gov/usao-edpa/pr/statement-united-states-attorney-william-m-mcswain-shooting-six-philadelphia-police.

513 Julia Terruso, "Civil Rights Attorney Larry Krasner: DA's Office Is 'Off the Rails,'" *Philadelphia Inquirer* (May 4, 2017), https://ww.inquirer.com/philly/news/politics/city/Longtime-civil-rights-attorney-Larry-Krasner-wants-to-reform-DAs-office.html.

514 Jennifer Gonnerman, "Larry Krasner's Campaign to End Mass Incarceration," *The New Yorker* (Oct. 22, 2018), https://www.newyorker.com/magazine/2018/10/29/larry-krasners-campaign-to-end-mass-incarceration.

515 *Ibid.*

516 *Ibid.*

517 Transforming Criminal Justice: Philadelphia D.A. Larry Krasner and Prof. Jody Armour Talk Reform, YouTube, https://www.youtube.com/watch?v=cfPSYQRHP9Y (last viewed July 16, 2022).

518 Memorandum, New Policies Announced Feb. 15, 2018, https://cdn.muckrock.com/outbound_composer_attachments/Lucasgsl/62919/Philadelphia-DA-Larry-Krasner-s-Memo.pdf.

519 Tom MacDonald, "Philly DA: City's 2022 Murder Rate Already Outpacing Record-Deadly 2021," WHYY (updated Jan. 25, 2022), https://whyy.org/articles/philly-da-citys-2022-murder-rate-already-outpacing-record-deadly-2021/.

520 *Ibid.*

521 Charles R. Davis, "Progressive Prosecutor Larry Krasner Is Taking on Gun Violence and 'Dirty Cops' in Philadelphia," *Insider* (Jun. 5, 2022, 6:45 AM), https://www.businessinsider.com/philadelphia-da-larry-krasner-interview-gun-violence-dirty-cops-2022-3; 100 Shooting Review Committee Report (Jan. 2022), https://phlcouncil.com/wp-content/uploads/2022/01/100-Shooting-Review-complete.pdf

522  100 Shooting Review Committee Report, *supra* note 12, 44.

523  Charles D. Stimson and Zack Smith, "'Progressive' Prosecutors Sabotage the Rule of Law, Raise Crime Rates, and Ignore Crime Victims," Legal Memo No. 275, The Heritage Foundation 12–13, footnotes 53–55 (Oct. 29, 2020), https://www.heritage.org/crime-and-justice/report/ progressive-prosecutors-sabotage-the-rule-law-raise-crime-rates-and-ignore.

524  Philadelphia Police Dept. Crime Statistics (last visited Jun. 27, 2022), https://drive. google.com/drive/folders/1gV8ivfKbcQqPoskcQiozESm71Eug_il1.

525  Mapping Philadelphia's Gun Violence Crisis, Office of the Controller, https:// controller.phila.gov/philadelphia-audits/mapping-gun-violence/#/?year=2018&layers=Point%20locations (last visited Jun. 27, 2022). There are very slight discrepancies between the Philadelphia Police Department's numbers and the controller's numbers. The reason for that slight discrepancy is not clear.

526  Mensah M. Dean, "'We Don't Have a Crisis of Crime.' DA Larry Krasner Says Philly Tourists Should Feel Safe Despite a Record Number of Killings," *Philadelphia Inquirer* (updated Dec. 6, 2021), https://www.inquirer.com/news/larry-krasner-homicide-rate-violent-crime-gun-20211206.html.

527  Michael A. Nutter, "Larry Krasner Owes an Apology to the 521 Families of Philly's Homicide Victims," *Philadelphia Inquirer* (Dec. 7, 2021), https://www.inquirer.com/ opinion/commentary/larry-krasner-michael-nutter-philadelphia-violence-20211207. html.

528  *Ibid.*

529  Mapping Philadelphia's Gun Violence Crisis, *supra* note 15.

530  Chris Brennan, "On Violent Crime, U.S. Attorney William McSwain and DA Larry Krasner Are Ready to Fight…Each Other," *Philadelphia Inquirer* (updated Aug. 16, 2019), https://www.inquirer.com/politics/clout/fox-news-tucker-carlson-william-mcswain-larry-krasner-gar-joseph-joe-sestak-20190816.html.

531  *Ibid.*

532  This is a reference to 18 U.S.C. § 922(g), which makes it a federal crime for anyone who has been previously convicted of a felony offense to ship, transport, or possess a firearm.

533  Panel, The Role of the Prosecutor, part of the Symposium, "Criminal Justice Reform: Pathways to a Safe and Just Society," hosted by the Penn Law Federalist Society on Apr. 2, 2022 (Cully Stimson participated in this panel.

534  Chris Palmer, Dylan Purcell, Mike Newall, and Mensah M. Dean, "Philly Gun Arrests Are on a Record Pace, But Convictions Drop Under DA Krasner," *Philadelphia Inquirer* (Mar. 30, 2021), https://www.inquirer.com/news/philadelphia-gun-arrests-2021-convictions-vufa-20210330.html.

535  *Ibid.*

536  *Ibid.*

537  *Ibid.*

538  *Ibid.*

539  *Ibid.*

540  "Length of Incarceration and Recidivism," United States Sentencing Commission (June 21, 2022), https://www.ussc.gov/research/research-reports/ length-incarceration-and-recidivism-2022.

541  *Ibid.*

542 *Ibid.*

543 Davis, "Progressive Prosecutor Larry Krasner Is Taking on Gun Violence and 'Dirty Cops' in Philadelphia," *supra* note 12.

544 Nutter, "Larry Krasner Owes an Apology to the 521 Families of Philly's Homicide Victims," *supra* note 17.

545 Sarah Morris and Malik Neal, "With a Second Term in Sight, Larry Krasner Has a Lot of Work Left to Do," *Philadelphia Inquirer* (Jun 17, 2021), https://www.inquirer.com/opinion/commentary/larry-krasner-district-attorney-juvenile-justice-cash-bail-reform-20210617.html.

546 Samantha Melamed, "Philly DA Larry Krasner Stopped Seeking Bail for Low-Level Crimes. Here's What Happened Next," *Philadelphia Inquirer* (Feb. 19, 2019), https://www.inquirer.com/news/philly-district-attorney-larry-krasner-money-bail-criminal-justice-reform-incarceration-20190219.html.

547 Larry Krasner, "The District Attorney's Office Is Using Cash Bail Strategically," *Philadelphia Inquirer* (Aug. 14, 2020), https://www.inquirer.com/opinion/commentary/larry-krasner-cash-bail-philadelphia-district-attorneys-office-coronavirus-20200814.html.

548 Stu Bykofsky, "Don't Fall for Larry Krasner's Cynical Bail-and-Switch Trick," *Philadelphia Weekly* (Apr. 21, 2021), https://philadelphiaweekly.com/stu-bykofsky-dont-fall-for-larry-krasners-cynical-bait-and-switch-trick/.

549 Jack Tomczuk, "Krasner Calls for Philly Court Change to Keep Alleged Shooters Locked Up," *Metro Philadelphia* (Oct. 18, 2021), https://metrophiladelphia.com/krasner-calls-for-philly-court-change-to-keep-alleged-shooters-locked-up/.

550 *Ibid.*

551 Angelina Sang, "DA Krasner Uses Tarik Bey Case to Exemplify Inadequacy of Cash Bail System," *The Davis Vanguard* (Oct. 20, 2021), https://www.davisvanguard.org/2021/10/da-krasner-uses-tarik-bey-case-to-exemplify-inadequacy-of-cash-bail-system/.

552 Matt Petrillo, "Philadelphia DA Larry Krasner Calls Out Those Who Set Bail After Man Accused of Shooting Ex-Girlfriend," CBS News Philadelphia (Nov. 15, 2021), https://philadelphia.cbslocal.com/2021/11/15/philadelphia-shooting-somerton-gun-violence-james-white-bail-larry-krasner/.

553 *Ibid.*

554 *Ibid.*

555 Ellie Rushing, "Friends and Professors Remember Slain Temple Student as Kind and Courageous: 'He Would Fight for Anybody,'" *Philadelphia Inquirer* (updated Nov. 29, 2021), https://www.inquirer.com/news/philadelphia/samuel-collington-temple-student-killed-philadelphia-20211129.html.

556 *Ibid.*

557 CBS 3 Staff, "17-Year-Old Latif Williams Turns Self in for Alleged Murder of Temple Student Samuel Collington," CBS News Philadelphia (Dec. 2, 2021), https://philadelphia.cbslocal.com/2021/12/02/latif-williams-arrest-samuel-collington-philadelphia-gun-violence-shooting-temple-university-attempted-robbery/.

558 Ralph Cipriano, "Krasner Strikes Again! Suspect in Murder of Temple Student Walked After D.A. Dropped Armed Carjacking Charges Against Him," BigTrial.net (Dec. 1, 2021), https://www.bigtrial.net/2021/12/krasner-strikes-again-suspect-in-murder.html.

559  *Ibid.*

560  *Ibid.*

561  Ralph Cipriano, "Under D.A. Krasner, Murders Up 79%; Gun Convictions Down 45%," BigTrial.net (Nov. 24, 2021), https://www.bigtrial.net/2021/11/under-larry-krasner-philly-has-almost.html.

562  Ralph Cipriano, "D.A. Set on Arrest Warrant for Abusive Man Who Killed Ex-Wife," BigTrial.net (Feb. 1, 2021), https://www.bigtrial.net/2021/02/da-sat-on-arrest-warrant-for-man-who.html.

563  *Ibid.*

564  *Ibid.*

565  *Ibid.*

566  Chris Palmer, Julie Shaw, and Mensah M. Dean, "Krasner Dismisses 31 from Philly DA's Office in Dramatic First-Week Shakeup," *Philadelphia Inquirer* (Jan. 5, 2018), https://www.inquirer.com/philly/news/crime/larry-krasner-philly-da-firing-prosecutors-20180105.html-2.

567  Chris Palmer, "Krasner Firings Stir Fallout in Court: Cases Stalled, Criticism Emerges," *Philadelphia Inquirer* (Jan. 8, 2018), https://www.inquirer.com/philly/news/crime/larry-krasner-da-philly-prosecutor-firings-fallout-court-cases-20180108.html.

568  *Ibid.*

569  *Ibid.*

570  *Ibid.*

571  *Ibid.*

572  Robert Lloyd, "'They Dig in Like Ticks': A New Doc Shows the Vexing Work of Criminal Justice Reform," *Los Angeles Times* (Apr. 20, 2021), https://www.latimes.com/entertainment-arts/tv/story/2021-04-20/philly-da-larry-krasner-pbs-review.

573  Samantha Melamed, Chris Palmer, and Dylan Purcell, "More than 70 Lawyers Hired by Philly DA Larry Krasner Have Left. Some Say the Office is in Disarray," *Philadelphia Inquirer* (Dec. 22, 2021), https://www.inquirer.com/news/philadelphia-district-attorney-da-larry-krasner-staff-turnover-20211222.html.

574  *Ibid.*

575  *Ibid.*

576  *Ibid.*

577  *Ibid.*

578  *Ibid.*

579  *Ibid.*

580  Miriam Krinsky (@miriamkrinsky), Twitter (May 19, 2021, 1:22 AM), https://twitter.com/miriamkrinsky/status/1394886205871837187.

581  John Nichols, "The Police Union Failed Miserably in Its Attempt to Beat Philadelphia DA Larry Krasner," *The Nation* (May 19, 2021), https://www.thenation.com/article/politics/larry-krasner-carlos-vega-win/.

582  Philly D.A., PBS Series, https://www.pbs.org/independentlens/documentaries/philly-da/ (last visited Jun. 27, 2022).

583  Zack Smith and Cully Stimson, "Philadelphia Isn't Los Angeles: Putting a Rogue Prosecutor's Primary Win Into Context," *The Daily Signal* (Jun. 3, 2021), https://www.dailysignal.com/2021/06/03/philadelphia-isnt-los-angeles-putting-a-rogue-prosecutors-primary-win-into-context/.

584 Ralph Cipriano, "2 Judges Call Out D.A. for Lack of Candor; Inky Covers for Krasner," Big Trial.net (May 31, 2022), https://www.bigtrial.net/2022/05/two-judges-call-out-da-for-lack-of.html; Ralph Cirpiano, "Judge Grills 3 Supervisors in D.A.'s Office About 'Lack of Candor,'" BigTrial.net (Jun. 23, 2022), https://www.bigtrial.net/2022/06/judge-grills-3-supervisors-in-das.html; R. Seth Williams, "Krasner Puts Ideology Over Duty in Pursuing Phony Innocence Claims," *Broad & Liberty* (Jun. 7, 2022), https://broadandliberty.com/2022/06/07/r-seth-williams-krasner-puts-ideology-over-duty-in-pursuing-phony-innocence-claims/.

585 Ellie Rushing, "Pa. House to Investigate Philly DA Larry Krasner's Office as Republicans Hunt for Impeachable Offenses," *Philadelphia Inquirer* (June 30, 2022), https://www.inquirer.com/news/philadelphia-da-larry-krasner-impeachment-pennsylvania-house-gop-20220629.html; Lee Brown, "Impeachment Process Started Against Progressive Philadelphia DA Krasner," *NY Post* (Jun. 14, 2022), https://nypost.com/2022/06/14/impeachment-process-started-against-philadelphia-da-krasner/.

586 *Ibid.*

587 Scott Calver, "Philadelphia District Attorney Larry Krasner Impeached by Pennsylvania House," *Wall Street Journal* (Nov. 16, 2022, 7:33 PM ET), https://www.wsj.com/articles/philadelphia-district-attorney-larry-krasner-faces-impeachment-vote-in-pennsylvania-house-11668604729.

588 List of the Members of the Pennsylvania Senate, https://www.legis.state.pa.us/cfdocs/legis/home/member_information/mbrList.cfm?body=S (last visited Jul. 22, 2022).

589 Chris Palmer, "Pa. Supreme Court Sides with Former Philly Cop Facing Murder Charges and Says DA Krasner Can't 'Rewrite the Law,'" *Philadelphia Inquirer* (Jul. 20, 2022), https://www.inquirer.com/news/ryan-pownall-police-shooting-pa-supreme-court-larry-krasner-20220720.html&cid=Philly.com+Twitter.

590 *Ibid.*

591 *Ibid.*

592 Remarks by United States Attorney William M. McSwain at the Citizens' Crime Commission of the Greater Delaware Valley's Quarterly Meeting, Enough of this Nonsense: Restoring Respect for the Rule of Law with Prosecution that Serves Law-Abiding Citizens and Victims, Not Criminals, U.S. Department of Justice (Nov. 7, 2019), https://www.justice.gov/usao-edpa/pr/enough-nonsense-restoring-respect-rule-law-prosecution-serves-law-abiding-citizens-and.

593 Joel Currier, "470 Years of Experience Gone: Kimberly M. Gardner Has Lost More Lawyers Than She Had When She Took Office," *St. Louis Post-Dispatch* (Sep. 18, 2019), https://www.stltoday.com/news/local/crime-and-courts/470-years-of-experience-gone-kimberly-m-gardner-has-lost-more-lawyers-than-she-had/article_c5b70e30-d3c3-551c-8a90-d1f03b47c1e3.html.

594 Nicholas Phillips, "Will St. Louis Circuit Attorney Kim Gardner Get Four More Years to Upend the Criminal Justice System," *St. Louis Magazine* (Jul. 5, 2020), https://www.stlmag.com/news/circuit-attorney-kim-gardner-longform-profile-2020-primary/.

595 Joel Currier, "Police Seek St. Louis Man After No-Show Prosecutors Forced his Release," *St. Louis Post-Dispatch* (Jul 22, 2021), https://www.stltoday.com/news/local/crime-and-courts/police-seek-st-louis-man-after-no-show-prosecutors-forced-his-release/article_c71c107e-ee5c-5711-8f64-7ff0caa474d4.html.

596 Christine Byers and Erin Richey, "'Kim Gardner is a poor excuse for a prosecutor': Family of Murder Victim Outraged After Charges Dropped, Suspect Freed,"

KSDK (Updated Jul. 21, 2021), https://www.ksdk.com/article/news/investigations/murder-charges-dropped-suspect-freed-kim-gardner/63-40aba7a5-5b36-410c-86bd-59ee93548b64.

597 Currier, "Police Seek St. Louis Man After No-Show Prosecutors Forced his Release," *supra* note 3.

598 Order, State of Missouri v. Brandon Campbell, No. 2022-CR02036-01, Div. No. 18 (Missouri Cir. Court, Twenty-Second Judicial Circuit Jul. 14, 2021), https://bloxim-ages.newyork1.vip.townnews.com/stltoday.com/content/tncms/assets/v3/editorial/d/cc/dcc563b8-7a77-53f7-867b-c0904ea12492/60f3526c4fe65.pdf.pdf.

599 *Ibid.*

600 *Ibid.*

601 *Ibid.*

602 *Ibid.*

603 Order, State of Missouri v. Brandon Campbell, *supra* note 6.

604 Joel Currier, "Dismissal of St. Louis Murder Cases Stems from Problems in Prosecutor's Office," *St. Louis Post-Dispatch* (Jul. 20, 2021), https://www.stltoday.com/news/local/crime-and-courts/dismissal-of-st-louis-murder-cases-stems-from-problems-in-prosecutor-s-office/article_00007592-fc29-5367-b07d-d7dc87e63662.html.

605 *Ibid.*

606 Byers and Richey, "Kim Gardner is a poor excuse for a prosecutor," *supra* note 4.

607 *Ibid.*

608 *Ibid.*

609 Currier, "Police Seek St. Louis Man After No-Show Prosecutors Forced his Release," *supra* note 3.

610 Byers and Richey, "Kim Gardner is a poor excuse for a prosecutor," *supra* note 4.

611 "U.S. Marshals Arrest St. Louis Man After Being Released from Prison on Dropped Murder Charges," Fox2Now (updated Jul. 23, 2021), https://fox2now.com/news/missouri/u-s-marshals-arrest-st-louis-man-after-being-released-from-prison-on-dropped-murder-charges/; Joel Currier, "Assistant Prosecutor in St. Louis Was Assigned Nearly 30 Felony Cases While on Leave," *St. Louis Post-Dispatch* (Jul. 21, 2021), https://www.stltoday.com/news/local/crime-and-courts/assistant-prosecutor-in-st-louis-was-assigned-nearly-30-felony-cases-while-on-leave/article_86592860-7bbd-5399-9c88-db5b778754b3.html#tracking-source=in-article.

612 Byers and Richey, "Kim Gardner is a poor excuse for a prosecutor," *supra* note 4.

613 *Ibid.*

614 Currier, "Dismissal of St. Louis Murder Cases Stems from Problems in Prosecutor's Office," *supra* note 8.

615 Currier, "Police Seek St. Louis Man After No-Show Prosecutors Forced his Release," *supra* note 3.

616 Phillips, "Will St. Louis Circuit Attorney Kim Gardner Get Four More Years to Upend the Criminal Justice System," *supra* note 2.

617 *Ibid.*

618 *Ibid.*

619 *Ibid.*

620 *Ibid.*

621 *Ibid.*

622 Tim Curtis, "Rep. Gardner Gets Aid from Soros in St. Louis Circuit Attorney Race, " *The Missouri Times* (July 21, 2016), https://themissouritimes.com/soros-gets-involved-in-st-louis-circuit-attorney-race/.

623 Joel Currier, "St. Louis Circuit Attorney Candidate Defends Accepting Super PAC Campaign Money From Liberal Billionaire," *St. Louis Post-Dispatch* (Jul 24, 2016), https://www.stltoday.com/news/local/govt-and-politics/st-louis-circuit-attorney-candidate-defends-accepting-super-pac-campaign-money-from-liberal-billionaire/article_11036aaf-4b1b-58cd-871f-4084f1ec1485.html.

624 *Ibid.*

625 Curtis, *supra* note 30.

626 Joel Currier, "Former Prosecutor Turned State Rep. Takes St. Louis Circuit Attorney Primary," *St. Louis Post-Dispatch* (Aug. 3, 2016), https://www.stltoday.com/news/local/crime-and-courts/former-prosecutor-turned-state-rep-takes-st-louis-circuit-attorney-primary/article_3f31a308-d84f-52bd-8d9e-f19e3dfb4ea3.html.

627 *Ibid.*

628 John Eligon, "No Charges for Ferguson Officer Who Killed Michael Brown, New Prosecutor Says" *New York Times* (July 30, 2020), https://www.nytimes.com/2020/07/30/us/michael-brown-darren-wilson-ferguson.html.

629 Currier, "St. Louis Circuit Attorney Candidate Defends Accepting Super PAC Campaign Money from Liberal Billionaire," *supra* note 31.

630 Report CRM0013-BY, Crime Comparison Based on UCR Reporting, St. Louis Metropolitan Police Department, https://www.slmpd.org/crimestats/CRM0013-BY_202012.pdf (last visited July 26, 2022) (showing 2020 crime statistics).

631 Zack Smith and Cully Stimson, "Meet Kimberly Gardner, the Rogue Prosecutor Whose Policies Are Wreaking Havoc in St. Louis," *The Daily Signal* (Apr. 14, 2021), https://www.dailysignal.com/2021/04/14/meet-kimberly-gardner-the-rogue-prosecutor-whose-policies-are-wreaking-havoc-in-st-louis/.

632 Erin Heffernan, *St. Louis Homicide Rate in 2020 Highest in 50 Years with 262 Killings,* St. Louis Post-Dispatch (Jan. 1, 2021), https://www.stltoday.com/news/local/crime-and-courts/st-louis-homicide-rate-in-2020-highest-in-50-years-with-262-killings/article_b3c323a7-bc38-55bc-812b-08990b0eb289.html#:~:text=trauma%20it%20causes.%E2%80%9D-,St.,%E2%80%94%20at%20267%20%E2%80%94%20but%20St.

633 *Ibid.*

634 NIBRS Crime Comparison by City, City Wide Crime Statistics Nov.–Dec. 2021, St. Louis Metropolitan Police Department, https://www.slmpd.org/crimestats/NIBRS001-C_211112.pdf (last visited Jul. 26, 2022).

635 NIBRS Crime Comparison by City, City Wide Crime Statistics June 2022, St. Louis Metropolitan Police Department, https://www.slmpd.org/crimestats/NIBRS001M-C_20220704.pdf (last visited Jul. 26, 2022).

636 Tom Hogan, "Cracking the Case of the 'Woke' Prosecutor," *New York Post* (updated Jan. 17, 2022), https://nypost.com/2022/01/17/cracking-the-case-of-the-woke-prosecutor-2/.

637 Jordan Duecker, "Gateway to the Wild West: The Accelerating Collapse of St. Louis, the Most Violent City in American," *City Journal* (July 21, 2020), https://www.

city-journal.org/st-louis-reigning-murder-capital-of-america;Z. Smith and Stimson, "Meet Kimberly Gardner," *supra* note 27.

638 Joel Currier, "Gardner Easily Wins Primary for St. Louis Circuit Attorney," *St. Louis Post-Dispatch* (Aug. 5, 2020), https://www.stltoday.com/news/local/crime-and-courts/gardner-easily-wins-primary-for-st-louis-circuit-attorney/article_84e24c99-6db7-5d69-99cf-80763b4994a8.html.

639 Joel Currier, "Voters Reelect St. Louis Circuit Attorney Gardner, Treasurer Jones and Sheriff Betts," *St. Louis Post-Dispatch* (Nov. 3, 2020), https://www.stltoday.com/news/local/govt-and-politics/voters-reelect-st-louis-circuit-attorney-gardner-treasurer-jones-and-sheriff-betts/article_9ec75961-2362-51aa-878c-bb0b12770df3.html.

640 Website, "Focused Office Resources on the Most Serious Offenses," Re-elect Kimberly Gardner Circuit Attorney, https://votekimgardner.com/2020/05/12/used-office-re-sources-efficiently/ (last visited Jul. 26, 2022).

641 Currier, "Dismissal of St. Louis Murder Cases Stems from Problems in Prosecutor's Office," *supra* note 8.

642 Z. Smith and Stimson, "Meet Kimberly Gardner," *supra* note 27; Robert Patrick, "St. Louis Prosecutor Declining More Cases and Issuing Fewer Arrest Warrants at Part of Reform Efforts," *St. Louis Post-Dispatch* (Jan. 30, 2019), https://www.stltoday.com/news/local/crime-and-courts/st-louis-prosecutor-declining-more-cases-and-is-suing-fewer-arrest-warrants-as-part-of-reform/article_915b1003-ea5f-5a45-ae88-e91257a97d09.html.

643 Lauren Trager, "Records Show Trial Conviction Rate for Circuit Attorney's Office Has Fallen Nearly 20% in 2 Years," KMOV 4 (Feb. 26, 2020), https://web.archive.org/web/20200701065633/https://www.kmov.com/news/records-show-trial-convic-tion-rate-for-circuit-attorneys-office-has-fallen-nearly-20-in-2/article_a1c0f8d2-5842-11ea-b7f6-d7598e1fc94e.html.

644 *Ibid.*

645 Janelle O'Dea and Joel Currier, "9 months into second term, St. Louis Prosecutor Can't Keep Attorneys on Staff," *St. Louis Post-Dispatch* (Sep. 26, 2021), https://www.stltoday.com/news/local/crime-and-courts/9-months-into-second-term-st-louis-prose-cutor-can-t-keep-attorneys-on-staff/article_a9b8b33a-a3c3-5a88-bc1e-7123f8b8aa85.html.

646 Michael Tobin, "St. Louis Circuit Attorney Kim Gardner's Office Dropping Slew of Felony Cases; Critics Say Criminals Can Walk," FoxNews (Aug. 3, 2021), https://www.foxnews.com/us/st-louis-circuit-attorney-kim-gardners-office-dropping-felony-cases-critics-criminals.

647 *Ibid.*

648 O'Dea and Joel Currier, "9 months into second term, St. Louis Prosecutor Can't Keep Attorneys on Staff," *supra* note 36.

649 Currier, "470 Years of Experience Gone: Kimberly M. Gardner Has Lost More Lawyers Than She Had When She Took Office," *supra* note 1.

650 Lauren Trager, "St. Louis Circuit Attorney Hasn't Disclosed Trips as Required by Law, Documents Show," KMOV 4 (July 27, 2020), https://web.archive.org/web/20200728213118/https://www.kmov.com/news/st-louis-circuit-attorney-hasnt-disclosed-trips-as-required-by-law-documents-show/article_bdee8a7a-d05f-11ea-b7c3-079ff4871843.html.

651 *Ibid.*

652 Z. Smith and Stimson, "Meet Kimberly Gardner," *supra* note 27.

653 Currier, "470 Years of Experience Gone: Kimberly M. Gardner Has Lost More Lawyers Than She Had When She Took Office," *supra* note 1.

654 *Ibid.*

655 Currier, "Dismissal of St. Louis Murder Cases Stems from Problems in Prosecutor's Office," *supra* note 8.

656 *Ibid.*

657 Order, State of Missouri v. Terrion Lamont Phillips, No. 1922-CR01583-01, Div. No. 23 & 1 (Missouri Cir. Court, Twenty-Second Judicial Circuit Jun. 24, 2021), https://bloximages.newyork1.vip.townnews.com/stltoday.com/content/tncms/assets/v3/editorial/e/81/e8123203-b7ea-5a53-8670-b95a3c7c17ce/60f5a5bc09a86.pdf.pdf.

658 Currier, "Dismissal of St. Louis Murder Cases Stems from Problems in Prosecutor's Office," *supra* note 8.

659 Joel Currier, "St. Louis Man Acquitted in 2018 Beating Death in City's Shaw Neighborhood," St. Louis Post-Dispatch (Jul. 16, 2021), https://www.stltoday.com/news/local/crime-and-courts/st-louis-man-acquitted-in-2018-beating-death-in-citys-shaw-neighborhood/article_79c75a09-3f3e-541f-8993-aceaaf002027.html.

660 *Ibid.*

661 *Ibid.*

662 Phillips, "Will St. Louis Circuit Attorney Kim Gardner Get Four More Years to Upend the Criminal Justice System," *supra* note 2.

663 O'Dea and Joel Currier, "9 months into second term, St. Louis Prosecutor Can't Keep Attorneys on Staff," *supra* note 36.

664 Joel Currier, "Investigator in Greitens Case Pleads Guilty to Evidence Tampering on Eve of Trial," St. Louis Post-Dispatch (Mar. 23, 2022), https://www.stltoday.com/news/local/crime-and-courts/investigator-in-greitens-case-pleads-guilty-to-evidence-tampering-on-eve-of-trial/article_936189af-4922-5771-8edc-ec41f2b312c6.html.

665 Phillips, "Will St. Louis Circuit Attorney Kim Gardner Get Four More Years to Upend the Criminal Justice System," *supra* note 2.

666 *Ibid.*

667 *Ibid.*

668 *Ibid.*

669 *Ibid.*

670 *Ibid.*

671 *Ibid.*

672 Currier, "Investigator in Greitens Case Pleads Guilty to Evidence Tampering on Eve of Trial," *supra* note 72.

673 Joel Currier, "St. Louis Circuit Attorney Denies Misconduct Charges Stemming from Greitens Probe," St. Louis Post-Dispatch (May 6, 2021), https://www.stltoday.com/news/local/crime-and-courts/st-louis-circuit-attorney-denies-misconduct-charges-stemming-from-greitens-probe/article_25838e7a-d2d3-530b-acf1-e39011733831.html.

674 *Ibid.*

675 *Ibid.*

676 Joel Currier, "Disciplinary Counsel Recommends Reprimand for St. Louis Circuit Attorney," St. Louis Post-Dispatch (Apr. 11, 2022), https://www.stltoday.com/news/local/crime-and-courts/

disciplinary-counsel-recommends-reprimand-for-st-louis-circuit-attorney/article_2b-5950fb-27ec-5bdb-bce3-024687ce6bba.html.

677 *Ibid.*

678 *Ibid.*

679 Staff Reports, "Panel Backs Reprimand for St. Louis Circuit Attorney Over Greitens Probe," *St. Louis Post-Dispatch* (May 10, 2022), https://www.stltoday.com/news/local/crime-and-courts/panel-backs-reprimand-for-st-louis-circuit-attorney-over-greitens-probe/article_4c6d4c19-3176-505a-8fa2-8cb4cb0aabf4.html; *see also* Jim Salter, *Missouri Supreme Court Reprimands St. Louis Prosecutor*, Wash. Post (Aug. 30, 2022, 4:18 PM EDT), https://www.washingtonpost.com/politics/missouri-supreme-court-reprimands-st-louis-prosecutor/2022/08/30/f5ffbbaa-28a0-11ed-a90a-fce4015dfc8f_story.html.

680 Complaint, Kimberly M. Gardner v. City of St. Louis, et al., No. 4:20-cv-00060, Dkt. 1 (Eastern Dist. Missouri Jan. 13, 2020), https://storage.courtlistener.com/recap/gov.uscourts.moed.177905/gov.uscourts.moed.177905.1.0.pdf.

681 Memorandum and Order, Kimberly M. Gardner v. City of St. Louis, et al., No. 4:20-cv-00060, Dkt. 84 (Eastern Dist. Missouri Sep. 30, 2020), https://bloximages.newyork1.vip.townnews.com/stltoday.com/content/tncms/assets/v3/editorial/6/7e/67e07373-1d69-53ce-929b-eb69727d663d/5f74d17bf316e.pdf.pdf.

682 *Ibid.*

683 Joel Currier, "Fox News Contributor Wins Judgment in Effort to Obtain Records from St. Louis Prosecutor's Office," *St. Louis Post-Dispatch* (Jul. 30, 2020), https://www.stltoday.com/news/local/crime-and-courts/fox-news-contributor-wins-judgment-in-effort-to-obtain-records-from-st-louis-prosecutors-office/article_31a2bcf6-96c1-5e38-8142-0425e5386cfc.html.

684 *Ibid.*

685 Chris Hayes, "Judge Calls Out Gardner's Office for 'Consistent Behavior' to 'Obfuscate the Process'," Fox2Now (updated Oct. 7, 2020), https://fox2now.com/news/fox-files/judge-calls-out-gardners-office-for-consistent-behavior-to-obfuscate-the-process/.

686 Joel Currier, "St. Louis Judge Disqualifies Gardner, Her Office from Prosecuting McCloskey Gun-Waving Case," *St. Louis Post-Dispatch* (Dec. 10, 2020), https://www.stltoday.com/news/local/crime-and-courts/st-louis-judge-disqualifies-gardner-her-office-from-prosecuting-mccloskey-gun-waving-case/article_6dd89413-e92e-54a7-ab32-ab1775c7ec3e.html.

687 Christine Byers, "Missouri Supreme Court Upholds Judge's Decision to Remove Kim Gardner from McCloskey Case," KSDK (updated Apr. 6, 2021), https://www.ksdk.com/article/news/local/missouri-supreme-court-ruling-gardner-mccloskey-case/63-9380d3d8-b63a-4a9b-a8cf-48ed82607c56.

688 Chris Nagus, "Kim Gardner Claims Police Held Her for 15 Minutes During Traffic Stop; Surveillance Video Show Differently," KMOV 4 (Jan. 23, 2020), https://web.archive.org/web/20200309233317/https://www.kmov.com/news/investigations/kim-gardner-traffic-stop-claim/article_ea9ce604-3cc4-11ea-8ff9-3fa786d28238.html.

689 Catherine Elton, "The Law According to Rachael Rollins," Boston Magazine (August 6, 2019), https://www.bostonmagazine.com/news/2019/08/06/rachael-rollins/.

690 *Ibid.*

691 Project Safe Neighborhoods, United States Department of Justice, https://www. justice.gov/psn (last accessed Aug. 14, 2022).

692 Elton, *supra* note 1.

693 *Ibid.*

694 The Rachael Rollins Policy Memo (Mar. 25, 2019), https://www.documentcloud.org/ documents/5980546-The-Rachael-Rollins-Policy-Memo.html (last accessed Aug. 14, 2022).

695 Samantha Michaels, "Boston's New DA Is a Black Woman Who is Out to Change the City's Racist Sentencing Disparities," Mother Jones (November 2, 2018), https:// www.motherjones.com/crime-justice/2018/11/a-black-woman-running-for-boston- da-is-out-to-change-the-citys-racist-sentencing-disparities/.

696 Elton, *supra* note 1.

697 Rollins4da.com, About Rachael, My Story https://rollins4da.com/meet-rachael/ about-rachael/ (last accessed Aug. 16, 2022).

698 *Ibid.*

699 Joe Battenfeld, "Rachael Rollins' Arrest as a College Student Bears Similarities to Another Biden Nominee," *Boston Herald* (Nov. 17, 2021), https://www.bostonherald. com/2021/11/17/battenfeld-rachael-rollins-arrest-as-a-college-student-bears-similari- ties-to-another-biden-nominee/.

700 *Ibid.*

701 Rollins, *supra* note 9.

702 *Ibid.*

703 *Ibid.*

704 Stephanie Saul, "2020 Candidates, Deval Patrick," *New York Times* (Apr. 27, 2020), https://www.nytimes.com/interactive/2020/us/elections/deval-patrick.html. Harvard Kennedy School, Harvard University, Deval Patrick, Co-Director, Center for Public Leadership, Professor of the Practice of Public Leadership, https://www.hks.harvard. edu/faculty/deval-patrick (last accessed Aug. 16, 2022).

705 Rollins, *supra* note 9.

706 Elton, *supra* note 1.

707 *Ibid.*

708 Fair and Just Prosecution, Parent Organization: Tides Center, Influence Watch, https://www.influencewatch.org/non-profit/fair-and-just-prosecution/#:~:text=- Fair%20and%20Just%20Prosecution%20(FJP,progressive%20approaches%20to%20 criminal%20justice (last accessed Aug. 19, 2022).

709 Michael Jonas, "Suffolk DA Hopeful Henning Reaches Out to Those He Helped Lock Up," Commonwealth Magazine (Aug. 30, 2018), https://commonwealthmaga- zine.org/criminal-justice/the-law-and-order-candidate-with-a-twist/.

710 *Ibid.*

711 Ballotpedia, Rachael Rollins, https://ballotpedia.org/Rachael_Rollins (last accessed Aug. 29, 2022).

712 Nik DeCosta-Klipa, "Elizabeth Warren Just Endorsed Rachael Rollins for Suffolk County District Attorney," Boston.com (Oct. 2, 2018), https://www.boston.com/news/politics/2018/10/02/ elizabeth-warren-rachael-rollins-suffolk-county-district-attorney/.

713 Jennifer Smith, "After Primary Victory, Rollins Hopes to Give DA Office 'Another Voice, Another Perspective,'" *The Dorchester Reporter* (Sept. 12, 2018), https://www.dotnews.com/2018/after-primary-victory-rollins-hopes-give-da-office-another-voice.

714 *Ibid.*

715 David Weigel, "Down the Ballot, Liberal Reformers Take Over the Criminal Justice System," The *Washington Post* (Sept. 5, 2018), https://www.washingtonpost.com/politics/2018/09/05/down-ballot-liberal-reformers-take-over-criminal-justice-system/.

716 That list no longer appears on her old campaign website. However, the authors printed a copy of the campaign website and list when it was available and have it in their possession. And though the list may no longer be on her campaign website, it does still appear in Appendix C of her policy memo (as previously mentioned).

717 Letter from National Police Association to Office of the Bar Counsel, In re: Formal Complaint and Demand for Investigation of Alleged Attorney Misconduct by Suffolk County District Attorney-Elect, Ms. Rachael Rollins, (Dec. 23, 2018), https://nationalpolice.org/main/wp-content/uploads/2018/12/DA_Rachael_Rollins_Complaint.pdf.

718 *Ibid.*

719 *Ibid.*

720 Rollins Policy Memo, *supra* note 6.

721 *Ibid.*, 2.

722 *Ibid.*

723 *Ibid.*, 16.

724 *Ibid.*, 18.

725 *Ibid.*, 20.

726 *Ibid.*, 22.

727 *Ibid.*, 30.

728 *Ibid.*

729 *Ibid.*

730 *Ibid.*

731 Simon Rios, "DAs Join Lawsuit That Seeks to Bar ICE Arrests At Local Courthouses," wibur.org (Apr. 19, 2019), https://www.wbur.org/news/2019/04/29/immigration-ice-courthouse-lawsuit-rachael-rollins-marian-ryan.

732 Jeremy C. Fox and Shelley Murphy, "Federal court overturns order blocking ICE arrests in Mass. Courthouses," *Boston Globe* (Sept. 1, 2020), https://www.bostonglobe.com/2020/09/01/metro/federal-court-overturns-order-blocking-ice-arrests-mass-courthouses/?p1=BGSearch_Advanced_Results&p1=Article_Inline_Text_Link.

733 Amanda Y. Agan, Jennifer L. Doleac, and Anna Harvey, "Misdemeanor Prosecution," National Bureau of Economic Research (Mar. 2021), https://www.nber.org/papers/w28600.

734 Rachael Rollins, "Holding Prosecutor Offices Accountable: The Suffolk County District Attorney's Office's Approach to Progressive Prosecution," *Stanford Journal of Civil Rights and Civil Liberties at 565* (Aug. 17, 2021), https://law.stanford.edu/publications/holding-prosecutor-offices-accountable-the-suffolk-county-district-attorneys-offices-approach-to-progressive-prosecution/.

735 David Alan Sklansky, *The Progressive Prosecutor's Handbook*, U.C. Davis Law Review Online, Vol. 50 (February 2017).

736  Rollins, "Holding Prosecutor Offices Accountable," *supra* note 46, 575.

737  Young-Jin Kim, "TIMELINE: Here's How Violence Erupted in Boston After Peaceful George Floyd Protests," NBC 10 Boston (Jun. 1, 2020), https://www.nbcboston.com/news/local/timeline-heres-how-violence-erupted-in-boston-after-peaceful-george-floyd-protests/2134787/.

738  *Ibid.*

739  *Ibid.*

740  Jeremy C. Fox and John Hilliard, "Boston Protests Against George Floyd Killing Begin Peacefully, End in Violence, Arrests," *The Boston Globe* (Jun. 1, 2020), https://www.bostonglobe.com/2020/05/31/metro/three-protests-against-george-floyd-killing-planned-boston-sunday/?event=event12.

741  *Ibid.*

742  *Ibid.*

743  *Ibid.*

744  *Ibid.*

745  *Ibid.*

746  DA Rachael Rollins (@DARollins), Twitter (May 30, 2020, 10:20 PM), https://twitter.com/DARollins/status/1266917323258109954?s=20.

747  Transcript: Suffolk DA Rollins Reacts to Boston Protests in Response to George Floyd's Death, WBUR (Jun. 1, 2020), https://www.wbur.org/news/2020/06/01/suffolk-da-rollins-boston-protests-george-floyd. The reference to Amy Cooper relates to an incident that occurred in Central Park in New York City on May 25, 2020, wherein Cooper, a white woman, was walking her unleashed dog and was asked by a black man named Christian Cooper (no relation) to put her dog on a leash. When Christian Cooper called the dog over to give him a treat, Amy Cooper yelled at him and called the police saying that Mr. Cooper was threatening her and her dog. Ultimately, she was charged with making a false police report, and the case was dismissed after she completed a five-session pretrial diversion course on racial identity. The incident happened on the same day that George Floyd was murdered.

748  *Ibid.*

749  *Ibid.*

750  *Ibid.*

751  Boston Police Patrolmen's Association (BPPA) (@BostonPatrolmen), Twitter (Jun. 2, 2020, 5:19 PM), https://twitter.com/BostonPatrolmen/status/1267928921489670146?s=20.

752  *Ibid.*

753  *Ibid.*

754  DA Rachael Rollins (@DARollins), Twitter (Jun. 2, 2020, 6:57 PM), https://twitter.com/DARollins/status/1267953560764985346?ref_src=twsrc%5Etfw%7Ctwcamp%5Etweetembed%7Ctwterm%5E1267953560764985346%7Ctwgr%5E5d5ee36bea60e292976d22ebb7573eec493dbb84%7Ctwcon%5Es1_&ref_url=https%3A%2F%2Fwww.masslive.com%2Fboston%2F2020%2F06%2Fboston-police-patrolmens-association-accuse-suffolk-da-rachael-rollins-of-inciting-violence-in-her-comments-on-police-brutality.html.

755  Paris Alston and Chris Citorik, "Suffolk DA Rachael Rollins Talks Police and Prosecutorial Reform," WBUR Radio (Jun. 23, 2020), https://www.wbur.org/radioboston/2020/06/23/rachael-rollins-reform.

756  *Ibid.*

757  *Ibid.*

758  UC Hastings College of Law, Hastings Journal of Crime and Punishment and Hastings Race and Poverty Law Journal Event, "Progressive Prosecution and the Carceral State," UC Hasting Panopto (Feb. 7, 2020, at 2:21:29) https://uchastings.hosted.panopto.com/Panopto/Pages/Viewer.aspx?id=917ae-0be-b80f-4084-aa10-ab58000cba7f&fbclid=IwAR1DpRUDFe4lx%20Hz5tOxiFHeV3LNA2Fc00baylYo92VYUISN2Zebg6BexPA. During this debate, Mosby said that a progressive prosecutor is "a person advocating for social reform not new liberal ideas; moving away from the tough on crime approach, the war on drugs, stop and frisk, zero tolerance and winning at all costs, which has led to mass incarceration and overcriminalization of black and brown people." Our intern emailed with the law school on 1/25/23 to request that the video, which had been archived, be reposted or that they provide us with a private link. On 1/26/23, they promised to provide our intern, a college student, with a private link to the archived video. After repeated attempts to get the law school to provide the video, as of March 12, 2023, we have been unsuccessful in getting a live link to the video.

759  *Ibid*; Danielle Eden Silva, "McGregor Scott Gets Hammered at UC Hastings Symposium After Claims Progressive Prosecutors Lead to Higher Homicide Rates," The Davis Vanguard (Feb. 8, 2020), https://www.davisvanguard.org/2020/02/mcgregor-scott-gets-hammered-after-claims-progressive-prosecutors-lead-to-higher-homicide-rates-at-uc-hastings-symposium/.

760  *Ibid.*

761  *Ibid.;* Role of the DA, California District Attorneys Association, https://www.cdaa.org/role-of-the-da (last accessed Aug. 15, 2022).

762  *Ibid.*

763  *Ibid.*

764  Hastings Event, *supra* note 70, at the 2:21:49 timeframe on video.

765  *Ibid.*

766  Ni, DeCosta-Klipa, "Following Backlash, Rachael Rollins Clarifies Comments Calling Public Defenders 'Overwhelmingly Privileged,'" Boston.com (May 7, 2020), https://www.boston.com/news/local-news/2020/05/07/rachael-rollins-public-defenders/.

767  *Ibid.*

768  *Ibid.*

769  *Ibid.*

770  *Ibid.*

771  Letter from Anthony Benedetti, Chief Counsel for Committee for Public Counsel Services, to Rachael Rollins, District Attorney for Suffolk County (May 1, 2020), https://media.wbur.org/wp/2020/05/DA-Rollins-WGBH-response-5-1-20.pdf.

772  Callie Patteson, "Video Resurfaces of New Biden US Attorney Berating News Crew," *New York Post* (Dec. 10, 2021), https://nypost.com/2021/12/10/video-resurfaces-of-new-biden-us-attorney-berating-news-crew/.

773  *Ibid.*

774  *Ibid.*

775  Cully Stimson and Zack Smith, "Rogue U.S. Attorney's Coming to a City Near You," The Heritage Foundation (Dec. 15, 2020), https://www.heritage.org/crime-and-justice/commentary/rogue-us-attorneys-coming-city-near-you.

776 The White House, "President Biden Announces Eight Nominees to Serve As U.S. Attorneys," (Jun. 26, 2021), https://www.white-house.gov/briefing-room/statements-releases/2021/07/26/president-biden-announces-eight-nominees-to-serve-as-u-s-attorneys/.

777 Fair and Just Prosecution, Joint Statement from Elected Prosecutors in Support of Rachael Rollins' Nomination for U.S. Attorney for the District of Massachusetts (Oct. 2021), https://fairandjustprosecution.org/wp-content/uploads/2021/10/Rollins-Nomination-Joint-Statement.pdf.

778 Andrea Harrington, the elected district attorney from Berkshire County, Massachusetts, signed the Fair and Just Prosecution letter.

779 Hatch Act, The United States Department of Justice, Prohibited Activities, https://www.justice.gov/jmd/political-activities#:~:text=Since%20partisan%20political%20activity%20in,engage%20in%20partisan%20political%20activities (last accessed Aug. 18, 2022). Rasheed Walters, "Rollins Deserves to be Called Out for DNC Party Attendance," *The Boston Herald* (July 21, 2022) https://www.bostonherald.com/2022/07/21/walters-rollins-deserves-to-be-called-out-for-dnc-party-attendance/.

780 Joe Dwinell, "Senator 'Demands' Investigation into Rachael Rollins Attending DNC Fundraiser," *The Boston Herald* (Jul. 18, 2022), https://www.bostonherald.com/2022/07/15/tom-cotton-calls-for-investigation-into-rachael-rollins-attendance-at-dnc-fundraiser/.

781 Joan Vennochi, "If This Were A Black Lives Matter Protest, Would the Response Have Been Different," *The Boston Globe* (Jul. 6, 2022), https://www.bostonglobe.com/2022/07/06/opinion/if-this-were-black-lives-matter-protest-would-response-have-been-different/.

782 Shelley Murphy, "US Attorney Investigates Quincy's Efforts to Block Long Island Bridge," *The Boston Globe* (May 22, 2022), https://www.bostonglobe.com/2022/05/22/metro/us-attorney-investigates-quincys-efforts-block-long-island-bridge/.

783 Adrian Walker, "US Attorney Rachael Rollins Opens Probe of Racism in Everett City Government," *The Boston Globe* (Jun. 3, 2022), https://www.bostonglobe.com/2022/06/03/metro/us-attorney-rachael-rollins-open-probe-racism-everett-city-government/.

784 Andrea Estes, "Newly Appointed Suffolk District Attorney Kevin Hayden Will Run to Permanently Succeed Rachael Rollins," *The Boston Globe* (Feb. 15, 2022).

785 Yawu Miller, "Is DA Hayden Reversing Rollins' Policies," *The Bay State Banner* (Jun. 22, 2022), https://www.baystatebanner.com/2022/06/22/is-da-hayden-reversing-rollins-policies/.

786 *Ibid.*

787 Joe Garofoli, *Chesa Boudin's Strategy to Remain San Francisco District Attorney: Run Against the Recall*, April 2, 2022, San Francisco Chronicle.

788 Michael Barba, *Judge Blasts Chesa Boudin for Disorganized DA's Office, Putting Politics Ahead of Prosecution*, September 29, 2021, San Francisco Examiner.

789 Megan Cassidy, "Deadly S.F. Hit-and-Run: Suspect Troy McAlister Pleads Not Guilty to All Charges," *San Francisco Chronicle* (updated Jan. 5, 2021), https://www.sfchronicle.com/crime/article/Deadly-S-F-hit-and-run-Suspect-due-in-court-15848170.php.

790 *Ibid.*

791 Rachel Swan and Megan Cassidy, "S.F. Parolee Accused of Killing Pedestrians Faced Life Sentence in Earlier Case, But Got Five Years," *San Francisco Chronicle* (updated Jan. 8, 2021), https://www.sfchronicle.com/crime/article/Fatal-hit-and-run-DA-Boudin-charges-suspect-15845917.php.

792 *Ibid.*

793 Susan Dyer Reynolds, "73 Felonies and 34 Misdemeanors in San Francisco Alone," Gotham, Substack (Sep. 9, 2021), https://susanreynolds.substack.com/p/73-felonies-and-34-misdemeanors-in?s=w.

794 Swan and Cassidy, "S.F. Parolee Accused of Killing Pedestrians Faced Life Sentence in Earlier Case, But Got Five Years," *supra* note 3; Susan Dyer Reynolds, "Chesa Boudin Released Troy McAlister Because 'He Worked Hard and Got his GED in Jail,'" Gotham, Substack (Mar. 23, 2022), https://susanreynolds.substack.com/p/chesa-boudin-*released*-troy-mcalister?s=r (noting that he received credit for the approximately five years he had served—a far cry from a sentence of thirty-five years to life).

795 Joe Vazquez, "San Francisco DA Boudin Once Represented Parolee Charged in Double Fatal Hit-and-Run," CBS Bay Area (Jan. 4, 2021), https://www.cbsnews.com/sanfrancisco/news/update-san-francisco-da-boudin-once-represented-parolee-accused-in-double-fatal-hit-and-run/.

796 Reynolds, "Chesa Boudin Released Troy McAlister Because 'He Worked Hard and Got his GED in Jail,'" *supra* note 6.

797 *Ibid.*

798 *Ibid.*

799 *Ibid.*

800 *Ibid.*

801 *Ibid.*

802 *Ibid.*

803 Cassidy, "Deadly S.F. Hit-and-Run: Suspect Troy McAlister Pleads Not Guilty to All Charges," *supra* note 1.

804 Recall Chesa Boudin—Yes on H—"Mrs. Abe," https://www.youtube.com/watch?v=mGUxZnjOFTc (last visited July 5, 2022).

805 Cassidy, "Deadly S.F. Hit-and-Run: Suspect Troy McAlister Pleads Not Guilty to All Charges," *supra* note 1.

806 Robert Hanley, "3 In Brink's Case Given Long Terms," *New York Times* (Oct. 7, 1983), https://www.nytimes.com/1983/10/07/nyregion/3-in-brink-s-case-given-long-terms.html.

807 The Megyn Kelly Show, Flashback: Megyn Kelly's Interview with the Man Who Raised Chesa Boudin, Former Terrorist Bill Ayers, https://www.youtube.com/watch?v=MQgBriIm8GA (last visited July 5, 2022).

808 Bay City News and Cheryl Hurd, "San Francisco DA's Father Granted Clemency by Outgoing NY Gov. Cuomo," NBC Bay Area (updated Aug. 24, 2021), https://www.nbcbayarea.com/news/local/san-francisco/san-francisco-das-father-granted-clemency-by-outgoing-ny-gov-cuomo/2639078/ ; Julian Mark, "San Francisco's Top Prosecutor Was 3 When His Dad Went to Prison. Cuomo Just Granted His Father Clemency," *Washington Post* (Aug. 24, 2021), https://www.washingtonpost.com/nation/2021/08/24/david-gilbert-clemency-cuomo-boudin/.

809 Terry Gross, "How San Francisco's D.A. Is Decreasing the Jail Population Amid COVID-19," NPR (Apr. 9, 2020), https://www.npr.org/2020/04/09/829955754/son-of-60s-radicals-is-the-new-d-a-in-san-francisco-facing-the-covid-19-crisis.

810 Maxwell Meyer, "Chesa Boudin: San Francisco's Lawless Revolutionary," *The Stanford Review* (Feb. 17, 2020), https://stanfordreview.org/chesa-boudin-san-franciscos-lawless-revolutionary/.

811 KQED News Staff and Wires, "S.F. Man Whose Case Upended California's Bail System Wins Release," KQED (May 4, 2018), https://www.kqed.org/news/11666269/s-f-man-whose-case-upended-californias-bail-system-wins-release.

812 Chesa Boudin, Chesa Boudin for San Francisco DA, 2019, https://www.youtube.com/watch?v=EL4HHmxuMP0 (last visited July 5, 2022); Tatiana Sanchez and Even Sernoffsky, "SF Public Defender Mano Raju, DA Chesa Boudin, Condemn ICE Courthouse Arrest," *San Francisco Chronicle* (Updated Mar. 5, 2020), https://www.sfchronicle.com/crime/article/ICE-arrests-defendant-outside-SF-courthouse-15107989.php;

813 Evan Sernoffsky, "DA Chesa Boudin Sets New Policies on SF Police Stops, Gang Enhancements, Three Strikes," *San Francisco Chronicle* (updated Feb. 28, 2020), https://www.sfchronicle.com/crime/article/San-Francisco-DA-Chesa-Boudin-sets-new-policies-15091160.php.

814 Daisy Nguyen, "Progressive Lawyer Boudin Wins San Francisco's DA Race," AP News (Nov. 10, 2019), https://apnews.com/article/ny-state-wire-us-news-ca-state-wire-politics-san-francisco-0eddc5267af84f6baebcfd7586a33dca.

815 Chesa Boudin (@chesaboudin), Twitter (Jun. 1, 2021), https://twitter.com/chesaboudin/status/1399775885834608640.

816 Elizabeth Weill-Greenberg, "D.A.s Are Asking Biden to End the Death Penalty. But Some are Still Wielding it Themselves," *The Appeal* (Apr. 5, 2021), https://theappeal.org/progressive-prosecutors-biden-letter-seeking-death-penalty/.

817 Letter from Fair and Just Prosecution-affiliated prosecutors, to Joe Biden, President of the United States (updated Jan. 26, 2021), https://fairandjustprosecution.org/wp-content/uploads/2021/01/FJP-Biden-Death-Penalty-Joint-Letter.pdf

818 Matt DeLisi, "Broken Windows Works," *City Journal* (May 29, 2019), https://www.city-journal.org/broken-windows-policing-works.

819 "Crime and Punishment: SFPD Battling Tidal Wave of Crime and Illegal Drug Sales in the Tenderloin Neighborhood," CBS Bay Area (May 25, 2021), https://www.cbsnews.com/sanfrancisco/news/crime-san-francisco-drug-sales-tenderlion-police-crackdown/.

820 News Release, "Official Declaration Allows the City to Waive Bureaucratic Hurdles to Quickly Implement Crucial Parts of the Mayor's Tenderloin Emergency Intervention Plan" City and County of San Francisco website (Dec. 17, 2021), https://sfmayor.org/article/mayor-london-breed-declares-state-emergency-tenderloin; Mallory Moench and Susie Neilson, "Mayor Breed's Tenderloin Drug Emergency is Ending. Does Data Show She Met Her Goals?," *San Francisco Chronicle* (updated Mar. 17, 2022), https://www.sfchronicle.com/sf/article/Mayor-Breed-s-Tenderloin-drug-emergency-is-17006934.php.

821 Moench and Neilson, "Mayor Breed's Tenderloin Drug Emergency is Ending. Does Data Show She Met Her Goals?," *supra* note 31.

822 Mallory Moench, "D.A. Chesa Boudin Joins Critics of Breed's Tenderloin Crackdown to Protest Plan," *San Francisco Chronicle* (updated Dec. 20, 2021), https://www.sfchronicle.com/sf/article/D-A-Chesa-Boudin-joins-critics-of-Breed-s-16717418.php.

823 *Ibid.*

824 *Ibid.*

825 *Ibid.*

826 *Ibid.*

827 *Crime and Punishment, supra* note 31.

828 Yoohyun Jung, "45 People Died in May in San Francisco from Accidental Overdoses," *San Francisco Chronicle* (Jun. 16, 2022), https://www.sfchronicle.com/projects/2021/san-francisco-drug-overdoses-map/.

829 Erica Sandberg, "Backlash by the Bay," *City Journal* (Jun. 27, 2021), https://www.city-journal.org/san-francisco-residents-fed-up-with-open-air-drug-use; Report on Accidental Overdose Deaths, Office of the Chief Medical Examiner (Jun. 21, 2021), https://sf.gov/sites/default/files/2021-05/2021%2005_OCME%20Overdose%20Report.pdf ; Report on Accidental Overdose Deaths, Office of the Chief Medical Examiner (May 17, 2022), https://sf.gov/sites/default/files/2022-05/2022%2005_OCME%20Overdose%20Report.pdf.

830 Jung, "45 People Died in May in San Francisco from Accidental Overdoses," *supra* note 36.

831 Yoohyun Jung, "San Francisco's Overdose Epidemic Disproportionately Affects Black People, Data Shows," *San Francisco Chronicle* (updated Oct. 5, 2021), https://www.sfchronicle.com/sf/article/San-Francisco-s-overdose-epidemic-16434757.php.

832 *Ibid.*

833 Jung, *45 People Died in May in San Francisco from Accidental Overdoses, supra* note 36.

834 Fentanyl Facts, Centers for Disease Control and Prevention, https://www.cdc.gov/stopoverdose/fentanyl/index.html (last visited Jun. 27, 2022).

835 Facts about Fentanyl, United States Drug Enforcement Administration, https://www.dea.gov/resources/facts-about-fentanyl (last visited Jun. 27, 2022).

836 *See supra* FNs 36 & 37.

837 *Ibid.*

838 Anna Tong and Josh Koehn, "DA Boudin and Fentanyl: Court Data Shows Just 3 Drug Dealing Convictions in 2021 as Immigration Concerns Shaped Policy," *The San Francisco Standard* (May 17, 2022, 2:04 PM), https://sfstandard.com/criminal-justice/da-chesa-boudin-fentanyl-court-data-drug-dealing-immigration/.

839 *Ibid.*

840 *Ibid.*

841 *Ibid.*

842 *Ibid.*

843 *Ibid.*

844 *Ibid.*

845 *Ibid.*

846 @bettersoma, Twitter (Nov. 5, 2021), https://twitter.com/bettersoma/status/1456651907858976768?s=20.

847 Tong and Koehn, "DA Boudin and Fentanyl: Court Data Shows Just 3 Drug Dealing Convictions in 2021 as Immigration Concerns Shaped Policy," *supra* note 43.

848 Stephanie Sierra, "Car Break-Ins on the Rise Across the Bay Area; How Some Are 'Risking it all' to Avoid It," ABC 7 News (Dec. 15, 2021), https://abc7news.com/san-francisco-car-break-ins-oakland-why-not-to-leave-your-trunk-open/11341223/.

849 S.F. Car Break-In Tracker, *San Francisco Chronicle* (updated July 4, 2022, 8:43 PM), https://www.sfchronicle.com/projects/sf-car-breakins/.

850 San Francisco Police Department CompStat Citywide Profile ending on 31-Dec-2021, https://www.sanfranciscopolice.org/sites/default/files/2022-01/SFPDCompstatDec2021-20220126.pdf.

851 *Ibid.*

852 "Smash-and-Grab Heist at San Francisco Neiman Marcus Another Retail Theft Red Flag," CBS Bay Area (July 6, 2021), https://www.cbsnews.com/sanfrancisco/news/update-smash-grab-heist-san-francisco-neiman-marcus-retail-theft-red-flag/.

853 Bradford Betz, "San Francisco Police Officers Association Blasts Far-Left DA Over Walgreens Thefts," Fox News (Jun. 15, 2021), https://www.foxnews.com/us/san-francisco-police-officers-association-blasts-da-walgreen-theft.

854 Monica Showalter, "Chesa Boudin's Free Pass for Shoplifters Drives San Francisco Store Owners to Lock All Goods Behind Glass Cases," *American Thinker* (Jun 19, 2021), https://www.americanthinker.com/blog/2021/07/in_san_francisco_chesa_boudins_freeforall_for_shoplifters_drives_store_owners_to_lock_all_goods_up_behind_glass_cases.html.

855 "All San Francisco Target Locations Reducing Operating Hours Due to Recent Spike in Crime," ABC 7 News (July 2, 2021), https://abc7news.com/target-hours-san-francisco-crime-shoplifting-sf/10851794/.

856 David Marchese, "San Francisco's D.A. Says Angry Elites Want Him Out of Office," *New York Times* Magazine (Feb. 28, 2022), https://www.nytimes.com/interactive/2022/03/01/magazine/chesa-boudin-interview.html.

857 *Ibid.*

858 *Ibid.*

859 *Ibid.*

860 Natalie Dreier, "Onlookers Watch as Man Fills Garbage Bag with Stolen Items from Walgreens Shelves," KIRO 7 (Jun. 15, 2021), https://www.kiro7.com/news/trending/onlookers-watch-man-fills-garbage-bag-with-stolen-items-walgreens-shelves/2ZHL5L-VQKRG5XG53TTQOYSOBLE/.

861 Megan Cassidy, "Man in Viral San Francisco Walgreens Shoplifting Video Sentenced to 16 Months in Prison; Released for Time Served," *San Francisco Chronicle* (Apr. 4, 2022), https://www.sfchronicle.com/crime/article/Man-in-viral-San-Francisco-Walgreens-shoplifting-17057408.php.

862 John Sexton, "San Francisco DA Chesa Boudin on Rampant Theft: 'It Has Nothing to Do with My Policies,'" HotAir (Mar. 1, 2022), https://hotair.com/john-s-2/2022/03/01/san-francisco-da-chesa-boudin-on-rampant-theft-it-has-nothing-to-do-with-my-policies-n452095.

863 *Ibid.*

864 Miriam Pawel, "How Chesa Boudin's Life Made Him a Lightning Rod for the Progressive Prosecutor Movement," *Los Angeles Times* (Mar. 30, 2022), https://www.latimes.com/politics/story/2022-03-30/chesa-boudin-san-francisco-recall-profile.

865 *Ibid.*

866 Evan Sernoffsky, "Deadly Crash Near SF's Lake Merced Followed a Lifetime of Crimes," KTVU (Feb. 5, 2021), https://www.ktvu.com/news/deadly-crash-near-sfs-lake-merced-followed-a-lifetime-of-crimes?utm_campaign=trueanthem&utm_medium=trueanthem&utm_source=facebook&fbclid=IwAR12I09oXagXO8cBPtzKO-33QyCFhQ12JvZNXO6OHcOT_4LcqvqPlD6eEaAE.

867 Madeleine Beck, "Pedestrian Killed in Lake Merced Collision Identified as Recent Dartmouth Grad," *San Francisco Examiner* (Feb. 5, 2021), https://www.sfexaminer.com/archives/pedestrian-killed-in-lake-merced-collision-identified-as-recent-dartmouth-grad/article_26173c68-4b14-5b67-b515-2933c781dedb.html.

868 Dion Lim, "Wife of Man Killed in SF Crash Tells Heartbreaking Story of California Dream Turned Nightmare," ABC 7 News (Feb. 6, 2021), https://abc7news.com/jerry-lyons-san-francisco-sheria-musyoka-sf-lake-merced/10317467/.

869 Beck, "Pedestrian Killed in Lake Merced Collision Identified as Recent Dartmouth Grad," *supra* note 81.

870 Lim, "Wife of Man Killed in SF Crash Tells Heartbreaking Story of California Dream Turned Nightmare," *supra* note 82.

871 Sara Gaiser, "Man Suspected of Fatally Beating 62-Year-Old Makes First Court Appearance," *San Francisco Examiner* (Sept. 26, 2019), https://www.sfexaminer.com/news/man-suspected-of-fatally-beating-62-year-old-makes-first-court-appearance/article_f7eec66a-d9d8-5ae3-8805-72577c92e5ee.html.

872 Susan Dyer Reynolds, "Two More Former Prosecutors Come Forward, This Time About a Boudin Plea Deal that Set a Killer Free," Gotham, Substack (Jun. 5, 2022), https://susanreynolds.substack.com/p/two-more-former-prosecutors-come?sd=fs&s=r.

873 *Ibid.*

874 Gaiser, "Man Suspected of Fatally Beating 62-Year-Old Makes First Court Appearance," *supra* note 71.

875 Reynolds, "Two More Former Prosecutors Come Forward, This Time About a Boudin Plea Deal that Set a Killer Free," *supra* note 72.

876 Lou Barberini, "Armed Robbery at Stow Lake," *MarinaTimes* (June 2021), http://www.marinatimes.com/armed-robbery-at-stow-lake.

877 Jay Barmann, "KPIX Reporter and Cameraman Robbed at Gunpoint at Twin Peaks," SFist (Mar. 4, 2021), https://sfist.com/2021/03/04/kpix-reporter-and-cameraman-robbed-at-gunpoint-on-twin-peaks/.

878 Thom Jensen, "Canadian Film Crew Robbed at Gunpoint at San Francisco's Twin Peaks," NBC Bay Area (Updated Mar. 28, 2022), https://www.nbcbayarea.com/news/local/canadian-film-crew-robbed-at-gunpoint-at-san-franciscos-twin-peaks/2848074/.

879 Louis Casiano, "San Francisco's New DA Pledges Not to Prosecute Public Urination, Other Quality-of-Life Crimes," Fox News (Nov. 11, 2019), https://www.foxnews.com/politics/san-franciscos-newly-elected-da-pledges-not-to-prosecute-public-urination-other-quality-of-life-crimes.

880 Gabe Greschler, "Why Did San Francisco's New District Attorney Fire Seven Prosecutors?," KQED (Jan. 12, 2020), https://www.kqed.org/news/11795676/why-did-san-franciscos-new-district-attorney-fire-seven-prosecutors.

881 *Ibid.*

882 Bigad Shaban, Robert Campos, Jeremy Carroll, and Mark Villareal, "Two SF Prosecutors Quit, Join Effort to Recall District Attorney Chesa Boudin," NBC Bay Area (Updated Oct. 31, 2021), https://www.nbcbayarea.com/news/local/

san-francisco/exclusive-two-sf-prosecutors-quit-join-effort-to-oust-former-boss-district-attorney-chesa-boudin/2698511/.

883 Heather Knight, "Why a Progressive Prosecutor Just Left D.A. Chesa Boudin's Office and Joined the Recall Effort," *San Francisco Chronicle* (updated Oct. 27, 2021), https://web.archive.org/web/20220506010847/https:/www.sfchronicle.com/sf/bayarea/heatherknight/article/She-s-a-progressive-homicide-prosecutor-who-16556274.php.

884 *Ibid.*

885 Rachel Swan, "S.F. Judge Blasts D.A. Chesa Boudin in Open Court, Citing Disorganization, Staff Turnover," San Francisco Chronicle (updated Sept. 29, 2021), https://www.sfchronicle.com/sf/article/S-F-judge-blasts-DA-Chesa-Boudin-in-open-court-16497522.php.

886 Michael Barba, *Judge Blasts Chesa Boudin for Disorganized DA's Office, Putting Politics Ahead of Prosecution,* S.F. Exam. (Sept. 29, 2021), https://www.sfexaminer.com/archives/judge-blasts-chesa-boudin-for-disorganized-da-s-office-putting-politics-ahead-of-prosecution/article_8d31d93d-d7a8-5f76-a682-572365240e56.html.

887 *Ibid.*

888 *Ibid.*

889 Heather Knight, "Why a Progressive Prosecutor Just Left D.A. Chesa Boudin's Office and Joined the Recall Effort," *supra* note 95.

890 *Ibid.*

891 Lindsay Kornick, "San Francisco DA Recall Effort: NY Mag Blasted for Blaming Republicans, 'Limits of Liberalism,'" Fox News (Jun. 6, 2022), https://www.foxnews.com/media/san-francisco-da-recall-ny-mag-blaming-republicans-liberalism.

892 Dept. of Elections, City and County of San Francisco, https://www.sfelections.org/tools/election_data/ (last visited June 12, 2022).

893 Heather Knight, "Chesa Boudin Blamed the Recall on the Right Wing. But S.F. Voters Who Ousted Him Just Want a City That Works," *San Francisco Chronicle* (updated Jun. 8, 2022), https://www.sfchronicle.com/sf/bayarea/heatherknight/article/Chesa-Boudin-blamed-the-recall-on-the-right-wing-17226645.php.

894 Brent Scher and Josh Christenson, "Soros Stiff-Arms Chesa Boudin After San Francisco Voters Kick Him to Curb," *Washington Free Beacon* (Jun. 10, 2022), https://freebeacon.com/democrats/soros-stiff-arms-chesa-boudin-after-san-francisco-voters-kick-him-to-curb/.

895 Charles D. Stimson & Zack Smith, "'Progressive' Prosecutors Sabotage the Rule of Law, Raise Crime Rates, and Ignore Victims," Legislative Memo 275, The Heritage Foundation (Oct. 29, 2020), https://www.heritage.org/crime-and-justice/report/progressive-prosecutors-sabotage-the-rule-law-raise-crime-rates-and-ignore.

896 Megan Cassidy, "Chesa Boudin Says He Won't Rule Out Running for San Francisco D.A., in First Interview Since Recall," *San Francisco Chronicle* (updated Jun. 28, 2022), https://www.sfchronicle.com/sf/article/Chesa-Boudin-says-he-won-t-rule-out-running-for-17271871.php.

897 *See* Mikenzie Frost, *Baltimore Takes Center Stage in Hogan's Police Funding Plan; Likely Town Hall Topic,* Fox 45 News (Oct. 18, 2021), https://foxbaltimore.com/news/local/baltimore-takes-center-stage-in-hogans-police-funding-plan-issues-likely-to-be-discussed.

898  *See* Stephen J.K. Walters, *Baltimore is Conducting a Dangerous Experiment in Law and Order*, Wash. Post (Apr. 16, 2021, 9:00 AM EDT), https://www.washingtonpost.com/opinions/local-opinions/baltimore-marilyn-mosby-low-level-crimes/2021/04/15/09bff31a-9c81-11eb-b7a8-014b14aeb9e4_story.html. Walters is the author of *Boom Towns: Restoring the Urban American Dream* and chief economist at the Maryland Public Policy Institute.

899  Maxine Streicher, "Dangerous Waiting Game: City Leaders Frustrated with Lack of Results in Crime Fight," FOX 45 News (Mar. 31, 2022), https://foxbaltimore.com/news/city-in-crisis/frustrations-running-high-over-crime-among-residents-and-city-leaders.

900  Mikenzie Frost (@MikenzieFrost), Twitter (Jan. 11, 2022, 8:21 PM). Embedded in the tweet is an interview by Frost of Luther Trent. Trent, riding in a car and wearing a mask, admits to setting his ex-girlfriend's house on fire. His statements, including his state of mind at the time of the offenses, can be used by the government in any subsequent state or federal prosecution for arson, attempted murder, or the like.

901  "Man Who Tried to Kill His Girlfriend Surprised by Plea Deal, Acknowledges He Should Be in Jail," Law Officer (Jan. 12, 2022), https://www.lawofficer.com/luther-trent-surprised-plea-deal/.

902  *Ibid.*

903  *Ibid.*

904  Mikenzie Frost, "Man Torches Ex-Girlfriend's Home; Says Plea Deals Like His Send Wrong Message to Baltimore," FOX 45 News (Jan. 11, 2022), https://foxbaltimore.com/news/local/man-torches-ex-girlfriends-home-says-plea-deals-like-his-send-wrong-message-to-baltimore.

905  *Ibid.*

906  Meet the U.S. Attorney, Erek L. Barron, United States Attorney's Office for the District of Maryland, https://www.justice.gov/usao-md/meet-us-attorney (last accessed Jun. 26, 2022).

907  Jeff Abell, "Demands for Criminal Case Outcomes Grow Louder," FOX 45 News (Apr. 19, 2022), https://foxbaltimore.com/news/city-in-crisis/demands-for-criminal-case-outcomes-grow-louder.

908  Maryland Code Ann., Pub. Safety § 3-524(d)(1).

909  Press Release from Baltimore City State's Attorney's Office, State Legislature Passes Maryland Police Accountability Act of 2021 (Apr. 15, 2021), https://web.archive.org/web/20210515160540/https://www.stattorney.org/media-center/press-releases/2249-state-legislature-passes-maryland-police-accountability-act-of-2021.

910  *Ibid.*

911  Telephone interview with Wicomico County Sheriff Mike Lewis on July 1, 2022. The authors have the notes from the call on file. In addition to the "necessary and proportional law" passed by the Maryland state legislature, Lewis noted that for the two previous years, the legislature had debated ending the legal doctrine called "qualified immunity" for law enforcement in Maryland.

912  Tim Swift and Keith Daniels, "Man Accused of Killing Deputy Was Out on Light Sentence for Baltimore Crime, Sheriff Says," ABC 7 News (Jun. 13, 2022), https://wjla.com/news/local/man-accused-of-killing-deputy-was-out-on-light-sentence-from-baltimore-crime-sheriff-says.

913  *Ibid.*

914 Isabel Hughes and Kristian Jaime, "Here's What We Know about the Shooting Death of Wicomico Deputy Glenn Hilliard," *Salisbury Daily Times* (Jun. 14, 2022), https://news.yahoo.com/heres-know-shooting-death-wicomico-172414716.html.

915 Swift and Daniels, *supra* note 16.

916 *Ibid.*

917 Baltimore City FOP (@FOP3), Twitter (Jun. 13, 2022, 4:22 PM), https://twitter.com/FOP3/status/1536443937627336704/photo/1.

918 Swift and Daniels, *supra* note 16.

919 Meet Marilyn Mosby, State's Attorney for Baltimore City, Office of the State's Attorney for the City of Baltimore, https://www.stattorney.org/office/meet-marilyn-mosby (last accessed Jul. 8, 2022).

920 Luke Broadwater, "Mosby's Focus on Crime Helped Unseat Bernstein," *The Baltimore Sun* (Jun. 25, 2014), https://www.baltimoresun.com/opinion/editorial/bs-md-ci-mosby-analysis-20140625-story.html.

921 "Meet the Candidates: Marilyn Mosby," The MSU Spokesman (Oct. 30, 2014), https://themsuspokesman.com/3648/special-coverage/meet-the-candidates-marilyn-mosby/.

922 Broadwater, *supra* note 24.

923 "Mosby Defeats Bernstein in Baltimore Prosecutor's Primary," *The Daily Record* (Jun. 25, 2014), https://thedailyrecord.com/2014/06/25/mosby-defeats-bernstein-in-baltimore-prosecutors-primary/.

924 Broadwater, *supra* note 24.

925 *See* Justine Barron, They Killed Freddie Gray: The Anatomy of a Police Brutality Cover-Up (2023). *See also* Kitria Stewart and Mary Ibeh, Freddie Gray, My Childhood Friend (2016); Mary Anne Whelan, Freddie's Last Ride: "What Really Happened to Freddie Gray?" (2020); Roberto E. Alejandro, The Crucifixion and Resurrection of Freddie Gray (Jan. 29, 2020); Sean Yoes, Baltimore After Freddie Gray: Real Stories from One of America's Great Imperiled Cities (Jul. 9, 2018); Ronald J. Leach, Baltimore Blue and Freddie Gray (Apr. 2016).

926 *See* Office of Governor Larry Hogan, Governor Larry Hogan Signs Executive Order Declaring State of Emergency, Activating National Guard (Apr. 27, 2015), https://governor.maryland.gov/2015/04/27/governor-larry-hogan-signs-executive-order-declaring-state-of-emergency-activating-national-guard/.

927 *See* Read the Transcript of Marilyn J. Mosby's Statement on Freddie Gray, Time (May 1, 2015), https://time.com/3843870/marilyn-mosby-transcript-freddie-gray/.

928 Lewis Interview, *supra* note 15.

929 Press Release, Office of Public Affairs, Federal Officials Decline Prosecution in the Death of Freddie Gray (Sept. 12, 2017), https://www.justice.gov/opa/pr/federal-officials-decline-prosecution-death-freddie-gray.

930 The words *juvenile, malicious, vindictive* come from an interview we conducted on July 5, 2022, with a former assistant state's attorney from the Baltimore City State's Attorney's Office. This attorney, who worked with Mosby when she was a line prosecutor and left the office after Mosby was elected state's attorney, told us the following: "She's not bright. She's angry, and she's juvenile, and she's malicious and vindictive."

931 Borzilleri v. Mosby, 874 F.3d 187 (2017).

932 Jessica Anderson, "City Reaches Tentative $75,000 Deal with Attorney Who Briefly Was Named a Deputy Baltimore Police Commissioner," *The Baltimore Sun* (Nov. 25,

2019), https://www.baltimoresun.com/news/crime/bs-md-ci-cr-michelle-wilson-set-tlement-20191126-mjs7nh5aazcnzawzojkzabb7li-story.html.

933 Charles D. Stimson and Zack Smith, "'Progressive' Prosecutors Sabotage the Rule of Law, Raise Crime Rates, and Ignore Victims," Heritage Foundation Legal Memorandum No. 275, 4–6 (Oct. 29, 2020), https://www.heritage.org/crime-and-justice/report/progressive-prosecutors-sabotage-the-rule-law-raise-crime-rates-and-ignore.

934 *Ibid.*

935 Interview, *supra* note 34.

936 Barry Simms, "Baltimore Police Commissioner Takes Issue with Prosecutor's Implementation of Policy on Misdemeanors," WBAL TV 11 (Jun. 28, 2022), https://www.wbaltv.com/article/baltimore-police-commissioner-prosecutor-policy-implementation/40447616.

937 Mikenzie Frost, "Baltimore Leaders Still Reluctant to Criticize Mosby As Crime Rises," FOX 45 News (May 12, 2022), https://foxbaltimore.com/news/local/title-05-12-2022.

938 Jessica Anderson, "Baltimore Police Aim to Be Among First Law Enforcement Agencies to Hire Civilian Investigators to Fill Vacancies, Improve Clearance Rates," *The Baltimore Sun* (Apr. 14, 2022), https://www.baltimoresun.com/maryland/baltimore-city/bs-md-ci-civilian-officers-20220414-hnfuvkjrxvfojebz65cxyq3wee-story.html.

939 *Ibid.*

940 Mark Reutter and Ian Round, "The Peripatetic Prosecutor: Marilyn Mosby Took 23 Trips in 2018 and 2019, Accepting $30,000 in Reimbursements," *Baltimore Brew* (Jul. 16, 2020), https://baltimorebrew.com/2020/07/16/the-peripatetic-prosecutor-marilyn-mosby-took-23-trips-in-2018-and-2019-pocketing-30000-in-reimbursements/.

941 Lee O. Sanderlin and Emily Opilo, "Feds File Superseding Indictment Against Baltimore State's Attorney Marilyn Mosby, Claim She Lied About Living in Florida," *The Baltimore Sun* (Mar. 11, 2022), https://www.baltimoresun.com/news/crime/bs-md-cr-mosby-superseding-indictment-20220310-ga3jnqc3rb-dldoftpw4wwda2g4-story.html. The website for the United States Attorney's Office for the District of Maryland does not contain the superseding indictment, only the original indictment. In the event they update their webpage, it can be found at https://www.justice.gov/usao-md.

942 Chris Berinato, Tim Swift, and Mikenzie Frost, "Feds Call Mosby's Defense a 'Tale of Victimhood to Deflect Attention," FOX 45 News (Mar. 11, 2022), https://foxbaltimore.com/news/local/feds-response-to-dismissal-motion-marilyn-mosby-is-a-victim-of-her-own-lies-and-choices.

943 Nigel Roberts, "Baltimore City States Attorney Marilyn Mosby Ordered to Appear in Court for Possibly Violating Gag Order," BET.com (Jun. 22, 2022), https://www.bet.com/article/r6j5vw/judge-orders-baltimore-prosecutor-marilyn-mosby-appear-violating-gag-order-keith-davis-case.

944 *Ibid.*

945 Tim Swift and Rebecca Pryor, "Judge Finds Mosby in Contempt of Court for Violating Gag Order in Davis Case," Fox 45

Baltimore (Aug. 12, 2022), https://foxbaltimore.com/news/local/judge-find-mosby-in-contempt-of-court-for-violating-gag-order-in-davis-case.

946  On the record phone interview with Tony Foreman on July 13, 2022. Notes of the call are with the authors.

947  Lee O. Sanderlin and Alex Mann, "A Threat to Public Safety: Staffing Shortage and Low Morale Plague Baltimore State's Attorney Marilyn Mosby's Office," *The Baltimore Sun* (Jun. 6, 2022), https://www.baltimoresun.com/news/crime/bs-md-ci-cr-marilyn-mosby-staffing-crisis-20220606-ln35rnzz5rbhlhaowpkxycibsa-story.html; Mikenzie Frost, "SA Mosby's Office Staffing Crisis Is Nothing Short of a Public Safety Emergency," FOX 45 News (Jun. 6, 2022), https://foxbaltimore.com/news/local/sa-mosbys-office-staffing-crisis-s-nothing-short-of-a-public-safety-emergency.

948  *Ibid.*

949  *Ibid.*

950  Sanderlin and Mann, *supra* note 51.

951  *Ibid.*

952  Memorandum Opinion, State of Maryland v. Kevin Hickson, Ronald Crawford, Davon Telp, Jarrell Docket, In the Circuit Court for Baltimore City, by Judge Jeffrey M. Geller (Jun. 28, 2022); Tim Swift, "Judge Details Egregious Failures On Staffing at Mosby's State's Attorney's Office," FOX 45 News (Jun. 30, 2022), https://foxbaltimore.com/news/local/judge-details-egregious-failures-on-staffing-at-mosbys-states-attorneys-office.

953  June 27, 2022, interview with Baltimore attorney who worked in the private sector and for the government in Maryland. The attorney did not want to be identified for fear of political retribution. Notes from the interview are on file with the authors.

954  Mikenzie Frost, "Gov. Hogan Set to Meet with Mayor Scott on Crime; Says City Receivership Not an Option," FOX 45 News (Nov. 29, 2021), https://foxbaltimore.com/news/local/gov-hogan-set-to-meet-with-mayor-scott-on-crime-says-city-receivership-not-an-option-yet.

955  *Ibid.*

956  Maxine Streicher, "No Press Spotted at Marilyn Mosby Press Conference," FOX 45 News (Oct. 14, 2021), https://foxbaltimore.com/news/city-in-crisis/marilyn-mosby-has-press-conference-where-it-appears-t.

957  Maxine Streicher, "It's a Disgrace: Frustration Rises Over Mosby's New Prosecution Policy," FOX 45 News (Apr. 21, 2021), https://foxbaltimore.com/news/city-in-crisis/frustration-with-mosbys-new-prosecution-policy-during-community-meeting.

958  Christina Tkacik, "Fed Up: Restaurant Owners Look to Baltimore State's Attorney's Race to Reverse City Crime Trends," *The Baltimore Sun* (Jul. 6, 2022), https://www.baltimoresun.com/food-drink/bs-fo-restaurateurs-states-attorney-20220706-onmndb6umnftvgbaxu7kgggg7u-story.html.

959  "City State's Attorney Race: Impact on Crime," FOX 45 News (Mar. 23, 2022), https://foxbaltimore.com/morning/city-states-attorney-race-impact-on-crime#:~:text=%22We%20just%20want%20a%20civil,do%20not%20overpromise%20and%20underperform.%22

960  *Ibid.*

961  Tim Swift, "Roland Park Residents Confront Marilyn Mosby at a Tense Community Meeting," Fox 45 News (Apr. 6, 2022), https://foxbaltimore.com/news/local/roland-park-residents-confront-marilyn-mosby-at-tense-community-meeting.

962 *Ibid.*

963 Mikenzie Frost, "Marilyn Mosby Goes on the Defense in Roland Park; Analysts Say Tone Shows Voter Frustration," FOX 45 News (Apr. 7, 2022), https://foxbaltimore. com/news/local/marilyn-mosby-goes-on-defense-in-roland-park-analysts-say-tone-shows-voter-frustration.

964 Keith Daniels, "Roland Park Residents React After Fiery Meeting with Marilyn Mosby," FOX 45 News (Apr. 7, 2022), https://foxbaltimore.com/news/local/ baltimore-city-states-attorney-marilyn-mosby-under-fire-by-some-roland-park-res-idents#:~:text=%22It%20is%20up%20to%20her,m%20sorry%20to%20 say%20that.

965 *Ibid.*

966 Foreman Interview, *supra* note 50.

967 *Ibid.*

968 The *Baltimore Sun* tracks the number of homicides per year in Baltimore. See Baltimore Homicides, *The Baltimore Sun*, https://homicides.news.baltimoresun. com/?range=7 (last visited Aug. 30, 2022); The Baltimore Police Department crime statistics page, https://www.baltimorepolice.org/crime-stats.

969 Elizabeth Janney, "Robbery Rate in Baltimore Is Highest in U.S.: Study," Patch (Apr. 5, 2019), https://patch.com/maryland/baltimore/ robbery-rate-baltimore-highest-us-study.

970 Tamar Larpin, Craig McCarthy, Carl Campanile, & Bruce Golding, "Manhattan DA Alvin Bragg reverses pair of Controversial Policies," *New York Post* (updated Feb. 4, 2022), https://nypost.com/2022/02/04/ manhattan-da-alvin-bragg-reverses-pair-of-controversial-policies/.

971 Lorena Mongelli, "Woman Accused of Killing Army Vet in 2018 Remains Free on Paltry Bail as Case Lingers," *New York Post* (updated Jun. 1, 2021), https://nypost. com/2021/06/01/woman-accused-of-killing-army-vet-in-2018-remains-free-on-pal-try-bail-as-case-lingers/.

972 *Ibid.*

973 Kevin Fasick and Anthony Izaguirre, "Son Dead, Dad Stabbed After Brawl Turns Fatal in Harlem," *New York Post* (updated Oct. 20, 2018), https://nypost. com/2018/10/20/son-dead-dad-stabbed-after-brawl-turns-fatal-in-harlem/.

974 Jack Morphet and Gabrielle Fonrouge, "Mother of Slain Army Vet Hason Correa Rips Manhattan DA Alvin Bragg for Giving Plea Deals in Case," *New York Post* (updated Jun. 10, 2022), https://nypost.com/2022/06/10/ mother-of-hason-correa-rips-da-alvin-bragg-for-giving-plea-deals/.

975 Kevin Sheehan and Jorge Fitz-Gibbon, "Grieving Mom of Slain Vet Berates Manhattan DA Alvin Bragg," *New York Post* (updated Jun. 29, 2022), https://nypost. com/2022/06/29/grieving-mom-of-slain-vet-berates-manhattan-da-alvin-bragg/.

976 *Ibid.*

977 Priscilla DeGregory, "Woman Charged in War Vet's Murder Gets Time Served After Plea Deal," *New York Post* (updated May 19, 2022), https://nypost.com/2022/05/19/ woman-charged-in-war-vets-murder-pleas-for-time-served/.

978 *Ibid.*

979 *Ibid.*

980 Morphet and Fonrouge, "Mother of Slain Army Vet Hason Correa Rips Manhattan DA Alvin Bragg for Giving Plea Deals in Case," *supra* note 5.

981 *Ibid.*

982 *Ibid.*

983 *Ibid.*

984 Anna D. Wilde, "The Anointed One: Students See Alvin Bragg as Conciliator," The Harvard Crimson (Jun. 8, 1995), https://www.thecrimson.com/article/1995/6/8/the-anointed-one-pon-the-evening/ (quoting then Dean of Students Archie C. Epps as saying, "I would push him toward elective politics because he's the perfect example of a crossover politician who can draw votes from both white and [b]lack voters").

985 Wedding/Celebrations, Jamila Ponton, Alvin Bragg Jr., *New York Times* (Nov. 2, 2003), https://www.nytimes.com/2003/11/02/style/weddings-celebrations-jamila-ponton-alvin-bragg-jr.html.

986 Tuition, Fees & Financial Aid, Trinity School, https://www.trinityschoolnyc.org/admissions/tuition-fees-and-financial-aid (last visited Aug. 23, 2022).

987 About, AlvingBragg.com, https://www.alvinbragg.com/about (last visited Aug. 23, 2022).

988 Jonah E. Bromwich, "Alvin Bragg Wins, Becoming First Black D.A. in Manhattan," *New York Times* (updated Feb. 23, 2022), https://www.nytimes.com/2021/11/02/nyregion/alvin-bragg-wins-manhattan-da.html.

989 *Ibid.*

990 Alvin Bragg, LinkedIn, https://www.linkedin.com/in/alvin-bragg-857327b/details/experience/ (last visited Aug. 22, 2022).

991 About, AlvingBragg.com, https://www.alvinbragg.com/about (last visited Aug. 23, 2022).

992 Dan M. Clark, "NY Chief Deputy AG Heading to New York Law School Teaching Post," Law.com (Dec. 10, 2018), https://www.law.com/newyorklawjournal/2018/12/10/ny-chief-deputy-ag-heading-to-new-york-law-school-teaching-post/?slreturn=20220721223631.

993 Chris Brunet, "Former NYPD Commissioner Criticizes New Manhattan DA Over Soros Ties," Daily Caller (Jan. 10, 2022, 12:58 PM), https://dailycaller.com/2022/01/10/eric-adams-alvin-bragg-manhattan-district-attorney/. Soros representatives have made a point to say that none of the $1 million Soros pumped into the race was funneled to Bragg. The Color of Change PAC expended funds as an independent expenditure supporting Bragg. The PAC though later halted expenditures because of allegations of impropriety against Bragg. Bragg denies any wrongdoing. Shawn Cohen, "Riddle of Why George Soros-Backed Political Action Committee Color of Change Pulled $500,000 in Funding from Super-Liberal Manhattan DA Alvin Bragg's Campaign After Disturbing Allegation Was Made Against Him by Unnamed Woman," DailyMail (updated Feb. 9, 2022), https://www.dailymail.co.uk/news/article-10490077/Color-Change-pulled-500-000-funding-DA-Alvin-Braggs-campaign-allegation.html.

994 Wilde, "The Anointed One," *supra* note 15.

995 Gus Saltonstall, "Manhattan District Attorney Race: Alvin Bragg Profile," Patch (Jun. 16, 2021), https://patch.com/new-york/washington-heights-inwood/manhattan-district-attorney-race-alvin-bragg-profile.

996 *Ibid.*

997 Achieving Fairness and Safety, Memorandum from Alvin L. Bragg, Jr. to All Staff, Jan. 3, 2022, https://www.manhattanda.org/wp-content/uploads/2022/01/

Day-One-Letter-Policies-1.03.2022.pdf (colloquially known as the "Day One Memo").

998 Erica Orden, "The Trials of Alvin Bragg," Intelligencer, New York Magazine (Apr. 13, 2022), https://nymag.com/intelligencer/article/manhattan-da-alvin-bragg-memo-trump.html.

999 Saltonstall, "Manhattan District Attorney Race: Alvin Bragg Profile," *supra* note 26.

1000 Joe Marino and Bruce Golding, "Ex-Con Would Have Faced 'Long Time in Jail' If Not for New Manhattan DA: Judge," *New York Post* (updated Jan. 12, 2022), https://nypost.com/2022/01/12/ex-con-would-have-faced-lengthy-sentence-if-not-for-alvin-bragg-judge/.

1001 Stephanie Pagones and Michael Ruiz, "Fallen NYPD Det. Jason Rivera's Grieving Widow Calls Out Manhattan DA Bragg in Heartbreaking Eulogy," FoxNews.com (Jan. 28, 2022), https://www.foxnews.com/us/widow-fallen-nypd-det-jason-rivera-manhattan-da-bragg.

1002 *Ibid.*

1003 Jonah E. Bromwich and William K. Rashbaum, "Conflict Quickly Emerges Between Top Prosecutor and Police Commissioner," *New York Times* (updated Jan. 10, 2022), https://www.nytimes.com/2022/01/08/nyregion/alvin-bragg-police-chief-eric-adams.html.

1004 Orden, "The Trials of Alvin Bragg," *supra* note 29.

1005 *Ibid.*

1006 *Ibid.*

1007 Bromwich and William K. Rashbaum, "Conflict Quickly Emerges Between Top Prosecutor and Police Commissioner," *supra* note 34.

1008 Orden, "The Trials of Alvin Bragg," *supra* note 29.

1009 Jonah E. Bromwich, "Manhattan D.A. Sharpens Crime Policies That Led to Weeks of Backlash," *New York Times* (Feb. 4, 2022), https://www.nytimes.com/2022/02/04/nyregion/manhattan-da-alvin-bragg-memo-prosecution.html.

1010 *Ibid.*

1011 *Ibid.*

1012 Tamar Lapin, Craig McCarthy, Carl Campanile, and Bruce Golding, "Manhattan DA Alvin Bragg Reverses Pair of Controversial Policies," *New York Post* (Feb. 4, 2022), https://nypost.com/2022/02/04/manhattan-da-alvin-bragg-reverses-pair-of-controversial-policies/.

1013 Orden, "The Trials of Alvin Bragg," *supra* note 29.

1014 Larry Celona and Jorge Fitz-Gibbon, "DA Alvin Bragg Cuts Break for Women Allegedly Caught on Video Attacking NYPD Cops," *New York Post* (updated Jun. 23, 2022), https://nypost.com/2022/06/23/da-alvin-bragg-cuts-break-for-women-allegedly-caught-on-video-attacking-nypd-cops/.

1015 *Ibid.*

1016 *Ibid.*

1017 *Ibid.*

1018 Rebecca Rosenberg, "New York City Prosecutor Defends Going Easy on Teen Who Brutally Attacked Cop," FoxNews.com (Jul. 28, 2022), https://www.foxnews.com/us/new-york-city-prosecutor-defends-going-easy-teen-brutally-attacked-cop.

1019 *Ibid.*

1020 *Ibid.*

1021 *Ibid.*

1022 *Ibid.*

1023 *Ibid.*

1024 *Ibid.*

1025 *Ibid.*

1026 *Ibid.*

1027 Marcia Kramer and Ali Bauman, "Hochul, Adams Not on Same Page After Video of Teens Fighting Transit Cops in Subway," CBS New York (updated Jul. 26, 2022), https://www.cbsnews.com/newyork/news/hochul-adams-not-on-the-same-page-after-video-of-teens-fighting-transit-cops-in-subway/.

1028 Jason Fisher, "'This is Lunacy!' Woke Manhattan DA Alvin Bragg Is Blasted for DEFENDING Decision to Free Boy, 16, Filmed 'Beating Cop at Harlem Subway Station' Just Two Days After He Was Charged with Mugging a Stranger," DailyMail (updated Aug. 1, 2022), https://www.dailymail.co.uk/news/article-11060047/DA-Alvin-Bragg-DEFENDS-decision-release-teen-brutally-battered-NYPD-cop-24-hours.html.

1029 Kramer and Ali Bauman, "Hochul, Adams Not on Same Page After Video of Teens Fighting Transit Cops in Subway," *supra* note 58.

1030 *Ibid.*

1031 Dean Balsamini, "Chelsea Victim 'Outraged' After Serial Gym Thief Gets Slap on Wrist," *New York Post* (updated May 14, 2022), https://nypost.com/2022/05/14/victim-outraged-as-serial-nyc-gym-thief-gets-slap-on-wrist/.

1032 *Ibid.*

1033 Joe Marino, Jack Morphet, and Jorge Fitz-Gibbon, "Macy's-loving 'serial shoplifter' gets charges downgraded thanks to soft-on-crime NYC DA Bragg," *New York Post* (Jun. 7, 2022), https://nypost.com/2022/06/07/nyc-da-downgrades-macys-loving-serial-shoplifters-charges/.

1034 *Ibid.*

1035 *Ibid.*

1036 *Ibid.*

1037 Larry Celona and Jorge Fitz-Gibbon, "DA Alvin Bragg Cut Deals that Freed NYC Career Criminal—Who Then Punched Woman in Random Attack," *New York Post* (updated Jun. 16, 2022), https://nypost.com/2022/06/16/da-bragg-cut-deal-to-free-nyc-criminal-who-then-assaulted-woman/.

1038 Tina Moore, *Manhattan* "DA Bragg Didn't Request Warrant for Man Who Later Used Gun in Slaying: Union Boss," *New York Post* (updated Mar. 22, 2022), https://nypost.com/2022/03/22/manhattan-da-bragg-didnt-issue-warrant-for-man-who-later-used-gun-in-slaying-union-boss/.

1039 *Ibid.*

1040 Valentina Jaramillo and Emily Crane, "Bodega Worker Jose Alba Too Scared to Leave Home After Murder Charge is Dropped," *New York Post* (updated Jul. 20, 2022), https://nypost.com/2022/07/20/bodega-worker-jose-alba-too-scared-to-leave-home-after-murder-charge-is-dropped/.

1041 Steven Vago, Georgett Roberts, and Melissa Klein, "NYC Bodega Clerk Jose Alba Tried to Avoid Confrontation that Led to His Arrest, New Video Reveals," *New York Post* (updated Jul. 9, 2022), https://nypost.com/2022/07/09/nyc-bodega-clerk-jose-alba-tried-to-avoid-confrontation-that-led-to-his-arrest-video/.

1042 Post Editorial Board, "Alvin Bragg's Prosecution of Jose Alba Looks Ever More Troublesome," *New York Post* (updated July 11, 2022), https://nypost.com/2022/07/11/alvin-braggs-persecution-of-jose-alba-looks-ever-more-troublesome/.

1043 Joseph Konig and Dean Meminger, "Manhattan DA Dismisses Murder Charges Against Harlem Bodega Worker," Spectrum News 1 (updated July 19, 2022), https://www.ny1.com/nyc/all-boroughs/news/2022/07/19/manhattan-da-set-to-dismiss-murder-charges-against-harlem-bodega-worker.

1044 Joe Marino, Tina Moore, Kyle Schnitzer and Jorge Fitz-Gibbon, "DA Feels Woman Who Allegedly Stabbed NYC Bodega Worker Jose Alba Was Defending Beau: Sources," *New York Post* (updated July 11, 2022,), https://nypost.com/2022/07/11/da-feels-jose-albas-accused-stabber-was-defending-beau-sources/.

1045 *Ibid.*

1046 Post Editorial Board, "DA Bragg Is Pro-Criminal for Letting the Perp Walk in Bodega Worker Jose Alba's Case," *New York Post* (updated July 12, 2022), https://nypost.com/2022/07/12/manhattan-da-bragg-is-pro-criminal-for-letting-the-perp-walk-in-bodega-worker-jose-albas-case/.

1047 Andrea Grymes, *New NYPD Statistics Show Shocking Crime Increase in Manhattan's 6th Precinct,* CBA New York (Aug. 18, 2022, 6:18 PM), https://www.cbsnews.com/newyork/news/new-nypd-statistics-show-shocking-crime-increase-in-manhattans-6th-precinct/.

1048 *Ibid.*

1049 Borough and Precinct Crime Statistics, NYPD, https://www1.nyc.gov/site/nypd/stats/crime-statistics/borough-and-precinct-crime-stats.page#manhattan (last visited Aug. 22, 2022).

1050 CompStat, Manhattan South, Report Covering the Week 8/15/2022 through 8/21/2022, Vol. 29, No. 33, https://www1.nyc.gov/assets/nypd/downloads/pdf/crime_statistics/cs-en-us-pbms.pdf.

1051 CompStat, Manhattan South, Report Covering the Week 8/15/2022 through 8/21/2022, Vol. 29, No. 33, https://www1.nyc.gov/assets/nypd/downloads/pdf/crime_statistics/cs-en-us-pbmn.pdf.

1052 Larry Celona, Conor Skelding, and Melissa Klein, "Crimefighter Exodus: Manhattan Prosecutors Flee DA Office After Bragg Takes Helm," *New Yor Post* (updated Jan. 15, 2022), https://nypost.com/2022/01/15/prosecutcrimefighter-exodus-manhattan-prosecutors-flee-da-office-after-bragg-takes-helmors-leave-manhattan-das-office-after-bragg-comes-in/.

1053 *Ibid.*

1054 Dean Balsamini, "Fellow NYC District Attorneys Not Embracing Alvin Bragg's Policies," *New York Post* (updated Jan. 8, 2022), https://nypost.com/2022/01/08/fellow-nyc-district-attorneys-not-embracing-alvin-braggs-policies/.

1055 *Ibid.*

1056 *Ibid.*

1057 Definition, *Merriam-Webster* Dictionary, https://www.merriam-webster.com/dictionary/racism (last visited Aug. 30, 2022).

1058 Michelle Alexander, *The New Jim Crow,* 184.

1059 Paul J. Larkin and Giancarlo Canaparo, *The Fallacy of Systemic Racism in the American Criminal Justice System* , 18 Lib. Univ.. L. Rev. (forthcoming 2023) (manuscript at 7, n.17) [hereinafter *Criminal Justice System*].

1060 *Ibid.*

1061 Adarand Constructors, Inc. v. Pena, 515 U.S. 200, 227 (1995).

1062 Grutter v. Bollinger, 539 U.S. 306, 328 (2003).

1063 Larkin and Canaparo, *Criminal Justice System, supra* note 3, at 26–30.

1064 Ibid. *supra* note 3, 4.

1065 *Ibid.* at 36–37(citing Batson v. Kentucky, 476 U.S. 79, 93–96 (1986), and its progeny).

1066 *Ibid.*, 6–7.

1067 *Ibid.*, 38.

1068 Personnel Administrator of Massachusetts v. Feeney, 442 U.S. 256, 260 (1979).

1069 Larkin and Canaparo, *Criminal Justice System, supra* note 3, 12–16.

1070 *Ibid.*

1071 *Ibid.*, 16–18.

1072 *Ibid.*,19, 26.

1073 *Ibid.*, 26, 27.

1074 *Ibid.*, 42–44 nn.186, 188 (citing Michael Tonry, *Malign Neglect: Race Crime and Punishment in America* (New York: Oxford University Press, 1995), 79 and Charles Murray, *Facing Reality: Two Truths About Race in America* (New York: Encounter Books, 2021), 51–52

1075 *Ibid.*, 47-48.

1076 *Ibid.*

1077 Latzer, *infra* note 41.

1078 Larkin and Canaparo, *Criminal Justice System, supra* note 3, 44 nn. 188–89.

1079 *Ibid.*, 38 n. 171 (citations omitted).

1080 *Ibid.*, 19.

1081 *Ibid.*, 18–19.

1082 *Ibid*, 17–21.

1083 *Ibid.*, 20–21.

1084 *Ibid.*, 19–20.

1085 *Ibid.*, 25.

1086 *Ibid.*, 42.

1087 *Ibid.*, 46 (citing statistics compiled by the U.S. Department of Justice).

1088 *Ibid.*

1089 *Ibid.*, 48 n.209.

1090 Gary A. Haugen, Victor Boutros, and Arthur Morey, *The Locust Effect: Why the End of Poverty Requires the End of Violence* (Brilliance Audio, 2014).

1091 13th (Netflix, 2016) (directed by Ava DuVernay), https://www.youtube.com/watch?v=krfcq5pF8u8.

1092 Fred Barbash and Harry Siegel, "Van Jones Resigns Amid Controversy," Politico (updated September 7, 2009), https://www.politico.com/story/2009/09/van-jones-resigns-amid-controversy-026797.

1093 Press Release, Princeton Univ., Former White House Advisor Van Jones Appointed Visiting Fellow (Feb. 24, 2010), https://www.princeton.edu/news/2010/02/24/former-white-house-adviser-van-jones-appointed-visiting-fellow; Van Jones, Political Commentator, Full Bio, CNN, https://www.cnn.com/profiles/van-jones-profile#about (last visited Aug. 30, 2022).

1094 #cut50, Change.org, https://www.change.org/o/cut50 (last visited Aug. 30, 2022).

1095 *Ibid.*

1096 Rafael Mangual, *Criminal [In]Justice: What the Push for Decarceration and Depolicing Gets Wrong and Who It Hurts the Most* (Nashville; Hachette Nashville/Center Street Publishing, 2022), 4.

1097 Barry Latzer, *The Myth of Overpunishment: A Defense of the American Justice System and a Proposal to Reduce Incarceration While Protecting the Public* (Washington, DC: Republic Book Publishers, 2022), 85.

1098 Definition, *Merriam-Webster* Dictionary, Ninth New Collegiate Dictionary (1991).

1099 *Ibid.*

1100 Latzer, *supra* note 42, 88.

1101 *Ibid.*

1102 *Ibid.*

1103 *Ibid.*, 89.

1104 *Ibid.*, 106.

1105 *Ibid.*, 91.

1106 *Ibid.*

1107 *Ibid.*, 73–74.

1108 *Ibid.*,106.

1109 *Ibid.*, 74.

1110 *Ibid.*

1111 *Ibid.*, 74–75.

1112 *Ibid.*, 77.

1113 *Ibid.*

1114 *Ibid.*, 83.

1115 *Ibid.*

1116 Alexander, *supra* note 3, 101.

1117 Latzer, *supra* note 39, 90.

1118 *Ibid.*

1119 *Ibid.*

1120 *Ibid.*

1121 *Ibid.*

1122 John F. Pfaff, "The War on Drugs and Prison Growth: Limited Importance, Limited Legislative Options," (Boston MA: Harvard Journal on Legislation 52, 2015), 173, 179.

1123 Latzer, *supra* note 39, 107.

1124 *Ibid.*

1125 *Ibid.* The fact that more people were admitted to prison than were arrested for this crime in 2019 might seem odd at first glance. But according to Latzer, "Prison admissions for rape include other sexual offenses…and [p]rison admissions in 2019 include some crimes committed and arrests made in previous years."

1126 *Ibid.*

1127 *Ibid.* at 108.

1128 *Ibid.*

1129 *Ibid.*

1130 U.S. Department of Justice, Bureau of Justice Statistics, "Reentry Trends in the U.S." (2004), https://bjs.ojp.gov/content/pub/pdf/reentry.pdf.

1131 Latzer, *supra* note 39, 110.

1132 *Ibid.*

1133 *Ibid.*, 113.

1134 *Ibid.*, 117.

1135 *Ibid.*

1136 *Ibid.*, 119.

1137 Gun Trace Report, City of Chicago, Office of the Mayor, (2017), https://www.chicago.gov/content/dam/city/depts/mayor/Press%20Room/Press%20Releases/2017/October/GTR2017.pdf (finding that in 95 percent of cases where the Chicago Police Department was able to identify the possessor of a gun used in a crime, "that individual was not the original, lawful possessor of the firearm...."); Megan E. Collins et al. 2017. "A Comparative Analysis of Crime Guns." *Russell Sage Foundation Journal of the Social Sciences*, 96. https://ccjs.umd.edu/sites/ccjs.umd.edu/files/pubs/COMPLIANT2-Megan%20E.%20Collins%2C%20Susan%20T.%20Parker%2C%20Thomas%20L.%20Scott%2C%20and%20Charles%20F.%20Wellford.%20A%20Comparative%20Analysis%20of%20Crime%20Guns.pdf (finding that most guns used in crimes are not possessed by the lawful initial purchaser at the time they are used in a crime).

1138 Zusha Elinson. 2021. "Gang Violence Drives Rise in Murder Rates in Some U.S. Cities." *Wall Street Journal*, Aug. 20, 2021. https://www.wsj.com/articles/gang-violence-drives-rise-in-murder-rates-in-some-u-s-cities-11629486712; Stephen Stock et al. 2022. "Number of Bay Area Freeway Shootings Spiking Due to Gang 'Hits'," NBC Bay Area, Feb. 8, 2022. https://www.nbcbayarea.com/investigations/number-of-bay-area-freeway-shootings-spiking-due-to-gang-hits-investigators/2804020/; Sara Cline, "Shootings Rise in Portland, as Police Blame Gang Violence," opb.org, June 11, 2021. https://www.opb.org/article/2021/06/11/police-say-gang-activity-fuels-portland-violence/.

1139 Latzer, *supra* note 39, 120.

1140 Latzer, *supra* note 39, 118.

1141 Dr. James Austin, Lauren-Brooke Eisen, James Cullen, Jonathan Frank, "How Many Americans Are Unnecessarily Incarcerated?," Brennan Center for Justice (2016), https://www.brennancenter.org/our-work/research-reports/how-many-americans-are-unnecessarily-incarcerated

1142 *Ibid.*

1143 Smart Justice, ACLU, https://www.aclu.org/issues/smart-justice#:~:text=The%20ACLU%20Campaign%20for%20Smart,in%20the%20criminal%20legal%20system.

1144 Latzer, *supra* note 39, 120.

1145 Criminal Justice Standards for the Prosecution Function, Part I, Standard 3-1.2(b), American Bar Association, 4th Ed. 2017, https://www.americanbar.org/groups/criminal_justice/standards/ProsecutionFunctionFourthEdition/.

1146 Adversarial Versus Inquisitorial System, The Doha Declaration, United Nations Congress on Crime Prevention and Criminal Justice, https://www.unodc.org/e4j/en/organized-crime/module-9/key-issues/adversarial-vs-inquisitorial-legal-systems.html#:~:text=The%20inquisitorial%20system%20is%20associated,has%20existed%20for%20many%20centuries.&text=The%20inquisitorial%20process%20can%20be-,defence%20to%20determine%20the%20facts (last visited Oct. 19, 2020).

1147 *Ibid.*

1148 *Ibid.* The inquisitorial system is associated with civil law legal systems and has existed for many centuries. It is characterized by extensive pretrial investigation and inter- rogations, with the objective of avoiding bringing an innocent person to trial. The inquisitorial process can be described as an official inquiry to ascertain the truth, whereas the adversarial system uses a competitive process between prosecution and defense to determine the facts. The inquisitorial process grants more power to the judge who oversees the process, whereas the judge in the adversarial system serves more as an arbiter between claims of the prosecution and defense.

1149 Conflicts of Interest, Criminal Justice Standards for the Prosecution Function, Part I, Standard 3-1.7(b), American Bar Association, 4th Ed. 2017, https://www.american-bar.org/groups/criminal_justice/standards/ProsecutionFunctionFourthEdition/.

1150 *Brady v. Maryland,* 373 U.S. 83, 87 (1963) (holding that criminal defendants have a constitutional right for prosecutors not to suppress evidence favorable to them where the evidence is material to either their guilt or their punishment—essentially, poten- tially exculpatory or mitigating evidence).

1151 Jencks Act, 18 U.S.C. §3500 (providing that after a government witness testifies at trial, the defense may request and receive any prior "statement" of that witness in the possession of the United States "which relates to the subject matter" of the testimony).

1152 *Giglio v. United States,* 405 U.S. 150, 154 (1972) (holding that evidence affect- ing a witness's credibility falls within the Brady Rule—essentially impeachment information).

1153 Olwyn Conway, "How Can I Reconcile with You When Your Foot Is on My Neck? The Role of Justice in the Pursuit of Truth and Reconciliation," 2018 Michigan State Law Review 1349, 1369 (2018).

1154 Note, "The Paradox of "Progressive Prosecution," 132 Harvard Law Review 748, 754 (2018).

1155 Definition, *Merriam-Webster* Dictionary Online, https://www.merriam-webster.com/dictionary/progressive (last visited Oct. 19, 2020).

1156 "Law Enforcement Legal Defense Fund, Prosecutorial Malpractice: Progressive Prosecutors, Public Safety, and Felony Outcomes" Policedefense.org (2020), http://www.policedefense.org/wp-content/uploads/2020/06/Prosecutorial-Malpractice.pdf (showing that in six cities where rogue prosecutors were elected, guilty verdicts decreased substantially, and those same offices dropped or lost cases by substantial percentages compared to when the offices were headed by independent, traditional law-and-order prosecutors); Paul G. Cassell, "Explaining the Recent Homicide Spikes in U.S. Cities: The 'Minneapolis Effect' and the Decline in Proactive Policing," Federal Sentencing Reporter (2020), https://papers.ssrn.com/sol3/papers.cfm?abstract_id=3690473.

1157 "Teen Courts: A Focus on Research," Juvenile Justice Bulletin, Office of Juvenile Justice and Delinquency Prevention, U.S. Department of Justice (Oct. 2000) (describing teen courts "as a voluntary alternative in lieu of more formal handling by the traditional juvenile justice system" where other "young people rather than adults determine the disposition, given a broad array of sentencing options"), https://www.ncjrs.gov/pdffiles1/ojjdp/183472.pdf; Teen Court, Montgomery County, MD, State's

Attorney's Office, https://www.montgomerycountymd.gov/SAO/other/teencourt.html (last visited Oct. 23, 2020).

1158 Sarah Schweig, Danielle Malangone, and Miriam Goodman, "Prostitution Diversion Programs," Center for Court Innovation (2012) (stating that "people arrested for prostitution tend to cycle through the justice system again and again. Recognizing this, some justice practitioners are trying new approaches—rather than fines and jail time—to address the problems, such as trauma, abuse, and drug addiction, that keep many women and girls in 'the life' of prostitution"), https://www.courtinnovation.org/sites/default/files/documents/CI_Prostitution%207.5.12%20PDF.pdf; Ana Ley, "The Impact of Specialty Courts: 'I've Seen Girls Go from Prostitution to College,'" *Las Vegas Sun* (June 8, 2014), (describing Nevada's specialty courts), https://lasvegassun.com/news/2014/jun/08/impact-specialty-courts-ive-seen-girls-go-prostitu/.

1159 "Mental Health Courts Program," Bureau of Justice Assistance, U.S. Department of Justice, https://bja.ojp.gov/program/mental-health-courts-program/overview (stating that the "Mental Health Courts Program funds projects that seek to mobilize communities to implement innovative, collaborative efforts that bring systemwide improvements to the way the needs of adult offenders with mental disabilities or illnesses are addressed"), (last visited Oct. 23, 2020); Treatment Court Locators, Substance Abuse and Mental Health Services Administration, U.S. Department of Health & Human Services, https://www.samhsa.gov/gains-center/treatment-court-locators (stating that "mental health courts for adults and juveniles work with people with mental illnesses who are involved in the justice system. These courts connect people to effective treatment and support after they undergo screening and assessments") (last visited Oct. 23, 2020).

1160 Family Justice Center Alliance website, https://www.familyjusticecenter.org/ (last visited Oct. 23, 2020) (stating that they "develop and support Family Justice Centers that help survivors and their children find the services they need in ONE place"); Your Safe Space, A Family Justice Center, San Diego Family Justice Center website, https://www.sandiego.gov/sandiegofamilyjusticecenter/fjcinfo/ (last visited Oct. 23, 2020), (stating that it is "dedicated to transitioning victims of domestic violence, sexual assault, and sex trafficking into survivors" and that it "is a team of professionals including therapists, nurses, attorneys, prosecutors, advocates, immigration attorneys, police, and other social service providers").

1161 John S. Goldkamp, Cheryl Irons-Guynn, and Doris Weiland, "Community Prosecution Strategies: Measuring Impact," Bureau of Justice Assistance, U.S. Department of Justice (Nov. 2002), (stating that "community prosecution initiatives deploy prosecutors or, in some jurisdictions, nonlegal staff in the community to identify the public safety concerns of residents and to seek their participation in developing and implementing strategies to address the problems that are the community's highest priorities"), https://www.ncjrs.gov/pdffiles1/bja/192826.pdf.

1162 George Soros, "Why I Support Reform Prosecutors," *Wall Street Journal* (July 31, 2022), https://www.wsj.com/articles/why-i-support-reform-prosecutors-law-enforces-jail-prison-crime-rate-justice-police-funding-11659277441?mod=article_inline.

1163 *Ibid.*

1164 *Ibid.*

1165 *Ibid.*

1166 *Ibid.*

1167 Sun Tzu, *The Art of War*, translated from the Chinese with Introduction and Critical Notes by Lionel Giles, (New York: Basic Books, 1974).

1168 *Ibid.* District Attorney Summer Stephan was interviewed by the author on August 10, 2022.

# ACKNOWLEDGMENTS

**B**oth of us are former federal prosecutors. One of us was also a local, state, and military prosecutor, defense attorney, and judge. We believe strongly in the rule of law, the presumption of innocence, the brilliance of the adversarial nature of our criminal justice system, and equal justice for all. The law is, and should be, colorblind. We are keenly aware that our criminal justice system is not perfect. We have, over the course of our careers, worked alongside other prosecutors, defense attorneys, and judges to continue to make positive reforms. We believe that victims have rights and should be protected, that all defendants are presumed innocent until proven guilty, and that they should receive a zealous defense. While those who commit any crime should be held accountable, we also believe in justice and mercy and redemption. Politics should not play any role whatsoever in the administration of justice. There are fantastic law and order elected district attorneys who are Democrats, Republicans, and Independents. What matters to us as lawyers—and as citizens—is that they are ethical, fair, reform-minded, honest, stand-up members of their local communities, and that they hold all criminals accountable for violating the law.

We have advocated for meaningful alternatives to incarceration, such as drug courts, domestic violence courts, and veterans courts, all of which provide services to those involved in crime but who want to reform their lives and become productive members of society. One of us worked as a drug court and domestic violence court prosecutor. The key to meaningful reform is holding people accountable for their actions, while providing incentives to get on the straight and narrow. Some heinous crimes, such as murder and rape, necessarily require long prison sentences. Long prison sentences reduce recidivism rates, as the U.S. Sentencing Commission has found over and over again.

This book is the culmination of our work in, and scholarship on, the criminal justice system. It would not have been possible without the assistance of many colleagues, friends, law enforcement professionals, concerned citizens, family members, and loved ones. It grew out of our rogue prosecutor series we wrote as scholars at The Heritage Foundation, the Washington D.C. think tank where we are both privileged to work.

We want to thank our Heritage colleagues for providing their time and insights as we worked on the book, including our bosses John Malcolm and Derrick Morgan. Special thanks also go to Jonathan Moy, Hans von Spakovsky, Jack Fitzhenry, Paul Larkin, Michael Gonzalez, Chris Byrnes, John Backiel, and Rob Bluey. We also want to thank our other Heritage colleagues who helped with research and promotion of our rogue prosecutor series, including Caroline Heckman, Katie Samalis, Tim Doescher, Andy Olivastro, Bridgett Wagner, Katie Trinko, Peter Parisi, Lauren Evans, Mark Guiney, Philip Reynolds, Tim Kennedy, Michelle Cordero, and Laura Falcon Pham.

We also had the great privilege of working with members of the Heritage Foundation Young Leaders Program who worked as interns in the Edwin Meese III Center for Legal and Judicial Studies and who conducted thousands of hours of research for this project. They included: Stephanie Neville, Maxwell Myrhum, Garrett Watts, Katherine Wygand Williams, Anna Klippert, Matthew Samilow, Samuel Bock, David Bainbridge, Nicole Imhof, Caitlin McDonough, Emma Nitzsche, Krishna Hedge, Courtney Baer, Tony Apolito, Naila Meese, Marcos Mullin, Holden Edwards, Bradyn Lawrence, Meaghen McManus, Matthew Rumsey, Isaac Bock, Louis Pham, Benjamin Oyer, Ross van Farowe, Anthony Truisi, Ashley Wilson, Frank Yang, and Abby Kassal.

We want to thank the many prosecutors, sheriffs, police officers, criminal defense attorneys, judges, academics, attorneys, public policy experts, and victims who spoke with us on and off the record for this book. In particular, we want to thank Los Angeles County Deputy District Attorneys Jon Hatami, Michelle Hanisee, Eric Siddall, and Kathy Cady, San Diego District Attorney Summer Stephan, former United States Attorneys Erin

Nealy Cox, Andrew Lelling, Richard Donoghue, McGregor Scott, and William McSwain. Thank you to those career prosecutors, public defenders, and criminal defense attorneys we spoke to off the record. You know who you are. We also are indebted to Pico Rivera City Council Member Andrew Lara, former Los Angeles County Sheriff Alex Villanueva, Frederick County (MD) Sheriff Chuck Jenkins, Wicomico County (MD) Sheriff Mike Lewis and other anonymous law enforcement officials across the country. We were privileged to speak with the following victims of violent crime, including Imelda Hernandez, Emma Rivas, Anna Estevez, and Tashika Hilliard, wife of Deputy First Class Glenn Hilliard, who was murdered by a career criminal, and the other victims who spoke to us off the record.

We want to offer a special thanks to Edwin Meese III, the 75th Attorney General of the United States, and former Alameda County Deputy District Attorney, who we have the privilege of working for at The Heritage Foundation. He is the most gracious, supportive, encouraging and kind person we have ever work for, and is, to quote President Ronald Reagan, the epitome of a "good man."

Finally, we want to extend our heartfelt thanks to our family members who supported us throughout this saga. Thank you to Cully's family (Laura, Sophia, Will, and Cate) and in particular, Ian, who helped with research. Thanks also to Zack's family (Anna, Debbie, Tommy, and Linda). We love you all.

In a book of this magnitude, despite the consultation, review, and editing that took place over a years' time, there are bound to be mistakes. Any mistakes, errors or omissions are our own.

# ABOUT THE AUTHORS

Charles "Cully" Stimson is a senior legal fellow at The Heritage Foundation. He served as a local, state, federal, and military prosecutor, a defense attorney, and a military trial judge. He served as Deputy Assistant Secretary of Defense for Detainee Affairs in the George W. Bush administration. After thirty years of active duty and reserve service, Stimson retired as a captain of the United States Navy JAG Corps where he was a two-time commanding officer and deputy chief judge of the Navy-Marine Corps Trial Judiciary.

**ZACK SMITH AND CHARLES D. STIMSON**

Zack Smith is a legal fellow at The Heritage Foundation. He served as an Assistant United States Attorney and has worked on a variety of criminal and civil matters in public service and private practice. He clerked for the Honorable Emmett R. Cox on the United States Court of Appeals for the Eleventh Circuit and during law school served as the editor-in-chief of the *Florida Law Review*.